State Building and Social Policies in Developing Countries

This book moves away from the orthodox neoliberal paradigm to suggest a new framework linking social policy with citizenship and transformation. The interjection of nation building, public society and public provisioning to the study of education, healthcare and employment caters to the needs of citizens equitably. By combining and coagulating these three broad arenas of politico-economic discussion, this book takes a new approach to the analysis of social policymaking in developing countries to indicate the drivers and triggers of transformation. It makes comprehensive, thorough critical comparisons between the trajectories of developed and developing countries, finds out the gaps in transformation and suggests drivers for changes.

The intentions of social policymaking, as proposed in the book, are to curb the growing inequalities in the forms of class, power and marginalisation. The chapters on education focus on provisioning of public goods for skills formation, innovation and citizenship education. The sections on healthcare centre on universal health care as opposed to universal health coverage by analysing access, healthcare-seeking behaviour, price setting, market provisioning etc. For the chapters on employment, propositions are posited regarding the expansion of productive capacity, factor mobility and social security to ensure work for all.

Besides theorising education, healthcare and employment based on public provisioning by the people's state, underwritten by a public society, the book provides feasible solutions through data sourced from all major international organisations. In addition, it recognises the unique postcolonial struggles and aspirations of the developing countries, and accordingly resorts to defining the normative principles, reflecting nuances, subtleties and peculiarities.

This book is a continuation of the author's *Fiscal and Monetary Policies in Developing Countries: State, Citizenship and Transformation* (Routledge) and will draw the attention of scholars and researchers who wish to gain a deeper understanding of, and pragmatic solutions to, social policies that address the transformational pathways of developing countries, accentuated by the COVID-19 pandemic.

Rashed Al Mahmud Titumir is a professor of economics at the Department of Development Studies, University of Dhaka, Bangladesh. He has led numerous projects for diverse organisations including governments, development partners and international organisations at home and abroad.

Routledge Studies in Development Economics

6 **The Economic Consequences of Globalization on Thailand**
Juthathip Jongwanich

7 **Cities and Economic Inequality in Latin America**
Intra-Urban Inequality in Argentina
Lena Simet

8 **Neoliberalism and Unequal Development**
Alternatives and Transitions in Europe, Latin America and Sub-Saharan Africa
Edited by Fernando López Castellano, Carmen Lizárraga and Roser Manzanera Ruiz

9 **Industrialization and Economic Diversification**
Post-Crisis Development Agenda in Asia and Africa
Banji Oyelaran-Oyeyinka and Kaushalesh Lal

10 **Digitalization and Economic Development**
Edited by Mohamed Sami Ben Ali

11 **The Political Economy of Universal Healthcare in Africa**
Evidence from Ghana
Philip C. Aka, Hassan Wahab, and Yvette M. Alex-Assensoh

12 **State Building and Social Policies in Developing Countries**
The Political Economy of Development
Rashed Al Mahmud Titumir

For more information about this series, please visit: www.routledge.com/series/SE0266

State Building and Social Policies in Developing Countries

The Political Economy of Development

Rashed Al Mahmud Titumir

Routledge
Taylor & Francis Group
LONDON AND NEW YORK

First published 2023
by Routledge
4 Park Square, Milton Park, Abingdon, Oxon OX14 4RN

and by Routledge
605 Third Avenue, New York, NY 10158

Routledge is an imprint of the Taylor & Francis Group, an informa business

British Library Cataloguing-in-Publication Data
A catalogue record for this book is available from the British Library

Library of Congress Cataloging-in-Publication Data
Names: Titumir, Rashed A. M., author.
Title: State building and social policies in developing countries : the political economy of development / Rashed Al Mahmud Titumir.
Description: 1 Edition. | New York, NY : Routledge, 2022. | Series: Routledge studies in development economics | Includes bibliographical references and index.
Identifiers: LCCN 2022002915 (print) | LCCN 2022002916 (ebook) | ISBN 9781032256108 (hardback) | ISBN 9781032256115 (paperback) | ISBN 9781003284222(ebook)
Subjects: LCSH: Equality—Developing countries. | Marginality, Social—Developing countries. | Developing countries—Social policy. | Developing countries—Politics and government.
Classification: LCC HN980 (ebook) | LCC HN980 .T58 2022 (print) | DDC 361.6/109172/4 23/eng/20220—dc10
LC record available at https://lccn.loc.gov/2022002915

ISBN: 978-1-032-25610-8 (hbk)
ISBN: 978-1-032-25611-5 (pbk)
ISBN: 978-1-003-28422-2 (ebk)

DOI: 10.4324/9781003284222

Typeset in Bembo
by Apex CoVantage, LLC

sister

Mahmuda Ashrafi Ferdousi

brothers

Rashed Al Habib Kamal
Rashed Al Amin Khaled
Rashed Al Ahmad Tarique

Contents

List of Figures xi
List of Tables xiii
List of Abbreviations xv
Preface and Acknowledgements xvii

PART I
Introduction 1

1 State and Social Policies in Developing Countries 3

Introduction 3
Public Society 6
Public Goods 11
Trends in Education, Healthcare and Employment 18
Summary 22
References 23

2 Social Policy, Public Society and Public Provisioning in Developing Countries 26

Introduction 26
Public Society and Public Goods 29
A Review 32
A Framework 44
Components 46
Summary 52
References 53

PART II
Education 57

3 Discourses on Investment in Human Capabilities 59

Introduction 59
A Review 61
A Framework 74
Summary 76
References 78

4 Education: Provisioning, Skill Formation and Citizenship 81

Introduction 81
Public Good and Market Provisioning 82
Skills Formation and Employment 93
Innovation and Education 100
Citizenship Education and Citizen State 104
Summary 105
References 106

5 Institutions and Transformational Pathways for Education in Developing Countries 108

Introduction 108
Political Settlement and Human Sociality 109
Education and Government Expenditure: A Simulation 119
Impact of COVID-19 120
Policy Roadmap 123
Summary 124
References 125

PART III
Healthcare 127

6 Debates on Provisioning of Healthcare in Developing Countries 129

Introduction 129
A Review 133
Stylised Facts 139
A Framework 141

Summary 142
References 143

7 Universal Health Care: Provisioning and Accessibility 145

Introduction 145
Socially Embedded Values 146
Firms and Price Setting 151
Market Provisioning and Universal Access 153
Country Spotlight: Accessibility Barriers in Bangladesh 155
Health Expenditure and Economic Life 157
Summary 164
References 165

8 Institutions and Transformation of Healthcare in Developing Countries 167

Introduction 167
Stability and Healthcare Provision 168
Transformability and Healthcare 171
Sustainability and Health Shocks 172
Policy Roadmap 176
Summary 177
References 178

PART IV
Employment and Social Security 181

9 Disquisitions on Employment and Social Security 183

Introduction 183
A Review 185
A Framework 198
Summary 203
References 204

10 Work for All: Skills, Productivity and Wages 207

Introduction 207
Productive Capacity and Skills Formation 210
Factor Mobility, Wages and Inequality 213
Productivity and Labour Extraction Function 216
Spotlight: Employment Trends in Bangladesh 221

Summary 234
References 235

11 Universal Social Security in Developing Countries 238

Introduction 238
A Framework 241
Social Security for All 243
Social Security Spending 248
Summary 252
References 253

12 Institutions and Transformation for Universal Employment and Social Security in Developing Countries 255

Introduction 255
Stability Conditions 256
Transformability Conditions 260
Sustainability Conditions 268
Policy Roadmap 273
Summary 274
References 275

PART V
Conclusions 279

13 Social Policy Agenda for Developing Countries 281

Index 287

Figures

1.1	Public society and the median voter	6
2.1	Citizens, state, market and public society	47
2.2	Rent-seeking and welfare cost	50
2.3	Cause-and-effect relationship in patron–client political accumulation	51
2.4	Interlocked factor and product market for public goods	52
3.1	Causal relationships between structures of governance, wealth inequality and economic performance	69
3.2	Some possible links between a child's well-being and the macro- and micro factors	70
3.3	Framework for state and market provision of education in creating public society	77
4.1	Market provisioning of education and excludability	82
4.2	Situation of employment, unemployment and labour force growth	93
4.3	Investment in quality education and skill	94
4.4	High R&D expenditure constituting innovation and growth	101
4.5	Innovation score	103
4.6	STEM graduates	103
4.7	Expenditure in R&D (per cent of GDP)	104
4.8	Citizenship education for public society	105
4.9	Tax–GDP ratio and corruption indices	106
5.1	Public expenditure on education by nature of spending, 2014–2015	117
5.2	Public expenditure on education as a percentage of GDP	118
5.3	Simulation result for education	120
5.4	COVID-19 shocks on education	122
5.5	Social policymaking roadmap for universal education	123
6.1	Citizens, state and healthy life	142
7.1	Socially embedded nature of individual affecting health-seeking behaviour	146
7.2	Oligopolistic health market structure	152

7.3 Market provisioning of health and exclusion 154
7.4 Scatterplot of current health expenditure versus inequality in life expectancy 155
7.5 Scatterplot of current health expenditure versus life expectancy 159
7.6 Distribution of curative visits by type of provider, for the poor and non-poor 163
8.1 Game theory matrix 170
8.2 COVID-19 related shocks 173
8.3 Policy roadmap 177
9.1 Transformational grid for employment 201
10.1 Productive capacity expansion and employment 210
10.2 (a) GDP per worker by broad economic sector (in BDT) (b) Labour productivity in Bangladesh, India and China 217
10.3 Extraction of labour and productivity 218
10.4 Labour productivity in selected countries 220
10.5 Shifts in population age structure in Bangladesh, 2000, 2025 and 2050 227
10.6 Percentage of total population by selected age groups in Bangladesh 229
10.7 First demographic dividend in Bangladesh and other South Asian countries 230
10.8 Public expenditure on health and education as a share of GDP 232
11.1 Universal social security 241
11.2 Social protection coverage 245
11.3 Targeting error of social security system in Bangladesh 246
11.4 Universal coverage and targeting approach 247
11.5 Social security spending versus coverage 249
11.6 Estimation of universal social security 251
12.1 Public order and human nature 267
12.2 COVID-19 related shocks 270
12.3 Policy roadmap 274

Tables

2.1	Approaches and underlying gaps	45
4.1	Attendance statistics	85
4.2	Number of private and public education institutions	86
4.3	Education infrastructure around the world	88
4.4	Teacher–student ratio of colleges in 2019	89
4.5	Comparative analysis between public and private universities	90
4.6	Government expenditure on education of some selected countries (2017)	91
4.7	Capital expenditure as a percentage of total expenditure in public institutions (2016)	92
4.8	Regression result on labour productivity	96
4.9	Employed population aged 15 or older by education level, area and sector	97
4.10	Occupational category by the level of education	98
4.11	Incongruity in qualifications	99
4.12	Share of under- and overeducated workers	99
4.13	Main reasons behind joblessness	100
4.14	Regression result on innovation	102
4.15	Correlation result between mean years of schooling and tax–GDP ratio	106
5.1	Human sociality and distribution of power	109
7.1	Percentage of availability of medical practitioners	149
7.2	Reasons behind choosing particular health service	149
7.3	Reasons behind non-treatment in terms of gender	150
7.4	Sources of financing medical expenses	156
7.5	The comparative evaluation of public and private provisioning	157
7.6	Proportion of nursing personnel and medical doctors per 10,000 population	164
9.1	Classification of theories	197
10.1	Factor mobility and productive capacity	213
10.2	Remittances as a share of GDP	214

10.3 Annual average growth rate of GDP, employment, labour productivity and real wage (per cent) 215
10.4 Employment and unemployment trend in Bangladesh 221
10.5 Unemployment by age group and gender 222
10.6 Youth unemployment by level of education 223
10.7 Unemployed youth aged 15–29 in total unemployment, by education level (per cent) 223
10.8 Employment by formal and informal sectors 224
10.9 Informal employment 224
10.10 Distribution of output (per cent of GDP) and distribution of employment (per cent of total employment) by broad economic sectors 225
10.11 Student–teacher ratio at primary and secondary levels 231
10.12 Education of the population aged 5 and over in Bangladesh (per cent) 233
10.13 Educational attainment of population aged 15 and over by 5-year age group, 2011 233
11.1 Social security spending in different parts of the world 250
11.2 Allocation for social security 250
12.1 Summarising conditions for stability, transformability and sustainability 272

Abbreviations

ADB	Asian Development Bank
BB	Bangladesh Bank
BBS	Bangladesh Bureau of Statistics
BC	Before Christ
BDT	Bangladeshi Taka
BNHA	Bangladesh National Health Accounts
CMC	Circulation of Commodities
CPD	Centre for Policy Dialogue
EU	European Union
GoB	Government of Bangladesh
GDP	Gross Domestic Product
GED	General Economics Division
GFI	Global Financial Integrity
HIES	Household Income and Expenditure Surveys
ICT	Information and Communications Technology
ICP	Investment Corporation of Pakistan
ILO	International Labour Organisation
IMF	International Monetary Fund
JDB	Japan Development Bank
MDG	Millennium Development Goals
MITI	Ministry of International Trade and Industry
MNC	Multinational Corporations
MP	Member of Parliament
NGO	Non-governmental Organisation
NHS	National Health Service
NPL	Non-Performing Loan
OECD	Organisation for Economic Co-operation and Development
OOP	Out-of-Pocket Expenditure
RMG	Ready-made Garments
R&D	Research and Development
SEA	Southeast Asia
SDGs	Sustainable Development Goals
SME	Small and Medium Enterprises

SSNP	Social Safety Net Programmes
USD	United States Dollar
VAT	Value-Added Tax
WHO	World Health Organization

Preface and Acknowledgements

The book intends to stir the discussion on social policies in developing countries. The evolution of social policy is deeply rooted in the direction of development, societal structure and prevailing political settlement in a society. State building and public society shape social policies, and are still in its infancy in developing countries.

The book challenges the definition of state building as ad hoc reforms and structural adjustment measures, and instead defines state building as relation between state and citizens. It becomes, therefore, imperative to understand the dynamics of power in a political settlement. For state building to be effective, it is required that power lies with the median voter.

Education, healthcare and employment have been viewed as the backbones of the development to break away from the cycles of poverty, and at the same time, as the building blocks of an equitable and sustainable trajectory of growth in human potentials. Currently pursued policies and mechanisms by a majority of developing nations, particularly in postcolonial states of Africa and Asia, have not succeeded in achieving the desired objectives, rather inflated inequalities exponentially. These have not been able to transform the developing countries due to failings in locating the loci of transformation problem, as the book will demonstrate. Rather consequential resultants have also given rise to widespread inequalities in educational, healthcare and employment outcomes in these countries as have done in the countries of origin. Simultaneously, social policies have also remained the centre of debates in developed countries in terms of modelling the benefits structure, financing social security or insurance, eligibility of key beneficiaries and recipients, and normative questions of morality, equity and justice.

On top of it, the COVID-19 pandemic has not only cost millions of lives around the globe and engendered unprecedented economic crisis but also laid bare the weaknesses of the existing structures and institutions to absorb the consequences of exposure to shocks. This calls for searching a new approach to examine the challenges, and the proposed book thus adopts a one-of-a-kind approach that relates education, healthcare and employment with nation building.

Besides theorising education, healthcare and employment based on public provisioning by people's state, underwritten by a public society, the book recognises the unique postcolonial struggles and aspirations of the developing economies, and accordingly resorts to defining the normative principles, reflecting nuances, subtleties and peculiarities, moving away from the orthodox neoliberal paradigm.

The analysis employs the evolution of institutions – formal and informal of past and present – to theorise the politico-economic structures in developing countries to comprehend the problems. In doing so, it undertakes a historical analysis of institutional structure that grids with the social relations in developing countries of precolonial, colonial and postcolonial eras. Rent-seeking nature of the political settlement has dismantled the formal institutions supposed to uphold rule of law and property rights to ensure the provision of public goods. The norms and values in the society over the years have made citizens conform to the discrimination, widening the alienation with the state while allowing the clientelist networks to accumulate power and capital.

Furthermore, it is necessary to be mindful of the heterogeneity amongst developing countries. Developing countries are not homogenous as they vary in histories, stages of development and policy directions. The book therefore mix-matches aggregation, at the subregional, regional or continental level, and single-country case studies, which also allows for decomposition of developing-country contexts. Aggregation provides a holistic overview and emerging stylised facts, while the detailed case studies offer readers a thorough understanding of the issue. This is further made comprehensive through critical comparisons between the trajectories of developed and developing countries, with the objective of finding out gaps in transformation and suggesting drivers for changes. In doing so, it takes Bangladesh as the case study. It also focuses on postcolonial states in Africa and Asia. Scandinavian and East Asian countries have been used as the parameter for development in social sector because of their achievements in education, healthcare and employment.

The chapters on education focus on provisioning of public goods for *skill formation, innovation and citizenship education*. The chapters on health centre on *universal health care* as opposed to universal health coverage by analysing access, healthcare-seeking behaviour, price setting, market provisioning etc. For the chapters on employment, propositions are posited regarding expansion of productive capacity, factor mobility and social security to ensure *work for all*.

I am thankful to the anonymous referees for their insightful observations for the development of the book.

I wish to express my gratitude to Adrina Ibnat Jamilee Adiba and Wahid Haider for their research assistance with unwavering dedication.

Two women – mother, Rawshan Ara Begum, and wife, Munira Nasreen Khan – both teachers – have been standing by my side, in sickness and health, in joy, and in sorrow. My father, Prof. Dr. M Arshad Ali, and my son, Muharrir Munir Arshad Titumir, have never missed the chance of reading my manuscript first. Two generational sources of constant inspiration!

I am alone responsible for any errors, inadequacies and omissions still remaining in the book.

Dhaka   Rashed Al Mahmud Titumir

Part I

Introduction

1 State and Social Policies in Developing Countries

Introduction

Education, health and employment have been viewed as the backbones of development to break away from the cycles of poverty. Currently pursued policies and mechanisms by a majority of developing nations, particularly in postcolonial states of Africa and Asia, have not succeeded in achieving the desired objectives, rather inflated inequalities exponentially. Besides theorising education, health and employment based on public provisioning by people's state, underwritten by a public society, the book provides cost, pragmatic and feasible solutions through collated evidence and recognises the unique postcolonial struggles and aspirations of the developing economies in question to endorse a more context-specific framework, beyond conventional paradigms. Through the entire length of the book, the discussion proposes new frameworks of drivers and triggers of transformation, necessary conditions, that is, factors of production, and sufficient conditions, that is, formal and informal institutions, power and political settlement.

The economic downturn triggered by global crises and pandemics, the likes of COVID-19, had sternly reinforced the need for an equitable distribution of public goods in society. The frailties of healthcare sectors across countries had been laid out in the open due to the pandemic whilst social distancing measures carried economies to a standstill. Global and national inequalities were more aggravated than ever and starkly manifested to the world. The efficacy in confronting the challenges posed by a global pandemic thus eventually depended on the preparedness and existing social policies of the countries, for example, adequate social security programmes, advanced testing facilities and the strength of its social contract. The virus, which originated in Wuhan of the Hubei Province in Mainland China, eventually moved across continents infecting large masses in Europe, the United States and South Asian countries as well following along the movement of individuals across borders. Overwhelmed at first, developed countries took a foothold eventually, only after a spike in affected cases and fatalities. Developing countries on the other hand were challenged by a dearth of resources to combat the pandemic, the result of it being higher death rates.

DOI: 10.4324/9781003284222-2

The proposed transformational pathway for education lies in three drivers: skill formation, innovation and citizenship formation. Quantitative objectives like enrolment rate have dominated policymaking in developing countries pushing aside factors like skills that can provide better work, innovation for transforming production and citizenship education for forming a public society. The book engages on the latter and proposes cause-and-effect layers of a paradigm shift in policymaking. COVID-19 has pushed back an already fragile health sector further in developing countries. Hence, the transformational pathway proposed in the book not only argues for universal health care that ensures access to healthcare for all with evidence but also delineates stages and steps for implementation for ensuring a need-based health system for the citizens. Jobless growth and resultant widespread unemployment have formed a sense of precarity in developing countries. The transformational pathway in employment is hence, the book argues, based on ensuring work for all for transformation as well as a universal life-cycle-based social security system to absorb systemic shocks, including those resulting from the pandemic and natural disasters.

The global economy is estimated to slow down by two per cent and is expected to cost around 1 trillion USD globally (UNCTAD, 2020). This will have serious ramifications for the pre-existing faultlines such as global inequality in income, health and education. The pandemic will further worsen the inequalities between the developed and developing countries. The fight against COVID-19 hinges upon the existing apparatuses in countries. These apparatuses are stark differences in healthcare structures and financing around the world. The number of doctors per 10,000 people is 42 in Germany and 28 in the United Kingdom; whilst in developing countries, the number is significantly lower, six in Bangladesh, nine in India and less than one in countries like the Democratic Republic of Congo and Tanzania. Government expenditure in healthcare in Germany in 2017 was 8.73 and in the United Kingdom, it was 7.65 per cent of the GDP. Expenditure in healthcare again in the developing countries is much lower, 0.38 per cent in Bangladesh, 0.96 per cent in India, 0.4 per cent in the Democratic Republic of Congo and 1.58 per cent in Tanzania (WHO, 2020). Spending on healthcare and education thus results in better social outcomes. Developed countries were thus better equipped to fight the Coronavirus compared to the developing ones. By the end of April 2020, Germany tested 30 people per thousand and the testing rate per thousand in the United Kingdom was 13. The testing rate per thousand people in Bangladesh at the same time was 0.39 and in India, it was 0.6. In African countries, the rate of testing was relatively much lower. Inability to undertake mass testing handicapped the developing nations in their fight against the virus.

Social distancing and closing down the economy due to COVID-19 have resulted in forced unemployment and furlough in countries affected. In such a situation, many countries have initiated unemployment benefits and have handed direct cash to the unemployed. The United States handed over paychecks of 1,200 USD as unemployment benefits during the stay-at-home order. A UNDP report projects income loss of well over 220 billion USD. People employed in the informal sectors have been the worst hit due to the economic shutdown. Around 2 billion workers or 61.2 per cent of the world's employed population work in the informal sectors. The percentage of informal workers in the total workforce in most of the developing countries is well above 80 per cent (ILO, 2020). The informal economy, due to its lack of regulation, cannot ensure the job security of those working. Stimulus programmes proposed by many countries are aimed towards the formal sector, mainly the large and medium industries. In such a scenario, initiatives like social security in the form of basic income provision or unemployment benefits may help ease the burden. Access to social protection albeit remains limited in the developing countries such that, globally, 55 per cent of the population have no access to social protection.

Many developing countries are yet to acknowledge healthcare, education and social security as people's rights. Often constitutions endorse these in fundamental principles, which pose no obligation on the state. There is much debate about allocating resources to healthcare, education and social security programmes. This debate, however, is silent about the issue of establishing healthcare, education and social security as citizens' rights. The discussion of this book will be limited to the public provision of education, health and employment. The failure of the state in providing these goods may lead to the private sector abusing market power. Privatising essential goods like education and health favours a select group, neglecting the majority of the population. When a state fails to effectively control and regulate the market for these goods and ensure equitable distribution, it results in a rise in infant mortality, fall in literacy rates, epidemics like Ebola and AIDS as seen in the African nations (Rotberg, 2002). Political settlement in the state also creates unequal economic opportunities. Such a notion is observed in both developed and developing countries. During the financial crisis of 2008, policies were put in effect to recover the economy by bailing out the very system that caused the crisis in the first place. The government prioritised Wall Street over Main Street and as a result, its ill-fated citizens suffered through the loss of their homes, jobs, pensions and savings. In developing countries, the scenario is rather grim as governments frequently offer to bail out financial institutions and the ruling elites as opposed to creating employment through providing equal economic benefits to all (Rotberg, 2002).

In order to understand the intersectionality of state-building and social policies, particularly in late-industrialising developing countries that envisage an inefficacy in their policies of education, healthcare and social security, the analysis disaggregates the context by focusing on a single country that represents the features of a least-developed country and is in a stage of transition. With regards to countries that fit the description, the book, therefore, attempts to provide a new framework for social policymaking in a developing country by illustrating the case of Bangladesh, and highlighting the key stylised facts in comparison with countries in East Asia and other developed countries.

The fundamental principles of a country's social policy originate from the aspirations of the people through their struggles. Hence, aspirational social policy is an understanding of the type of society people want to live in. The evolution of social policy is deeply rooted in the direction of development, societal structure and prevailing political settlement in a society. There are, therefore, continuous contradictions and struggles between the two polar opposites: aspirations vis-à-vis impositions. This book focuses on public goods and tends to excavate the optimum logic of the importance of public goods to be served as public goods indeed. In this context, the significance of public society is a prerequisite to undertake comprehensive social policy where people get the benefit of the public goods. This book puts its concentration on education, health and employment particularly with congruent pieces of evidence of the current state of these public goods in developing countries like Bangladesh and other countries. There will be a critical comparison between developed and developing countries in this regard to find out where the principal problems are rooted.

Public Society

Public society in its simplest form promotes social justice and equal rights for the citizens. The power lies with the median-income citizen in public society. Public society emerges when the power lies in the median population, similar to the normal distribution. In reality, power is exercised by those on the extreme right of the distribution (Figure 1.1). The ideal public society envisioned in this book entails the accessibility to basic human rights including education, health and employment for the citizens. The accessibility is guaranteed by the state through public provisioning. Citizens on the other hand provide funds to the state through taxation for the provisioning. Hence, the state and citizens embody a relationship that requires a give and take.

The notion of human sociality as expressed throughout this book originates from theories based on justice but transcends beyond utilitarianism. In terms of normative ethics, utilitarianism served the purpose of forming the moral basis of economic behaviour. However, it also entailed that during maximum

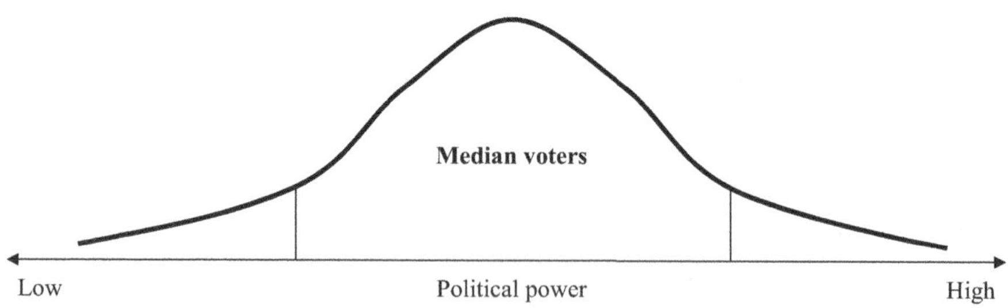

Figure 1.1 Public society and the median voter

Source: Prepared by author

capacity or full employment, higher satisfaction of one individual would be brought about at the expense of a lower level of satisfaction of another. On this stripped utilitarianism on the ground of justice, Rawls (1971) asserted that if people had to choose principles of justice from behind a veil of ignorance that restricted what they could know of their own positions in society, they would not choose principles designed to maximise overall utility, because this goal might be attained by sacrificing the rights and interests of groups that they themselves belong to. Instead, they would safeguard themselves against the worst possible outcome, first, by insisting on the maximum amount of liberty compatible with the same liberty for others, and, second, by requiring that any redistribution of wealth and other social goods is justified only if it improves the position of those who are worst off. This second principle is known as the "maximin" principle because it seeks to maximise the welfare of those at the minimum level of society. The notion of the normative concept of human sociality adopts the maximin principle but also moves beyond it by stressing the need for egalitarianism in society. It does so by assuming that households and labour form the necessary conditions for human sociality, but these conditions will not lead to a virtuous cycle on their own unless accompanied by an egalitarian approach of ensuring every citizen with adequate resources. The discussion throughout the book suggests that the provision of public goods by the state to all citizens in a collective process will likely bring about the egalitarian improvement in well-being.

A public good is highly political in terms of benefits and coverage. From the very ancient period to the present time, it is quite common and rampant that people who got most of the privileges in case of abiding in a particular society tend to deprive others. It is a basic instinct of powerful and privileged people in most countries. In fact, the government itself does not want to provide public goods to the general people deliberately. Generally, the public good is a good, which is both non-rival and non-excludable. Education, health, employment opportunities and environmental benefits like fresh air, water and rivers are all public goods. If public goods like education and health are considered in retrospect from the old and recent history, the proposition will become bona fide that public good was always a matter of conquering from the powerful people.

For instance, in Bangladesh, during British colonial rule, the landlords worked under the supervision and support of the British employees of the British East India Company. They extracted revenue as much as possible from the peasants and labourers. In return, their basic needs like food, shelter, education and employment were neglected. Revolts emerged due to the deprivation of basic needs of living and survival. Farmers and peasants were compelled to cultivate indigo in their fields in spite of knowing that it was detrimental to the crops and the fertility of the harvesting field. Thus, their food amenities were disrupted. They were deprived of educational advantages. Health benefits were very trivial for them. In terms of getting employment, the people of Bengal were always deprived of getting a high-class job. They were kept distressed deliberately by the coercive authority. In fact, religious polarisation was created by the British rulers through which riots occurred between Hindus and Muslims. Consequently, aggression turned into a volcano, which erupted later through mass protest and agitation. People came out to stand against the authoritative and oppressive rule of the British intruders. They had to fight for their basic needs. After a long and sacrificing movement, the British left the Indian subcontinent through which the scope of getting public goods comprehensively was created.

Afterwards, in the Pakistan period, earlier exploitation lingered. The colonial nature of the state did not change. In the case of education, health, employment, freedom of speech, business, export–import, quota, tariff and other aspects, the then East Pakistani (currently Bangladesh) people were acutely deprived by the West Pakistani (currently Pakistan) government. There was a clear presence of discrimination in every aspect, which will be demonstrated later in this chapter. The crucial point is that people of East Pakistan were deprived of public goods and social development in that period. This situation gave birth to myriad movements, mass protests, agitation and comprehensive grievances in East Pakistan. The constant bulge of exploitation and oppression turned into a war of liberation for the people of East Pakistan in 1971. This war was a massive effort to emancipate and to become independent from the grasp of socio-economic exploitation in terms of basic needs and freedom of life. Not only do poor and developing countries face this turmoil of public good provision but developed countries also have examples in this regard.

The quandary of racism is an age-old trend in the United States. Even after the end of the civil war (1861–1865) which took place to relinquish slavery, discrimination prevailed in American societies. Racism entered in the form of slavery around 1619 in the United States through bringing slaves from the African subcontinent for the advantages of the then colonial tenure. Slavery spread rapidly throughout the American colonies. The civil war led to the passage of the civil rights act in 1866 by Congress but the problem prevailed severely. There was labour entrance discrimination between Black and white. The Black people were deprived of getting equal opportunities towards education, living, health facility, wages, retirement benefits at work, access to savings, investment and business. Even while moving by public transport, the Blacks were restricted to sitting beside the white and if a white person told the Black one to leave his/her seat, he/she was compelled to do it. After so many movements, violence, political war and farce and chivalrous protest, the rights-based condition in the United States ameliorated. Still, there is a muffled depression between Black and white. The social security system of the United States ensures civil rights but has not been updated for the people all over the states irrespective of class and race. In 1953, the net worth of the typical Black household was only 20 per cent of that of white households (Kuhn et al., 2020). The black population was institutionally excluded from higher-paid jobs – while they were paid almost the same as their white counterparts in unskilled labor, they were believed to be less skilled in general than the whites in better-paid occupations (Wright, 2013). To entrench this skill-based discrimination, the landowning classes believed that public schools should not be made accessible to the black population, as better education would develop their level of skills, and make them less suitable to work as cheap labor. Therefore, the attitude led to a lower quality of education for the blacks, while the whites were assumed to be better-skilled, exposing the marginalized population to greater bias. The lower quality of education in turn led to a more inferior level of skill among the black population, trapping them in a vicious cycle of lower wages, and legitimizing these wage differentials on the grounds of race (Wright, 2013).

At present, there is widespread acclaim for American Blacks in politics, arts, economy, sports and other parts. Even the US citizens got their first Black president in 2009 Barack Obama, who was elected twice and had been in power in successive two terms. Discrimination has been mitigated to a large extent but this is not the full story depicting the present condition of all African Americans in the United States. By 2013, the wealth of the median Black family of the United States had fallen to a mere 10 per cent of that of their white counterpart. In 1953, four-fifths of white families made more than the typical Black households, now it has become nine-tenth in this context. The typical Black households are poorer than 90 per cent of white households. In the case of earning opportunity, disparity still prevails. By 2013, the median Black households still made only 58 per cent of what the median white households did. In fact, after the devastating recession period in 2008, the relatively poor Americans were less capable to thrive and invigorate their living conditions and earning opportunities. Despite civil rights having been established, social welfare and development have not occurred as powerful elites and corporations still represent the white class who are very much reluctant and unwilling to provide equal opportunity. This condition has led to silent grievances and ongoing arguments and counterarguments.

Coercion in general terms means inducing someone to comply with one's wishes and can be done by threatening the person. The Weberian definition of state has the absolute monopoly on the use of forces. Thus one can perceive that state by nature is coercive. Government rules and regulations can sometimes be coercive in nature. Coercion again can be replaced in a society. The ultimate motive of the state is to get a job done and to do so it can use two methods. First, the state can be coercive and somewhat force a citizen to comply with the regulations. On the other hand, the state can provide incentives to the citizens to motivate them to comply (Morris, 2011). The acceptance criterion of coercion capability of a state is usually defined in the constitution of a nation. Thus in a democracy, there are limited opportunities for the state to be coercive on its citizens. The coercive role of the government against freedom of speech and other basic rights violates the constitution by which the state receives its power. In underdeveloped and developing countries, people suffer from a lack of social security and their basic needs. People have to struggle for their relevant and acclaimed public goods. The government remains coercive and tends to be highly authoritative. For example, the living standard in African countries is very minimal and miserable due to civil war and unrest amongst different groups of guerrillas and militants and governments. Low standard of living coupled with widespread corruption in Mali, Sudan, South Sudan, Demographic Republic of Congo, Central Africa, Liberia and in some other countries causes health crises, illiteracy, insecurity, lack of food and shelter among people especially children and women. A military coup is very common in these countries. Various forms of oppression and brutality on general people are prevalent where human rights are being extremely violated. Such a phenomenon was also prevalent in other countries outside Africa where states were driven by the tendency of giving less and taking more and hence unwilling to provide public goods. People's movement and the struggle for an aspirational public society, however, is ascertained in every case in order to secure the rights and provisions from the state. It is, however, observed that check and balance in government can significantly offset the coercive nature of the state. For instance, the administrative system in the United States works in a way that makes it hard for the state to be coercive. The president is elected through electoral colleges that are voted by the citizens. Members of both the legislative branch of Congress and Senate are selected through direct election. The cabinet selected by the president has to go through the approval process by the Senate. The Supreme Court reserves the authority to nullify any executive order of the president. Supreme court justice picks on the other hand are selected by the president and must ensure a majority in the Senate. Such an intricate system makes coercion difficult in the United States.

Public accountability refers to a social relation where an actor has to justify the conduct to a significant other (Day and Klein, 1987; Romzek and Dubnick, 1998; Pollitt, 2003). Accountability between the citizen and the state is one of the principal–agent problems, where citizens act as the principal who delegates public duty to agents or political representatives. Accountability between the principal and the agent enhances the performance and ensures the legitimacy of the public office (Bovens, 2005). Institutions become autocratic in the absence of accountability and the welfare of the citizens is seldom prioritised under the shade of non-accountable government. If some initiatives are taken which unleash as in favour of the citizens, they are mainly some strategic stand to linger the power. For example, decentralisation of power and the emergence of local government in the 1980s in Bangladesh is a remarkable incident in its political history. Apparently, it seemed that the ultimate purpose was to ensure more benefits through the provision of public goods for the people abiding in both remote rural places and urban areas. Later, it appeared that the action was mainly enacted to create a supporting syndicate and group of patrons for perpetuating power and authority by the military government.

A common attribute of public goods is the moral hazard. Freeriding problems emerged whenever a provision of goods like education, health, food, freedom of speech, environmental benefits, skills and employment was involved. Freeriding exists on both sides, the provider and the recipient, in Bangladesh. On one hand, the government, the provider of public goods, assumes that citizens evade taxes. On the other side, citizens or the recipients of public goods suspect that the taxes they pay to the government fail to be utilised properly and are subjected to corruption and capital flight. Lack of accountability and transparency in the system strengthens the belief of both sides. Politicising institutions has seriously damaged accountability. The injustice caused by a lack of accountability in the system often results in public agitation. Henceforth, the likes of quota reform and road safety movements spread like wildfire and held the government accountable. By dint of forced accountability, the ruling authority enacted an ordinance of abolishing quota in entrance of government jobs. The Civil Rights Movement in the United States forced the government, in the same way, to put forward the Civil Rights Act. On the other hand, accountability in the political system of developed and western countries has resulted in many leaders resigning from their respective posts for failure to do the job properly. Both British Prime Ministers David Cameron and Theresa May resigned from their posts because of their failure to deliver "Brexit".

Public Goods

Even though the concept of "public goods" can be traced to the likes of Aristotle, Plato or Confucius, it was first theorised by Paul Samuelson in the 1950s (Hazelkorn and Gibson, 2019). A good can be "public" when the consumption by an individual does not reduce the consumption of any other individual. Hence, *non-rivalry* is the first property of "public goods". The second property, non-excludability, means that no one individual can be excluded from the consumption of the good (Samuelson, 1954). The absence of any of these two properties makes it a private one.

The current approach to social policy is about imposition and thus dominated by varieties of neoclassical traditions, namely public choice theories while the governments across the world including Bangladesh are undertaking market-centric reforms in public goods provision as a part of ideological project of neoliberalism, being principally designed by the multilateral banks such as World Bank, initiated through structural adjustment reforms. Bangladesh has been implementing neoliberal structural adjustment policies since the early 1980s. Neoliberal policies became the norm as International Financial Institutions (IFIs) aligned with the economic and political interests of civil-military elites in various sectors such as employment, health and education. The neoliberal policies continued despite the advent of democratic regimes since the 1990s, supported by IFIs, and thus began the implementation of market-driven economic policies. The reform policies had proved to be financially beneficial mainly for the elites in Bangladesh as benefits were not distributed among the different societal groups. This is particularly evident as compared to the 24 affluent families of hitherto United Pakistan, there are now around 40 to 50 families with ownership and control over almost the total industrial and financial assets in the country, leaving the vast majority out (Kabeer, 2013). The absence of policies directed at equitable distribution has aggravated the disparities in income and wealth between different societal groups. Inequality has increased gradually. As a part of neoliberal reforms, the privatisation process has been undertaken, with the purpose of ensuring skill development, increased quality and price competitiveness. These efforts were complemented by tax exemption, subsidy and tariff exemption of import of equipment, but still privatisation did not deliver promised outcomes in most of the countries. Bangladesh is an example. Since 1990, government investment in social sectors has declined over the years (Raymond, 1994). A key objective of the structural adjustment programmes was to streamline the size of the public sector as a service delivery mechanism by reducing costs (Haque, 1998). In the sub-Saharan region, only two categories of investors are capable of making an easy entrance into the process of privatisation. The first category comprised national leaders who were mainly military officials, both serving and retired as well as quasi-military civilians and paternalistic groups and their cronies. The secondary category constituted multinational corporations (Nwankwo and Richards, 2001). Groups from both categories tended to use their optimum power and lobbying capacity to loot money in an egregious form and made the public sector impermeable to general people. Thus, public goods were confiscated by the powerful groups. Privatisation, opposite of public provision, has also failed in the region of Africa. Private investors have drifted away from investing in water and electricity utilities. Private investors cared little about fulfilling the expectation of the poor people and only focused on their private interests. Their focus was on cost recovery, which did not facilitate the social objectives such as poverty reduction and promoting equity and employment (Bayliss and Mckinley, 2007). Upon gaining independence, the national governments of sub-Saharan African nations dominated the provisions of utilities. In the 1980s, the debt crisis and the ensuing contraction of the budget prompted a reappraisal of public sector provision. The tendency of lobbying among the donors for the restructuring of public services was remarkable. By the 1990s, the donors demanded full-scale privatisation. Contrarily, implementation of the projects undertaken by the private donor agencies slowed down and the outcome was not satisfactory. People were ultimately unable to come under the coverage of public utilities like safe drinking water, electricity facilities as well as quality education, health and other public services. Between 1990 and 2003, less than four per cent of global private investment in infrastructure went to sub-Saharan Africa (Bayliss and Mckinley, 2007). Participation in the private sector has been expensive and inflexible in these countries. For instance, the privatisation of Dar es Salaam's water supply began in the mid-1990s in Tanzania. The first attempt collapsed in 2000 while a second attempt was initiated from a consortium led by a UK firm Biwater. This treaty existed for only 18 months from the signing year of 2003 and was terminated with very negligible service provision. Later, the management of this sector was handed over to a specially created public company under the leadership of a new CEO. Significant improvement emerged during that period (Bayliss and Mckinley, 2007). Privatisation had a pernicious consequence on service provision in this region in the long run. People were deprived of basic utilities.

The financial difficulties of many state utilities in the 1980s, due to reduction in subsidy, compelled them to focus on achieving financial sustainability. Attaining social objectives was relegated to a later stage. Poor households as a consequence suffered enormously. The cost recovery purpose of the private corporations led to greater inequality in sub-Saharan Africa. In Namibia, price increases have varied geographically depending on how expensive it was to supply water. Inevitably, the price increase was lower in wealthy regions and higher in poor regions based on water availability in each region (Bayliss and Mckinley, 2007). Ironically, it became like a grinding machine that trampled the poor people struggling for their sheer existence each and every day and getting jeopardised by the high cost of service provision which was supposed to be availed by them as their fundamental needs.

Among Asian countries, Bangladesh, India, Korea, Philippines and Thailand have epitomes of the state being supportive to private sectors in terms of marketing, investment, negotiation and finance (Haque, 2008). In Latin American countries, there has been a tendency of reducing the role and power of the state in some public good provisions. The state became minimalist in those countries and the market became the ultimate decision maker regarding goods and services. Different market-driven policies like privatisation, contracting out of services, liberalisation of trade and investment, deregulation of finance and price control were adopted (Martin, 1993). Among these policies, privatisation played a dominant role during the 1980s and 1990s. In the 1980s, there was a tendency of making state-private capital alliances which turned into public–private partnership programmes in countries such as India, Korea, Thailand, Vietnam, China, Indonesia and others. Partnership with foreign investors emerged. Bangladesh followed that path of PPP (Public–Private Partnership) in some respects (e.g. Biman Bangladesh Airlines became a part of it). Because of these initiatives, the post-war strategy of reducing foreign ownership and enhancing economic self-reliance got hindered (Haque, 2008). In the 1980s and 1990s, many countries introduced market-based restructuring of social security allowing the private sector to play a salient role. Chile, Peru, Colombia, Brazil and Argentina were pioneers of these market-oriented reforms regarding social security (Nitsch and Schwarzer, 1996). Situations become worse for underprivileged populations, especially women and children due to the diminishing role of the state in the public provision of public goods. The rising predilection for such anti-welfare policies led the states prone to embrace the neoliberal strategy more than before in Asia, Africa and Latin America (Haque, 2008). One unique feature of the neoliberal state is that it tends to consider institutional objectives and structures in the image of the corporate business sector (Haque, 2008). This kind of approach makes social goods difficult to be achieved by people abiding by society. The dogmatic process of the market-led approach prioritises private or individual interests mostly. Public goods were supposed to be provided in a public society where people from all sectors would have access to their benefits. Education, health and employment became costlier due to privatisation. In the case of privatisation, it has appeared that the personal interest of corporate business came forth in lieu of providing citizenship qualities and skills. In Bangladesh, due to the massive privatisation of the educational sector, many institutions have sprouted. The problem is most of the institutions aim at collecting as much money as they can. Recent research shows that a guardian in Bangladesh has to spend more for his/her son/daughter for pursuing education. In the United States, a guardian has to spend 5.18 per cent of his/her total income for the son's/daughter's educational activity whereas in Bangladesh the rate is 80 per cent of total income which is more than 15 times that of the United States. In Bangladesh and some African countries, health facilities have been strenuous due to very high prices and also less quality. On the other hand, countries, which have instigated universal health facilities, have gained a lot. If health facilities can be provided for the public good, they can be well managed by most of the developing countries keeping their existing size of budget, while the opposite is true in developing countries. Out-of-pocket expenditure in the health sector has been very high in this region. Out-of-pocket expenditure is 67 per cent of total health costs in Bangladesh which is more than that of neighbouring countries like India (62 per cent), Pakistan (56 per cent), Nepal (47 per cent), Bhutan (25 per cent) and Maldives (18 per cent). In the United Kingdom and the United States, it is 9 per cent and 11 per cent, respectively (WHO, 2019).

Social safety net programmes, in the form of a "targeted approach", do not cover all citizens and cause severe exclusion. Such an approach leads to selection bias, as it requires a comprehensive process in selecting the beneficiaries. Selection of the beneficiaries also requires defining the beneficiaries group which can be problematic (Zohir, 2002). The government provisions for subsidised services like education and health must be expanded and the cost of acquiring benefits from these sectors should be waived. This prospect becomes crucial for the most vulnerable groups like children, women and old-aged people who suffer from severe economic poverty very often and have no access to the service provided by the private sector due to high expenditure (Haque, 2008).

Many Latin American countries were compelled to adopt neoliberal policies under the intense pressure from international agencies. Neoliberal policies became hegemonic and unpopular (Topik, 1999). The notion of citizenship became constituent of larger social movements related to people's democratic rights (Dagnino, 1998). During the 1990s, a remarkable upsurge in popular resistance emerged against neoliberal policies of Latin American governments. The privatisation process made mass people aggrieved and distressed especially those who could not afford to gain the facilities of privatised products. The privatisation of public enterprises, worker layoffs, dismantling of reform laws and other concomitant unpopular initiatives raised waves of mass protest (Harris, 2000). Between 1976 and 1992, due to adverse impacts of neoliberal structural adjustment policies, there were 146 public demonstrations directly against the then existing neoliberal policies in 39 developing countries (Abugre, 2000).

The provision of public goods differs from country to country. Provision of goods like health, education and security depends greatly on the political system of the country. In the United States, education is provided by both the public and private sectors. Cost of private education though is more expensive than the public one. Publicly funded colleges and universities are accessible to all because of their low cost. Healthcare in the United States on the other hand is more complicated than in many developed nations. The cost of healthcare is much higher than the developed nations as it is mostly provided by the private sector. The provision of private health insurance exists in the United States. Unlike the United States, most of the European nations provide healthcare publicly at low cost. The National Health Service or NHS in the United Kingdom is responsible for providing healthcare to the public. The NHS is heavily subsidised by the government. Scandinavian countries, with democratic socialist political systems, also follow the same rule in terms of public good. European countries are able to provide public goods universally because of the higher rate of taxes. Citizens get the return from taxes in the form of public healthcare and education. Number of socialist countries has significantly gone down after the fall of the Soviet Union. Cuba, one of the very few remaining socialist countries, has public provision of both healthcare and education. The government in Cuba heavily invested in human capital. As a result, the country has one of the highest ratios of doctors per 10,000 population. There are 85 doctors per 10,000 people in the country compared to 26 in the United States, 28 in the United Kingdom, 42 in Germany and 6 in Bangladesh.

Postcolonial states have followed the footsteps of the colonial rulers in the beginning. As time went by, failure of the state in the developing countries to provide public goods has opened the door for much expensive private provision of goods like health and education. Primary reasons for failures are linked to weak infrastructure, poor technological advancement, poor quality and outcome. (Cline and Luiz, 2013; Shah et al., 2018). Health expenditure in developing countries averages at 4 per cent of the GDP whereas in the developed countries, often the number shoots to 17 per cent (OECD, 2022).

Provision to basic needs gets hurdled in the presence of acute inequality. For example, if there is a huge income gap between rich and poor in a particular country, health facilities may not be accessible to people working in marginal sectors. Besides, in some cases, race, caste, clan and religion make influence over access to public goods. Income inequality is severe in Bangladesh. In 2016, the magnitude of the Gini index was 0.48, which increased from 0.458 of 2010 (BBS, 2016). If the value of Gini coefficient tends to be at 0.5, it means there is a high propensity of inequality. In Bangladesh, the income share of the poorest 5 per cent of people is 0.23 per cent of total income, which came down from 0.78 per cent of the year 2010 (BBS, 2016). On the contrary, the richest 5 per cent of the population have increased their income share of total income to 27.89 per cent from 24.61 per cent in 2010. Inequality situation is more severe in rural areas than urban ones. In this situation of social and economic insecurity, access to public goods becomes questionable due to the lack of a comprehensive social welfare programme. Again, if the state becomes the responsible one to initiate the universal health scheme, conditions may ameliorate through frequent steps and supervision accompanied by well-defined policies. Thailand, South Africa and Turkey have been able to introduce universal health prospects in their countries. Economic growth in Cuba is not very high but they have been able to provide public goods. Cuba has emphasised social development and their social safety net programmes are operated with the purpose of reaching people of all spheres. Education and health costs are very minimal there. It has been estimated that in 2016, OOP of health was only 10.3 per cent of current health expenditure in Cuba. In order to provide health service for all, public spending in health service should be increased to a satisfactory level. The case of developed countries, particularly the United States and the United Kingdom, provides obvious differences in comparison to developing counterparts. Failure of developing countries in following the steps of developed countries creates the difference in public good provision. The reform of the health sector in Columbia was in action in 1993 on the internationally advocated paradigm of privatisation of healthcare delivery. From the experience of trivially positive outcomes of this model in other countries, Columbia tended to adopt a theoretically sound model. Some ten years after the implementation of this scheme named "Law 100" resulted in a negative manner. The objective of universal health coverage was not achieved and people could not avail of healthcare services due to huge expenses. Forty per cent of the population was left out of health insurance coverage (Groote et al., 2005). Besides, key health indicators like disease control programmes gradually deteriorated. This is not only the case of Columbia but also applicable for other lower and lower-middle-income countries that could not bring a larger section of people under the shade of universal health provision (Groote et al., 2005). In the name of coverage prospect, people from the wealthier portion of population got more opportunities to avail themselves of public services than the poor and marginalised section.

During the 1960s and 1970s, education was generally assumed to be a public responsibility and it was assumed that financing for required improvements in access and quality of this sector would be managed by public financing like progressive income taxes (Jallade, 1979). In the early era of neoliberal reforms, the full weight of public policy was brought to bear on supporting fees, often instituting an additional, national user fee for primary school attendance (Klees, 2008). The World Bank recommended user fees for primary and secondary education, which was implemented in the following year (Thobani, 1984; Klees, 1984). This situation gave birth to inequality problems where poor families could not send their children to schools with higher education becoming expensive as well. The government did little to ensure the quality of education and focused more on loans. Thus, burdens and liabilities were imposed by the donor agencies where quality and access to the basic education sector were not the prime focus but loan extraction was.

The goal of universal health coverage is deeply embedded in politics, ethics and international law (Sachs, 2012). According to article 25 of the 1948 universal declaration of human rights, everyone has the right to a standard of living adequate for medical care and the right to security in case of illness or disability. The constitution of the World Health Organization called health as a fundamental right of every human being regardless of his or her race, religion, political belief, economic and social condition. Though universal health coverage has some substantial commitments, access to healthcare facilities depends on social and economic conditions either (Sachs, 2012).

Neoclassical economics propounds that there might be market failure, the incidence of externality in provision of public goods. Neo-Keynesian economics emphasises that market failure is inevitable to occur and calls for a target-based price system to maximise the welfare of the people. In reality, the targeted approach has failed saliently in many countries. The problem with targeted approach lies in discrimination in the provision. Targeting a certain group may create polarisation in that regard. Targeted approach comes with the problem of selection bias. Selection of beneficiaries can be problematic for two reasons. First, the *classification of* the target beneficiaries is complex work. For instance, the definition of poverty varies across different lines. It can be defined by the asset holding and can also be defined by the monthly income and so on. Such classification of poverty leads to the second problem. *Exclusion* of beneficiaries in targeted approaches in most cases results in failure of the programme. Exclusion can occur for many reasons. As explained before, classification of target groups can lead to exclusion. Selection bias at the same time can result in exclusion of vulnerable groups. Lack of accountability and transparency of the executing agency as well as political intervention often results in nepotism while selecting the beneficiary group. Targeted approach overall fails to incorporate all the citizens in need of social protection. In most cases, targeted approaches require coordination among different agencies which often creates hindrance in developing countries because of weak institutions.

There are other differences between the developing countries and developed countries. For example, a student of primary grade in the United States is trained to cut grass, how to sew clothes or how to do the job of a plumber. In some developed countries, students are taught basic skills of business through practical orientation. On the contrary, in developing countries like Bangladesh, life skill training is not taught in the similar manner which becomes a vital problem in the case of searching for jobs. This situation creates a vacuum in different multidimensional skill-based sectors like research, management and many private sectors. The resulting skill mismatch and the lack of employment generation at the same pace as increasing youth unemployment ensue a mounting population in need of social security. There are several social safety net programmes in Bangladesh and in developing countries that actually do not cover the whole population stream. This proposition becomes pragmatic when it is seen that inequality is increasing randomly and both education and health costs are rising simultaneously.

Very often some developing countries have tended to initiate targeted approaches for a particular group of people such as social safety net programmes for the marginalised people in India. In this case, the situation didn't ameliorate rather discrimination sprouted. Through targeted approach, neither proper fulfilment nor skill development occurred. It can be termed as a temporary solution to a permanent predicament. In terms of outcome provision, universalisation of social goods should be instigated. Skill development should be authorised by the state itself to ensure comprehensive welfare from which social benefits can be attained.

Trends in Education, Healthcare and Employment

Both the state and market have been coercive and unaccountable which declined the opportunity of equal and free access to public goods. Policies in this regard have only helped a certain group and kept the general citizens out of the benefit cycle. As a result, poverty increased and national assets occupied by the richest class increased. Most of the developing countries have not been able to ameliorate skills as well as citizenship capability. For example, in Bangladesh, while the national income increased in recent times, income of middle- and lower-income groups barely increased. Real wages did not increase in most of the countries. Informalisation of the economy has occurred in many countries resulting in job insecurity. In sub-Saharan African countries, the situation is worse than in others. In those countries, the state has been mostly coercive and violent. People have been suffering from the deficiency of basic needs like education, health, employment, water and sanitation. Some emerging stylised facts regarding social policies of Bangladesh and other developing countries are discussed with a view to portraying the issues of overall economic and social sectors related to education, health and employment.

Rising Inequality

Global inequality around the world has increased in the recent decade. Resources have gone in the palm of the richest ones whereas the poorest ones have lost access to assets. Per capita income in some developing countries is rising but mostly because of the mountainous amount of assets occupied by the richest class. In 2016, the top 10 per cent of the total population in sub-Saharan African countries possessed 54 per cent income shares. In India, the Middle East and Brazil, the share is 55 per cent, 61 per cent and 55 per cent, respectively (Alvaredo, 2018). The rise of global inequality has not been steady. The income shares of the top 1 per cent at the global level increased from 16 per cent to 22 per cent during the 1980–2007 period. After the recession, the share declined slightly to 20.4 per cent in 2016. On the other hand, the share of the bottom 50 per cent of the global population oscillated around 9 per cent with a very trivial increase from 1980 to 2016 (Alvaredo, 2018). In Bangladesh, the income share of the poorest population was 0.23 per cent of overall income. This is a sharp fall from 0.78 per cent in 2010. On the contrary, the richest people's share of income has risen to 27.89 per cent in 2016 from 24.61 per cent in 2010. This means that the bottom 5 per cent have lost their share of income in the total economy. Again, the Gini coefficient of 0.48 illustrates the persistence of high inequality. The ultimate situation inhibits that people are being deprived and the richest class are occupying most of the income shares. This condition excavates the real scenario of state and market phenomenon of failure to benefit their population equality in terms of basic needs. This book thus proposes that per capita income be measured by "median" indicator as "mean" indicator does not exhibit the real phenomenon and hides the persistence of inequality and tendency of reverse growth

Increase in Educated Unemployment

The number of educated unemployed people is on a rise. There is a lack of skill development which attributes to a deficiency of teachers' efficiency. Opportunities for getting jobs are decreased due to a lack of necessary expertise and goal orientation. Research and Development in many developing countries are unsatisfactory. Education provided to the students often does not match with skill requirements of the jobs in the economy. While technological advancement, as well as innovation, has occurred in most of the developed countries, developing ones have not reached that position yet. In 2018, Bangladesh was ranked as the least innovative country in Asia. It stands in 17th position in Asia while countries like Brunei, the Philippines, Indonesia, Sri Lanka, Cambodia, Nepal and Pakistan are ahead of Bangladesh. Singapore, South Korea and Japan are ranked as the most innovative countries in Asia (Global Innovation Index, 2018). Bangladesh ranked 116 across the world in terms of capability and success in innovation. Sub-Saharan African countries, as well as Latin American ones, lack innovation which results in less productivity in the competitive market. In Bangladesh, according to the Survey of Manufacturing Industries 2019 conducted by BBS, during the 2012–2019 period, the number of new employment opportunities in large and mediocre industries is 482,971. It means every year on average almost 80,000 people are getting employed in the industrial sector. On the other hand, every year almost 20–22 lacs job applicants are entering into the job market. Therefore, the lion's share of the job applicants remains unemployed due to scarcity of job opportunities. The rate of unemployment among people completing education up to tertiary level has increased to 11.2 per cent in the 2016–2017 fiscal year from 9 per cent a year earlier (BBS, 2017). The country has almost failed to utilise the largest demographic dividend due to mismanagement, undergrowth of skills and low job opportunities. The demographic dividend is the economic growth potential that can result from shifts in a population's age structure, mainly when the share of the working-age population (15 to 64) is larger than the non-working-age share of the population (14 and younger, 65 and older). In sub-Saharan Africa, the rate of unemployment decreased slightly in 2013 from 6.024 per cent to 5.925 per cent. Again, in 2015, the rate went higher and in 2018 the rate was 6.096 per cent (World Bank, 2018). In 2017, the global unemployment rate was 5.6 per cent corresponding to 192.7 million unemployed people which is an increase of 2.6 million people compared with 2016 (ILO, 2018b). On the other hand, countries like China, Korea Republic and Japan are comparatively in a better and more constant position than that of other developing countries (ILO, 2018b).

Low Quality and High Price in Health Sector

Low quality and high price of public goods is a vital problem in developing countries. Out-of-pocket expenditure is higher than that in developed countries. Countries that have been able to reduce health expenditure have succeeded to ensure health facilities for larger sections of a society. In 2016, out-of-pocket expenditure as a share of current health expenditure was high in developing countries like Bangladesh, India and Pakistan. This phenomenon illustrates that health situations in those countries have been in a good manner where people are getting necessary health treatments based on high quality and low price. In several developing countries, different kinds of approaches have been taken like targeted approaches for a peripheral group, privatisation of the health sector and others. These approaches failed at the end of the day as inequality still persists. Universalisation of the health sector is a basic prerequisite for proper health facilities. Besides, due to technological lags, developing countries are falling behind in terms of quality.

Low Absorption and Decrease in Real Wage

The labour force is growing at a much faster rate than the employment potential. The implied fragility of absorption capacity and vulnerability of labourers to low wages would worsen the human condition of living hence falling short of the fulfilment of "good society" criteria as water, food, protection from harsh weather (clothing and shelter) and safety from harm. Employment creation has slowed down in recent years, along with low productivity growth in the manufacturing sector with an overall persistently low level of productivity.

There is acute wage inequality in developing as well underdeveloped countries. According to the Global Wage Report 2018/19, in high-income countries, the Gini coefficient for wage inequality ranges from 19.5 for Sweden to 38.7 for Chile (ILO, 2018a). Among low-income countries, the Gini coefficient is 53.6 in the United Republic of Tanzania while South Africa, ranked as an upper-middle-income country, has a Gini coefficient of 63.9. In Bangladesh, the Gini coefficient is 33 which is less than Mongolia and Vietnam. The real wage growth at the same time declined to 3 per cent in Bangladesh which was less than India (5.5 per cent), Nepal (4.7 per cent) and Sri Lanka (4 per cent). Women participate in part-time job sectors more than men. The gender pay gap is comparatively better in Bangladesh but mostly negative in other developing countries. Due to the contrasted job sector and increase of informal job sectors, workers are paid less than their expectations. Moreover, due to lack of skills and proper communication, educated workers are also getting deprived of expected salaries. As a result, they have to cling to low-salary-based jobs. From the recent volatile condition of the agricultural sector of Bangladesh, it has become conspicuous that farmers are paid less in contrast with their labour and dedication. After day-long arduous labour and efforts, a farmer in Bangladesh gets only 386 BDT on average (BBS, 2019). Based on the per capita income of 160,060 BDT per year, per capita income is 438 BDT per day. Besides, there is gender discrimination in regard to real wages per day. A female farmer gets 346 BDT per day which is 42 BDT less than that of a male worker (BBS, 2019). This ironic quandary reveals the miserable condition of almost 3 crore families whose livelihood and basic needs are dependent on the daily income made from the agricultural sector. This situation leads a large number of farmers to informal jobs to get more money.

Informalisation of Economy

Informal employment has increased more than formal employment in the developing countries. Many men and women due to poverty are driven to participate in the informal job sector to have a mere profit in order to run their daily life. Besides, lagging in adroitness is another reason which leads them to indulge in the informal sector. In order to increase productivity, the workers need to be well trained to get expertise, the work environment needs to be improved and job motivation needs to be enhanced through job security (Amin and Sultana, 2013). In the last two decades in the twentieth century, informal employment comprised one-half to three-quarters of non-agricultural employment in developing countries (ILO, 2002). The proportions tend to show the upper trend in this context when developing countries are even getting an estimate of better GDP growth (ILO, 2002; Beneria, 2001; Castells and Portes, 1989). Different sorts of informal workers like agricultural day labourers, urban street vendors, paid domestic workers, at-home clothing producers and other manufacturing producers are seen in the informal job sector. It has been evident that due to lack of skills and proper training facilities, people are not getting their expected job which drives them away from the mainstream job sector. As a consequence, they try to get their earnings from the informal sector. The existence of an informal sector so large that it employs the majority of the employed labour force is why the quality of jobs in developing countries have remained poor, with most workers involved in unpaid or subsistence-level agriculture jobs. An individual's access to a decent job will depend on their location and education level such that those living in urban areas with higher educational qualifications will be able to secure a better quality job than someone with lower skills in a rural setting.

Unequal Power, Coercive Nature of the State and Market

Provider of the public goods, either market or state, has been coercive in most cases serving the interest of a particular group of people. The situation is worse in sub-Saharan countries where power has been concentrated. In the Central African Republic, Mali, South Sudan, Sudan and other lower-income African countries, several times military has taken over, blood has been shed and people have been the ultimate sufferers. Even though the formal colonisation has ended, still pseudo-colonial features are prevalent in these countries. Neoliberal policies have been introduced in these countries in the form of market-oriented approaches. People have been suffering from deficiency of basic needs. They are not getting proper education, training and skills, health facilities and a satisfactory real wage. Not only in sub-Saharan Africa but also in other developing countries power concentration has been prevalent. The states have mostly remained coercive, alienating from the general people. When alienation occurs, the problems multiply, whereas solutions are mostly not offered. Identification of problems and finding out solutions are mutually inclusive process. If the state and people stay well connected, solutions come through interaction with people. Added to this, there are authoritarian populism in many developed and developing countries where the issues such as inequality are not acknowledged and general massess fall prey into blame games and "alternative truths". Due to this unaccountable situation, people get affected and remain deprived of their basic needs. The same goes for the market. Examples demonstrate that markets have worked for a particular group of people who have been arriviste and have a closed link with the incumbent authority. The avarice for power and rent makes the providers of the public goods coercive and unaccountable. Through the process of concentration of power, the coercive nature of the ruling authority gets unleashed. Coercive nature of either state or market gets enhanced when unaccountability prevails. Accountability does not allow the incumbent authority to take arbitrary decisions which mainly goes against the interest of the general people.

Summary

This book attempts to challenge a number of theoretical positions regarding social policy and public goods, particularly for developing countries. The main argument is that the universal provision of public goods and the resulting well-being of people in developing countries are necessary and their efficacy is contingent upon the intensity of "public society". The analysis employs the evolution of institutions – formal and informal of past and present. In doing so, a historical analysis of institutional structure finds that the social contract in developing countries of the precolonial, colonial and postcolonial eras is alienating between the state and her citizens. The rent-seeking nature of the political settlement has dismantled the formal institutions supposed to uphold rule of law and property rights to ensure the provision of public goods. The norms and values in the society over the years have made citizens conform to the discrimination, widening the alienation with the state while allowing the clientelist networks to accumulate power. Thus, for "provision of public goods", it is necessary to understand the notions of configuration of power, politics, political settlement and pro-social behaviour of human beings that play a vital role in social policymaking. The configuration of power in society is a crucial variable in determining the allocation and distribution of public resources.

With the advent of "Development Economics", following WWII, it had been argued that economic progress would lead to the betterment of the society through the application of the "trickle-down" mechanism. Economic growth in terms of GDP was considered to be the sole indicator of a nation's state of progress. This Western-led motto of development brought signs of progress but at the cost of widening the gap between individuals and groups in terms of economic resources. In addressing the ever-increasing inequality, attention has been given to education, health and employment, providing an alternative framework in terms of ideas for the redistribution of income and allocation of public goods.

In order to examine the trends of public goods provisioning and social policies of developing countries, this book has attempted to test hypotheses, derived from propositions, through empirical examinations in the succeeding chapters. The three main components – education, health care and employment and social security – are divided into three parts with each part providing a thorough review of existing literature, an analysis and a summary for the policymakers for transformative changes in developing countries.

References

Abugre, C. (2000). Still sapping the poor: A critique of IMF poverty reduction strategies. World Development Movement.

Alvaredo, F. (2018). *The world inequality report*. Cambridge, MA: Harvard University Press.

Amin, A.T.M.N., and Sultana, S. (2013). *The informal economy of Bangladesh an exploratory study of five selected sectors for moving towards formalization*. Dhaka: ILO.

Bangladesh Bureau of Statistics. (2017). *Bangladesh labour force survey*. Dhaka: Bangladesh Bureau of Statistics.

Bangladesh Bureau of Statistics. (2019). *Report on household income and expenditure survey 2016*. Dhaka: Bangladesh Bureau of Statistics.

Bayliss, K., and McKinley, T. (2007). Providing basic utilities Africa in Sub-Saharan: Why has privatization failed? *Environment: Science and Policy for Sustainable Development*, 49(3), pp. 26–32.

Benería, L. (2001). Shifting the risk: New employment patterns, informalization, and women's work. *International Journal of Politics, Culture, and Society*, 15(1), pp. 27–53.

Bovens, M.A. (2005). *From financial accounting to public accountability*. Retrieved March 22, 2022, from https://citeseerx.ist.psu.edu/viewdoc/download?doi=10.1.1.503.3621&rep=rep1&type=pdf

Castells, M., and Portes, A. (1989). World underneath: The origins, dynamics, and effects of the informal economy. In A. Portes, M. Castells, and L. Benton (Eds.), *The informal economy: Studies in advanced and less developed countries* (p. 12). Baltimore: Johns Hopkins University Press.

Cline, G.B., and Luiz, J.M. (2013). Information technology systems in public sector health facilities in developing countries: The case of South Africa. *BMC Medical Informatics and Decision Making*, 13(1), pp. 1–12.

Dagnino, E. (1998). 'Culture, citizenship, and democracy: Changing discourses and practices of the Latin American Left', in S.E. Alvarez, E. Dagnino and A. Escobar, (eds), *Cultures of politics/politics of cultures: Revisioning Latin American social movements*, Boulder: Westview Press.

Day, P., and Klein, R. (1987). *Accountabilities: Five public services* (Vol. 357). London, New York, and Tavistock: Taylor & Francis.

De Groote, T., De Paepe, P., and Unger, J.P. (2005). Colombia: In vivo test of health sector privatization in the developing world. *International Journal of Health Services*, 35(1), pp. 125–141.

Dutta, S., Lanvin, B., and Wunsch-Vincent, S. (Eds.). (2018). *Global Innovation Index 2018: Energizing the world with innovation*. Geneva: WIPO. Retrieved March 22, 2022, from https://www.wipo.int/edocs/pubdocs/en/wipo_pub_gii_2018-chapter1.pdf

Haque, N.U., Montiel, P., and Sheppard, S. (1998). *Public sector efficiency and fiscal austerity*. Washington, DC: International Monetary Fund. Retrieved March 22, 2022, from https://www.elibrary.imf.org/view/journals/001/1998/056/001.1998.issue-056-en.xml

Haque, S. (2008). Global rise of neoliberal state and its impact on citizenship: Experiences in developing nations. *Asian Journal of Social Science*, 36(1), pp. 11–34.

Harris, R. (2000). The effects of globalization and neoliberalism in Latin America at the beginning of the millennium. *Journal of Developing Societies*, 16(1), pp. 139–162. https://doi.org/10.1163/156852200512021

Hazelkorn, E., and Gibson, A. (2019). Public goods and public policy: What is public good, and who and what decides? *Higher Education*, 78(2), pp. 257–271.

ILO. (2002). Decent work and the informal economy. *In the international labour conference, 90th session, item VI*. Geneva: International Labour Organisation.

ILO. (2018a). Global Wage Report 2018/19: What lies behind gender pay gaps. *International labour office*. Retrieved November 20, 2021, from www.ilo.org/wcmsp5/groups/public/-dgreports/-dcomm/-publ/documents/publication/wcms_650553.pdf

ILO. (2018b). *World employment and social outlook*. Geneva: ILO. Retrieved March 22, 2022, from https://www.ilo.org/global/research/global-reports/weso/2018/lang--en/index.htm

ILO. (2020). *ILOStat*. Retrieved from https://ilostat.ilo.org

Jallade, J.P. (1979). Financing education for income distribution. *Finance and Development*, 16(1), p. 33.

Kabeer, N. (2013). *Intersecting inequalities, the MDGs and what comes next*? London: Overseas Development Institute.

Klees, S.J. (1984). The need for a political economy of educational finance: A response to Thobani. *Comparative Education Review*, 28(3), pp. 424–440.

Klees, S.J. (2008). A quarter century of neoliberal thinking in education: Misleading analyses and failed policies. *Globalisation, Societies and Education*, 6(4), pp. 311–348.

Kuhn, M., Schularick, M., and Steins, U.I. (2020). Income and wealth inequality in America, 1949–2016. *Journal of Political Economy*, 128(9), pp. 3469–3519.

Martin, B. (1993). *In the public interest? Privatization and public sector reform*. London: Zed Books.

Ministry of Finance. (2018). Social safety net programmes: Budget 2016–17, 2017–18 (revised) & budget 2018–19. Government of Bangladesh.

Morris, S.D. (2011). Forms of corruption. *CESifo DICE Report*, 9(2), pp. 10–14.

Nitsch, M., and Schwarzer, H. (1996). Recent development in financing social security in Latin America, issues in social protection. Discussion Paper 1. Geneva: ILO.

Nwankwo, S., and Richards, D.C. (2001). Privatization – the myth of free market orthodoxy in sub-Saharan Africa. *International Journal of Public Sector Management*, 14(2), pp. 165–180.

OECD. (2022). *Health expenditure in relation to GDP.* Retrieved March 22, 2022, from https://www.oecd-ilibrary.org/sites/592ed0e4-en/index.html?itemId=/content/component/592ed0e4-en

Pollitt, C. (2003). *The essential public manager.* Maidenhead: Open University Press.

Rawls, J. (1971). *A theory of justice.* Cambridge, MA: Harvard University Press.

Raymond, S. (1994). The disappearing third world. *Economic Reform Today*, No. 4.

Romzek, B., and Dubnick, M. (1998). Accountability. In Jay M Shafritz (Ed.), *International encyclopedia of public policy and administration* (Vol. 1, pp. 6–11). Boulder: Westview Press.

Rotberg, R.I. (2002). Failed states in a world of terror. *Foreign Affairs*, pp. 127–140.

Sachs, J.D. (2012). From millennium development goals to sustainable development goals. *The Lancet*, 379(9832), pp. 2206–2211.

Samuelson, P.A. (1954). The pure theory of public expenditure. *The Review of Economics and Statistics*, 36(4), pp. 387–389.

Shah, H., Meghji, A.F., and Mahoto, N.A. (2018). Healthcare services in developing countries of the South Asian region: Present and future perspectives, in Bit, A. (ed.) *Design and development of affordable healthcare technologies* (pp. 1–22). Hershey, Pennsylvania, USA: IGI Global. doi: 10.4018/978-1-5225-4969-7.ch001

Thobani, M. (1984). Charging user fees for social services: Education in Malawi. *Comparative Education Review*, 28(3), pp. 402–423.

Topik, S. (1999). The construction of market society in Latin America: Natural process or social engineering? *Latin American Perspectives*, 26(1), pp. 3–21.

UNCTAD. (2020). The Covid-19 shock for developing countries. *UNCTAD/GDS/INF/2020/2.* Retrieved September 7, 2021, from https://unctad.org/en/PublicationsLibrary/gds_tdr2019_covid2_en.pdf

WHO. (2019). *Global spending on health: A world in transition* Retrieved April 22, 2021, from https://www.who.int/publications-detail-redirect/WHO-HIS-HGF-HFWorkingPaper-19.4

WHO. (2020). *WHO database.* Retrieved December 1, 2021, from www.who.int/healthinfo/statistics

World Bank, World Bank Indicators. (2018). *Unemployment, total (% of total labor force) (Modeled ILO estimate) – Sub-Saharan Africa.* Retrieved December 1, 2021, from https://data.worldbank.org/indicator/SL.UEM.TOTL.ZS?locations=ZG

Wright, G. (2013). *Sharing the prize.* Cambridge, MA: Harvard University Press.

Zohir, S. (2002). *Wider impacts of microfinance institutions: Towards defining the scope and methodology.* Retrieved March 22, 2022, from https://www.findevgateway.org/sites/default/files/publications/files/mfg-en-paper-wider-impacts-of-microfinance-institutions-towards-defining-the-scope-and-methodology-2002.pdf

2 Social Policy, Public Society and Public Provisioning in Developing Countries

Introduction

Developing countries have been afflicted with being trapped in low-level provision of public goods due to various complications. Due to failure in the privatisation of public goods like education, health, water and electricity, the governments were compelled to reorganise the pattern of providing and distributing public goods. Besides, the states have been responsible for the failure in the public sector because of incessant experimental tendency without considering the practical situation of mass people. Many a time, it has been evident that ulterior motives and self-interests of individuals are the vital elements in determining the provision of public goods. There have been murky policies provided by the international donor agencies and IFIs like IMF and World Bank, which did not bear fruit in the developing countries. Rather, citizens have suffered the most due to labyrinthian nature of the public sector and monopolisation of the market, while extractive nature of the institutions has been leading to low-level trap of public goods. Most of the schools of thought have argued for and against the question of providing public goods. In this chapter, attempts are made to understand various schools of thoughts and their substantial criticisms with a view to comprehending the universalisation of public goods.

For institutions, either state or market, the ultimate purpose is assumed to be the optimal delivery of public goods to all the common people of the society at a low price and with good quality. It is evident that both state and market have had flaws in providing public goods. Markets have adopted predatory pricing. Again, the state has been proved as coercive in most cases, especially in developing countries. Different schools of thoughts like classical, Keynesian, neoclassical and new institutional have argued on the typical mode, institutional setting and its format, but issues relating to coerciveness are quite absent in these theories. Both market and state have been evident to act coercively when these are given the power of authority to provide public goods to the people. Generally, power makes the authorities coercive. When coerciveness remains embedded in the hands of the powerful, either conspicuously or in a camouflaged form, distribution and quality of public goods get

DOI: 10.4324/9781003284222-3

disrupted. Without a struggle by an active public society, both state and market remain unaccountable which is prone to make arbitrary decisions in favour of vested interest and against the well-being of mass people. Both classical and neoclassical economics have argued the importance of markets to provide social or public products. For example, Adam Smith (1776) has stressed enhancement of capability of human being, particularly through education, if needed by means of public finance. If a person gets proper education, capability and skills get developed and ultimately s/he is able to produce more output than before. Though it has devoted much on human capital, the neoclassical economics does not emphasise on public provisioning. Rather it focuses on the importance of the market that it should be free of government intervention. The Keynesians argue for state interventions. Public choice theory opines that common people are deprived of public goods due to the network among the powerful which revolve around the bureaucrats, lobbyist groups or businessmen, politicians and civil society. In this process, mass people remain out of the need-based service as the vicious network becomes the ultimate consumer, scraping away the people from their basic needs like education, health, employment and so forth. New institutional economics argues for institutional rearrangement, incorporating both formal and informal institutions and their coordinated interaction in the case of public service delivery. The political settlement analysis, focusing on the distribution of power, demonstrates that dysfunctions of institutions create misallocation. This chapter advances on the premise that politics and economy of a country are interrelated. There is evidence that if the political ambience is not in favour or a fiasco prevails in a particular country, the economy gets affected. On the other hand, if the political environment is favourable to common people and there remains participation of common people, the economy thrives and people benefit. The issue is the economy is highly susceptible to damage or downflow if the political setting is not accountable and well-functioned.

Again, it is not about the institutions that will deliver the public services to the people, the most important factor is the pattern of service delivery, which is contingent upon the powers of the median voters and their capacities to mute coercion and ensure accountability to them. The forthcoming analysis is thus different from the public choice theory, which has also criticised the state for making a vested interest network and suggests customer-oriented service provision. Again the loophole here is the marginalisation of common people for being reduced to "customer", from the entitlement of being "citizens". It is, thus, important to make a distinction between citizen and customers while the focus must be on comprehending coercion. In his lecture "Politics as a Vocation" (1918), the German sociologist Max Weber defines the state as a "human community that (successfully) claims the monopoly of the legitimate use of physical force within a given territory". Weber stated three elements of the state – territoriality, violence and legitimacy. He opines that the state has the monopoly of violence in a legitimate form and it can execute it when people tend to show less allegiance to them or any kind of menace occurs. State very often makes misuse of this privilege with the purpose of perpetuating the power holding nature through being coercive and violent towards mass people. In *The German Ideology* (1846), Karl Marx characterises the power of state as exploitative. He further says in *The Communist Manifesto* (1848) that: "The executive of the modern state is nothing but a committee for managing the common affairs of the whole bourgeoisie".

The conceptual addition to the political settlement analysis is that struggle is a prerequisite to avail need-based services. By dint of struggle and movement for education, health, employment and other basic needs, accountability gets generated. Otherwise, coerciveness gets thrived which is inherent in the nature of the ruling class, whether it is state or market. An analytical framework is crafted along the lines, showing the positive correlation between public society and public goods. Moreover, an effort is placed to lay out a pathaway – stability, transformability and sustainability. Without stabilising the basic needs of the people, the transformation proves to be difficult. Again, the process of transformation should be pursuing a pathway, which is process-led and advances towards sustainability.

The book pursues universal approach to social policies, and thus, it necessitates discussions and examples relating to welfare state. The welfare state can be seen from a narrower or broader point of view. The former incorporates traditional domains, like income transfer and social services, while the latter focuses on the state's role in managing the entire economy, like employment wage and other macroeconomic activities. The activities which are often shaped by institutions are often determined by the welfare states. Of such institutions, employment and the labour market are crucial ones. Social policies are also formulated to act as a protection to the risks and uncertainties that one might face in terms of his/her work life due to various incapabilities. Esping-Anderson (1990) takes into account different countries in a cluster based on their regime type. The United States serves as a representative of the liberal regime, Sweden as the social democratic regime and Germany as an illustration of the conservative regime. In Scandinavia, the welfare states have been actively expanding the horizon of social services. This also creates an enabling environment for female participation in the labour market. Esping-Anderson (1990) further suggests that the regime type associated with the United States (market model), even though, ensures democratic participation in the labour force, has created an environment where different racial or ethnic groups are engaged in good or white-collar jobs and junk or odd jobs differently. Hispanics were found to fill those vacancies by the women and the Blacks. Further analysis suggests that Hispanics and other immigrants are perhaps becoming the new proletariats. The theorisation of the welfare state is not free from severe criticisms. The conservatives fear that welfare rights require the government to participate in the market, which might hamper the market equilibrium. Also, such rights may bring severe fluctuations in the motivations or incentives to work.

Public Society and Public Goods

Understanding the relationship between public society and public goods is crucial, since literature from all sides suggests that public funds are being captured through the concentration of power, resulting in inequality, deprivation of basic services and rights. As the state is responsible for the supply of public goods, it has to build up the connection with its citizens who claim or demand public goods. State and citizens are engaged in a bonding that incorporates mutual rights, duties and obligations. Citizens help build state institutions through taxation. If the distribution of power and resources remains unequal, the society turns out as an unequal society with inequality widening day by day. Thus, the understanding of the political context of public good provisioning is important in order to explain why inequality is rising. Accordingly, the essential component of the analytical framework for provisioning of public good is public society, where equality and rights of citizens can be ensured through human sociality.

Human sociality is the tendency of people to be concerned with and associate with each other, broadening the analysis of human decision-making and behaviour. The most salient trait of *Homo sapiens* is that in a human society, people do not act as rational and individualistic beings rather they live collectively which leads to human sociality. Individuals are social animals, influenced by social preferences, social networks, social identities and social norms. Many people have social preferences for fairness and reciprocity and possess a cooperative spirit. General economic policies assume individuals are self-regarding, autonomous decision makers, these policies often focus on prices. Human sociality however implies that behaviour is also influenced by social expectations, social recognition, patterns of cooperation, care of in-group members and social norms. Indeed, the design of institutions, and the ways in which they provide services, may provoke motivation for cooperative tasks, such as community development and school monitoring. It is important to note that people often behave as conditional cooperators – that is, individuals who prefer to cooperate as long as others are cooperating.

For social order to function, French sociologist Durkheim advocated two different forms of solidarity that are characteristic of primitive and industrial societies. Primitive societies nurtured mechanical solidarity that entails a community with similar thoughts and actions. It was assumed that in primitive societies social relationships are weak and homogenous, therefore laws are required to be repressive and punitive to impose controls on offences of the common conscience. Industrial societies consisted of a division of labour among individuals according to the merit that rewarded them accordingly. In such societies, Durkheim suggested that moral and economic regulation is required in order to maintain organic solidarity in society (Durkheim, 1893; Bowring, 2016).

Social preferences and social influences can lead societies into self-reinforcing collective patterns of behaviour. Humans are inherently social. In making decisions, often affected by what others are thinking and doing and what is expected. Human foraging groups typically have culturally transmitted norms and practices, that is, food sharing. Social meanings and norms, and the social networks that humans are a part of, pull towards certain frames and patterns of collective behaviour. Thus, human societies develop social norms as a means of coordinating and regulating behaviour as well as expressing community values, and these informal governance mechanisms have profound consequences for societies (Bowles, 2016). Bowels make the original and interesting argument that such "levelling mechanisms" of collective work act like redistributive taxes to reduce the disadvantage of engaging in costly prosocial behaviour. The absence of these kinds of levelling mechanisms in primate groups may explain why human societies differ from those of other primates.

In every human society, people cooperate with many unrelated individuals. Division of labour, trade and large-scale conflict is common. The sick, hungry and disabled are cared for, and social life is regulated by commonly held moral systems that are enforced, albeit imperfectly, by third-party sanctions (Boyd, 2006). Human groups maintain a high level of sociality despite a low level of relatedness among group members (Gintis, 2000). Reciprocal altruism leads to a high level of cooperation in human societies, and many behavioural scientists believe that reciprocal altruism is sufficient to explain human sociality. The manifestation of *strong reciprocity* is evident in the propensity of humans to engage in episodic collective action towards transforming social norms and political regimes. Movements for civil rights, civil liberties and political democracy in authoritarian states are responsible for creating modern liberal democracies, yet participation in such movements cannot usually be explained in terms of self-interest or reciprocal altruism (Bowles and Gintis, 1986). Robert Trivers introduced the concept of *reciprocal altruism* in order to understand cooperative and altruistic behaviour that occurs between unrelated individuals rather than kin. Reciprocal altruism requires individuals to respond in kind – do for others what was done for them – if the behaviour is to continue. Reciprocal altruism is based on the principle "You scratch my back and I'll scratch yours". They cooperate with each other extensively and frequently behave altruistically. It can even be said that cooperation and help are just as fundamental a part of human nature and human society as selfishness and competition. Indeed, cooperation is fundamental to social life (Trivers, 1971).

Inequality has the same effect on society. Inequalities create an inefficient structure in society which fails to deal with public goods and justice. The collective and political capacity of state and market cannot work within that structure (Atkinson and Piketty, 2007, 2010). The distribution of income and wealth in the society depends on the power and politics within the government and the fiscal activities taken by them. Other than politics, rent-seeking activities also impact the income and wealth distribution as political activities can lead to the accumulation of wealth by a few. This is commonly observed in developing countries.

Inequality affects how state and market institutions function, as well as how institutions deliver public goods. Particularly, high levels of inequality may lead to institutional failures when resources and power are captured by few elites at the expense of poorer and more vulnerable sections of the people (Bardhan, 2005; Ostrom, 1990; Platteau, 2004). These effects are of particular concern in developing countries where institutions (formal or informal) are central to the distribution of resources when governments are unable to provide adequate public goods and insurance (Ostrom, 1990; Townsend, 1994). There is also strong evidence that income and wealth inequalities are closely related to political inequalities, the distribution of political power and influences over political outcomes (Stiglitz, 2013). Thus, inequalities in income and wealth may result in harmful social, economic and political outcomes in the form of increased poverty and social exclusion, lower economic growth, and sociopolitical instability and insecurity. Furthermore, institutions like family and immediate social circumstances shape the aspirations, perceptions and attitudes, which tend to transmit values, wealth, tastes and beliefs across generations (Bowles et al., 2006). Inequality in wealth inheritances results in generations with little initial wealth and limited opportunities (Piketty, 1998, 2015).

The state has an important role to play in reducing inequality in society. State through its available policy mechanisms can improve the distribution of wealth. With the help of fiscal policy, states can introduce progressive taxation and education system that can enhance human capital through provision of equal opportunities. Property rights, if regulated properly, can also reduce unequal distribution of wealth (Atkinson, 2014; Piketty, 2015; Stiglitz, 2013).

Equality and citizenship are interlinked, and the concept of citizenship has received renewed attention (Kymlicka and Norman, 1994). Thomas H. Marshall was perhaps the first who focused on the conflict inherent in modern industrial societies: the tension between *equality*, as an assumption of the notion of citizenship, and *inequality*, as a consequence of class structure of the capitalist system. Marshall in *Citizenship and Social Class* (1950) states three elements of citizenship. First, the *civil element* of citizenship propagates the rights of freedom. This includes the freedom of speech, personal liberty, right to own property and right to justice. These rights are upheld by the courts of justice in a state. Second, the *political element* gives an individual the right to participate in political processes. This includes voting rights of citizens as well rights to representation in parliament. Parliament and local government is the associated institution for political rights. Lastly, the *social element* deals with rights associated with economic welfare and the right to live to the standards prevailing in society. Educational institutes and social services are the corresponding institutions for social rights. Social rights can eliminate inequality in society (Marshall, 1965).

Marshall (1950) introduced a notion of positive liberty into citizenship through the concept of social rights, such as rights to well-being, rights to health, education and services regardless of the person's position in the economy. For him, access to such basic social welfare and resources was a right *per se*. He also argued that access to social rights is essential to exercise civil and political rights as it enables them to engage in civil and political life.

A Review

There are numerous theories with regard to provision of public goods. The debates are also full of partial readings. While hardly these abstractions account for situations or courses of actions in developing countries.

Adam Smith was not only an advocate of a laissez-faire market where a minimal state has no more role than the protective function but also a pragmatic social thinker of economic growth (Reisman, 1998). In his book "Wealth of Nations", laissez-faire has been considered as the only qualified presumption rather than a hard-and-fast rule where the natural order appears in an imperfect mode (Reisman, 1998). He advocated a market-based approach in order to achieve economic growth and recommended the trivial role of the state, doing nothing but protecting the environment of the market. He did not anticipate that market freed from the state could go under the dominance of large corporations and cartels such as the East India Company (Reisman, 1998). Smith had demonstrated some reasons behind his aversion to state authority and intervention in economic activity. First, he believed that the government was ignorant of trade and the outcome had been counterproductive enactments leading to low-returning allocations. Second, according to Smith, the government was wasteful of capital which frequently encroached upon the funds destined for more necessary expenses. Third, the government was vulnerable to the clamorous importunity of partial interest (Smith, 1776; cited in Reisman, 1998). Fourth, the government is largely dependent on the network of salaried officials. Smith entitled those bureaucrats as idle and profligate (Reisman, 1998).

The thinkers of classical school of economics put their interest concretely in the conditions of their own time. They are, however, confronted with the facts of economic and social changes taking place in contemporary English society as well as in previous historical periods (Harris, 2007). From their perspective, progress was conceived within a format of need to preserve private property and hence the interest of property-owning class. They conceived that the exercise of individual initiative under free competitive conditions will result in individual achievement which will consequently end up in social well-being. They recognised the accumulation and investment of social products as the main driving force of economic growth (Harris, 2007). Smith emphasised the process of extension of the division of labour. He advocated the public provision of education with partial contributions from the enrolled students (Thomas, 2018). He calls for education for all believing that it would offset the harmful effects of the division of labour on the workers, and therefore, education had to be accessible to the workers (Thomas, 2018). In short, Smith supports the enhancement of human ability that promotes prosperous life. It was assumed that workers consumed their wages for subsistence, capitalists reinvested their profits and landlords spent their rents on "riotous living". Accumulation makes an impact on the distribution of income as the economy expands over time (Harris, 2007). Ricardo admitted that with better education and improved habits, natural wages could rise (Garegnani, 1983).

The fact is though the classical school of thought has propagated a market-based economy free of state intervention, both Smith and Ricardo felt the need for education for comprehensive development of skill and human capability. Instead of promoting this aspect and its pathways, neoclassical economics rather exaggerated the theory of free market economy and free competition. The focus has been put on market-based public goods instead of equal distribution. Classical economics conceived that individual achievement would give rise to comprehensive well-being but in reality, it did not happen; rather capital accumulation and concentration have become rampant in societies. Most of the common people are being deprived of their basic needs and if they can avail themselves, they have to spend a herculean amount of money. Even sometimes, they do not get the desired service they are worth getting. Classical economics did not say anything about coercion and accountability. The notion of public society and how the vast number of people can be brought under the shade of public goods opportunity are also absent in classical economics. The statement Smith and Ricardo made on education and human capability has not been brought to the broad discussion rather the succeeding schools highlighted on either market or state.

John Maynard Keynes advocated for increased government expenditures and lower taxes to stimulate demand and pull the economy out of depression. Keynesians assert that wage responds slowly with the change of supply and demand which results in shortage and surpluses, especially of labour, conceiving unemployment is subject to the caprice of aggregate demand (Blinder, 1988). The Keynesian economics advocates active government policy in order to resolve the quandary of recession or economic depression. The gap in Keynesian school is that it did not mark the situation of monopolisation of power in terms of providing public services. Again, Keynesian economics did not specify the responsibility of the government in terms of expenditure for the mass people ensuring basic needs like health, education, employment etc. People in developing and underdeveloped have a reverse narrative that they feel discouraged to pay tax as they get very little service in ratio with what they pay. Besides, the coercive attitude and monopoly of violence, which is many a time misused through exploitation and deprivation of common people are absent in Keynesian economics.

The neoclassical school of thought has been distinguished as a mainstream or orthodox form of economics. Most of the developing countries have opted for market-oriented reforms of the economy, based upon neoclassical economics. It is a reshaped form of classical economics in the perspective that free market or perfect competition results in efficient resource allocation which regulates economic attributes and makes an equilibrium through market forces of demand or supply. The individual ambition of market participants, that is, buyers and sellers perform in the market through self-regulating appropriation which is termed as the "invisible hand" by Adam Smith (Sullivan and Sheffrin, 2003; Agboola, 2015). In neoclassical economics, the presupposition of the existence of an individual who strives to augment his/her utility is made by methodological individualism under the shade of rational choice theory (Kjosavic, 2003 cited in Agboola, 2015). Neoclassical economics emphasises rationality and employs utility maximisation through this process (Dequech, 2007; cited in Agboola, 2015). Like the classical school of thought, neoclassical economics aims at focusing on individual interest through which the well-being of the larger group will be achievable. A major condition of general equilibrium is free competition which is a consequence of laissez-faire. In this respect, the unrestricted supply and demand of goods would unconditionally give rise to the exchange values of each and every product (Daal and Jolink, 1993). They further add that in this realm, buyers and sellers do not only have perfect information about the price of the product but can also participate in market transactions whilst the utility maximising nature of human agents clears the market and enables it to move towards an equilibrium state. Critics argue that the state represents the interest of bureaucracy, which guards the authority's jealousy and seeks benefits when restricting economic activity (Krueger, 1974; cited in Reyes and Galarza, 2018). Therefore, it is not able to intervene efficiently. Public policies for development have resulted in an inferior mode of outcome (Krueger, 1990). The underlying reason is that bureaucracy has autonomous interest holding the supreme power more than other groups or agents (Krueger, 1990). Dorfman, Solow and Samuelson (1958) argued in their "Turnpike Theorem" that the fastest growth path is the one following balanced growth. Even if that path does not play an adequate role to enhance the welfare of the population, it is efficient to follow the course and create adjustments when the economy has achieved the most desirable outcome.

Several scholars have extrapolated the conception of individual behaviour from diverse perspectives. There has been a plethora of critical discussions regarding rational human behaviour provided by the neoclassical school of thought. In the words of Karl Marx, and his general conclusion in his Preface to *A Contribution to the Critique of Political Economy* (1859), "men enter into definite, necessary relations, which are independent of their will", and "the totality of these relations of production constitutes the economic structure of society", thus forming the framework upon which the superstructure (state, institutions, traditions, norms and values) is based, and evolves and transforms according to changes in economic foundation. According to him, the essence of man is no abstraction inherent in every single individual. In reality, it is the ensemble of social relations (Engels, 2010). "Human nature" ought to be defined as an attribute of the human species that is uniquely or distinctly human (Byron, 2016). Marx says,

> Species-activity and the species-spirit whose real, conscious and authentic existence consists in social activity and social enjoyment. Since the essence of man is the true community of man, men, by activating their own essence, produce, create this human community, this social being which is no abstract, universal power standing over against the solitary individual,

> but is the essence of every individual, his own activity, his own life, his own spirit, his own wealth.
>
> (Karl Marx, *Economic and Philosophic Manuscripts of 1844*; cited in Byron, 2016)

His argument is that human essence is the ability to produce within a community in a way that serves the community and oneself. This characteristic disproves the notion of neoclassical school that individual interest gradually tends to social well-being. Marx contemplates the idea of human nature and production altogether and doesn't want to segregate them. Human being has a natural instinct to produce both for himself and for the community (Byron, 2016). In producing a unique product, individuals affirm their uniqueness and in distributing their products, they gratify others. This phenomenon creates a mutual and interdependent relationship among the members of the society. Since human nature is distinctive and unique in operational mode, they make an attempt to produce goods for the other fellows. Marx posits that utilitarians never consider human nature in general, which would alert them to the harmful nature of capitalist utilitarianism (Byron, 2016). Criticising capitalism Marx implies that in this format workers do not produce for their fellow species. Their objective turns into satisfying individual interests for their subsistence. "One consequence of the peculiar nature of labour-power as a commodity is, that its use-value does not, on the conclusion of the contract between the buyer and seller, immediately pass into the hands of the former" (Marx, 1885) – the value of the labour power is determined by the value of the commodities – the minimum value of labour power is such that it covers the means of subsistence that is essential, and any fall in the value of labour power below this minimum is the marker of a "crippled state". In abstract political economy and in the real world, as Marx says, workers work for themselves and not for their human beings. "Free, conscious activity" becomes non-existent which was previously a characteristic of labour. Labour becomes coerced and since it is done in a perfunctory manner, free and conscious activity gets diminished (Byron, 2016).

Post-Keynesian economics makes rigorous criticism of neoclassical economics. It opposes the neoclassical school of thought calling it unrealistic, since reality is non-linear, dynamic and subject to uncertainty. The world is about imperfect competition and incomplete information, and debt plays a major role in determining aggregate demand. Irrational consumers and irrationality in expectations constantly hone in on a state of disequilibrium (Olshansky, 2015). According to neoclassical economics, when a rational consumer chooses any option, he chooses the best option available, since a consumer knows what is the best option for her/him so s/he makes the selection accordingly. On the other hand, the Post-Keynesians argue that humans do not have the mental capabilities to figure out the level of utility from each option they make. Rather, they make consumption decisions based on heuristics (Olshansky, 2015). A society cannot be termed as a model of independent individual choices because an important part of a society is how humans with diverse characteristics interact with each other. This interaction includes the impact of one's choice-making and spending on others. The neoclassical theory ignores the idea of interactions (Olshansky, 2015).

Neoclassical school also misreads Adam Smith on the point of self-interest and nature of human beings. Though Smith advocated market-centric approach and minimalist state, he called for public provision of goods, among which education is worth mentioning. Smith proposed that education should be equally accessible for all so that this can offset the harmful effects of the division of labour. Through this statement, Smith also tended to assure the issue of job security through proper education and skill development. Human beings are mainly purposive, cooperative and creative through the functioning of solidarity and interaction. Neoclassical economics diverted this "purposiveness" to self-interest. While making the economy liberal was supposed to be their prime objective, it has been proved gradually that demand-supplier authoritarianism originated acutely in lieu of liberalisation. Akerlof and Shiller extend their critical discussion to Adam Smith implying that Adam Smith was correct that people rationally pursue their interests. According to Akerlof and Shiller, this thought experiment of Adam Smith and later neoclassical economics missed the point of non-economic motivation that guide human beings and they also fail to take into account the extent to which humans are susceptible to become irrational or misguided. They ignore the "animal spirits" (Akerlof and Shiller, 2009). Animal spirit refers to people's peculiar relationship with ambiguity or uncertainty. Akerlof and Shiller compared the condition economy with a family. They argue that just like a family faces happiness, sorrow, disarray, success and failure, the economy also has this sort of diverse moment which can be termed as good times and bad times. In this realm of ups and downs, the issue of self-sacrifice and effort must be taken into account. People use the information at hand to make rational decisions. Then they make rational decisions based on rational predictions. Through this pathway, trust and confidence are mandatory. Confidence is more beyond rationality. Even a truly trusting person may discard or discount information. He/she may hide information either and information might be fabricated. Even if the person proceeds the information rationally, there is a possibility that he/she may not act rationally. In reality, he/she acts according to what he/she trusts to be true (Akerlof and Shiller, 2015). Neoclassical school of thought has averted this trust issue which is an indispensable part of an economy.

Sen criticised traditional economics for containing too little structure. According to him, a person is given one preference ordering which comes forth on the occasion of his need of interest. Thus his welfare is also reflected, the idea of what should be done is summarised and his actual choices and behaviour are described. A person thus termed as "rational" might be true in a limited sense of revealing no inconsistencies in his choice behaviour but if he has no use for these distinctions between quite different concepts, he must be a bit of a fool (Sen, 1977). Sen refers to John Harsanyi's distinction between ethical preferences and subjective preferences. Ethical preference means what the individual prefers on the basis of impersonal social considerations and subjective preference incorporated what an individual actually prefers. Generally, sympathy goes towards the subjective preference but one thing is unclear in this respect, that is, the role of commitment (Sen, 1977). Normally a person's subjective preference is taken to define his/her utility function whereas commitment is excluded from the functioning process. Moreover, ambiguity gets revealed from the fact that these are defined to "express his preferences in the full sense of the word as they actually are" (Sen, 1977). Sen argues that sometimes lack of personal gains in particular acts is accepted by considering the value of rules of behaviour. He further points out that even within a consequentialist act, evaluation framework, the exclusion of any consideration other than self-interest seems to impose a wholly arbitrary limitation on the notion of rationality (Sen, 1977). Sen tends to recapitulate that not only subjective preference but also ethical preference is highly significant and mandatory to conceive while making utility-based decisions. Absence of rules or behaviour which are socially constructed mostly creates the possibility of making irrational choices. Thus, the notion of "individual knows what is best for him" does not work in many socio-economic practical phenomena.

Another dimension of critical analysis of rational human behaviour is that people are irrationally pro-social (Bowles et al., 1997). In laboratory settings, this consistently appears to contribute more than the rational actor model predicts in public goods games (Schneider and Pommerehne, 1981; Isaac and Walker, 1988; cited in Bowels, Boyd et al., 1997). Bowles, Boyd, Fehr and Gintis introduced the term "homo reciprocans". Ostrom et al. have propounded the theory in favour of the existence of reciprocal fairness in various forms of social institutions. According to this approach, strategic interactions involving coordination problems with a propensity to cooperate, they respond to the cooperation of others by maintaining or increasing their level of cooperation they make response on the part of others through retaliation against them at any cost who have offended them before, even if they cannot expect future gains from such kind of retaliation, they are not stanched (Bowles et al., 1997). If certain forms of punishments are unavailable for a particular period, individuals respond to defection with defection. Such agents can be termed as homo reciprocans which stands in contrast with the homo reciprocans definition provided by traditional economics.

There have been further challenges to the rationality assumption by notable scholars. The same choice problem may evoke different kinds of preferences, depending on inconsequential variations in the formulations of options (Tversky and Kahneman, 1986) or in the procedure used to elicit choices (Tversky et al., 1990). Kahneman (1994) has found two obstacles to the maximisation of experienced utility. First, people lack skills in the task of predicting how their tastes might change and second, maximisation is a tendency to use the effect associated with particular moments as a proxy for the utility of extended outcomes. Kahneman (1994) identified this sort of peculiarity as a trait included in the cognitive treatment of time which delineates the importance that people attach to the emotions of transactions and may cause other forms of myopia in decision-making. Besides, maintenance of coherent beliefs and preferences is a very crucial and indispensable task for limited minds (Simon, 1955; Tversky and Kahneman, 1986). The assumption of rational decision is often defended by the argument that people will learn to make correct decisions accompanied by further argument that rational decision makers will drive out the irrational ones. Tversky and Kahneman imply that affecting learning works only under certain conditions. It requires accurate and immediate feedback about the relation between the situational conditions and the appropriate response. These conditions are very often cannot be satisfied by managers, entrepreneurs and politicians while facing problems since outcomes are very common to get unleashed late and are not easily attributable to a particular action, variability in the environment deteriorates the reliability of the feedback, no information or lack of information may occur during alternative decision-making process and most important decisions are unique and provide little opportunity for learning (Einhorn and Hogarth, 1978; cited in Tversky and Kahneman, 1986). The claim that the market can be trusted in correcting errors made by individuals and the effect of individual irrationalities cannot be made without supporting evidence. Moreover, the burden of specifying a plausible corrective mechanism should rest on those who make this claim (Tversky and Kahneman, 1986).

Kenneth J. Arrow has emphasised on trust. In the absence of trust, it would become very costly to arrange for alternative sanctions and guarantees, and many opportunities for mutually beneficial cooperation would have to be forgone (Arrow, 1969). Lack of trust is indeed a major cause of underdevelopment (Banfield, 1958; cited in Arrow, 1969). Moreover, all the individuals are not the same. If the choices of all the individuals were the same, there would not be any trade to take place. Though Arrow implied the importance of difference of choice and diversity of people's interest, he did not particularly mention the coerciveness of state and market. He denoted state as coercive from the perspective that state has coercive power and that power can be used to economise transactions. Arrow did not call the state an entity rather a system of individual agents. While talking about allocation by market or state, he elucidated that if an allocative process is to take place through majority voting, it will create a paradox. According to him, if a majority could do what he wanted then it would be optimal to win with a bare majority and take everything. Any such bargain can be broken up by another proposed majority (Arrow, 1969). Arrow misses the differences between demand and need, as a sick person requires healthcare irrespective of her/his capacity to pay for services while demand refers to the willingness and ability of consumers to purchase goods at different prices. In terms of public goods, with people's needs, equity and efficiency also come forth. Individuals may differ from one another, their choice may be disparate but everyone needs education, everyone needs proper health facilities and desired wage so that he/she can run his/her livelihood in a decent manner.

The neoclassical school of economics has been criticised from various grounds by heterodox schools. It has been argued that the notion of group well-being by individual well-being is questionable as persons may act cynically and only work for his/her own interest. As a result, both capital accumulation and capital concentration occur. Besides, neoclassical economics has talked about human capital but did not discuss citizenship building. Not only education is required to enhance economic output but also to develop citizenship, which allow people to share responsibilities, give taxes and follow rules and regulations. The whole process can be regarded as a virtuous cycle of economy. Neoclassical economics did not bring forth the issue of equal opportunity. Apart from that, it fails to explain the way social characteristics are acquired by individuals (Kjosavic, 2003).

New Institutional Economics (NIE) shares some assumptions with neoclassical economics but differs from it based on several methodological standpoints. New institutional economics has made an attempt to graft institutional content onto mainstream economics by effectively extending conventional economics thoughts (Furubotn and Richter, 1986). It does not challenge the fundamental assumptions of conventional economics regarding methodological individualism and economic maximising rationality (Furubotn and Richter, 1986). The NIE holds that individuals do not get complete information, their mental capacity to process information is limited, their motivation is more complicated and their preferences are subjective and less stable than assumed in neoclassical theory (North, 1990; cited in Agboola, 2015). In this way, NIE nullifies the instrumental rationality provided by neoclassical theory and implies bounded rationality. Coase (1960) makes his point by saying that in order to carry out a market transaction it is necessary to discover who it is that one wishes to deal with, inform them in a compatible way through discussing of terms, conduct negotiations leading up to a bargain, draw up the contract and undertake the inspection to make certain that the contracts are well observed. He further argues that rearrangement of property rights could be processed through the market price system whenever it would lead to an increase in the value of production assuming a costless market transaction process. Where property rights are well defined and transaction cost is zero, allocation of resources becomes efficient and not dependent on the pattern of ownership or private property rights. In congruence with Coase's work, the focus has been put on governance structures of firms which are necessitated by the cognitive limitation and opportunism of human agents (Williamson, 2002). The institutional arrangement of a market is directly related to the level of transaction cost in the market (Buitelaar, 2004). Institutions and the effectiveness of enforcement determine the cost of transacting (North, 1990; cited in Agboola, 2015). According to Coase (1984), in the absence of transaction costs – the costs of identifying potential trading partners, negotiating contracts, monitoring for compliance and so forth – it does not matter how property rights are allocated. Following North, a broad definition has been explicated, that is, systems of established and embedded social rules that structure social interactions (Hodgson, 2006; cited in Meramveliotakis, 2018).

According to NIE, efficient allocation can be achieved if the transaction is zero or very minimal and property rights are well-defined. NIE is concerned about the well-defined ownership of property rights. Again, its focus on transaction cost considering that zero transaction cost would result in efficient allocation creates some basic foibles. Transaction cost is rarely zero and it gets bigger when many firms get involved in the determination of the ownership of property rights and getting relative benefits. Again, NIE has talked about the typical form of debate, that is, choice and provider. They extended their thoughts to the rearrangement of institutions but did not highlight the basic problem of "coercion". Again, the debate is not about the choice and provider, rather it is regarding the needs of the common people which must be ascertained by the responsible authority through the practice of accountability. The NIE jots about skills but not about citizenship. As a whole, NIE shirks the issue of social construction and overall well-being through establishment of public society. Rather, it is almost symmetrical to prior orthodox and conventional theories with an extension that, if institutions are well formed with concrete property rights, they will operate smoothly and individuals will get the benefit.

Public education serves a similar function by lowering the cost to the government of getting its citizens to further the government's interest. Through public education, the government gets more control over the educational system and public education makes the educators government employees who work for further government interest. It works as a tool to socialise the students by teaching a curriculum which illustrates that government as an institution furthers public interest (Holcombe, 1997). Paul Samuelson (1954) suggests that public goods are government-produced goods which imply that goods with the characteristics of jointness in consumption and non-excludability ought to be produced by the government. Markets fail to allocate resources Pareto-efficiently.

Government itself can become a failure because of not being able to allocate goods properly. Samuelson has followed the customary path of choice regarding public goods and has taken a side without considering the issue of accountability and equality. It has been evident from many developing countries that the government itself may capture public goods for its own interest and may deprive general people by providing basic facilities to a particular group of people. Sub-Saharan African countries are epitomes in this respect. In these countries, throughout the years either military regime or bureaucratic power has confiscated power in order to serve a particular network that has an intimate connection with the powerful one. Thus people get deprived and their needs remain unfulfilled.

Political economy is concerned with the conflicting roles of individuals in the market and state. Individuals while operating in the market usually are engaged in activities with self-interest. On the other hand, within the boundary of state, an individual embarks on collective action (Balaam and Veseth,

1996). Political economy also deals with the problem of choices and distribution in state and market. Karl Polanyi argued that the emergence and subsequent development of a "market society" were made possible by the enormous and incessant intervention of the state. Similarly, Charles Tilly's work *Coercion, Capital, and European States, AD 990–1990*, showed that the development of the modern state in countries such as Britain and France paved the way for capitalist development. Albert O. Hirschman (1977) argued that the "invention of capitalism depended on the creation of a new type of political actor – an individual liberal subject who was the product of a liberal state" (Blyth, 2009). The government in a capitalist economic system has to provide public goods like education, health and employment even though capitalism is a self-regulating system (Scott, 2006). Capitalism is described as a three-level system comprising political authority, institutional foundations and economic markets from upper to lower case. Economic markets comprise product markets and factor markets. Principal economic actors can be termed as factor owners, firms and consumers (Scott, 2006).

In modern economics, this approach has massive importance in studying the accumulation, price mechanism and distribution process in public society and public goods provisioning sector through an economic lens which is why this book has concentrated on this approach. In the economic realm, individuals or classes compete with each other in order to gain personal interest or to keep control over productive resources in a political way. Thus, political economy describes the process of accumulation on the basis of the economic realm where the political system gives the directions to the process. The classical understanding of economic behaviour, however, is being termed as classical political economy. Attention has been given to the political economy that originates from Karl Marx. To understand the power relationship in the contemporary world, the ideas of Marx are highly relevant theoretical constructs.

Marxian theories are often being termed as conflict theories (Sears and Cairns, 2015) – the theories that draw attention to power differentials, such as class conflict, and generally contrast historically dominant ideologies. According to Marx, the "material basis of the state is relative scarcity". Relative scarcity is a condition in which the productivity of labour enables a group of people to produce a surplus that is more than enough to enable them to survive, yet not enough to allow everyone to live in true abundance. When productivity reaches such a point, society gets divided into two classes: proletariat class – the vast majority, who spends most of their time working, while receiving minimum wages that barely enables them to live; and bourgeoisie class – a tiny minority who exploit the majority – that is, appropriate surplus and live in luxury without performing productive labour. The division of society into such classes, in turn, gives rise to the state. According to the Marxian view, the state is controlled by the economically dominant class, enabling it to maintain its control over the exploited classes. In another way, the states' rights were being allotted according to wealth.

The Neo-Marxist theorists differ significantly from the classical Marxist notion. Power, according to Neo-Marxist theorists, possesses a significant degree of autonomy whereas the function of the capitalist state is believed to maintain coherence, cohesiveness and stability of the economic system. Marxian literature, however, is not flawless. For example, in postcolonial states, the class cannot be divided strictly into bourgeoisie and proletariat; rather "intermediate classes" dominate in the developing countries in the state formation and transition process.

A few studies have been conducted so far to explain the class struggle and state in postcolonial societies (e.g. Alavi, 1972; Riaz, 2005; Sen, 1999, 2009; Saul, 1974). Saul (1974) states in this regard, the problem of "the state" as it presents itself in the context of "underdevelopment" has been under-theorised and little researched. Alavi (1972) claims that the exploiting class – the "bourgeoisie" – should be divided into three classes in postcolonial societies as the Indigenous bourgeoisie, Metropolitan neocolonialist bourgeoisie and Landed classes. Bureaucracy acts as an interwoven among the interests of these three social classes. And, the key common phenomenon of such societies, as he identified, is the special role of military – bureaucratic oligarchy. Another important facet of postcolonial states is that it inherits the "overdeveloped" state apparatuses and their institutionalised practices through which the colonial powers mainly regulated and controlled the indigenous social classes. The overdevelopment of the bureaucratic-military state apparatus in the colonial period originated from exercising supremacy over the native social classes. The state, in the postcolonial period, remains autonomous because of the failure of any single class to overcome the rule of the overdeveloped state.

Rent-seeking becomes a particularly important process in a country in transition in driving the evolution of property rights when that evolution is seen in the context of political organisation and mobilisation (Khan, 2000b). In neoclassical economics, rent is always inefficient. But, the precarious point is that rent is only efficient under some specific and well-defined circumstances and if those conditions get changed or do not exist, it may be turned into inefficient rent. Creating stable property rights is seen to be effective in preventing rent dissipation. But, in the context of a developing economy, in the absence of a well-defined property rights structure, there is a tendency to capture the resources or the rent-seeking is practised by the rentiers. Public society and public goods provisioning become vulnerable because of rent-seeking behaviour. Rent-seeking refers to unproductive, confiscating activities that convey positive returns to the individual but not to society (Krueger, 1974, cited in Chakraborty and Dabla-Norris, 2006). It refers to the tasks that seek to create, maintain or change the rights and institutions on which particular rents are based (Khan, 2000). Rent-seeking tempts unequal distribution of wealth and income in the economy and the consequence of widespread rent-seeking is that resources are being confiscated which are not used in productive sectors. Rent-seeking has severe consequences for developing countries as it can turn in to illicit forms (bribing, coercion etc.) and is more detrimental to growth.

In most of the developing countries or in transient economies, the relatively wealthy people are engaged in rent-seeking through abusing power. Such power is not derived from their wealth, rather acquired through creating a nexus with political and administrative power.

Thus, the idea of political settlement becomes important in analysing the correlationship between politics and economy. Khan (2010) defines: "A political settlement is a combination of power and institutions that is mutually compatible and also sustainable in terms of economic and political viability". Thus, the "political settlement" describes a specific distribution of power between relevant organisations in a country. The political settlements in developing countries are structurally different from most advanced countries and also considerably different from each other. Development involves institutional solutions that address the market failures relevant for that country and that can be implemented in that particular political settlement. Identifying critical aspects of the "macro-political equilibrium" is vital as it affects the "micro" analysis of particular institutions and organisations located within that macro-equilibrium. The analysis of "political settlements" identifies relevant aspects of the macro-political equilibrium that can affect the operation of particular institutions and organisations at the micro level (Khan, 2010). The political settlements framework denotes a degree of influence in shaping the direction and balance of power in elite politics that in turn shapes development, security and governance institutions. This approach focuses on the central structure of power that determines the overall pace and direction of development and change in a country.

The concept refers to elite equilibrium in the existing type of political settlement and clarifies that the power is being concentrated in the hands of authoritative entities. The motive of the ruling elite is simply to have a state with a concentration of power. This results in the coercive power of the state. Di John and Putzel (2009) referred to political settlement as the balance or distribution of power between competing social groups and social classes. The concept of "double balance" stems from the social order framework where the organisations produce a string between the distribution and management of political power on the one hand, and the distribution and management of economic power on the other (NWW, 2009).

The idea of political settlement stems from "double balance". Resource distribution in a political settlement works through the formation of institutional arrangements. Elite groups compete with each other for control over resources. Two kinds of orders arise, Limited Access Order (LAO) and Open Access Order (OAO), which differ primarily in the way conflict is mediated by the elites and the nature and role of rents in managing such conflict. In LAO, conflicts are managed through elite negotiations in a personalised and discretionary way while rents are generated by limiting access (exclusiveness) to critical social, economic and political resources. OAO refers to pluralistic, open, competitive political and economic arrangements, which ensure the rule of law, universal protection of property rights and the impersonal organisation of social, economic and political transactions (NWW, 2009). The principal supposition of the social-order framework is that elite has the motivation to manage violence and this is done through strategic rent allocations among powerful elites forming legitimacy through non-economic means, to explain how elite political settlements are maintained. In developing states, however, the nature of political settlement is clientelist. This can be defined as one where substantial holding power is based on sources *outside* the incomes generated by formal institutions which belong to the intermediate class of the developing states. This explains why informal organisations based on patron–client networks are important in limiting the access to resources.

Rent-seeking activity can be also linked to the discussion of "primitive accumulation" by Marx (Khan, 2000). Primitive accumulation is enfolding the property (land), by dispossession. The Marxian argument was that by using coercion (state power), the state steals some capital from people and provides it to the hand of the private sector to accelerate industrialisation. Khan (2000) stated that the same process of wealth transfers or appropriation in developing countries can be described as rent transfer and rent-seeking. By exercising organisational and political power, the intermediate class is mainly involved in this process of capital accumulation. This results in inequality in society as rents are not turned into productive sectors to enhance growth and development.

So, the distribution of political power determines which individuals or groups are likely to gain in distributive contests. In an exchange economy, therefore, power is the fundamental actor to the economic outcome. The political economy approach not only helps apprehend the distributional aspects of public resources of a country, rather it guides to clarify reasons of inequality among different countries and this can lead to a more rigorous understanding of the economics of public resources at inter, intra and global contexts.

There are demonstrated gaps in different approaches, warranting a new framework (Table 2.1).

A Framework

The book discusses three areas of social policies: health, education and employment. The key solution lies in education. Without proper health and nutrition, people will not be able to obtain the skills they need to learn. A public society is a prerequisite for accountability for the certainty of provisioning of public goods for all. The configuration of power in developing countries is the main source of all types of inequality, as power holders capture the significant amount of rent for their personal desire which is actually meant for the citizens. Different approaches and models have been propagated but did not work in developing countries. Liberal, neoliberal policies pursued through Washington Consensus and post-Washington Consensus could not ensure people with public goods. Precisely, public goods have not become public literally. Privatisation has been undertaken and the outcome is quite dissatisfactory.

Table 2.1 Approaches and underlying gaps

Approaches		*Concept about state and society*	*Concept about citizenship*	*Underlying gaps*
Market-centric approach	Classical economics	The state is an instrument to fulfil the self-interest of individuals.	Citizens seek to pursue their self-interests	Fails to recognise coerciveness of the institutions, human beings as social-beings who live in communal solidarity and state as an instrument to fulfil the universal needs and the collective interest of a society
	Neoclassical economics	Believes in laissez-faire economy with privatisation and non-interventionist state	Rational individuals seek to maximise their utility and profit	Eliminates public spending on education, healthcare and employment creation which rises inequality in the society and coerciveness of either market or state is not mentioned
	New institutional economics	A set of institutions that permit individuals to benefit personally from doing what will also serve the (material) interests of society as a whole and acknowledge the market inefficiencies	Individuals and society as a whole seek to benefit through a set of institutions	Ignores the weak governance and the political transaction cost in developing countries
	Public choice	Applies the methods of economics to the theory and practice of politics and government showing that collective action is modelled with individual decision makers using the political process to further their self-interests	Individuals are political beings with self-interests	Fails to capture the complex political structure of developing countries due to a narrow economic lens
Political economy		The state is responsible for providing public services to all and ensuring minimum rights to its citizens.	Passive citizenship.	Lack the civic, political and social elements of citizenship

Source: Prepared by author

A handful of rent-seeking groups were the ultimate beneficiary of privatisation. As a result, a larger section of people could not avail the daily necessary needs like water, electricity, education, health and other needs. Government failure is another important aspect to attribute. The institutional rearrangement in both informal and formal sectors could not provide the ultimate solution about how to provide public goods for every section of society. This book makes a diverse and multifaceted interplay among different approaches where nullifying the approaches is not the purpose rather the focus is given on aspiration for a public society where general people can get necessary benefit from public goods. Accountability is a must for the provider of public goods, whether it is state or market. This book has tended to address the issue of "coercion" which is inherent in the ruling authority. Without movement and aspiration for a public society, accountability cannot be ascertained. Thus, the intention of this book is to develop a new understanding of the state and society for the efficient provision of public goods.

Components

The political-institutional features of developing countries can influence the institutional outcome. The unequal power relations of different agents will be made endogenous in the model for explaining the function of efficient public provisioning that will lead to the construction of public society in developing countries. A flow chart on necessary conditions, sufficient conditions and outcomes shows the path towards the high provision of public goods where agents, market and state head through the path of stability, transformability and finally towards sustainability (Figure 2.1).

Agents

Market and state, both agents, need to be stabilised through necessary conditions for making the price of health and education low while increasing quality so that people from every class get the opportunity to avail the optimum benefit from these public goods. Besides, skill development alongside citizenship building is necessary to ensure job opportunity. It has been deemed that public goods provider, whether market or state, is mainly coercive. Hence, establishing accountability is a prerequisite to ensure universalisation and equal opportunity to public goods. Through this process, a citizen state can be formed where equity, efficiency, human dignity, justice, aspiration and struggle are extant. The sufficient condition comprises, amongst others, institutions and political settlements. These components conflate with each other to maintain the citizen state. The ultimate purpose should be to achieve a stable, transformed and sustainable milieu of public goods provisioning.

State–society relations are reflected in the interactions between state institutions and societal groups in terms of negotiation between them in order to allocate basic rights and public services. The state derives its authority through

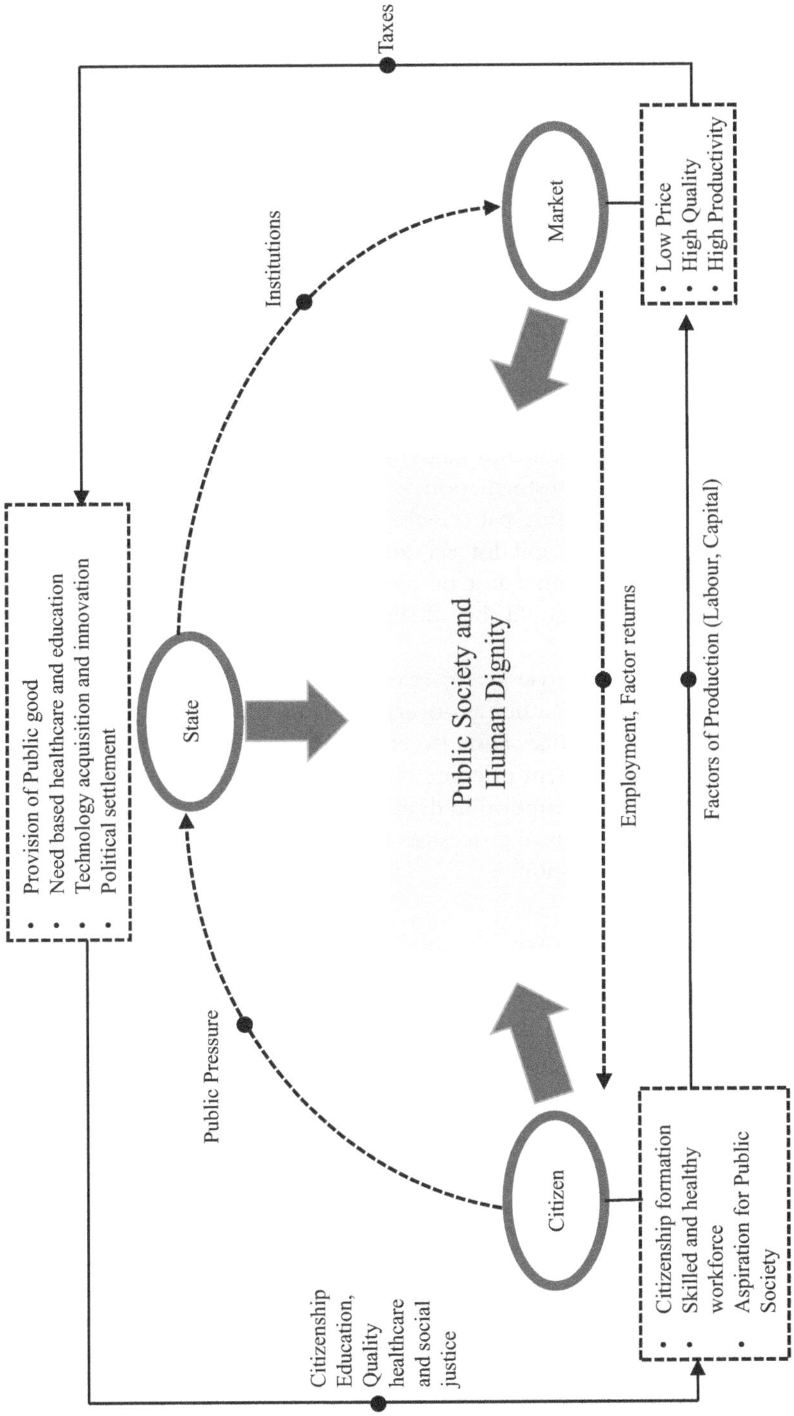

Figure 2.1 Citizens, state, market and public society

Source: Prepared by authors

its interaction with citizens. Citizens enjoy certain rights in society. Such rights include the right to vote and participate in political process and public life. A citizen is also provided with access to education, health and other basic human rights from the state. State also provides a citizen the security of residence and freedom to move freely. These rights are bestowed on citizens through citizenship.

Political settlement deeply impacts the relationship between the state and society. This relation is usually based on patronage, corruption and lack of accountability in fragile states. The presence of informal institutions in such states results in the deterioration of formal laws. Informal institutions tend to create a political elite in the society. Such elite groups directly benefit from patronage and income from natural resource rents without caring for the citizens. This group holds the power and tries to limit the participation of citizens in the political process and public life. This can be done with help from the state in the form of repression and state-mandated violence. Such a nature of political power results in weak and fragile states.

Success in economic transformation is acquired through bounding governance capabilities in managing patron–client politics in ways that allow political stability sufficient for capitalist accumulation to continue. Rent-seeking and unfair interventions could not be reduced unless the privileges of rent-seeking and corruption could be challenged through accountability and democratisation.

First, in developing countries, transaction costs are high not only because of government interventions, rather as governments usually lack the institutional capacity to reduce transaction costs by effectively protecting property rights and thus efficient enforcement of contracts.

Second, the political corruption in developing countries originates from the difficulty in managing the fiscal processes. The patron–client politics come into play from structural corruption.

Power and Politics

In developing countries, in the case of institutions and state, power is mostly associated with the idea of patron–client politics. It has its place in developing countries regardless of culture, politics or economic strategies as it allows the governing group to identify the most critical, the best organised, the most troublesome or simply the most dangerous constituencies to them threatening their power to hold and buy them off selectively which cannot be done under formal budgetary institutions. By critically discussing the propositions regarding transaction cost by neoclassical economics, Bowles and Gintis (1993) argue that in the process of transaction, the price and other terms of exchange often include a payment that exceeds at least one agent's next best alternatives. As there remains an unequal sharing of information, an asymmetric information problem arises in the exchange. Thus, the distribution of power is important as it is related to the issue of political settlement.

However, state and powerful elites using their patron–client network and other dimensions of means try to capture the public goods that are actually meant for the citizens. This process ultimately leads to rent-seeking and underdevelopment.

Means

The provider of public goods, whether it is state or market, tends to capture the flow of the goods through various means. They might benefit in terms of individual interest through capital accumulation. This sort of phenomenon has been experienced in sub-Saharan African countries and in some developing countries. The ruling authority tends to confiscate and concentrate public goods which result in an artificial crisis of public goods in the market. Another means that public goods are subjected to is coercion. Coerciveness is inherent in the ruling authority. Through coerciveness, the malpractice of unaccountability grows higher. As a result, low provision of public goods occurs.

In this circumstance, two conditions function towards the way of achieving the high provision of public goods, that is, necessary condition and sufficient condition. People's aspiration for a public society is a sufficient condition in this respect. Without the aspiration of public society, public goods cannot be delivered appropriately on an equal basis. The coercive state or market does not want to provide public goods in an ambience of unaccountability. Hence, a constant struggle is required to ensure high provision of public goods. Ruling authority and the elite class through coercion often dictate the terms of the transaction in a market which may lead to inefficient outcomes.

Outcome

Basically, the state is linked to the economy through the processes of rent creation, distribution of resources and basic rights and facilities. The role of the state machinery is to provide public goods efficiently to the citizens. But, in developing countries, because of the rent-seeking behaviour of public officials and powerful agents, citizens are deprived of social welfare. They have to bear the cost which benefits the extractors (powerful elite) in the form of "Rent".

Economic transformation is achieved through the continuation of capitalist accumulation. Political stability through managing the patron–client relation is required to attain productive accumulation. Rent-seeking and unfair interventions exist because of privileges given to a selected few. Hence, accountability and democratisation can challenge corruption, and undue advantages can reduce rent-seeking.

Rent results in a significant amount of welfare costs (deadweight loss). Restriction on supply (reducing supply from *Q1* to *Q2*) raises the price level from *Pc* to *Pm* point. Total rent is being shown by the shaded area. It is worth stating that the rent itself is not a loss as far as society is concerned. It

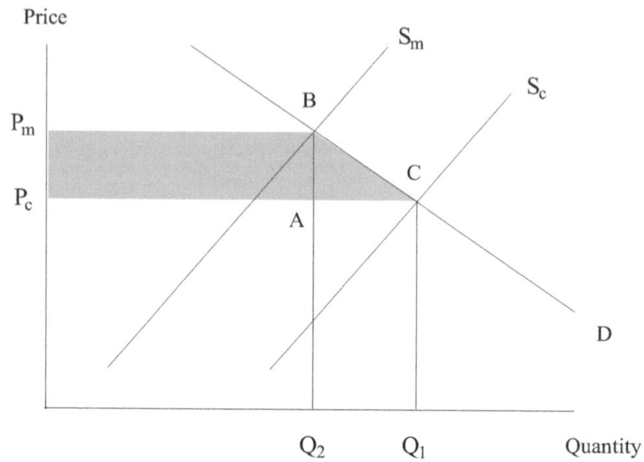

Figure 2.2 Rent-seeking and welfare cost

Source: Prepared by authors

is notionally a transfer from consumers and factor suppliers to the owners of the firm since it is composed of what was previously part of the consumer and producer surplus. The social cost of the monopoly is the net social benefit that is lost as a result of the monopoly (Figure 2.2).

In the figure, the lost net social benefit (known as the deadweight welfare loss) is measured by the little triangle *ABC*. The magnitude of the transfer of wealth from consumers to rent-seekers is depicted by the box *PmPcAB*. In developing countries, often the government authority or bureaucrats and politicians tend to earn rents in different ways. Simply, by exercising power, they succeeded in managing rent through state-created monopoly.

In developing countries, rent is not used in a productive way that will lead to growth. In developing countries, a significant part of the rent-seeking is spent within patron–client networks and the rents produced and distributed within these networks (Khan, 2000). One of the main reasons why developing countries diverge significantly from good governance conditions is that there is an unending gap between the reality of developing country politics and theoretical policy prescription. There is a systematic dearth in the practice of democracy and accountability in developing countries. Political parties use personalised power to establish a patron–client relationship with agents, that is, bureaucracy. Consequently, politically driven accumulation is high which leads to fractionalisation and economic inequalities (Engerman and Sokoloff, 2002; Blair, 2005). The principles of impersonal politics can however keep developing countries free from patron–client politics (AFD et al., 2005)

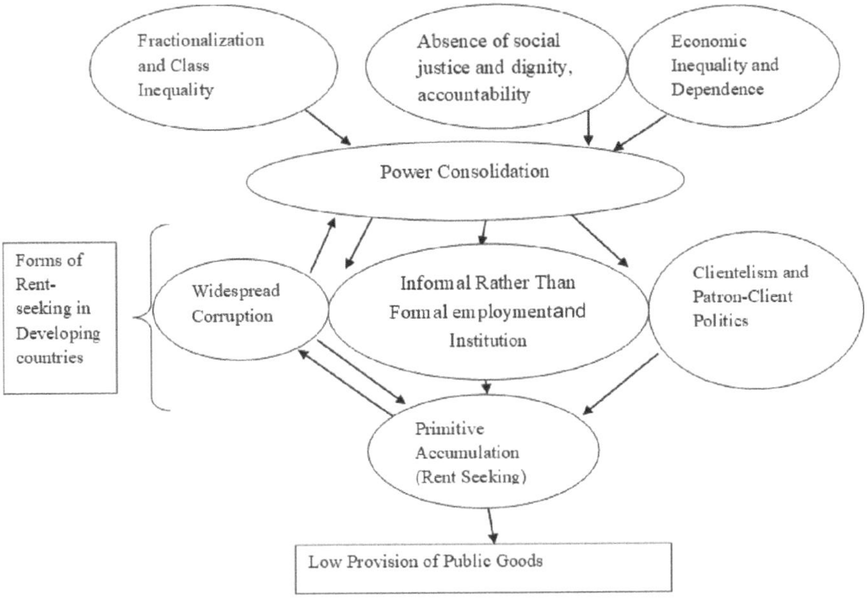

Figure 2.3 Cause-and-effect relationship in patron–client political accumulation

Source: Prepared by authors

As a result of rent-seeking tendency, the public goods are being captured by a few powerful. So, because of the contested interplay of the agents of developing countries, resources are captured by a few, retarding the growth or transition process of the postcolonial states, in the absence of pluralism and accountability. Due to the rent-seeking process, masses of this region are most vulnerable as they are not getting their services, wages and return of their labour or human capital cannot pave the way towards growth. The whole process of rent accumulation by state and elite and their process of using means (power) are depicted. As a process of holding power and rent-seeking behaviour, there is a low provision of public goods to citizens and they also get lower wages, which in turn leads to the underdevelopment of mass citizens (Figure 2.3).

State creation of monopoly over economic resources leads to the lower provision of public goods. The political elite groups tend to distribute state resources in a manner that results in the accumulation of resources by the elites. Hence, higher accumulation for the elite means lower public goods for the citizens. Lower provision of public goods on the other hand results in low levels of productivity. Productivity depends on education, health and employment opportunities created by the state. Lower productivity hence reduces the earnings of the citizens. Lower earnings eventually lead to low investment and savings. This impacts the economy greatly as low investment in general

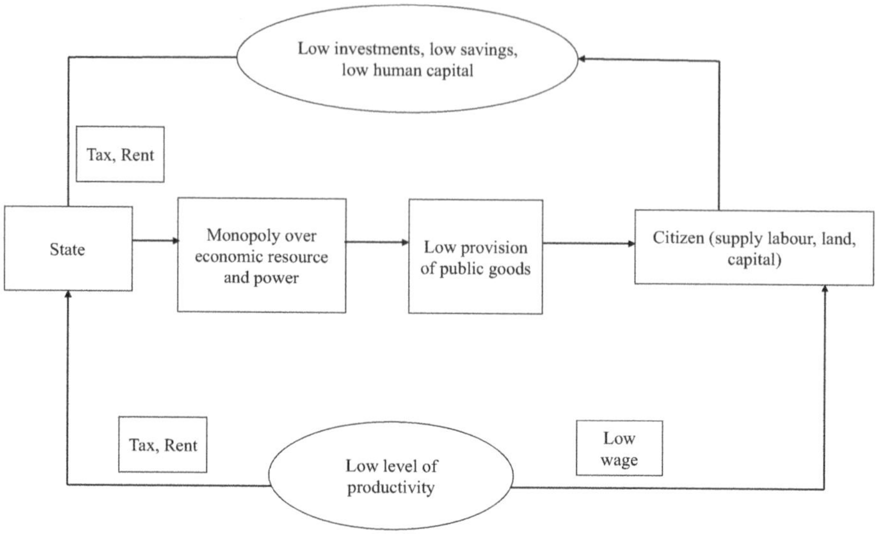

Figure 2.4 Interlocked factor and product market for public goods

Source: Prepared by authors

slows down the economy. Hence, the state receives lower tax returns from the citizens. The political elite that concentrates power creates a vicious cycle in public provisioning (Figure 2.4).

Summary

The provision of public goods is hampered or flowed at a low stream due to the coercive nature of the provider. It could be the market or state that turn out to be predatory. In this realm of tilted political settlement, a particular class or group of powerful people become the ultimate beneficiary who work against the needs of the general people.

For curbing the concentration of power, a pathway is a public society and constant movement. Without movement, accountability cannot be established. Through the fulfilment of necessary and sufficient conditions towards the pathway of stability and transformability, sustainability will be achieved, resulting in high provision of public goods for every one of the society. Socially and politically powerful groups tend to extract resources from the rest of the population in inefficient ways and thus set up bad institutions. Thus, this process leads to lower provision of public goods and hampers citizen welfare. Such a nature of power relations in developing countries acts as a hindrance towards economic transformation. High inequality in developing countries exists because of the unequal distribution of resources due to power relations. The necessity for provisioning of public goods comes because of unequal distribution. The provision of public goods can significantly improve the living standard of those living in the lower echelon of the society. A nation state cannot sustain high inequality. Hence, it is imperative for the state to formulate policies that respond to the existing inequality in society. The welfare of the society relies on the relation between the state, market and citizens.

References

AFD, D., German Development Policy and World Bank. (2005). *Pro-poor growth in the 1990s: Lessons and insights from 14 countries.* Retrieved March 22, 2022, from https://documents1.worldbank.org/curated/en/421141468027836341/pdf/328850Pro1poor1growth1in1the11990s.pdf

Agboola, A.O. (2015). Neoclassical economics and new institutional economics. *Property Management*, 33(5), pp. 412–429.

Akerlof, G., and Shiller, R.J. (2009). *Animal spirits. How human psychology drives the economy, and why it matters for global capitalism.* New Jersey: Princeton University Press.

Akerlof, G., and Shiller, R.J. (2015). *Phishing for phools: The economics of manipulation and deception.* Princeton, NJ: Princeton University Press.

Alavi, H. (1972). The state in post-colonial societies Pakistan and Bangladesh. *New Left Review*, 74, p. 59.

Aroche Reyes, F., and Ugarteche Galarza, O. (2018). The death of development theory: From Friedrich von Hayek to the Washington consensus. *Journal of Post Keynesian Economics*, 41(4), pp. 509–525.

Arrow, K.J. (1969). The organization of economic activity: Issues pertinent to the choice of market versus non market allocation. *The Analysis and Evaluation of Public Expenditure: The PPB System*, 1, pp. 59–73.

Atkinson, A.B. (2014). *The colonial legacy: Income inequality in former British African colonies (No. 2014/045).* WIDER Working Paper. Retrieved March 22, 2022, from https://www.econstor.eu/bitstream/10419/96303/1/778819191.pdf

Atkinson, A.B., and Piketty, T. (Eds.). (2007). *Top incomes over the twentieth century: A contrast between continental European and English-speaking countries.* Oxford: Oxford University Press.

Atkinson, A.B., and Piketty, T. (Eds.). (2010). *Top incomes: A global perspective.* Oxford: Oxford University Press.

Balaam, D.N., and Veseth, M. (1996). *Introduction to international political economy.* New Jersey: Prentice Hall.

Banfield, E.C. (1958). *The moral basis of a backward society* (with the assistance of Laura F. Banfield). Glencoe, IL: The Free Press.

Bardhan, P. (2005). Institutions matter, but which ones? *Economics of Transition*, 13(3), pp. 499–532.

Blair, H. (2005). Civil society and pro poor initiatives in rural Bangladesh: Finding a workable strategy. *World Development*, 33(6), pp. 921–936.

Blinder, A.S. (1988). The fall and rise of Keynesian economics. *Economic Record*, 64(4), pp. 278–294.

Blyth, M. (Ed.). (2009). *Routledge handbook of international political economy (IPE): IPE as a global conversation.* London: Routledge.

Bowles, S. (2016). *The moral economy: Why good incentives are no substitute for good citizens*. New Haven, CT: Yale University Press.

Bowles, S., Boyd, R., Fehr, E., and Gintis, H. (1997). Homo reciprocans: A research initiative on the origins, dimensions, and policy implications of reciprocal fairness. *Advances in Complex Systems*, 4(2/3), pp. 1–30.

Bowles, S., Durlauf, S.N., and Hoff, K.R. (Eds.). (2006). *Poverty traps*. New York: Russell Sage Foundation.

Bowles, S., and Gintis, H. (1986). *Capitalism and democracy*. Nova Iorque: Basic Books.

Bowles, S., and Gintis, H. (1990). Contested exchange: New microfoundations for the political economy of capitalism. *Politics and Society*, 18(2), pp. 165–222.

Bowles, S., and Gintis, H. (1993). The revenge of homo economicus: Contested exchange and the revival of political economy. *Journal of Economic Perspectives*, 7(1), pp. 83–102.

Bowring, F. (2016). The individual and society in Durkheim: Unpicking the contradictions. *European Journal of Social Theory*, 19(1), pp. 21–38.

Boyd, R. (2006). The puzzle of human sociality. *Science*, 314(5805), pp. 1555–1556.

Buitelaar, E. (2004). A transaction-cost analysis of the land development process. *Urban Studies*, 41(13), pp. 2539–2553.

Byron, C. (2016). Essence and alienation: Marx's theory of human nature. *Science and Society*, 80(3), pp. 375–394.

Chakraborty, S., and Dabla-Norris, E. (2006). Rent seeking. *IMF Staff Papers*, 53(1), pp. 28–49.

Coase, R.H. (1984). The new institutional economics. *Zeitschrift für die gesamte Staatswissenschaft*, 140, pp. 229–231.

Coase, R.H. (1960). The problem of social cost. In *Classic papers in natural resource economics* (pp. 87–137). London: Palgrave Macmillan.

Dequech, D. (2007). Neoclassical, mainstream, orthodox, and heterodox economics. *Journal of Post Keynesian Economics*, 30(2), pp. 279–302.

Di John, J., and Putzel, J. (2009). *Political settlements*. Birmingham, UK: GSDRC, University of Birmingham. Retrieved March 22, 2022, from https://gsdrc.org/publications/political-settlements-2/

Durkheim, É. (1893). *The division of labour in society, contemporary social theory*. Illinois: The Free Press of Glencoe.

Einhorn, H.J., and Hogarth, R.M. (1978). Confidence in judgment: Persistence of the illusion of validity. *Psychological Review*, 85(5), p. 395.

Engels, F. (2010). *The origin of the family, private property and the state*. London: Penguin.

Engerman, S.L., and Sokoloff, K.L. (2002). Factor endowments, inequality, and paths of development among new world economics. *Economía*, 3(1), pp. 41–109.

Esping-Andersen, G. (1990). *The three worlds of welfare capitalism*. Princeton, NJ: Princeton University Press.

Furubotn, E.G., and Richter, R. (1986). The new institutional economics symposium June 12–14, 1985 Saarbrücken: Editorial preface. *Journal of Institutional and Theoretical Economics (JITE)/Zeitschrift für die gesamte Staatswissenschaft*, 142(1), pp. 1–3.

Garegnani, P. (1983). The classical theory of wages and the role of demand schedules in the determination of relative prices. *The American Economic Review*, 73(2), pp. 309–313.

Gintis, H. (2000). Strong reciprocity and human sociality. *Journal of Theoretical Biology*, 206(2), pp. 169–179.

Harris, D.J. (2007). The classical theory of economic growth. In Vernengo, M., Caldentey, E. P. and Rosser Jr., B. (eds.) *The new Palgrave dictionary of economics*. London: Palgrave Macmillan.

Hirschman, A.O. (1977). A generalized linkage approach to development, with special reference to staples. *Economic Development and Cultural Change*, 25, p. 67.

Holcombe, R.G. (1997). A theory of the theory of public goods. *The Review of Austrian Economics*, 10(1), pp. 1–22.

Isaac, R.M., and Walker, J.M. (1988). Group size effects in public goods provision: The voluntary contributions mechanism. *The Quarterly Journal of Economics*, 103(1), pp. 179–199.

Kahneman, D. (1994). New challenges to the rationality assumption. *Journal of Institutional and Theoretical Economics (JITE)/Zeitschrift für die gesamte Staatswissenschaft*, 150(1), pp. 18–36.

Khan, M. (2000a). Rents, efficiency and growth. in *Rents, rent-seeking and economic development: Theory and evidence in Asia* (pp. 21–69). Cambridge: Cambridge University Press.

Khan, M. (2000b). Class, clientelism and communal politics in Bangladesh. In K.N. Panikkar, T.J. Byres, and U. Patnaik (Eds.), *The making of history: Essays presented to Irfan Habib* (pp. 572–606). Delhi: Tulika.

Khan, M. (2010). *Political settlements and the governance of growth-enhancing institutions*. Retrieved March 22, 2022, from https://eprints.soas.ac.uk/9968/1/Political_Settlements_internet.pdf

Kjosavic, D. (2003). Methodological individualism and rational choice theory in neoclassical economics: A review of institutionalism. *In Forum for Development Studies*, 80(3), pp. 202–245.

Krueger, A.O. (1974). The political economy of a rent seeking society. *American Economic Review*, 64(3), pp. 291–303.

Krueger, A.O. (1990). Government failures in development. *Journal of Economic Perspectives*, 4(3), pp. 9–23.

Kymlicka, W., and Norman, W. (1994). Return of the citizen: A survey of recent work on citizenship theory. *Ethics*, 104(2), pp. 352–381.

Marshall, T.H. (1950). *Citizenship and social class*. Cambridge: Cambridge University Press.

Marshall, T.H. (1965). The right to welfare. *The Sociological Review*, 13(3), pp. 261–272.

Meramveliotakis, G. (2018). New institutional economics: A critique of fundamentals and broad strokes towards an alternative theoretical framework for the analysis of institutions. *Asian Journal of Social Science Studies*, 3(2), p. 50.

North, D.C. (1990). A transaction cost theory of politics. *Journal of Theoretical Politics*, 2(4), pp. 355–367.

North, D.C., Wallis, J.J., and Weingast, B.R. (2009). *Violence and social orders: A conceptual framework for interpreting recorded human history*. Cambridge: Cambridge University Press.

Olshansky, G. (2015). *Taking down the totem: A post-keynesian behavioral critique of neoclassical economics*. Economics Honors Papers 20. Retrieved from https://digitalcommons.conncoll.edu/econhp/20

Ostrom, E. (1990). *Governing the commons: The evolution of institutions for collective action*. Cambridge: Cambridge University Press.

Piketty, T. (1998). Self-fulfilling beliefs about social status. *Journal of Public Economics*, 70(1), pp. 115–132.

Piketty, T. (2015). About capital in the twenty-first century. *American Economic Review*, 105(5), pp. 48–53.

Platteau, J.P. (2004). Decentralized development as a strategy to reduce poverty? *Poverty, Inequality and Growth*, p. 253.

Reisman, G. (1998). *Capitalism: A treatise on economics*. Ottawa, IL: Jameson Books.

Riaz, A. (2005). *Unfolding state: The transformation of Bangladesh*. Whitby, ON: de Sitter Publications.

Samuelson, P.A. (1954). The pure theory of public expenditure. *The Review of Economics and Statistics*, 36(4), pp. 387–389.

Samuelson, P.A. (1958). Aspects of public expenditure theories. *The Review of Economics and Statistics*, 40(4), pp. 332–338.

Saul, J.S. (1974). The state in post-colonial societies: Tanzania. *Socialist Register*, 11.

Schneider, F., and Pommerehne, W.W. (1981). Free riding and collective action: An experiment in public microeconomics. *The Quarterly Journal of Economics*, 96(4), pp. 689–704.

Scott, R.E. (2006). The law and economics of incomplete contracts. *Annual Review of Law and Social Science*, 2, pp. 279–297.

Sears, A., and Cairns, J. (2015). *A good book, in theory: Making sense through inquiry*. Toronto: University of Toronto Press.

Sen, A.K. (1977). Rational fools: A critique of the behavioral foundations of economic theory. *Philosophy and Public Affairs*, 6(4), pp. 317–344.

Sen, A.K. (1999). Democracy as a universal value. *Journal of Democracy*, 10(3), pp. 3–17.

Sen, A.K. (2009). *The idea of justice*. Cambridge, MA: Harvard University Press.

Simon, H.A. (1955). A behavioral model of rational choice. *The Quarterly Journal of Economics*, 69(1), pp. 99–118.

Smith, A. (1776). *An inquiry into the nature and causes of the wealth of nations: Volume one*. London: printed for W. Strahan; and T. Cadell.

Stiglitz, J.E. (2013). Equal opportunity, our national myth. *New York Times*, p. 16.

Sullivan, A., and Sheffrin, S.M. (2003). *Economics: Principles in action*. New Jersey: Pearson Prentice Hall.

Thomas, A.M. (2018). Adam Smith on the philosophy and provision of education. *Journal of Interdisciplinary Economics*, 30(1), pp. 105–116.

Townsend, R.M. (1994). Risk and insurance in village India. *Econometrica: Journal of the Econometric Society*, 62(3), pp. 539–591.

Trivers, R.L. (1971). The evolution of reciprocal altruism. *The Quarterly Review of Biology*, 46(1), pp. 35–57.

Tversky, A., and Kahneman, D. (1986). Rational choice and the framing of decision. *The Journal of Business*, 59(4), pp. 251–278.

Tversky, A., Slovic, P., and Kahneman, D. (1990). The causes of preference reversal. *The American Economic Review*, 80(1), pp. 204–217.

Van Daal, J., and Jolink, A. (1993). *The equilibrium economics of Léon Walras*. London: Routledge.

Williamson, O.E. (2002). The theory of the firm as governance structure: From choice to contract. *Journal of Economic Perspectives*, 16(3), pp. 171–195.

Part II
Education

3 Discourses on Investment in Human Capabilities

Introduction

In ancient Greece, two kinds of education prevailed: formal and informal. Formal education consisted of an official paid enrolment in a public school primarily for males and non-slaves, whilst informal education referred to more indirect forms of gaining knowledge such as from a social setting. Higher education in Athens was mostly limited to the wealthy households that were able to afford to pay for the education delivered by sophists, imaging a wide prevalence of inequality of access to formal education. Sophists often even advertised their services to reach a higher number of potential pupils. This left out the peasant classes due to a lack of affordability, and women and slaves due to being barred from admission.

Much unlike the unequal state of education in ancient Greece, present-day education in Finland is a manifestation of inclusive quality education. Finnish education policy hinges on equal educational accessibility, Education for All initiative, regardless of an individual's physical or cognitive ability, socio-economic background or ethnicity. Policies are designed to achieve minimum differences between schools and negligible variation in class-level scientific reasoning skill. Through the reforms of 1994, the Finnish education system underwent decentralisation and restructuring of educational institutions which led to desired harmonisation of central decision-making and local autonomy.

On the other hand, education in Myanmar has been marred with limitations such as inaccessibility of quality education for all, weak infrastructure of educational institutions and obsolete teaching methods. Many children remain out of school who either dropped out or were never enrolled. A 2014 census revealed that one in five children between the ages of 10 and 17 – about 1.7 million young people – were working instead of attending school (Reuters, 2016). Many families need children to earn an income, and often parents cannot afford the cost of books, uniforms and other school-related fees.

Education is a fundamental human right and essential for the exercise of all other human rights. As a tool to sustain the economic growth of a country, education has a much wider impact than simply improving earnings or employment opportunities which is why it is a component of the human development

DOI: 10.4324/9781003284222-5

index. It has been observed that in all countries with comparable data, adults with lower literacy skills are far more likely to report poor health, have less trust in their fellow citizens and perceive themselves as objects – rather than actors – in the political process. Countries failing to equip their residents with proper skills and technological progress are unlikely to accelerate economic growth, and large swaths of the population risk languishing on the margins of society (Schleicher, 2015).

The United Nations Development Programme (UNDP) in its flagship publication titled Human Development Report identifies three indicators for human development. These are education, health and wealth. Education is measured by mean years of schooling and health by life expectancy. Lack of education is identified as the major barrier out of the three towards an equal society. Overall, inequality in education has contributed the most to the loss of human development. (UNDP, 2016). The unequal access to education has led to a global call for universal primary education. Accessibility also relies on public provision of financial resources to establish educational infrastructure and invest in quality enhancement, including training teachers.

Far from the requirement, the developing countries are gradually raising spending in education as a part of GDP. For example, real education expenditures in a sample of 26 African countries grew by an average of six per cent annually from 2000 to 2009 (UNESCO, 2011). Similar patterns of growth in education expenditure can be observed in South Asia while the total education budget in India doubled between 2004 and 2009 (Muralidharan et al., 2017). As a result of this increased budgetary investment, countries in sub-Saharan Africa, Latin America and the Caribbean regions spend about 4.7 per cent of GDP on education, which compares favourably to North American and European countries that spend about 4.8 per cent of GDP on education (UNESCO, 2020).

However, South Asian countries such as India lag behind their African and Latin American counterparts by spending only 4 per cent of GDP on education in 2018 (Ramberg, 2021). This rise in education spending in developing countries has mostly been channelled towards initiatives that improve schooling access, and school inputs such as classrooms, textbooks and teachers. As a result, the global proportion of primary students who were out of school fell from 19 per cent in 1999 to 8 per cent in 2018 (Ramberg, 2021). Although enrolment rates in sub-Saharan Africa lag behind other regions, enrolment rates in primary school have risen from just 55 per cent in the mid-1990s to almost 80 per cent at present. While education spending levels and enrolment rates in schools have increased across the developing world, a variety of research and datasets show that learning levels remain low. For instance, in India and East African countries, half of the fifth-grade students have failed to read a second-grade text (Mbiti, 2016; Pratham, 2014; Uwezo, 2013). The low level of learning can be attributed to the high rates of teacher absenteeism, financial transfer leakages and ineffective school monitoring systems (Mbiti, 2016; World Bank, 2003). While developing countries as a group have made substantial steps in raising enrolment and committing more resources to education, subsequent reforms need to focus on initiatives that increase accountability and incentives across the education system, improve the effort and pedagogical practice of teachers, support the more efficient use of the existing resources and leverage the growing private sector (Mbiti, 2016).

The education system is of central importance to the economic future of developing countries, both because of the important role in accelerating economic growth and because of its critical role in analysing the citizenship, a central component of nation building.

Politics influenced by the colonisers act as a deterrence to education policies in developing countries. For instance, the education system of Bangladesh is still influenced by the British colonial education policy in India, which aimed to create a group of educated people to serve the interest of the colonial rulers. Following the partition of British India in to India and Pakistan, Bangladesh became the Eastern part of Pakistan. In the Pakistan period, the discriminatory policy in the education sector resulted in lower allocation in education, lessened supply of teachers and decreasing number of schools in East Pakistan. The Constitution of Bangladesh stipulates that the state shall adopt effective measures for the purpose of establishing a uniform, mass-oriented and universal system of education. Yet the country has not been able to ensure universal education for all.

This chapter attempts to assess the state of education in developing countries taking Bangladesh as a case study in light of education as a right, a vehicle for productive employment and a means of unleashing human potential for a public society. The chapter has made distinctions between the economic demand and basic human need for education by exploring the nature of state and private sector in educational provisioning and the outcomes in economic, social and political arenas.

A Review

The emerging issues in the education sector call for a transformative change. The mainstream theories suggest different types of educational provisioning which are plagued with limitations. In order to construct an alternative framework suitable for the education sector in developing countries, those limitations need to be factored in along with their theoretical underpinnings. The mainstream theories can be classified into two subgroups: market-centric approach and political economic approach.

Market-Centric Approach

The following approaches can be clustered as market-centric as these approaches to education rely on market provisioning. These promote the values of rationalism and individualism.

The mainstream neoclassical school which propagates market provision, yet such provisioning could create the problems of rivalry and excludability. If education is referred to as a public good, it is theoretically to be both non-excludable and non-rival such that individuals cannot be effectively excluded from use and where use by one individual should not reduce availability to others. Public good is assumed to be an important example of market failure, in which market-like behaviour of individual gain-seeking does not produce efficient results. The production of public goods results in positive externalities which are not remunerated. Hence, private organisations will not be able to profit, which gives them zero incentives to produce the goods. On the other hand, the neoclassicals argue that citizens enjoy "free ride" or goods without any contribution, and when the number of "free riders" are high, the costs exceed the profit and again makes the venture unviable (Powell, 2008).

Thus, Coase (1960) describes the economic efficiency of an economic allocation or outcome in the presence of externalities. The theorem states that if trade in an externality is possible and there are sufficiently low transaction costs, bargaining will lead to a Pareto-efficient outcome, a state of allocation of resources in which it is impossible to make any one individual better off without making at least one individual worse off. The contrasting perspective suggests that if voluntary provision of public goods will not work, then the obvious solution is public provisioning. This saves each individual from the tendency to be a free rider, while also ensuring that no one else will be allowed to free ride. For that reason, governments or states need to impose taxation to fund the production of public goods. Public provisioning of public goods like education and healthcare would create equal access for individuals to education and healthcare and there are positive externalities associated with these public goods for which citizens should pay tax (Stiglitz, 2000). In case of market provision of education, Pigouvian tax can correct an inefficient market outcome, and does so by being set equal to the social cost of the negative externalities. For example, a tax shifts the marginal private cost curve up by the amount of the tax. If the tax is placed on the quantity of emissions from a factory, the producers have an incentive to reduce output to the socially optimal level. If the tax is placed on the percentage of emissions per unit of production, the factory has the incentive to change to cleaner processes or technology.

The Pigouvian tax, as is argued, cannot internalise the externality in the long run in case of market provisioning of public goods. In the short run, individual firm output can be controlled by Pigouvian tax by which marginal social cost and marginal private cost coincides. In the case of long run, output of each firm cannot be different in competitive equilibrium because of Pigouvian tax only. With the tax difference in the long run, the government can only control the number of firms, not the output of firms (Carlton and Loury, 1980). As a result, the issue of market provisioning of education requires an incentive (e.g., subsidy) from the government to internalise the externalities. This incentive might motivate the private sector in the short run. But in the long run, the government cannot ensure the quality of education only by subsidising the private education sector. It requires regulation and quality management to ensure optimal output in the education sector.

For a refined articulation within the neoclassical economics, Gary Becker (1964) comes up with a novel formulation and coins "human capital", to refer to resources such as knowledge, talents, skills, abilities, experience, intelligence, training, judgement and wisdom possessed individually and collectively by individuals in a population. Human capital is a means of production, into which additional investment through education, training, healthcare etc. yields additional output. Becker also points out that formal education is not the only way to invest in human capital. Workers also learn and are trained outside schools, especially on the job. Thus, education increases human capital which helps a person to invest more and get more wage or income than others. And those who are unable to afford an education generally receive much lower wages. The justification for this is that a lack of education leads directly to lower incomes, and thus lower aggregate savings and investment (Becker, 1964). Conversely, education raises incomes and promotes growth because it helps unleash the productive potential of the poor. But is education only important to create human capital? Knowledge, health and other basic needs cannot be narrowly treated as human capital. In modern Human Capital Theory, all human behaviour is based on the economic self-interest of individuals operating within freely competitive markets. Other forms of behaviour such as cooperation and collectivism, which are related to human sociality, are excluded or treated as distortions of the model. Galbraith who is a pioneer of the idea of human capital, however, perceives education as a way to eradicate poverty and to improve people's living standard (Pressman, 2007). As increased access to education and enhancement of quality require more money, increasing taxes in order to finance public education is necessary (Galbraith, 1998).

The emergence of the concept of social capital is largely stimulated by the work of Pierre Bourdieu (1986) and James S. Coleman (1988). Social capital helps dominant groups to maintain the social solidarity and the position of the group. Social solidarity is derived of Bourdieu's concepts on cultural capital, habitus and field. Cultural capital is the knowledge or skills of a person that assist the person to be a part of the dominant group of society. It can be embodied, objectified or institutionalised (educational qualification). These knowledge or skills are sometimes inherited by a person that is known as habitus. Habitus differs from one another based on the familial or cultural context (Bourdieu, 1986). Finally, the field is a social setting where the position of groups is determined by "the rules of the game", habitus and cultural capital. The "rules of the game" is the understanding of how the system operates by using the inherent knowledge which depends on the economic, cultural and social class (Dika and Singh, 2002). Education can be helpful in building social capital and bringing about positions or the title of nobility. This social capital can be convertible to economic capital (Bourdieu, 1986). The three forms of capital are often overlapping and, in some cases, causing confusion. The concept also remains economic by not engaging in social terrain. Social capital, thus, is a reduction to economic thinking (Haynes, 2009).

Coleman sees social capital as an investment that eventually turns into human capital. Social capital needs a social structure where there should be obligations, trustworthiness, proper information channel and effective norms. Closure of social structure and appropriate social organisation ensures effective social capital that turns into human capital. In the creation of human capital, Coleman talks about the social capital in the family and outside the family. Family background, education of parents and intergenerational connection affect the children in achieving positive outcomes in education. The social capital of a community also has an effect on the development of children. Thus, the social capital not only benefits an individual but also benefits the people who are a part of the structure. In this sense, social capital cannot be considered as a private good (Coleman, 1988). Since an individual does not invest spontaneously or consciously in social capital for the benefit, it is neither a public good. Social capital cannot fulfil the criteria of club good too because individuals are already a part of it. It is then considered as a common collective good (Poder, 2011).

Robert Putnam's concept of social capital is built on the idea of James Coleman and social networks. The definition of social capital is the "features of social organisations such as networks, norms and social trust that facilitate coordination and cooperation in mutual benefit" (Putnam, 1995). His work emphasises on civic culture which is Coleman's idea of norms of reciprocity and trust and on social network that creates connection and bonding between individuals. As voluntary organisations are regarded as socially organised groups with mutual trust with the members, Putnam considered these organisations as a way of creating social networks. Thus, the involvement of civil society has decreased to some extent. The theory, nonetheless, fails to incorporate the conflicts between different voluntary associations, the role of mass media and other forms of communication and the challenges of power relations in political society (Siisiäinen, 2000). The definition of social capital is to an extent contradictory and too broad that the clarity and validity are difficult to examine. Moreover, the concepts of obligation and trust in social capital are vague and unmeasurable by nature (Smart, 1993).

Information asymmetry has become a pronounced area of research. This contrasts to perfect information, which is a key assumption in neo-classical economics. Spence (1973) investigates how (potential) employees send a signal about their level of ability to employers through educational qualifications. Spence suggests that even if education does not contribute anything to an employee's productivity, it could still have value to both the employer and the employee. If the appropriate cost–benefit structure exists (or is created), "good" employees will buy more education in order to signal their higher productivity. The increase in wages associated with obtaining a higher credential is sometimes referred to as the "sheepskin effect" (Hungerford and Solon, 1987), since "sheepskin" informally denotes a diploma. It is important to note that this is not the same as the returns from an additional year of education. The "sheepskin" effect is actually the wage increase above what would normally be attributed to the extra year of education. Spence's insight is that these actions can occur in equilibrium, even if they are costly and unproductive. Trade may occur with gross inefficiencies because of unproductive signaling. Crucially, the theory of signalling only works if the signal is credible: if low-productivity workers found it easy to get a degree, then they could masquerade as clever types. Nevertheless, obtaining an educational degree in order to convey a signal requires a certain level of socio-economic advantages. Thus, in the real competitive job market, the disadvantaged group will lag behind. Again, the problem arises where the two parties have different interests and asymmetric information. For example, the principal cannot directly ensure that the agent is always acting in the principal's best interest, particularly when activities that are useful to the principal are costly to the agent, and where elements of what the agent does are costly for the principal to observe. Often, the principal may be sufficiently concerned at the possibility of being exploited by the agent that they choose not to enter into the transaction at all, when it would have been mutually beneficial: a suboptimal outcome that could lower overall welfare. And altogether these contexts may lead to results such as unemployment and underemployment.

The most orthodox within the neo-classical economics is the branch of public choice. The basic behavioural assumption of public choice stands the same as for any other market-centric approaches like individualism, rationalism and profit maximisation. However, this theory explains how public goods like education and healthcare are demanded and supplied. Here, the government works as a marketplace wherein citizens trade taxes for public goods. Between citizens and politicians, the relationship works as an exchange of support (i.e., votes, propaganda etc.) for benefits. The theorists argue that people freeload public goods wherever they can which leads to waste of resources. And according to this genre, freeloading rather than market exchange is the main political motive and all government activity is actual or attempted plunder which can be termed as "legitimate theft" (Stretton and Orchard, 1994). On the other hand, this narrow self-interest model does not explain much about other humanistic behaviour such as the redistribution activities of government. Social services like old allowance programmes, free primary education and unemployment compensation appear to be widespread popular support that goes beyond the rational self-interest of the government.

In 1980s, most of the developing countries embark upon market-centric neoliberal reforms, with the ideological premise that the rational individuals enjoy the greatest freedom in the free market economy. Under the political project, the countries have witnessed cuts in public spending in education and healthcare, the removal of price controls and subsidies, particularly on food; and the privatisation of public enterprises. The neoliberalism also experienced backlash, with children being withdrawn from schools due to rising cost of education and getting lessened healthcare owing to price escalation in privatised facilities, encumbering well-being. Mothers of poor families, who played the role of caregivers for their children, had to leave this role to enter into the labour market to earn money so that families can meet the rising living cost.

The capability approach introduced by Sen is more holistic. Amartya Sen (1997) scrupulously makes a distinction between human capability and human capital. Human capital refers to the agency of people in augmenting production possibilities. Yet human capability is more important because it refers to the substantive freedom of people to lead the lives they have reason to value and to enhance the real choices they have. Education, for example, is crucial beyond its role in production; its most important role being that of increasing human capability and therefore choice. Raising human capability improves: the choices, well-being and freedom of people; their role in influencing social change and their role in influencing economic production. Hence, Sen stresses on the positive role of the market and opposes regulations that impede the freedom of people to decide where to work, what to produce and what to consume. But it has been argued before that the market creates inequality in access to the substantive freedom to acquire human capability. And the concept is too idealistic to be realistic. But Nussbaum criticises Sen's idea of freedom as freedom does not always yield good capabilities (Saito, 2003). For better understanding, some argue that the capability approach needs another complementary theory of obligations, rules and set of functioning (Clarke, 2006).

Political Economy Approach

These approaches are different from market-centric schools as these support government intervention in education. They emphasise on equity and other humanistic values. These are not also homogenous. Some are in direct conflict with others.

The term "animal spirit" was first introduced by John Maynard Keynes, prominent British economist who tended to urge other economists both traditionally and non-traditionally to pay attention to the thought pattern that animate people's ideas and feelings and their animal spirits. It was quite ironic that most economists of that time did not realise the significance of this issue and fell back on the typical and artificial implications of economic events. They presumed that variations in an individual's behaviour, feelings, impression and passion do not matter in the aggregate and that economic events are driven by inscrutable economic factors or erratic government action (Akerlof and Shiller, 2009). According to traditional economics, the free market is the only solution to resolve and mitigate the economic crisis. This shape of the economy appears to be stable and perfect. There is little, if any, need of government intervention that state should play a role in a minimalist way. On the other hand, excessive government interference is not detrimental to the health of the economy. According to both classical and neo-classical economics, people rationally pursue their own interest, and through individual welfare of the basic needs, gradually society becomes the beneficiary of it as a whole. On the contrary, non-economic motivation of human being, animal spirit, has been shirked by these two schools of thoughts. Keynes sought to explain the departure from full employment and he emphasised the importance of animal spirits. He stressed their fundamental role in business man's calculations.

> Our basis of knowledge for estimating the ten yield years hence of a railway, a copper mine, a textile factory, the goodwill of patent medicine, an Atlantic liner, s building in the city of London amounts to little and sometimes to nothing.
>
> (Keynes, 1936)

Question arises, if people are uncertain, how do they make decisions? The answer is, they make their decisions by the nature of animal spirit. They are the result of a spontaneous urge to action. They are not, as rational economic theory makes a proposition, "the outcome of a weighted average of quantitative benefits multiplied by quantitative probabilities" (Keynes, 1936, cited in Akerlof and Shiller, 2009). Animal spirit has become an economic term which refers to a restless and inconsistent element in the economy. It refers to people's relationship with ambiguity or uncertainty. Conventional economic theories exclude the changing thought patterns and modes of doing business that brings on a crisis. It has been visible that they even exclude the loss of confidence and trust. They exclude the sense of fairness that inhibits the wage and price flexibility that could possibly stabilise an economy (Akerlof and Shiller, 2009). Moreover, corruption and its rules are condoned and further excluded as well as the sale of bad products in booms, and role of their revelation when the bubbles burst. Additionally, the role of the story that interprets the economy is averted either. All of these exclusions are responsible for several economic crises that emerged from the conventional thoughts. As a result, the changing pattern of the economy did not seem to be penetrable and understandable. This phenomenon led to further disbelief and deep crisis in myriad economic occasions. Without considering the notions of animal spirit, very often economists, traditional mostly, fail to deal with disparate modes of economic depression and crises. The issue of trust, confidence, diverse feelings and corruption are not isolated from the economy nor are they alien to the perception of understanding the changing shape of current and future economic status. Classical and neoclassical schools should have brought the theme of animal spirit and its substantial provisions in theorising and making practical affairs of economic models.

Unlike the neoclassical approach, the post-Keynesians believe in an economic world where large oligopolistic firms control the markets which are not subject to the dictates of consumer. Rather, consumer preferences and choices are moulded by large firms. Thus, Post-Keynesians go for state provision in merit goods like education which cannot be provided by the private sector. And these goods cannot be measured by their demand; rather every human being has a need for these and has the basic right to get education, employment and healthcare. Second, Post-Keynesianism considers uncertainty and history. Post-Keynesians noted that, given uncertainty, the investment decision in education is driven by the "animal spirit" and families tend to choose schools or any other medium of education similar to their ancestors. So, from a Post-Keynesian perspective, it can be understood why low educational access, high dropouts or inferior quality of education is associated with low-income families and parents with no or little education. Thus, it has been advocated for government interventions which would invest in young children for disadvantaged groups as post-Keynesians understand the need for the state to provide money for developing human capital and bringing the children from poor families out of poverty. Thus, Post-Keynesianism believes in the virtue of equity and this approach to education opposes the existing social stratification and income inequality. This approach fits better for the countries with proper taxation but in the case of developing countries where the preference of tax avoidance is high, it is not an easy job for the government only to finance education expenditure. On the other hand, the market oligopoly cannot ensure good quality of education (Pressman, 2007).

Marxists have served to theorise and criticise education in the reproduction of capitalist society and advocate for alternative methods of equal education system. They argue that the education system in the capitalist world is highly unequal. For instance, Samuel Bowles (1972) demonstrates that market incentives destroy cooperation and are less efficient than voluntary, altruistic behaviour, and unequal education in the free market economy derives from the social division of labour. Bowles and Gintis (1976) state that children inherited the productive skills and "adapted to the social relations of production through learning by doing within the family". As the capitalist system grew, families were uprooted from the land and thrown into the oppressive factories to work as labour. Ownership of the means of production was heavily concentrated in the hands of landlords and capitalists which increased the inequality of wealth (Bowles and Gintis, 1976). In this regard, Piketty in "Capital in the Twenty-First Century" calls the era as "patrimonial capitalism", a society dominated by oligarchs who inherit their wealth which leads to heavy wealth inequality. It is argued that the relationship between inequality and how productively a society uses its resources is mediated by the structure of economic governance. Governance structures also critically influence the degree of inequality. Correspondingly, the feasibility of distinct forms of governance is itself strongly influenced by the degree of inequality and, in particular, by the nature and distribution of property rights (Bowles and Gintis, 2012) (Figure 3.1).

The capitalist society undermining the role of the family in socialisation and production establishes the system of schooling as a socialisation process. The emphasis of school on discipline, punctuality, acceptance of authority outside the family and accountability taught the youths to believe in the benevolence of the government, to accept the authority of state and its agents and to uphold the bourgeoisie ideology. Public elementary and secondary education becomes dominated by the capitalist class. A system of class stratification was developed as children of the social elite attended private schools while children from the working class tended to drop out. And the public high schools go fully under the control of the social elite. And it is acknowledged that an important factor

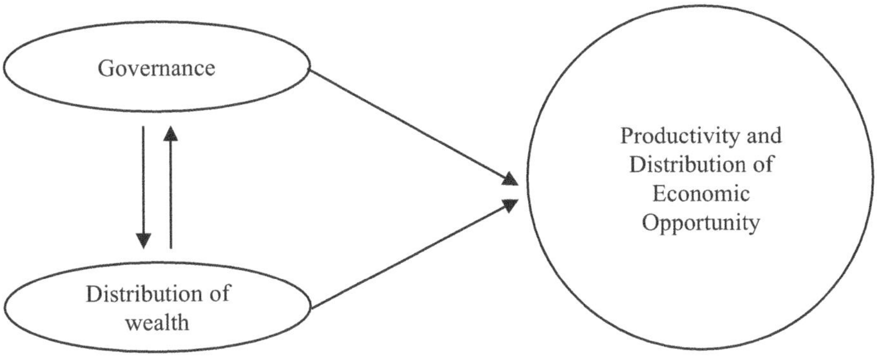

Figure 3.1 Causal relationships between structures of governance, wealth inequality and economic performance

Source: Prepared by authors; adopted from Bowles and Gintis (2012)

in the creation of inequality in society is the difference in individuals' access to education as education generates human capital (Bowles, 1972).

It is argued that equalising children's developmental opportunities to public goods is a difficult task, since it involves the investment of government and family concomitantly. Some possible outcomes of children's well-being and the factors behind them have been depicted. It can be observed that government investment along with family's investment in child's well-being, family's assets and the other characteristics of the family lead to greater investment in the child's human capital which raises the income of the child (Bowels et al., 2005).

Raising poor parents' incomes would presumably lower the amount of conflict and stress in poor children's homes. Ensuring that working mothers have predictable schedules that are compatible with their children's schedules would also improve children's lives. It also argued that the schools which are situated in areas inhabited by affluent families are equipped with more qualified teachers than other schools and this creates differences in well-being between the children from poor and affluent families. Thus, equalising parents' incomes or providing more social services would fully equalise children's developmental opportunities. In order to redistribute the income from rich to poor, tax is an efficient tool as redistributive tax spreads incomes among the population more fairly by taxing the rich people more and poor people less (Figure 3.2). Besides redistributing income, the income tax also finances the public provision of a set of goods and services that are valued by individuals. Though higher taxes reduce private consumption, they increase the supply of the goods furnished by the government (Bandyopadhyay and Esteban, 2007). And all at once, it is also argued that in the presence of positive externalities all citizens benefit from the public provisioning of education and healthcare but if they do not pay for it through paying tax, the state may undersupply the public goods.

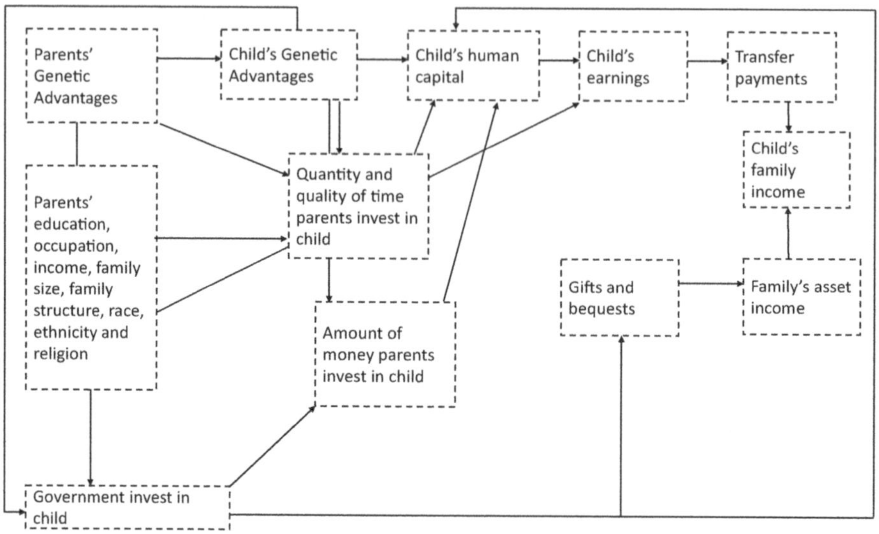

Figure 3.2 Some possible links between a child's well-being and the macro- and micro factors

Source: Prepared by authors; adopted from: Bowles et al. (2005)

A complete opposite perspective is presented by Nozick, stating that each child is entitled to the full untaxed benefits of his family resources, insofar as he chooses to use those resources for his benefits. Thus, Nozick advocates for private education paid for individually matching to its resources and preferences (Coleman, 1976) while Rawls proposes to erase the good fortune inherited by a person from his/her family such as social advantages like wealth, connections or access to better-than-average education or inherited natural advantages like intelligence, creativity or athletic ability which would create equal opportunity for all children from any family. Hence, Rawls supports taxation to support programmes that expand opportunities (like public education) and opts for public provisioning what he calls a "social minimum" (what is known generally as "social safety net" programmes).

Human sociality is the idea that has identified the loopholes in the basic assumption of market-centric approaches that human beings act in accordance with their self-interests. Sociality defines the tendency of individuals to cooperate in social groups. By cooperation, it is meant that an individual's behaviour incurs personal costs in order to engage in a communal activity that confers benefits exceeding these costs to other members of one's group. This cooperation is unique in nature (Bowles and Gintis, 2002). Humans engage in cooperative behaviour induced by prosocial emotions which include emotions, such as shame, guilt, empathy, and sensitivity to social sanction, that induce agents to undertake constructive social interactions, and others, such as the desire to punish norm violators, that reduce free-riding when the prosocial emotions fail to induce sufficiently cooperative behaviour in some fraction of members of the social group (Hirshleifer, 1987).

This pro-social behaviour is rooted to the existence of human society, otherwise all would become sociopaths, however strong the institutional arrangements are. Pro-social behaviour dictates human beings to be responsible to each other and to carry out caring acts. Hence without representative government, civil liberties, due process, women's rights, respect to minorities, education for all and other altruistic institutions and activities, human dignity will be impossible (Bowles and Gintis, 2002).

The liberals have also purported to convention as a process of cooperation. Theory of convention has been implicated at an embryonic stage by David Hume and his primary concern was to deem a remedy for the chaos that would reign in the state of nature. This remedy is supposed to bring stability of possession in a competitive environment with scarce resources (Latsis, 2009). Hume says in his "A Treatise of Human Nature",

> This can be done after no other manner, than by a convention entered into by all the members of the society to bestow stability on the possession of those external goods, and leave everyone in the peaceable enjoyment of what he may acquire by his fortune and industry. By this means, everyone knows what he may safely possess; and the passions are restrained in their partial and contradictory motions.
>
> (Hume, 1739)

In a precise manner, Humean convention is a general sense of common interest which all the members of the society express to one another and which induces to regulate their conduct by certain rules (Hume, 1739 cited in Latsis, 2009). Self-interest or avidity of acquiring goods and possessions for the members of the society and their kith and kin is insatiable, perpetual, universal and directly destructive of society. Though the lens of justice was put from a minimal point of view, he demands to get self-interest checked so that anarchy and arbitrary consumption of a particular group of people does not happen. Therefore, morality and an accepted set of rules of behaviour are necessary indeed to practice just for all (Hume, 1739). The concept of convention forms a mechanism which neutralises the conflicting interests of the non-socialised individuals through agreement on some principle of self-interested reciprocity. Hume's theory of convention has been criticised either for not making a comprehensive and thoroughgoing exegesis of convention and justice but the apothem of the theory is quite significant which should have been discussed and analysed by the neoclassical school of thought. Hence, this notion gives another challenge to the neoclassical school of economics.

In recent years, evolutionary game theory has supplanted the classical games. The aim here is to make a model which would be able to predict the equilibrium choice. Evolutionary game theory of this sort accounts for the emergence of conventions without relying on strategic behaviour or standard rationality assumptions. Instead, conventional behaviour is modelled as a self-organising system that is independent of its own history. Coordination occurs in situations where agents' immediate interests are in some sense harmonious before the game is engaged. Selection of one behavioural regularity amongst several alternatives would be impossible if different agents had strong and incompatible preferences for specific equilibrium strategies or for non-coordinated outcomes. Hume basically focused on cooperative behaviour which would be prone to social interest. The natural attitudes of confined generosity such as caring and making interest based on the preferences of the near ones, friends and family, might bring destruction directly but it would promote social cooperation gradually and benefit the members of the society (Latsis, 2009). The convention comes out in situations where a number of people each stand to gain from the institution or perpetuation of a particular social practice among them. They adopt a principle that regulates their interaction with each other. It has been argued that during Hume's period not that much concern was put on self-interest as people did not get oriented with that perspective till then. Still, his minimalist notion of common interest and regulatory attributes which works on mutual interaction buttresses the applicability of a set of principles, rules and as a whole, convention. Herbart Gintis shows how such is better explained as correlating devices rather than Nash equilibrium. This is ultimately helpful in explaining human sociality rather than self-interest and human beings as a cooperative species. The social norms of social choreographers have two attractive properties that are lacking in the social norms as Nash equilibrium. First, the stated conditions under which rational agents play Nash equilibrium are generally complex and implausible, however, rational agents in a very natural sense play correlated equilibrium. Second, the social norms as Nash equilibrium approach have been unable to explain why compliance with social norms is often based on other-regarding and moral preferences in which agents are willing to sacrifice on behalf of social norms. In this sense, morality plays a right role even if no one is caring about it at all (Gintis, 2009). Classical theory has wrong implications regarding social norms and their conditioning devices. It focuses on Nash as opposed to correlated equilibrium and hence ignores the rich social fabric of potential conditioning devices where each device corresponds to a distinct social structure of interaction. Additionally, the theory renders salient the epistemic conditions for the existence of social norms, conditions that are fulfilled only in an idealised, fully equilibrated social system. In general, social norms will only be contested and only partially implemented. Through this process, the passage from one choreographed equilibrium to another will be mediated by forms of collective action and individual heroism that cannot be currently explicated in terms of game theory (Gintis, 2009).

Social cooperation is an indispensable part of the society as human beings cannot solely afford to make all the requirements for their respective survivals which must be provided through mutual cooperation among the members of the society. Thus society, according to Hume, becomes advantageous to human beings. Three factors are primarily responsible for the benefits of social cooperation. First, the division of labour increases the productive capacity of the society beyond which could be achieved individually by its members. Second, specialisation enables people to increase their skills beyond what could be possible in a solitary state. Third, society provides a remedy in times of emergency such as during natural disasters or mental and physical illness which cannot be managed to overcome solely most of the time (George, 2017). Thus, people make a social network of intimate relationships where friends and family play a vital role which is interdependent to assure each other's existence and thrive. Affection originates in the family ambience where natural affection is delivered by a parent to the offspring and then circulated in the society as they learn to behave in an affectionate manner (Hume, 1739). They acquire the social habits, skills and temperament which contribute to establishing social cooperation. Difference occurs when behaviour towards strangers comes forward as there will be partiality regardless of justice. As Hume mentioned, justice is an artificial concept which tends to restrict favouritism and propounds disinterested passion towards people. Benevolence is largely partial as it is mostly shown to the dear ones like friends and family. It is a natural instinct of human beings not to treat others equally. In this regard, justice is required as a mode of social virtue and convention. Hume stressed property rights through the statement of mutual cooperation which is basically not promised but maintained through mutual understanding. As people become aware of the advantage of this reciprocity, they adjust their behaviour accordingly (George, 2017). Thus, people may be naturally self-interest-driven and selfish agents of their basic utilities, they behave in a cooperative way where mutual understanding and well-mannered relationships are maintained. Justice forbids illegal undertaking of others' needs and property rights. In the society, social harmony cannot be achieved so long as man's natural passions, which give preference to themselves and their friends and family, are not restrained by any convention or agreement. People's partial self-interest, if kept unrestrained by reason, generates the anti-social passion of avidity – the ultimate desire to acquire goods and services for the person himself and his friends and family. Avidity is insatiable, perpetual, universal and directly destructive to society. On the other hand, benevolence is regarded as too weak to counter the balance the love to gain (George, 2017). In this respect, social harmony should be escalated through establishment of mutual cooperation and convention where mutual sympathy will conduct as a structural setting for both parties, regardless of people's nature of partial benevolence towards their near and dear ones. Therefore, it is important to assure disinterested benevolence where pursuit of subjective self-interest should not be the ultimate goal, not even through doing well to others temporarily to make strong pretence of being good and benevolent in the eyes of others, rather, they should make juxtaposition of social sympathy through a systematic structure of social convention. In this context, both classical and neoclassical theories fall into follies as social sympathy and disinterested benevolence are not discussed in either of the thoughts. Human being is naturally self-interest-driven and he/

she has an insatiable tendency to acquire goods thinking less about others or sometimes indulging in nepotism. Therefore, to assure equitable distribution of goods and services, people have established an environment of mutual cooperation and social harmony which should not be averted anyway.

A Framework

Increasing gross enrolment is one of the significant facts of the education sector. However, the question remains whether quality is ensured along with access. In recent years, an upward trend is noticed in overall gross and net enrolment rates in secondary, higher secondary and tertiary levels of education all over the world. While the enrolment statistics show an upward trend, other indicators of the education sector have not shown such a trend.

A significant feature of the education sector in developing countries is low quality of education. There is inadequacy in physical infrastructures, teachers and supporting materials. Average pupil–teacher ratio remains high meaning there are higher numbers of students per teacher. The average teacher–pupil ratio in low-income countries stands at 1:40 in primary schools while the ratio is much lower at 1:12 in high-income countries (UNESCO, 2020). This high teacher–pupil ratio in low-income countries yields a low quality of education as the number of teachers is very low in comparison with the number of students. Also, the large class size and small learning time combine to limit effective contact hours and undermine learning achievement of students.

An emerging matter of concern in developing countries is the increasing unemployment among educated youths. The growth of the labour force has not surpassed the growth of unemployment. And unfortunately, a huge portion of youths is working in informal sectors, where the wage and working conditions are low. Meanwhile, the employers are unable to employ the graduates as youths fail to meet the job requirements. Gross entry ratio into tertiary programmes is only 11 per cent in low-income countries and 39 per cent in lower-middle-income countries. High-income countries see a higher ratio of 61 per cent (UNESCO, 2020). In terms of creating a skilled workforce, developing countries in Asia and Africa fall much behind the developed ones. In Southeastern Asia, only 6 per cent of the youths enrolled in Technical and Vocational Education and Training (TVET). In sub-Saharan Africa, it is barely a per cent. European countries on the other hand have 18 per cent of the youths enrolled in TVET (UNESCO, 2020).

The education sector of these countries is facing low public funding, which deters further development in this sector. To create equal access to education, there is no substitute for public provisioning of education. Government expenditure in education has been on the rise in both low and lower-middle-income countries with the government now focusing on educating the population. But improving quality and developing physical infrastructure require major further investments to meet the rising demand of the growing population. Still the majority of the schools in low- and lower-middle-income countries do not have facilities like electricity and Internet (UNESCO, 2020). As the demand for education increased much faster than the public education system could cope with, the profit-seeking private sector has increased exponentially in the education sector.

Fragile democracy and primitive accumulation dominate policies in the education sector of most of the developing countries. For instance, in Bangladesh, the state under various governments tried to revive the education system and over the last 44 years, a total of seven national education commissions and committees have been established by the various political and military governments and the policies articulated so far have upheld the sustained political-ideological interest of the leading class (Chowdhury and Kabir, 2014).

Based on the review of the literature and the stylised facts, a new framework is devised in this chapter. The framework discussed here will be elaborated in the following chapter with empirics. It has identified education as a basic human need which is different from the economic term "demand". In economics, demand means the quantity of a commodity or a service that people are willing or able to buy at a certain price (Sullivan and Sheffrin, 2003). Moreover, the need for education is universal and it has to be fulfilled though many human beings may not be willing or able to pay for it.

Achievements in education are measured with quantitative indicators such as enrolment and completion rate, which tell nothing about the quality of education provided. The focus lies in defining and measuring education based on the quality and outcome of education. For this purpose, education is judged on its ability to create a skilled workforce and ability to form innovation, both of which lead to the economic growth of a country as well as its citizens. The current education system should be moulded through provisioning of citizenship education. Global citizenship is being promoted by the UN and its sister concerns like UNESCO and others. A student should be taught citizenship education which incorporates human rights, rule of law, public order, legitimacy, representativeness of the members of the parliament and also social and national responsibilities. A proposition on citizenship will be discussed in the following chapter where it will also be delineated that when a student is taught and trained with citizenship attributes, he/she will be more likely prone to culminate national responsibilities while during studentship and after entering the job sector.

The outcome from education is defined as long-term benefits derived from education in an economy. Universal education is required in an economy to provide equal opportunity to all its citizens. This has the potential to generate a workforce that can raise the output. At the same time, skill-oriented education and training increase both the economic output and return on labour. Skilled workforce coupled with technology acquisition and innovation will raise the overall economic return to the state. When the economic output is on the rise, the state generates more income through taxes. Citizenship education on the other hand raises public awareness and leads to a public society that forces the state to intervene and provide public goods such as education and health.

The transformative conditions to achieve the outlined outcomes from education rely on state provisioning. State provisioning of education opens the door for education to all, making it more accessible to the vulnerable groups in the society. Open access to education benefits not only the individual but the society as a whole. State provisioning allows for higher investment in the education sector for fulfilling the needs of the citizens. This also results in higher modernising the education sector in order to focus more on skills and innovation. Finally, citizenship education can only be provided when the state has an active role in the education sector (Figure 3.3).

Ramesh (2004) puts forward the importance of well-designed economic policies in promoting economic development. A strong positive relationship exists between investment in education and growth of the economy in all countries regardless of their development status (OECD, 2003). Education leads to advancement in technologies and globalisation of the economy which in turn contributes to economic competitiveness of the country. Furthermore, it also contributes to slowing population growth and improving overall health of the population. The clustering of Hong Kong and Singapore in one group, and Korea and Taiwan in the other, is more pronounced in education than in other social policies. While economic development was the education system's key goal in all the NIEs, Korea and Taiwan emphasised more on vocational and technical education (Morris, 1996). Again, national unity has been promoted through the education system in the NIE governments. The public and private sectors have played different roles with respect to provision and financing of education across the NIEs. The provision of education is dominated by the state at different levels in different countries. The NIEs do not necessarily spend on education which is concentrated at the primary and secondary levels. Rather they devote a smaller percentage of the GDP to education than do OECD countries. Tertiary education opportunities are limited in the city states compared to their Northeast Asian counterparts. Insufficient higher education opportunities in the countries result in the shortage of skilled and technical personnel. High demand for skilled workers due to rapid industrialisation aggravated income inequality between university graduates and non-graduates.

Summary

Education widens choices and freedom. The public choice school has also assumed education as a marketable good and state as a market where citizens pay tax for education. But in the 1980s, the market-centric approach of the neoliberal reforms cuts the government subsidy in education which led to many unexpected outcomes like high dropouts in poor families, unemployment and so on. Post-Keynesians, on the contrary, have supported state intervention like subsidy etc. to bring equity. Marxists have advocated for an alternative equitable education system, arguing that the market-driven education destroys the virtue of collectivism and altruism. They believe that the contemporary capitalist education system is reproducing the social division

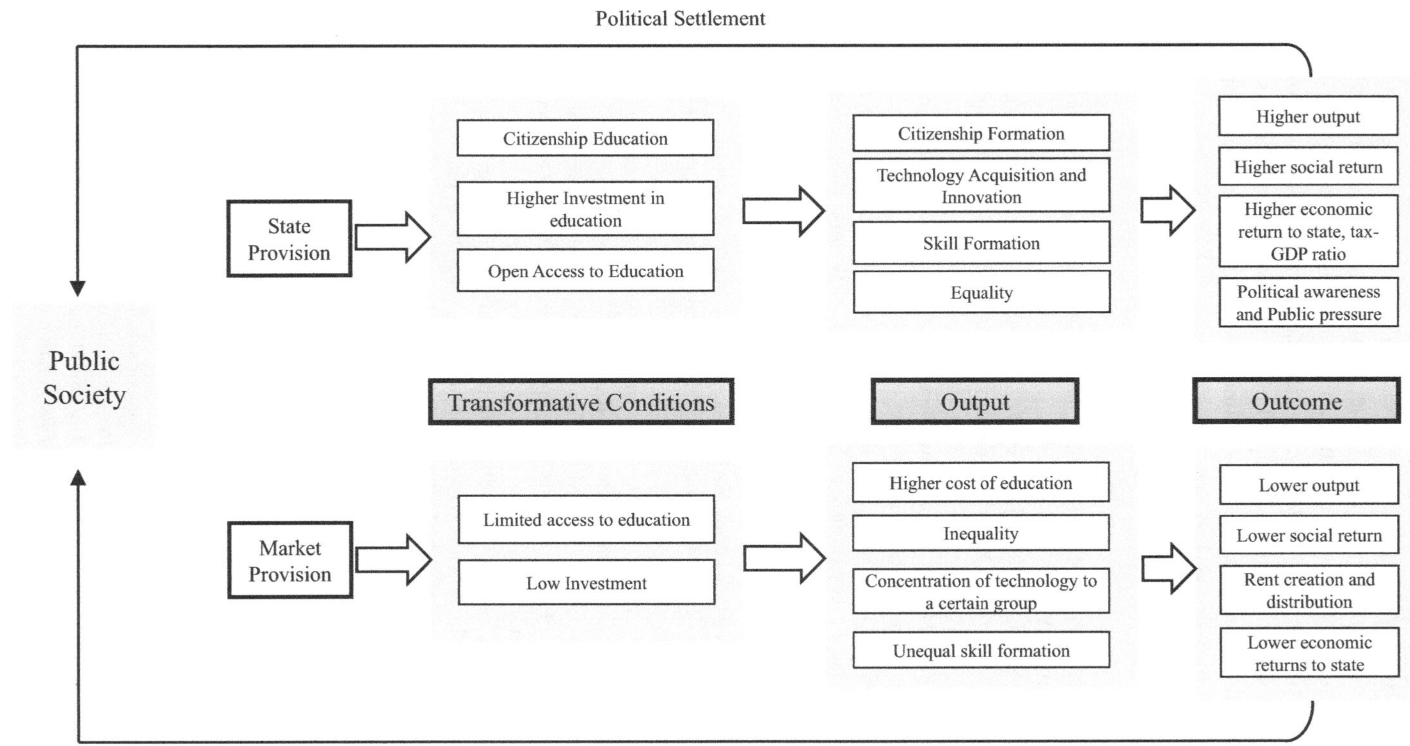

Figure 3.3 Framework for state and market provision of education in creating public society

Source: Prepared by author

of labour and maintaining the existing status quo. The political economic approaches also emphasise on the correlation between the access to education and the inequality in the society. These assume that education provisioning is the function of the government. Human sociality, as opposed to self-interest, is identified as the altruistic virtue of human nature which keeps human beings together in a society. Human beings, hence, believe in altruistic activities and institutions like representative government, establishing human rights, universal access to education and so on.

References

Akerlof, G.A., and Shiller, R.J. (2009). *Animal spirits: wie wirtschaft wirklich funktioniert.* Frankfrut: Campus Verlag.

Bandyopadhyay, S., and Esteban, J.M. (2007). *Redistributive taxation and public expenditures.* LSE STICERD Research Paper, 95. Retrieved March 22, 2022, from http://eprints.lse.ac.uk/6537/

Becker, G.S. (1964). *Human capital.* New York: National Bureau of Economic Research: Distributed by Columbia University Press.

Bourdieu, P. (1986). The forms of capital. In John G. Richardson (Ed.), *Handbook of theory and research for the sociology of education* (pp. 241–258). New York: Greenwood Press.

Bowles, S. (1972). Schooling and inequality from generation to generation. *Journal of Political Economy*, 80(3, Part 2), pp. S219–S251.

Bowles, S., and Gintis, H. (1976). *Schooling in capitalist America: Educational reform and the contradictions of economic life.* New York: Basic Books.

Bowles, S., and Gintis, H. (2002). Social capital and community governance. *The Economic Journal*, 112(483), pp. F419–F436.

Bowles, S., and Gintis, H. (2012). *Democracy and capitalism: Property, community, and the contradictions of modern social thought.* London: Routledge.

Bowles, S., Gintis, H., and Groves, M.O. (Eds.). (2005). *Unequal chances: Family background and economic success.* Princeton, NJ: Princeton University Press. Retrieved from www.jstor.org/stable/j.ctt7tbdz

Carlton, D.W., and Loury, G.C. (1980). The limitations of Pigouvian taxes as a long-run remedy for externalities. *The Quarterly Journal of Economics*, 95(3), pp. 559–566.

Chowdhury, R., and Kabir, A.H. (2014). Language wars: English education policy and practice in Bangladesh. *Multilingual Education*, 4(1), p. 21.

Clarke, D. (Ed.). (2006). *The Elgar companion to development studies.* Cheltenham: Edward Elgar Publishing.

Coase, R.H. (1960). The problem of social cost. In *Classic papers in natural resource economics* (pp. 87–137). London: Palgrave Macmillan.

Coleman, J.S. (1976). Differences between experiential and classroom learning. *Experiential Learning*, pp. 49–61.

Coleman, J.S. (1988). Social capital in the creation of human capital. *American Journal of Sociology*, 94, pp. S95–S120.

Dika, S.L., and Singh, K. (2002). Applications of social capital in educational literature: A critical synthesis. *Review of Educational Research*, 72(1), pp. 31–60.

Galbraith, J.K. (1998). *The affluent society.* Boston: Houghton Mifflin Company.

George, H.S. (2017). *Self-interest and social order in classical liberalism.* Washington, DC: CATO Institute.

Gintis, H. (2009). *The bounds of reason: Game theory and the unification of the behavioral sciences.* Princeton, NJ: Princeton University Press.

Haynes, P. (2009). *Before going any further with social capital: Eight key criticisms to address.* Retrieved April 20, 2022, from https://www.ingenio.upv.es/sites/default/files/working-paper/before_going_any_further_with_social_capital__eight_key_criticisms_to_address.pdf

Hirshleifer, J. (1987). *Economic behaviour in adversity.* Chicago: University of Chicago Press.

Hume, D. [1739] (1978). A treatise of human nature. *British Moralists*, 1650(1800), p. 443.

Hungerford, T., and Solon, G. (1987). Sheepskin effects in the returns to education. *The Review of Economics and Statistics*, 69(1), pp. 175–177.

Keynes, J.M. (1936). *The general theory of employment, interest, and money.* London: Palgrave Macmillan.

Latsis, J. (2009). Hume and the concept of convention. *Recherches sur la Philosophie et le Langage*, 26, pp. 217–234.

Mbiti, I.M. (2016). The need for accountability in education in developing countries. *Journal of Economic Perspectives*, 30(3), pp. 109–132.

Morris, P. (1996). Asia's four little tigers: A comparison of the role of education in their development. *Comparative Education*, 32(1), pp. 95–110.

Muralidharan, K., Das, J., Holla, A., and Mohpal, A. (2017). The fiscal cost of weak governance: Evidence from teacher absence in India. *Journal of Public Economics*, 145, pp. 116–135.

OECD. (2003). *Financing education: Investments and returns: Analysis of the world education indicators 2002.* Paris: Organisation for Economic Cooperation and Development.

Poder, T.G. (2011). What is really social capital? A critical review. *The American Sociologist*, 42(4), p. 341.

Pratham. (2014). *Annual status of education report (rural) 2013.* New Delhi, India: Pratham.

Pressman, S. (2007). A prolegomena to any future Post Keynesian education policy. *Journal of Post Keynesian Economics*, 29(3), pp. 455–472.

Putnam, R.D. (1995). Tuning in, tuning out: The strange disappearance of social capital in America. *PS: Political Science & Politics*, 28(4), pp. 664–683.

Ramberg, J. (2021). *UNESCO – Global Education Monitoring Report 2021: Inclusion and education: All means all.* Retrieved March 22, 2022 from https://unesdoc.unesco.org/ark:/48223/pf0000373718

Ramesh, M. (2004). *Social policy in East and Southeast Asia: Education, health, housing and income maintenance.* London: Routledge.

Reuters. (2016). *One in five children in Myanmar go to work instead of school – Census.* Retrieved November 29, 2021, from www.reuters.com/article/myanmar-youth-labour-children-school-idINKCN0WU184

Saito, M. (2003). Amartya Sen's capability approach to education: A critical exploration. *Journal of philosophy of education*, 37(1), pp. 17–33.

Schleicher, A. (2015). Education in an uncertain world. *Project syndicate and human development report.* Retrieved March 24, 2022, from https://www.project-syndicate.org/commentary/education-technological-skills-more-important-by-andreas-schleicher-2015-12

Sen, A. (1997). Human capital and human capability. *World Development*, 25(12), pp. 1959–1961.

Siisiäinen, M. (2000). Social capital, power and the third sector. In M. Siisiäinen, P. Kinnunen, and E. Hietanen (Eds.), *The third sector in Finland* (pp. 3–25). Helsinki: University of Lapland.

Smart, A. (1993). Gifts, bribes, and guanxi: A reconsideration of Bourdieu's social capital. *Cultural Anthropology*, 8(3), pp. 388–408.

Spence, M. (1973). Job market signaling. *The Quarterly Journal of Economics*, 87(3), pp. 355–374.

Stiglitz, J.E. (2000). Capital market liberalization, economic growth, and instability. *World Development*, 28(6), pp. 1075–1086.

Stretton, H., and Orchard, L. (1994). *Public goods, public enterprise, public choice*. London: The Macmillan Press Ltd.

Sullivan, A., and Sheffrin, S.M. (2003). *Economics: Principles in action*. NJ: Pearson Prentice Hall.

UNDP. (2016). *Human Development Report 2016: Human development for everyone*. United Nations Development Programme.

UNESCO. (2011). *Financing education in Sub-Saharan Africa: Meeting the challenges of expansion, equity and quality*. The United Nations Educational, Scientific and Cultural Organization. Paris. France.

UNESCO. (2020). *UNESCO Institute for Statistics (UIS)*. The United Nations Educational, Scientific and Cultural Organization. Paris. France. Retrieved November 25, 2021, from http://data.uis.unesco.org/

Uwezo. (2013). *Are our children learning? Literacy and numeracy across East Africa*. Uwezo, Nairobi, Kenya.

World Bank. (2003). *World Development Report 2004: Making services work for poor people*. Washington, DC: World Bank.

4 Education

Provisioning, Skill Formation and Citizenship

Introduction

The chapter, based on the theories discussed in the previous one, adopts a framework for understanding the education sector in developing countries. The chapter also looks in greater detail into the demand and supply side variables of the education sector that dominate current market provisioning policies. A careful analysis of market structures suggests barriers to entry protect incumbent firms and restrict competition, resulting in distortionary prices and price discrimination through charging different prices to customers for the same product or service. This has ramifications in creating a public society built on the idea of social justice and equality. Exclusion stemming from market provisioning of education worsens the gap between the richest and the poorest of the society as education offers increased capability. Raising human capability through education and training results in higher economic returns. Developing countries tend to have an economy that has more labour incentives than capital. As a result, skill formation and technology acquisition can increase higher returns on labour. For developing countries, this could reduce income and wealth gaps in society.

Public provisioning, as demonstrated, creates positive externalities and spillover effects. The transformational pathway for education lies in public provisioning that can ensure accessibility to all through universal education. An important reason for public provisioning of education is citizenship education. Such an education is necessary for state-building and public society. The formation of a citizen-state could ensure check and balance in political process as well as policymaking. Citizenship education at the same time gives the citizens a sense of their basic human rights mandated by the state in the social contract (Titumir, 2021). For instance, a lack of such citizenship education is visible during the time of pandemic when citizens in many cases failed to comply with social distancing and hygiene.

In light of the discussion in the previous chapters, the following section proposes new propositions and produces comparative assessments on the experiences of different countries in the sphere of education. These include the economic aspect of education such as skill formation and innovation as well

DOI: 10.4324/9781003284222-6

as the sociopolitical aspect such as citizenship education. The propositions are proved with empirical evidence in the next section.

Public Good and Market Provisioning

Education, a public good, if provisioned through market, there is a possibility of excludability in forms of access leading to unequal distribution due to imperfect market and entry barriers.

Since education is assumed to be a basic universal need, every human being has the right to get access to education irrespective of their ability to pay, socio-economic status, gender or any other racial identities. When education is provided by market alone, people face price discrimination and excludability. Demand for public goods can be encouraged by reducing the price paid by consumers. For example, subsidising the tuition fees of students will encourage more families to send their children to school, which will generate a positive externality for future generations.

Education is assumed here to be provided as a *pure* public good. When it is being provided as a pure public good, individual benefit remains unchanged as the number of users increases. In the horizontal line of Figure 4.1(a), the number of beneficiaries on the horizontal axis and on the vertical axis there is the price or individual benefit. Universal public provision of education keeps the benefit constant and the number of beneficiaries does not change, which means no excludability occurs in public provision. The benefit, however, does not remain constant when education is provisioned through the market. In

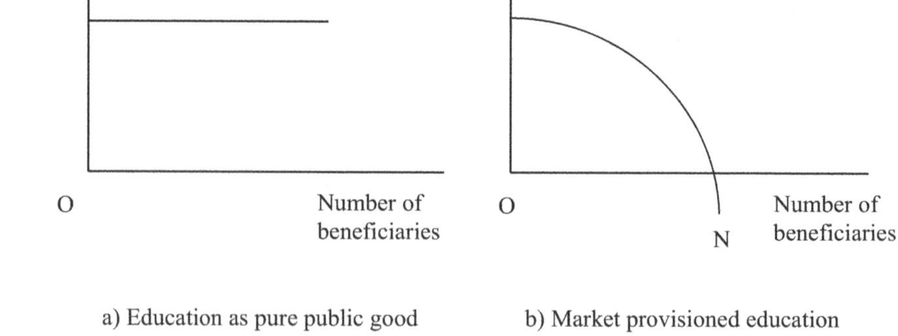

Figure 4.1 Market provisioning of education and excludability

Source: Prepared by author

market-provisioned education, the constant benefit goes to a small number of beneficiaries (Figure 4.1b). People irrespective of their ability to pay, socio-economic status, gender or any other identities cannot afford the prices set by the market. Those who have the ability to demand from the market can have access to education and others remain excluded. Market provisioning thus allows *N* people to get access to education who are able to buy services from the market. Hence many people become excluded.

The hypothesis is that instead of acknowledging education as people's need, therefore, a consequential basic right, the market provisioning considers it as people's demand which leads to price discrimination and exclusion.

A = education, a public good being provisioned through market
B = excludability
C = restriction in entry
D = spillover effect or negative externality

Logically,

$(A \to B \to C \to D) \to (A \to D)$

A	*B*	*C*	*D*	*A→B*	*B→C*	*C→D*	*(A→B)∧(B→C)∧ (C→D)*	*A→D*	*(A→B)∧(B→C)∧ (C→D)→(A→D)*
T	*T*	*T*	*T*	*T*	*T*	*T*	*T*	*T*	*T*
T	*T*	*T*	*F*	*T*	*T*	*F*	*F*	*F*	*T*
T	*T*	*F*	*T*	*T*	*T*	*T*	*F*	*T*	*T*
T	*T*	*F*	*F*	*T*	*F*	*T*	*F*	*F*	*T*
T	*F*	*T*	*T*	*F*	*T*	*T*	*F*	*T*	*T*
T	*F*	*T*	*F*	*F*	*T*	*F*	*F*	*F*	*T*
T	*F*	*F*	*T*	*F*	*T*	*T*	*F*	*T*	*T*
T	*F*	*F*	*F*	*F*	*T*	*T*	*F*	*F*	*T*
F	*T*	*T*	*T*	*T*	*T*	*T*	*T*	*T*	*T*
F	*T*	*T*	*F*	*T*	*T*	*F*	*F*	*T*	*T*
F	*T*	*F*	*T*	*T*	*F*	*T*	*F*	*T*	*T*
F	*T*	*F*	*F*	*T*	*F*	*T*	*F*	*T*	*T*
F	*F*	*T*	*T*	*T*	*T*	*T*	*T*	*T*	*T*
F	*F*	*T*	*F*	*T*	*T*	*F*	*F*	*T*	*T*
F	*F*	*F*	*T*	*T*	*T*	*T*	*T*	*T*	*T*
F	*F*	*F*	*F*	*T*	*T*	*T*	*F*	*T*	*T*

Source: Author

All values in the last column are true. Hence, it is proved that if public goods are provisioned through the market, it creates negative externality.

The provisioning through market has become dominant since the 1980s, with the adoption of neoliberal policies of privatisation and reduction of public spending in the sector. The reduction in public spending, as discussed before, creates unemployment and increases dropouts from schools from poor households, amongst others. Inequalities, thus, both between states and within states have increased dramatically during the era of neoliberalism. Markets have exacerbated these existing inequalities. A historical contextual snapshot of Bangladesh is given to illustrate the evolution.

During the British period, the demand for education was very low. Since access to public sector employment started rising in the British and Pakistani Period, this initiated a motivation to educate boys. Independence from Pakistan brought many social changes. The huge growth of population, declining farm size, increasing landlessness, an increasingly strained labour market and the growing commercialisation of agriculture altogether gradually push the economy to shift from small-scale peasant ownership and localised labour markets into a more monetised one based on more impersonal wage labour relationships. Micro-level studies from the late 1970s and early 1980s observed a skewed distribution of education with school attendance largely associated with boys from well-off urban families. In the long run, these males get formal jobs with higher returns. The reduced returns to unskilled labour induced the families to educate their children, especially boys. Later, inflow of remittances from abroad and cities as well as microcredit revolution work as incentives for families to send their daughters to school. Since education plays a great role in social mobility, the idea of mass education to tackle poverty gets popular in Bangladesh. Education can transform the huge population of this country into a productive workforce. Support for mass education, hence, is viewed as a wider national interest (Hossain and Kabeer, 2004). Robust population growth along with the socio-economic changes creates a large demand for education in Bangladesh.

Education in Bangladesh is supplied by a mix of providers. Schools are run by government, private organisations and NGOs. Primary education spans grades 1–5, Junior secondary grades 6–8, secondary grades 9–10, higher secondary grades 11–12 and tertiary education grades 13 and above. Along with the change in political discourse, the unmet demand has led to market provision of education in Bangladesh. The understanding is that prevalence of markets in the education sector would open more choices, competition and diversity and if it is properly understood and properly systemised would create a virtuous cycle and human capital for the society (Narayan, 2010). However, many children receive no schooling. Poor quality, organisational mismanagement and failed school administration are rampant, though there are mushrooming of high-cost, high-fee schools for the new rich in the towns and cities.

The difference in enrolment in secondary education is wide between the developing and the developed nations. Moreover, the completion rate is much lower compared to most of the developed states. The scenario is even more dismal in the African nations with a gross completion ratio much lower than the developed ones. In terms of the dropout rate, there is a high percentage of dropout rate in the African nations. Dropout rate is significantly lower in developed countries. Bangladesh still has a much higher dropout rate compared to nations like Norway and South Korea (Table 4.1).

Table 4.1 Attendance statistics

Countries	*Net enrolment rate (per cent)*		*Gross completion ratio (per cent)*		*Dropout rate (per cent)*	
	Primary	*Secondary*	*Primary*	*Secondary*	*Primary*	*Secondary*
Bangladesh		66.55	94.97	71.05		7.04
Burundi	92.80	27.52	57.96	30.48	56.24	25.55
Hong Kong	95.45	96.14	103.68	106.85	1.3	1.03
Cuba	97.74	84.18	90.43	101.88	3.6	4.09
Germany	90.14	85.30		87.36		
India	92.26	61.63	76.75	70.13	8.76	4.88
Malaysia	99.65	72.21	97.52	80.34	3.62	7.81
South Korea	97.26	98.01	97.90	103.10	0.52	0.66
Norway	99.88	95.61	100.20	101.66	0.9	1.24
Senegal	75.38	37.67	37.04	29.43	39.67	32.39
United Kingdom	99.49	97.13	100.25	97.11	0.25	

Source: UNESCO (2020)

The net enrolment rate of students in the primary level stands at more than 90 per cent in almost all the countries except Senegal. The differentiation starts from the secondary level. African countries are the lowest in enrolling students at the secondary level of education. South Asian countries stand at a medium level in this case and the developed countries show a higher rate of enrolment. The gross completion ratio is similar in the case of both primary and secondary levels of education in the African nations. The South Asian countries have a greater percentage of completion of primary level than that of the secondary level. The developed countries have a very high amount of completion ratio at both levels. Low enrolment and completion rate in secondary education show that focus should now shift from primary to secondary level in order to create a skilled workforce. The dropout rate is very high in African countries at both levels. All the other countries have a very low ratio of dropout which shows a good amount of progress in the educational attainment (Table 4.1).

The private educational institutions in Bangladesh like in India are burgeoning day by day. And the number of private institutions is far higher than the public educational institutions. There are now 19493 schools managed by the private sector whereas the number of public schools is 804 (Table 4.2). The mounting growth of private educational institutions is due to the adoption of neoliberal reforms and high population growth.

Remarkably, the ratio of students enrolled in private institutions is lower than the public ones which means that the number of students in one private school is lower than the number of students in public schools. And it can be observed that though there are 86 private universities in Bangladesh whereas there are only 37 public universities, approximately 13,327 students study in

Table 4.2 Number of private and public education institutions

Institutions	*Private*	*Public*
School	19,493	804
College	3,811	302
University	86	37
Madrasah	9,316	3
Technical educational institution	5,538	252
Medical college	64	29
Dental college	23	9
Law college	71	0
Professional training institution	83	132

Source: Adopted from BANBEIS, 2015

one public university whereas only about 4,416 students study in one private university. Public institutions worldwide have a higher percentage of students. In the United Kingdom, 93.7 per cent of students study in publicly managed schools (UNESCO, 2020).

The argument for privatisation of education in developed countries has relied on competition and associated quality. Developed countries have been able to implement universal enrolment. However, developing countries are still far away from establishing universal enrolment.

Since colonial era, provision of education was limited to an elite class and the situation did not get much better even during the Pakistani period. After independence, the successive governments took certain initiatives to enhance access to education for mass people. This is linked to the aspirations and struggles of the general masses of Bangladesh. But, it becomes difficult for the government alone to provide education to its citizens due to huge population and low financial capacity. The increasing dependence on private provisioning also stems from the unmet demand due to huge population as the public sector has limited capacity owing to fiscal constraints. The private provisioning is largely concentrated in urban areas.

Children from rural regions are disproportionately affected. As a result, inequality between the rich and the poor as well as rural and urban population widens, and the impact is felt in the long term. If public school can accommodate all students, private schools could become competitive by offering either higher quality education or value-added products. In developing countries, private schools fill in the gap due to limited absorption capacity of the public education institutions, without having any thrust to improve quality in absence of competition. Both the systems exhibit low quality, though for different reasons.

In the developed countries, a new form of social division has emerged due to the prevalence of market and state in the education sector (Bowles, 1972). Since the privatisation of education, the rich secure education at a private school, or at one of the high status publicly funded schools by using their social, economic and cultural capital, reinforcing class divisions (Robertson and Lauder, 2001). Others have to accept neighbourhood schools or underchosen schools which perform poorly, and eventually these schools have little or limited "value" when it comes to other kinds of transactions in the education and wider labour market (Whitty et al., 1998). Thus, a new form of social stratification takes foothold due to the difference in quality of education. These perpetuate the vicious cycle of inequality and deprivation.

In Bangladesh, per household expenditure on education in urban areas is higher than similar expenditure in rural areas. In urban areas, per household educational expenditure is 1,796 BDT whereas such expenditure in rural areas is 604 BDT (BBS, 2019) as there are more private schools, colleges, universities etc. in urban areas than in rural areas. Annual Education Survey 2015 reveals that there are 162 English medium schools in Bangladesh. Among them 38 are "O" level, 99 are "A" level and only 25 are junior secondary level. Most of the schools are located in Dhaka city (138) followed by Chittagong (13) (BANBEIS, 2015). A survey over 1,000 households finds that monthly educational expenses in Dhaka are around $50, and private tution accounted for over half the cost. The households with a monthly income of $ 193 or less spend $2 on monthly school fees and $33 on tuition ($35 a month), whereas households with an income over $257 pay $6 as school fees and a staggering $141 on private tuition) (May, 2014). The increasing out-of-pocket expenditure also indicates the lack of quality in teaching in schools, coercing parents to send their children to private tuition centres. Households of all economic strata spend a substantial part of their income on children's education, even when the children attend public or publicly assisted schools. This clearly indicates that people are willing to get quality and productive education and also to pay any price for it but still they are not getting it. The teachers are dissatisfied with their job, have poor incentive and motivation, function in adverse working conditions and have no career and professional development path ahead of them. Demoralised and demotivated teachers can hardly make their contribution to a functioning school system that can serve the interest of learners and society. The prevalence of multi-typed provisioning has failed to provide the desired quality education to people of Bangladesh and this can be also observed in higher secondary and tertiary education.

Most of the students of private universities incur more money on tuition fees, housing and living conditions whereas the students of public universities live in university-allocated residences almost for free and pay significantly low tuition fees. In 2010, the monthly expenditure of a student of private universities was 18,831 BDT, wide ranging between 11,000 and 36,000 BDT and with a standard deviation of 4,923 BDT. The mean monthly expenditure of a student of a public university was only 4,443 BDT, varying from 1,540 to 8,040 BDT and had a standard deviation of 1,248 BDT. The students of private universities had to pay for higher tuition fees and housing rent, resulting in such a huge difference. Unlike public, private universities charged on an average 1,200 USD per year (May, 2014). The privatisation has led to higher cost in education.

There is a significant variance between parents' income of the students of private universities and public ones. The average monthly income of parents of private universities in 2010 was 99,061 BDT, ranging from 25,000 to 546,000 BDT and with a large standard deviation of 89,403 BDT, meaning a difference in income of parents within the private universities. On the contrary, the mean income of parents of public university students is 70,010 BDT with a range between 12,000 and 350,000 BDT and with large standard deviation of 80,121 BDT (Barman et al., 2012).

The students of secondary level of the developed countries have the complete privilege of having the access to developed school resources like electricity, Internet, computer and drinking water (Table 4.3). But, African countries like Burundi and Senegal provide less access to the resources than all the other countries. South Asian countries like Bangladesh and India provide higher access than that of the African countries but not the levels of the developed ones. Bangladesh has a poor percentage in providing Internet and computers in the secondary level of education mainly.

The institutions offering post higher secondary education in Bangladesh are included in college education. The types recognised are: intermediate colleges, degree colleges, honours colleges and master's colleges (Table 4.4). The total number of institutions involved in college education has been increasing. The number was 3,150 in 2005, 3,324 in 2010, 3,547 in 2012, 3,793 in 2013, 3,985 in 2014 and 4,113 in 2015. Majority (92.66 per cent) were privately managed

Table 4.3 Education infrastructure around the world

Countries	*Percentage of secondary schools with access to electricity*	*Percentage of secondary schools with access to Internet*	*Percentage of secondary schools with access to computer*	*Percentage of secondary schools with access to drinking water*
Australia	100	100	100	100
Bangladesh	92.3	35.3	83.4	97.3
Burundi	41.9*	0.7*	1.7*	72.1*
China	99.4	98.1	98.0	99.6
Cuba	100	48.7	100	100
Germany	100	100	100	100
India	67.7		48.1**	87.6*
South Korea	100	100	100	100
Norway	100	100	100	100
Senegal	76.9	43.5	69.9	83.5
United Kingdom	100	100	100	100
United States	100	100	100	100

Source: UNESCO (2020)

Table 4.4 Teacher–student ratio of colleges in 2019

Type of college	*Teacher–student ratio*	*Average student per college*	*Average teacher*
School & college (college section)	1:17	270	16
Higher secondary	1:15	264	18
Degree (pass) college	1:27	937	35
Degree (honours)	1:44	1,955	45
Master's college	1:103	7,930	77
Total (college education)	1:33	894	27

Source: BANBEIS (2019)

and 7.34 per cent were managed by government. Among all institutions, 96 per cent had electricity and 80 per cent had multimedia facilities. There were 30,103 desktop computers and 6485 laptop computers in 4,113 colleges which is not quite satisfactory as it means that on an average there are only about 9 computers in one college though 93 per cent of colleges had computer Internet and 19 per cent had solar panels. Teacher–student ratio is comparatively lower in college education, which is 1:33. But in master's college, it is quite depressing as one teacher is assigned for 103 students. There were 4,113 colleges in 2015. In total, 3,535 colleges (86 per cent) have principals and among them 7.38 per cent were female. Vice principal was only in 1,060 (26 per cent) colleges, professors were 519 (0.13 professor/college), associate professors were 2815 (0.68/institution), assistant professors were 18,462 (4.48 /institution) and lecturers were 78,222 (19/institution) (BANBEIS, 2015).

Absence of quality assurance mechanism is a critical issue in Bangladesh. University Grants Commission (UGC) as the apex body of the government for higher education is responsible for funding the public universities. Though private universities do not get any government assistance in terms of funding, they need to receive approval from the UGC to operate and award degrees. Annual Education Survey, 2015 reveals that there were 122 universities in Bangladesh, 37 (30 per cent) were public and 85 (70 per cent) were private. Total number of students was 872,891. Average number of students per university was 7,154, the average number of students in public universities was 13,327 and private universities was 4468. Overall gender parity index was 47.55, with 60 per cent in public and 37 per cent in private universities. Total teachers in 122 universities were 26,319. Among them only 25.47 per cent were female. In public universities, this percentage was 21.92 per cent and in private universities this percentage was 28.64 per cent. Variation was large among the universities. Average number of teachers in 2015 was 336 in public, 164 in private and 216 in both public and private universities. Teacher–student ratio was 1:40.33 in public universities, 1:27 in private and 1:33 in both public and private universities which indicates that in private universities one teacher finds it easier to pay attention than public ones. In 2015, there were 12,414 teachers in public universities. Among them 27.4 per cent were professors, 16.94 per cent were associate professors, 30.56 per cent were assistant professors and 25.06 per cent were lecturers.

The traditional teaching method is a common feature in universities. And sharing of knowledge and students' participation in the learning process is minimal. Moreover, the monologue teaching and learning system, gap and lack of communication between teachers and students act as barriers in creating the congenial atmosphere for learning in the universities of Bangladesh. Simultaneously, modern teaching methods and facilities like Internet, multimedia and sound system are in short supply in public universities. Furthermore, financial crisis, lack of residential halls, shortage of seats against the demand and involvement of teachers in other activities are also identified as the barriers to quality education in Bangladesh. The quality and facilities in both the library and laboratory are poor and outdated. There is a shortage of modern equipment in the laboratory. On the other hand, recent text and reference books, professional journals are hardly available in libraries. The government allocation for universities is mostly spent on salary and allowances of the faculty and staff members. As a result, due to a weak financial base, the universities of Bangladesh cannot play their assigned role in research, innovation, skills development and citizenship education.

These also confirm that despite higher education costs in private universities, these institutions are failing to provide their students a well-equipped campus, library facilities, teachers with higher qualification and adequate resource funding (Table 4.5).

Senegal has the lowest expenditure on education and Norway has the highest. The developed countries generally spend a reasonable amount of their GDP on education at both secondary and tertiary levels (Table 4.6). On the other hand, countries like India and Burundi have lower government expenditure

Table 4.5 Comparative analysis between public and private universities

	Public university	*Private university*
Number of universities	37	85
Average number of students per university	13,327	4,468
Per cent of female students	37 per cent	28 per cent
Gender parity index	60	37
Teacher–student ratio	1:19	1:23
Number of teachers with PhDs	4,178 in 32 public universities	2,719 in 75 private universities
Research funding	All public universities have	22 private universities do not have any
Own campus	All public universities have	68 private universities do not have any
Accommodation facility for students	Provided to 38 per cent of students	Very rarely provided

Source: UGC (2014)

Table 4.6 Government expenditure on education of some selected countries (2017)

Countries	*Government expenditure on education as a percentage of GDP*		*Government expenditure on education as a percentage of Total government expenditure*	
	Secondary	*Tertiary*	*Secondary*	*Tertiary*
Australia	1.65	1.41	4.31	3.69
Bangladesh	0.99	0.51	7.35	3.80
Burundi	1.61*	1.45*	4.62*	4.18*
Germany	1.98	1.25	4.51	2.84
India	1.59*	1.10*	5.81	4.01
Japan	1.34	0.63	3.52	1.66
Norway	2.28	2.13	4.56	4.27
Senegal	0.78**	0.94**	3.62**	7.07**
UK	2.08	1.41	5.23	3.54
USA	1.71	1.21	4.68	3.32

Source: UNESCO (2020)

on education. Most of the countries here have higher government expenditure at the secondary level. In the case of Bangladesh, expenditure on secondary education is almost double that of tertiary education.

Bangladesh has the highest percentage of capital expenditure in public institutions with 14.2 per cent and the United Kingdom has the lowest capital expenditure in education. Japan and Norway have very high amounts of capital expenditure in all three levels of education. On the other hand, other countries have higher expenditure in the tertiary level than that of the secondary and primary levels. Bangladesh here has the highest capital expenditure in the secondary level of education which is more than three times that of the tertiary level (Table 4.7).

The investment of households in education becomes burdensome as educated youth unemployment is very high. The percentage of educated unemployment in Bangladesh was 14 per cent in 2010 which is higher than that of India (11 per cent) and Vietnam (5 per cent). The rate of unemployment is increasing in Bangladesh which was 2.5 per cent during 1995–1996 and increased to 4.5 per cent in 2010 whereas underemployment increased from 16.6 per cent to 20.3 per cent during 2000–2010 (Figure 4.2). During this period, 20.1 million new labourers joined the labour force whereas in 2010 the rate of employment was only 3.1 per cent which is less than the rate of growth of labour force and rate of unemployment. Along with this increasing unemployment growth rate, increasing educated unemployed people has worsened the situation. Equally worrying is that a huge chunk of youths with full of possibilities migrates to other countries by being dissatisfied with the quality of higher education and employment opportunities. The high unemployment and underemployment, particularly among young people, are belying a potential "demographic dividend" for Bangladesh as such is

Table 4.7 Capital expenditure as a percentage of total expenditure in public institutions (2016)

Countries	*Capital expenditure as a percentage of total expenditure in public institutions*			
	Total	*Primary*	*Secondary*	*Tertiary*
Australia	7.7*	5.3	5.2	11.1
Bangladesh	14.2		27.2	8.1
Germany	6.7	6.3	5.5	8.4
Japan	11.3	12.6	10.6	10.4
South Korea				12.9
Norway	12.4	13.3	13.6	12.7
Senegal	5	1.3	2.9	9.9
UK	2.3	2.3	2.2	
USA	8.7**	8.6	8.6	4.7

Source: UNESCO (2020)

feasible since the largest share of population is from the economically active age group.

The total employed population was only 13 per cent in the formal sector and 87 per cent in the informal sector in 2013 (BBS, 2013). This informal employment is mostly characterised by low productivity, low pay and precarious conditions. In 2013, the youth unemployment rate was 10.3 per cent, higher than the regional South Asian average (9.45 per cent). More than 95 per cent of youths work in the informal sector, of which many work as self-employed (31.7 per cent), or in unpaid family work (11.1 per cent) whereas more than 75 per cent of businesses leaders claimed that a scarcity of skilled young workers was a challenge to hiring youth (S4YE, 2015). There is a miss-match between the qualifications attained by the graduates and the desired skills required by the employers, indicating failure by the education system in contributing towards skills formation.

Social policy also requires a feminist approach, which considers intersectionality that encumbers "a grassroots benchmark to the strategy of political coalition-building in order to support transformative social policy" (Enriquez, 2021). The policies should be designed in a manner that not only improves living standards but also addresses the sources of inequality production (Enriquez, 2021). The enrolment and survival rate of girls in primary and secondary education have increased progressively over the years in developing countries, inching closer to gender equity. However, there still exist 5.5 million more out-of-school girls than boys (UNESCO, 2020). Sub-Saharan Africa still lags behind in terms of gender parity in primary education. Bangladesh has seen an increasing rate of female enrolment and educational attainment over the years. In 2015, the gross enrolment ratio in secondary level rose to 77.84 per cent for girls and the pass rates of female students were higher in many public examinations (BANBEIS, 2015). However, the

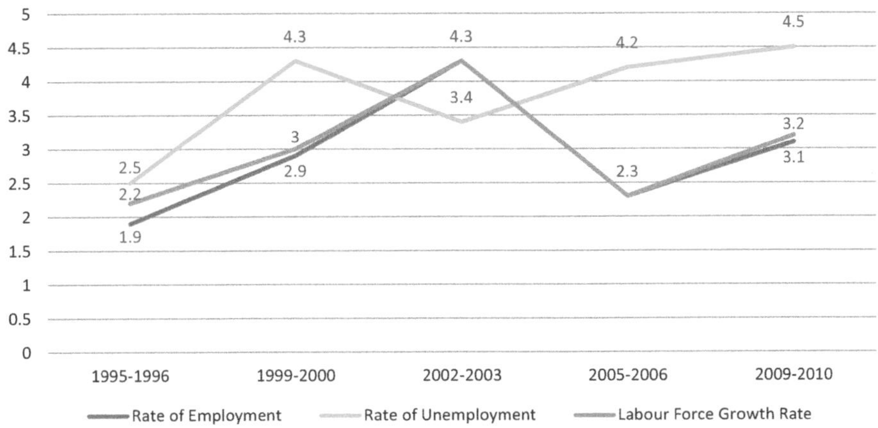

Figure 4.2 Situation of employment, unemployment and labour force growth

Source: *Prepared by authors*

high rate of educational attainment has not matched in the labour market as women still constitute the majority of unemployed young NEETs (Not in Education, Employment, or Training). Two-thirds of young women are NEET and two-thirds of school dropouts are women. Labour force participation for females remains much lower in South Asian and African countries. However, sub-Saharan countries have a higher rate of female labour force participation, much owed to the rural agricultural sector (ILO, 2020). Lack of security and early marriage still persist as the reason for high dropouts and lower share in the labour force (Munshi, 2015). Female labour force participation is quite low compared to male. At the same time, female employees are given lower wages than their male counterparts. They earn up to 60 per cent less than the male. The gender gap widens more in male-dominated works like managerial positions where women constitute only 27 per cent of the positions worldwide (ILO, 2020). Gender discrimination in the workplace needs to be looked at if the developing countries want to improve female labour force employment.

Skills Formation and Employment

Low level of skill formation, as an outcome of low level of quality education and insufficient investment, results in underemployment and unemployment. Productivity of labour depends on skill formation. Labour force with lower skill results in lower output. The hypothesis demonstrates that lack of quality education with low levels of investment cannot generate skilled labour force as demanded by the market, which forges unemployment and underemployment problems in the economy as well.

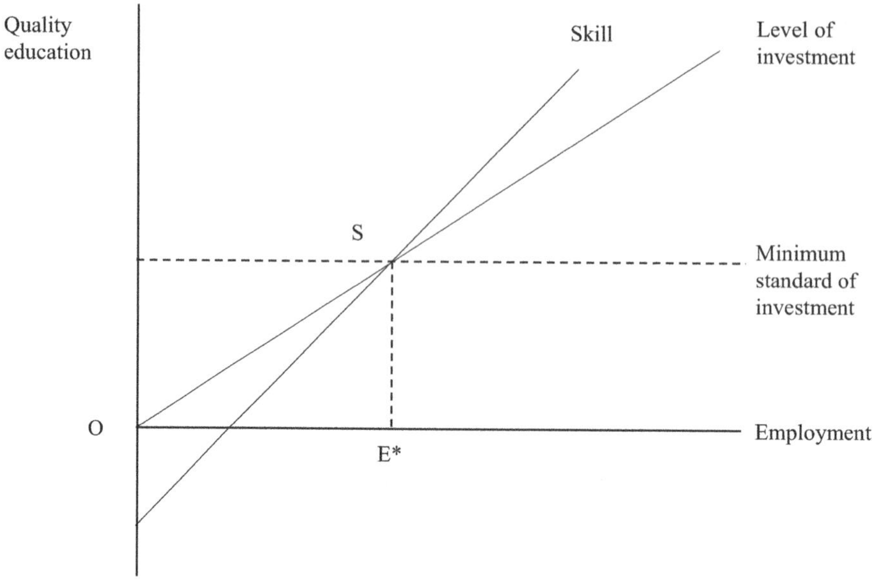

Figure 4.3 Investment in quality education and skill

Source: *Prepared by author*

When the level of investment in quality education increases, the skill of the labour force also develops. A minimum level of investment in quality education develops skill up to the point S which guarantees employment up to the point E* (Figure 4.3). Increasing trend of investment and quality education boosts skill as well as employment in the economy.

The quality of education depends on certain parameters. Let us consider a society where quality education depends on three parameters. And these are technological support, favourable environment and training opportunities. Consider,

Q=quality education
C=technological support
B=favourable environment
A=training opportunities
S=skill
U=public funding
R=regulation
R=return from investment

$$\frac{dA}{dt} = \tau_1 \frac{dU}{dt} + \tau_2 \frac{dR}{dt} \tag{1}$$

$$\frac{dA}{dt} = \alpha A \tag{2}$$

$$\frac{dB}{dt} = \tau_1 \frac{dU}{dt} + \tau_2 \frac{dR}{dt} \qquad (3)$$

$$\frac{dA}{dt} = \beta B \qquad (4)$$

$$\frac{dC}{dt} = \tau_1 \frac{dU}{dt} + \tau_2 \frac{dR}{dt} \qquad (5)$$

$$\frac{dA}{dt} = \gamma C \qquad (6)$$

$$\frac{dQ}{dt} = \alpha A + \beta B + \gamma C \qquad (7)$$

$$\frac{dQ}{dt} = \mu Q \qquad (8)$$

$$\frac{dS}{dt} = \mu Q \qquad (9)$$

$$\frac{dS}{dt} = \sigma S \qquad (10)$$

$$\frac{dE}{dt} = \sigma S \qquad (11)$$

With initial values, $A\ (0)>0, B(0)\ >0, C(0)>0, U(0)>0, R(0)>0$

Here τ_1 *and* τ_2 are the rate of growth of public funding and regulation, respectively.

And

α=growth rate of training opportunities
β=growth rate of favourable environment
γ=growth rate of technological support
μ=growth rate of quality education
σ=growth rate of skill

And *consider* $\tau_1, \tau_1, \alpha, \beta, \gamma, \mu, \sigma \geq 0$

In Equation (*1*), the training opportunities depend on public funding and regulation. Here, τ_1 and τ_2 are the rate of growth of public funding and regulation, respectively.

Case 1:

If τ_1, τ_2=0, then in Equations (*1*), (*3*) and (*5*), the increase or decrease in regulation and public funding will not occur. Consequently, the growth rate of A, B and C in Equations (*2*), (*4*) and (*6)* will be zero. Hence, in Equation (*7*), the quality education will not increase. It will remain as it was initially.

So, with no growth of quality education in Equation (*8*), the rate of growth of quality education μ will be zero. As a result in Equation (9), the skill will remain as it was initially, keeping the rate of growth of skill to be zero in Equation (*10*). Hence, in Equation (*11*), employment will not increase.

Case 2:

If τ_1,τ_2 is increasing then in Equations (*1*), (*3*) and (*5*), *A*, *B* and *C* will increase. As a result, in Equations (*2*), (*4*) and (*6*), the growth rate of *A*, *B* and *C* will increase.

Consequently, in Equation (*7*), the quality education will change positively. Equation (*8*) shows the increased rate of quality education. As a result, in Equation (*9*), skill will change positively and resulting in an increased growth rate of skill in Equation (*10*).

Employment finally increases in Equation (*11*) because of the increase in skill.

The previous section discussed how education has been commoditised in Bangladesh and how it is creating price discrimination along with other negative externalities. The inferior quality of education is creating unskilled labourers who cannot enter into job market or are working in underpaid informal sectors despite attaining higher education. Labour productivity is here measured by the outcome per worker by GDP. The labour productivity, the dependent variable in the equation and a measure of skill are positively affected by mean years of schooling. The exercise, comprising panel data of 34 countries, a mix of both developed and developing countries, shows that low skill level is significant at one per cent and reduces labour productivity by 2.3 per cent (Table 4.8).

Government expenditure in education demonstrates a positive impact on labour productivity. A per cent increase in education expenditure increases the labour productivity by 13.9 per cent (Table 4.8).

Table 4.8 Regression result on labour productivity

Variables	*Labour productivity*
Life expectancy	0.0699**
	(0.0288)
Government education expenditure	0.139*
	(0.0763)
Mean years of schooling	0.261***
	(0.0592)
Employment in skill level 1 (low skill)	-0.0233*
	(0.0118)
Constant	1.986
	(1.945)
Observations	33
R-squared	0.886

Source: Standard errors in parentheses
*** p<0.01
** p<0.05
* p<0.1

Education plays a vital role to form knowledge and skill. If education attainment can signal his or her level of competency, a higher level of education, therefore, helps a person to get a higher paid job.

The outcome of the current scenario of education can be measured by the status of engagement in the workforce. According to the Quarterly Labour Force Survey Report 2015, among 106.1 million working-age population (aged 15 years and older), only 59.5 million are engaged in various sectors of the economy. The numbers varying with education level, gender, area and economic sector are given in Table 4.9.

In most of the developed countries, the highest share of employed population has only secondary level of education. In case of Bangladesh, the top position is held by the workers, having primary education as the country has recently achieved universal primary education (Table 4.9).

The phenomenon of overeducation, on the contrary, tends to take place when an insufficient number of jobs match a certain level of education. The mismatch in supply and demand forces some of the degree holders to take up available work that they are subsequently overqualified to perform. In Bangladesh, overeducated youths were found primarily in elementary occupations (13.9 per cent) and to a lesser degree in clerical (5.9 per cent) and sales (3.1 per cent) work. The consequence is that overeducated youths are likely to earn less than they otherwise could have and are not making the most of their productive potential. Many younger people held positions for which they were undereducated. Approximately two-thirds (66.1 per cent) of young managers, as well as 62.0 per cent of young professionals and 91.6 per cent of young technicians and associate professionals did not hold the necessary level of education expected for the job. Most of the other occupations also showed high shares of undereducated workers. The undereducation of workers can have a severe impact on labour productivity and can be a significant hindrance to economic growth, but can also impact young workers in terms of their self-confidence (Toufique, 2014).

One means of measuring the mismatch between the jobs people do and their level of educational qualification is to apply the normative measure of

Table 4.9 Employed population aged 15 or older by education level, area and sector

Education level	*Rural*		*Urban*		*Sector (per cent)*		
	Male	*Female*	*Male*	*Female*	*Agriculture*	*Industry*	*Service*
None	34.1	38.9	19.4	28.7	57.1	15.3	27.6
Primary	27.6	24.0	24.0	24.6	40.7	25.2	34.1
Secondary	28.6	32.0	34.5	30.8	34.7	23.1	42.2
Higher secondary	5.5	3.3	9.6	7.3	15.1	17.9	67.0
Tertiary	3.6	1.7	12.2	8.6	5.1	15.4	79.4
Others	0.5	0.1	0.2	0.0	17.9	14.3	67.8

Source: Labour Force Survey Report, 2016

occupational skills categories of the International Standard Classification of Occupations (ISCO), a tool for organising jobs into a clearly defined set of groups according to the tasks and duties undertaken in the job. ISCO-08 includes the categorisation of major occupational groups (first-digit ISCO levels) by level of education in accordance with the International Standard Classification of Education (ISCED). It is alarming that 64 per cent of workers' qualifications do not match with their job requirements (Table 4.10).

Those who have a higher level of education are considered overeducated and those with a lower level of education are considered undereducated. For instance, a university graduate working as a clerk (a low-skilled, non-manual occupation) is overeducated, while a secondary school graduate working as an engineer (a high-skilled, non-manual occupation) is undereducated. The result for surveyed Bangladeshi youth was that a minority of young workers were in occupations that matched their level of education (36.0 per cent), compared to workers in occupations for which they were overeducated or undereducated (64.0 per cent). In total, 2.4 per cent of young working Bangladeshis were overeducated and 61.6 per cent were undereducated (Table 4.11). The results are, in part, a reflection of the levels of education attained by youth in the country. A substantial share of employed youths complete education below the secondary level. It is not surprising that youths are classified as more undereducated than overeducated.

In Bangladesh, 6 per cent of the workers are overemployed while 59 per cent are undereducated. The number of workers overeducated goes as high as 20 per cent in developed countries. For example, the United Kingdom has 22 per cent of workers who are overeducated (ILO, 2020). This is mainly due to the high number of tertiary graduates in the developed countries. At the same time, the number of people undereducated for work is high in developing countries whereas the number is quite low for the developed ones.

Developing countries have a higher share of undereducated workers due to having low skilled workers (Table 4.12). On the other hand, developed countries have more highly skilled workers. Overall there are 935 million

Table 4.10 Occupational category by the level of education

ISCO major groups	*Broad occupation group*	*Educational level*
Managers Professionals Technicians & associate professionals	High-skilled non-manual	Tertiary
Clerical support workers Service & sales workers	Low-skilled non-manual	Secondary
Skilled agricultural & fishery workers Craft & related trade workers Plant & machine operators and assemblers	Skilled manual	
Elementary occupations	Unskilled manual	Primary

Source: Cited in Toufique (2014)

Table 4.11 Incongruity in qualifications

Major occupational category (ISCO-08)	*Overeducated*	*Undereducated*
Legislators, senior officials, managers	0.0	66.1
Professionals	0.0	62.0
Technician and professionals	0.0	91.6
Clerks	5.9	17.1
Service workers and shop market sales workers	3.1	55.9
Skilled agriculture and fishery workers	0.4	69.7
Craft and related trade workers	0.5	61.9
Plant & machine operators and assemblers	0.0	76.6
Elementary occupations	13.9	36.4
Armed forces	0.0	84.0
Total	2.4	61.6

Source: Cited in Toufique (2014)

Table 4.12 Share of under- and overeducated workers

Countries	*Share of workers overeducated*	*Share of workers undereducated*
Bangladesh	6	59
India	14	48
Nepal	11	46
Vietnam	20	28
United Kingdom	22	22
Norway	15	20
Egypt	8	49
Uganda	2	85

Source: ILO (2020)

workers in the world whose job does not match with the educational level (ILO, 2020). Hence, there is a large deadweight loss in the economy.

High graduate unemployment also comes from a shortage of graduates with specialised skills (EIU-BC, 2014). Demand for university education is not uniform across disciplines. The business and management degree, for example, at both undergraduate and postgraduate levels, continues to be most popular, fuelled by students eagerly anticipating jobs in banking and other private firms, or looking to carve it on their own as entrepreneurs. At the same time, there remains a familiar desire of students looking to work in the public service and this drives demand for degrees within the social sciences whereas the capacity of the civil service to absorb graduates is limited.

More than half (61.8 per cent) of unemployed youths singled out the lack of required education as the most crucial obstacle to finding work (Table 4.13). Given that the least educated youths had the highest chance of finding work implied that these youths were referring to the difficulty of getting more skilled jobs. Lack of training was mentioned by 15.7 per cent of unemployed youths.

Table 4.13 Main reasons behind joblessness

Lack of required education	61.8 per cent
Lack of training	15.7 per cent
Lack of practical experience	9.9 per cent
Low wages	5.3 per cent
Scarcity of jobs	2.7 per cent

Source: SWTS-Bangladesh (2013), cited in Toufique (2014)

Other obstacles included lack of practical experience (9.9 per cent), low wages (5.3 per cent) and scarcity of jobs (2.7 per cent) (Toufique, 2014).

The absence of quality education and less than the required skill development programmes are hindering in generating skilled youth who can be employed in formal jobs with decent wage. There is also shortage of specialised skills. Moreover, the growth of the labour force has surpassed the growth of the job market. There are paucity of jobs for graduates with specialised degrees (i.e., limited public jobs for a large number of social science students). Furthermore, employers complain that graduates are endowed with key soft skills and English language abilities. Besides skills, for an economy to transform from the low-level trap is to require talents, who are innovative, risk-taking, adaptable and responsive to changing environments.

Innovation and Education

A higher level of education with higher level of research and development (R&D) expenditure tends to raise the innovation level, a necessary condition for higher economic growth. Education influences innovation in an economy, which is considered a necessary condition for economic growth. Innovation requires higher investment in R&D. Increased expenditure in higher education and R&D is the precursor for technological acquisition and innovation in an economy.

When expenditure in R&D increases, it promotes innovation. The quality of higher education also gets boosted, fermenting further innovation that results in higher economic growth. After a certain period of time (point I), the innovative capacity of the economy and its outcome exceed the level of R&D expenditure (Figure 4.4).

The lower investment in higher education with low levels of R&D expenditure hinders innovation and thus affects economic growth negatively. Government intervention in the form of higher R&D expenditure and higher level of education tends to raise the innovation level.

A=the higher R&D expenditure
B=higher level of education
C=raise to the innovation

The proposition implies that $(A \wedge B) \rightarrow C$ *or* $\sim (A \wedge B) \vee C$

Here,

No.	*A*	*B*	*C*	*(A^B)*	*~(A^B)*	*(A^B)→C*	*~ (A^B)VC*
1	*T*	*T*	*T*	*T*	*F*	*T*	*T*
2	*T*	*T*	*F*	*T*	*F*	*F*	*F*
3	*T*	*F*	*T*	*F*	*T*	*T*	*T*
4	*T*	*F*	*F*	*F*	*T*	*T*	*T*
5	*F*	*T*	*T*	*F*	*T*	*T*	*T*
6	*F*	*T*	*F*	*F*	*T*	*T*	*T*
7	*F*	*F*	*T*	*F*	*T*	*T*	*T*
8	*F*	*F*	*F*	*F*	*T*	*T*	*T*

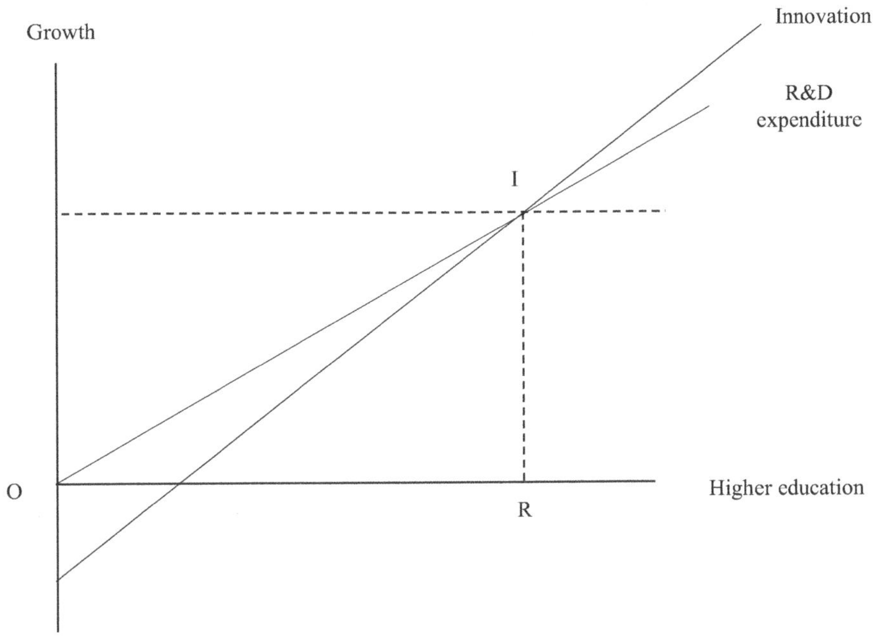

Figure 4.4 High R&D expenditure constituting innovation and growth

Source: Prepared by author

1. Either there is no higher R&D expenditure and higher level of education or there is a raise in innovation level.
2. Here, ~ *(A∧B)* is *F* which implies that it is not possible for innovation not to rise when there is higher R&D expenditure and higher level of education.
3. Either there is no R&D expenditure or there will be a rise in innovation.
4. If there is no higher R&D expenditure and higher level of education, there is no rise in innovation.
5. Either there is no higher R&D expenditure and higher level of education or there is a raise in innovation level.

A regression with panel data for 34 countries is run to measure the impact of different variables on innovation. The dependent variable innovation is quantified by using the Global Innovation Index. Independent variables are government education expenditure, R&D expenditure, scientific publications and science, technology, engineering, and mathematics (STEM) graduates.

R&D expenditure by the government demonstrates a significant relationship with innovation. A per cent increase in R&D expenditure increases innovation by 9.48 per cent. A per cent increase in STEM graduates augment innovation by 42.3 per cent (Table 4.14). The insignificant relation between government expenditure in education and innovation is due to the fact that primary and secondary education along with tertiary education are lumped together as government education expenditure. Thus, the result is in line with the argument that it is imperative for the government to spend more in R&D and especially in higher education as this also increases the number of STEM graduates and scientific publications at the same time.

Innovation largely depends on the knowledge capital of the population. In recent times, innovation has gained momentum as countries are now looking towards every resource for increased productivity. In this milieu, many indices have been introduced to measure the innovativeness of a country. These indicators use extensive methods in calculating innovation and rank countries based on different criteria. Bangladesh stands 116th out of 129 countries portraying a dismal picture (WEF, 2019). The lower rank is mainly attributed to weakness in human capital and research capacity.

Table 4.14 Regression result on innovation

Variables	*Innovation*
Government education expenditure	0.385
	(0.846)
Scientific publications	0.0176***
	(0.00297)
R&D expenditure	9.482***
	(1.268)
STEM graduates	0.423***
	(0.138)
Constant	21.59***
	(5.355)
Observations	27
R-squared	0.931

Source: Standard errors in parentheses
*** $p<0.01$
** $p<0.05$
* $p<0.1$)

There exists a stark difference between the developed and developing countries in terms of innovation (Figure 4.5). Countries with higher levels of innovation tend to have better tertiary education with increased percentage of students graduating from STEM subjects. Developing countries lag far behind than the developed ones in terms of enrolling students in STEM subjects (Figure 4.6). Southeast Asian countries have started to reap the benefits of having a higher percentage of STEM graduates.

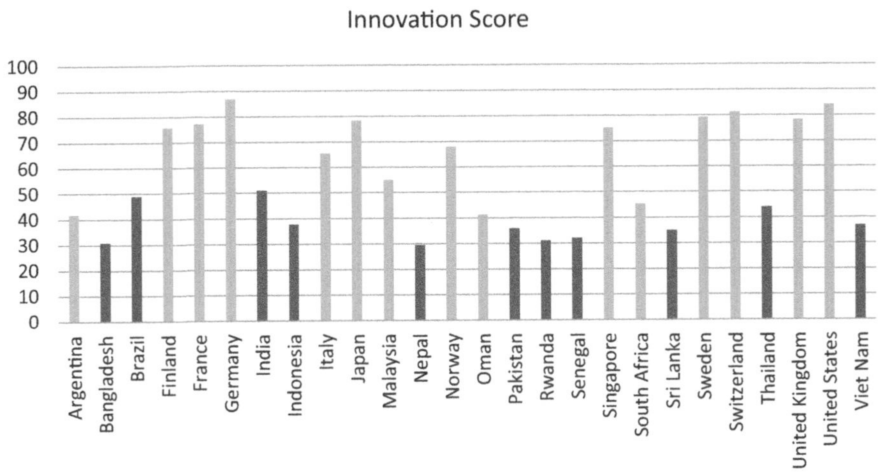

Figure 4.5 Innovation score

Source: World Economic Forum, 2019

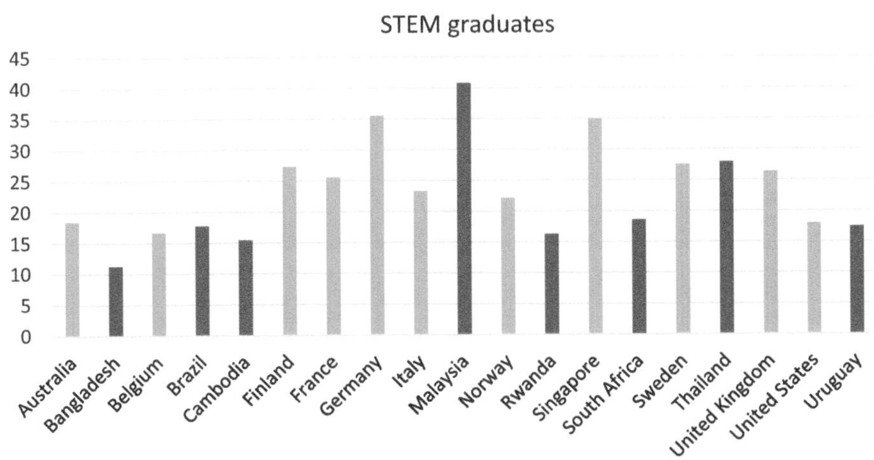

Figure 4.6 STEM graduates

Source: UNESCO, 2020

The paucity of a better quality of education and research puts the country in the lower rank. Expenditure in R&D is also much lower in developing countries than in the developed ones. In most cases, the difference between the developing and developed countries is 5 to 10 times (Figure 4.7). The outcome of such low expenditure is low innovation for the countries.

Citizenship Education and Citizen State

Citizenship education promoting a sense of norms, values, customs, conventions and human sociality strengthens civic engagement and contract between citizen and state, which leads to establishing a public society and citizen state.

Citizenship attributes the entitlement of rights from, and the duties towards, the state, which is manifested by the social contract. In order to make citizens aware of their rights and duties, citizenship education is a prerequisite. This education helps grow the sense of norms, values, customs, conventions, human sociality etc. within the society, which enforces social contract between citizen and state and increases civic engagement. The strong sense of citizenship, effective social contract and civic engagement lead to a strong public society. The state becomes a citizen state ensuring rights as well as enforcing duties (Figure 4.8).

The formation of human capabilities and social transformation of China and East Asian countries owes much to education than trade liberalisation (Sen,

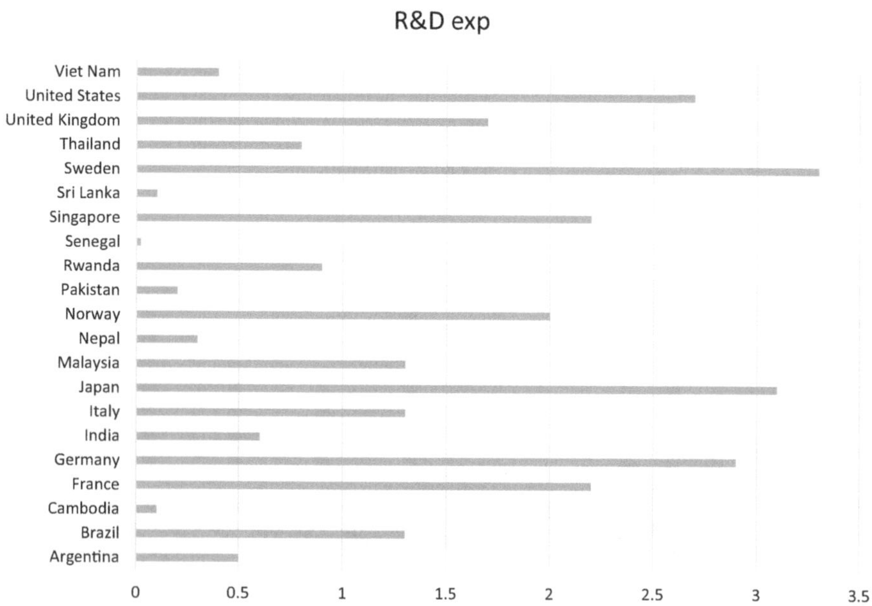

Figure 4.7 Expenditure in R&D (per cent of GDP)

Source: WEF, 2019

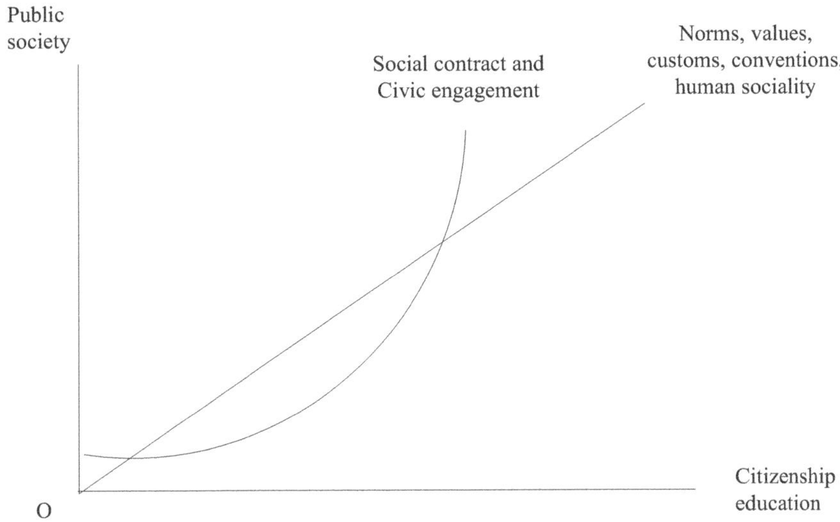

Figure 4.8 Citizenship education for public society

Source: Prepared by author

1999). Confucian system of education in the East Asian countries strengthened their societies. East Asian countries have lower corruption and hold human rights in high regard. Higher tax–GDP ratio in these countries also results in higher public spending as well as higher value in ensuring rights.

An ideal citizen state has a higher tax–GDP ratio and low corruption perception score. High corruption coupled with low tax–GDP ratio puts the developing countries at the bottom (Figure 4.9). Both these variables have positive strong correlation with mean years of schooling or education. This means that an increase in mean years of schooling is likely to positively affect tax–GDP ratio (Table 4.15).

Summary

Education has two features that make it different from any other private goods which are non-excludability and non-rivalry. When market is introduced, it would always target to maximise its profits, which will eventually raise the cost of education and create excludability through price discrimination. Barriers to entry protect incumbent firms and restrict competition in a market, thus contributing to distortionary prices and price discrimination leading to charging different prices for the same product or service. The market provisioning does not create any positive externalities or spill-over effects whereas the government can provide subsidies to encourage the production of public goods which have positive externalities as evident from the experience.

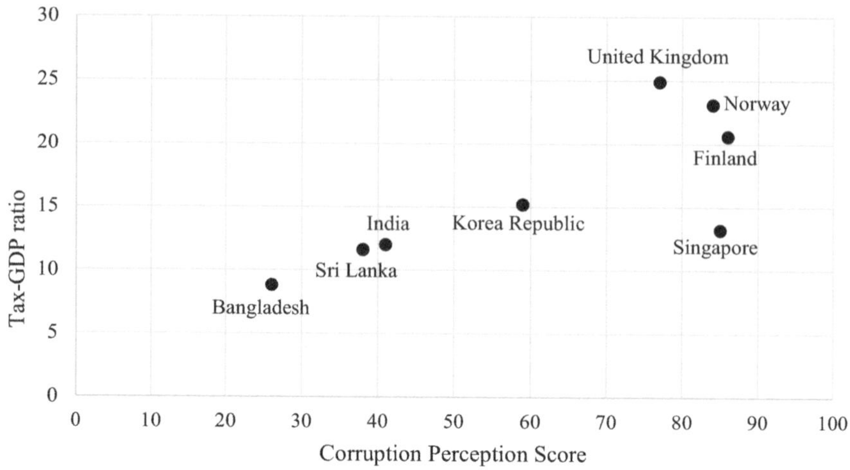

Figure 4.9 Tax–GDP ratio and corruption indices

Source: Prepared by author

Table 4.15 Correlation result between mean years of schooling and tax–GDP ratio

	Mean years of schooling	*Tax–GDP ratio*
Mean years of schooling	1	
Tax–GDP ratio	0.814721	1

Source: Calculated by author

Developing countries are still in the early stages as goals of educational policies still remain focused in attaining higher enrolment and completion rates, with hardly any attention for improvement of the quality of education. The absence of quality education and less than the required skill development programmes are hindering in generating skilled youth who can be employed in formal jobs with decent wage. There is also shortage of specialised skills. Innovation requires higher investment in R&D. Increased expenditure in higher education and R&D is the precursor for technological acquisition and innovation in an economy. Citizenship education promoting a sense of norms, values, customs, conventions and human sociality strengthens civic engagement and contract between citizen and state, which leads to establishing a public society and citizen state.

References

BANBEIS. (2016). *Bangladesh Education Statistics 2015*. Dhaka: BANBEIS. Retrieved July 10, 2021, from http://lib.banbeis.gov.bd/BANBEIS_PDF/Bangladesh%20Education%20Statistics%202015.pdf

BANBEIS. (2019). *Bangladesh education statistics*. Dhaka: Bangladesh Bureau of Education Information and Statistics.

Barman, D.B., Sharmin, I., and Dey, D. (2012). A comparative study of the cost of higher education in private and public universities in Bangladesh. *East West Journal of Business and Social Studies*, 3, pp. 47–67.

BBS. (2013). *Labour Force Survey 2010*. Dhaka: Bangladesh Bureau of Statistics.

BBS. (2019). *Household Income and Expenditure Survey 2016*. Dhaka: Bangladesh Bureau of Statistics.

Bowles, S. (1972). Schooling and inequality from generation to generation. *Journal of Political Economy*, 80(3, Part 2), pp. S219–S251.

EIU-BC. (2014). *High university enrolment, low graduate employment: Analysing the paradox in Afghanistan, Bangladesh, India, Nepal, Pakistan and Sri Lanka*. London, New York, Hong Kong, and Geneva: The Economist Intelligence Unit.

Enriquez, C.R. (2021). Global social policy. In Berik, G. and Kongar, E. (eds.) *Routledge handbook of feminist economics* (pp. 450–458). London: Routledge.

Hossain, N., and Kabeer, N. (2004). Achieving universal primary education and eliminating gender disparity. *Economic and Political Weekly*, 39(36), pp. 4093–4100.

ILO. (2020). *ILO statistics*. Geneva, Switzerland: International Labour Organization. Retrieved from https://ilostat.ilo.org/

May, M.A. (2014). *Making education attainable for all: Why Bangladesh needs low-cost, private schools*. Dhaka: BRAC.

Munshi, F. (2015). *S4YE Flagship report: Bangladesh case study*. Washington, DC: World Bank.

Narayan, V. (2010). The private and the public in school education. *Economic and Political Weekly*, 45(6), pp. 23–26.

Robertson, S.L., and Lauder, H. (2001). A class choice? Restructuring the education/social class relation. In R. Phillips and J. Furlong (Eds.), *Education, reform and the state: Twenty Five Years of Politics, policy and practice*. Oxford: Routledge.

S4YE. (2015). *Toward solutions for youth employment: A 2015 baseline report*. Washington, DC: Solutions for Youth Employment.

Sen, A. (1999). *Commodities and capabilities*. Oxford: Oxford University Press Catalogue.

Titumir, R.A.M. (2021). *Education in Bangladesh* (pp. 131–158). Springer Books.

Toufique, K.A. (2014). *Labour market transitions of young women and men in Bangladesh*. Geneva: International Labour Office.

UGC. (2014). *Annual Report 2014*. Dhaka, Bangladesh: University Grants Commission.

UNESCO. (2020). *UNESCO Institute for Statistics (UIS)*. The United Nations Educational, Scientific and Cultural Organization. Paris, France. Retrieved from http://data.uis.unesco.org/

WEF. (2019). *Global Competitiveness Report 2019*. Davos, Switzerland: World Economic Forum.

Whitty, G., Power, S., and Halpin, D. (1998). *Devolution and choice in education: The school, the state and the market*. Australian Education Review No. 41. Australian Council for Educational Research (ACER) Limited, 19 Prospect Hill Road, Camberwell, Melbourne, Victoria 3124, Australia.

5 Institutions and Transformational Pathways for Education in Developing Countries

Introduction

After the "Blackship Turmoil" in 1853 where Japan was forced to open up their boundary to the western countries, the Meiji regime intended to awaken Japanese nationalism in the face of the crisis. This was the first time that Japanese sovereignty was threatened by an outer force. As a result, the regime transformed the indigenous religion into a political ideology that would bind the Japanese as a single entity, known as Shinto. Shinto can be characterised as a Japanese ancient religion based on a mingling of nature worship with ancestor worship. It has no definite doctrine for the code of morals. The government embedded Confucian ethics into Shinto to systematise its theology as a political device. The government also stressed the organic unity of society and the state, a "family state" – people with common ancestry headed by the emperor, a direct descendant of the unbroken imperial lineage. On the other hand, the government attempted to enrich the nation and strengthen the military through the adoption of Western knowledge. Thus, the national ideology developed within this synthesis of indigenous metaphysical accounts and partial but strong faith in the Western ways of thinking (Shibata, 2004).

While the education system relies on the power and wealth distribution of a given society, such could extenuate the trigger to form a cooperative society. As evident from the story of Japan, state formation depends on the policies and citizenship of that state, where political groups play a major role in determining the transformational path. The importance of norms, values and informal institutions in state formation is enormous. The composition of power in a society determines human sociality, comprising norms, values and other informal institutions. This dimension of co-dependence in human nature however has been ignored by the demand and supply-based market-centric approaches. The role of education in forming both formal and informal institutions cannot be ignored. Hence, education cannot be studied from the lens of market-centric approach only.

This part hence identifies education as a human right necessary to form human sociality that will transform both the lives of the citizens and the overall economy. The gaps in transforming education in developing countries have

DOI: 10.4324/9781003284222-7

largely focused on access, and too little on the institutional capacities to generate skills, innovation and citizenship. It elucidates on the unaddressed grid of the transformational pathways by examining social construction of education and human sociality.

Political Settlement and Human Sociality

A society should go for that education system which they aspire for. This proposition is found upon the ideology of human sociality. Due to human sociality, human beings depend upon social relationships and interaction with each other. People do not live alone; they rather live in a society where they have to rely upon one another even in the case of fulfilling their self-interests. People all aspire for equal rights to education and equal opportunity to work. Hence, a system is required to create equal access to quality education and desired employment opportunities for all citizens. This education would teach citizens the essence of communal solidarity for their own good alike from the spirit of individualism taught by the education which is treated as a commodity or capital. So, the key argument here is that the education system relies on the power and wealth distribution of the society, which depends upon the tendency of individual human beings to associate in social groups and form cooperative society. The relationship among education system, power distribution and human sociality works as follows:

Human beings in society, if they believe in social collectivism and want to live in communal solidarity, tend to associate in social groups and rely upon each other. This high sociality brings an equal distribution of power so that everyone can be better off in society. In this type of society, citizens get equal access to education and equal opportunity to employ their potential in productive ways. The low tendency to associate in social groups and individualistic behaviour, whereas, leads human beings to think about their own well-being only. They, thus, only think about maximising their own profit and distribution of power is ultimately unequal which creates unequal access to education. This unequal access to knowledge keeps reproducing the social stratification of labour and helps prevail the status quo in the society (Table 5.1).

Human sociality indicates the inclination of members of a society to live in social harmony. However, for the past three decades, neoliberal reforms have

Table 5.1 Human sociality and distribution of power

	Human sociality	*Distribution of power*
Equal access to education and equal employment opportunity	If there is high tendency to associate in social groups	Equal
Unequal access to education and reproduction of social division of labour	If there is low tendency to associate in social groups	Unequal

Source: Prepared by author

overturned the human vision of education. Education has now become a tool in the market whereas previously it was viewed as a tool for nation building. Privatisation and competition have created ever competing individuals overtaking a societal individual (Lawson and Spours, 2011). It needs to be kept in mind that higher education not only contributes greatly to a person's achieved "functioning" but also provides an institutional space to exercise a person's freedom – capability – to choose between alternative combinations of "functioning". People choose what to do and what people choose to do is what people become (Nixon, 2011).

A public society exists when there is a greater willingness to build relationships among societal beings, and reinforce the society to combat "social recession". The attainment of these goals depends on the ability of the citizens to take control over their lives and communities. Education, hence, needs to be provided in the ways citizens want it to be provided. The perceptions of mass people regarding education require attention in terms of policy formulation in the education sector. In 2015, the Bangladesh government proposed to impose value added tax on private educational institutions. Since the ultimate burden will be on the customers or the students, students of private universities organised mobilisation to repeal the taxes with the slogan "No VAT on Education" which was supported by a significant majority of the mass. The Government had to change the decision in the end and later scrapped the idea. The success of this movement ultimately represents the fact that people aspire for a society where education must not be commoditised. Contrary to the popularly held belief that all private university going students are from well-off families, only about 20 per cent of the students come from the upper intermediate class society. The remaining students come from the struggling middle and lower-income groups. A large number of students also have to depend on part-time jobs to pay for the already expensive education. Most of these young individuals have to be at their respective universities till 3–4 pm on weekdays and then work evenings as well as on weekends to make ends meet. But on the issue of imposing VAT, students from all socio-economic backgrounds came together (New Age, 2015).

Turning to the primary students, economic barriers alone are not stopping children from attending schools. Discriminatory attitudes towards students also act as an impediment to enrolment. This act occurs from both sides as often parents feel that schools are not cut for their children and schools as well often feel that some children hesitate to prepare for schools (Seel, 2007). For example, street and migrant children make up the largest share of out-of-school children. In most cases, these children are ignored in the system. There need to be specific policies in place to bring these children into mainstream education. For instance, in Nepal, schools have adopted a school mapping mechanism to identify the out-of-school children in a society. In Bangladesh, NGOs have been involved in educating street children, but without any government supervision and hence remain out of the mainstream education system. Bangladesh also initiated tailored education programmes to increase female enrolment in primary and secondary education. These programmes include scholarships and tuition-free education. As a result, the female enrolment rate in Bangladesh has surpassed the male enrolment rate. Such grassroot programmes however require an active participation from the local population. Community support programmes always tend to carry positive results.

The deliberate adoption of the principle of meritocracy exhibited an aspect of historical discontinuity within Japanese society. Meiji Japan imposed political, economic and social transformation on itself. After the introduction of the Western cabinet system in 1885, the preferential policy for civil service recruitment from court nobles disappeared. The state bureaucracy came to be staffed predominantly by graduates of Tokyo Imperial University. They were academic elites who had survived a series of extremely competitive entrance examinations before entering into this apex institution newly founded by the Meiji government. Western learning was heavily emphasised in the curriculum of the university. The government hired a large number of foreign teachers in Tokyo. There in 1877, the ratio of Japanese professors, Japanese associate professors and foreign professors was 4:3:17 in the Faculties of Law, Science and Letters on average. The government paid extremely high salaries to foreign teachers, in comparison with Japanese professors and also some ministers in the Japanese Cabinet. Recognising the validity of the "universal" value of Western civilisation in the nineteenth-century world, Meiji Japan understood that "Competition with the West had to take place on the West's own terms". Thus, the Meiji restoration was not an "aristocratic revolution", comparable to the Prusso-German unification in the Kaiserreich or the Kemalist modernisation project in Turkey. Nor did Meiji leaders enjoy the "advantages of the ruling class in the ancient regime" in Barrington Moore's Dictatorship thesis. Robert Bellah captured well the political aspirations of Meiji leaders.

Japan's economic and military development had taken firm hold from the 1880s. In Japan, no organised movement had arrested Westernisation, unlike some other non-Western "catching-up" states. The cultural contradictions and ideological ambiguity of national leaders were the side effect of the formation of the Japanese modern state in the political, economic and cultural contexts of the nineteenth-century world. While creating a new national elite through the adoption of Western ideas, the government inculcated national identity in all Japanese. For this purpose, the Meiji regime identified universal schooling as the best means for the ideological consolidation of the new state (Shibata, 2004).

The state education system became the key institution of the Meiji regime based on its political assumptions about the formation of the Japanese Emperor state. Initially, early Meiji leaders, such as Mori Arinori, believed that all Japanese should share the same sense of patriotism and see themselves as Japanese citizens, regardless of their social origins, gender, religious beliefs or political ideas. The underlying idea of these leaders was their strong admiration for the US education system and its philosophical basis in American liberalism. Thus, the government quickly established the Ministry of Education in 1871. By enacting the Fundamental Code of Education in 1872, the government shaped the institutional keystone of the modern education system. The code stated that "Learning is the key to success in life, and no man can afford to neglect it. . . . There shall, in the future, be no community with an illiterate family, nor a family with an illiterate person". The universalisation of primary education was a core part of the state political project of the Meiji government. The Ministry of Education actually pioneered the formation of modern Japan.

However, it is important to note that the wide dissemination of education was not new to the Meiji education system. It is estimated that almost all Samurais, 50–70 per cent of merchants and 20–60 per cent of peasants could read and write. These literacy rates of the nineteenth-century Japanese were astonishing even for the British and the French at that time. Confucian learning was taught in the Samurai school as well as in the Terakoya (commoners' school). In the Tokugawa period, 97.3 per cent of Terakoya schools taught children the cartography of Confucian books as the prime subject and 91.5 per cent of the schools taught Confucian reading as the second major subject. The development of the modern Japanese education system was laid on a solid basis of learning from the Tokugawa period, as Ronald Dore has shown. Yet, as seen in his study, Tokugawa education was provided for individuals of various social strata in diverse forms, contents and standards. The occasional opportunities given to commoners for Samurai education were exceptional (Shibata, 2004).

The innovative aspect of the Meiji state education system was the provision of uniform educational content for the children of all social strata and all regions. This was a great leap forward from Tokugawa education to a concept of modern education in a state education system. In the creation of that education system, the key role of primary education was to ensure that all Japanese would share the same sense of national identity and unify the Japanese within the new ideological framework of the Emperor state. Along with the development of the state bureaucracy, initial, liberal ideas faded out within the governmental policy for education. The central state bureaucracy exerted greater control of education than in the early Meiji period. Given the clear signs of development in the national economy, criticisms of this governmental policy came neither from inside the government nor from the Japanese people. In 1890, the Emperor promulgated the Imperial Rescript on Education, defining educational principles of his state. It was asserted that the people as the subjects of the emperor ought to maintain the virtues of the state as well as filial piety to parents and benevolence to others. After the promulgation of the rescript, the related rituals, such as the recitation of the script and bowing to the Imperial Portrait, were enforced (Shibata, 2004).

As a consequence of the establishment of the state education system, Japan was equipped with a reliable and solid network for the dissemination of the national ideology to all citizens. Within the governmental policy for education, the political dogmas of state Shinto and the idea of a "family-state" became the important elements of Japanese national identity.

The expansion of educational access has been a public policy success in Bangladesh. Since the mid-1990s, there have been enough primary school places for the entire school-age population, gender disparities in primary schools have been eliminated and secondary enrolments have begun to rise. There remain problems of exclusion and poor quality, but the massive expansion of education has been widely acknowledged as a major achievement. Processes of national identity creation have played out in education policy through the compulsion of successive governments to imprint their own brands of nationalism on the population. An incentive has been the positive vision of how the masses can be transformed through education, a vision shared among the educated upper and middle classes from which politicians and bureaucrats are drawn (Hossain et al., 2002).

In recent years, public budgetary allocation in Bangladesh, both under revenue and development heads, to the education sector has been the highest compared to other broad sectors (Campe, 2007). The literacy rate and enrolment rate of both the female and male populations are always showing an upward trend. Aiming for all children's access to quality education, particularly girls and children from disadvantaged backgrounds, many initiatives have been taken in the last two decades. Curriculum and textbook development and distribution of free textbooks to all primary school children have been major efforts. But, due to systemic corruption and inefficiencies, there have been substantial leakages, wastages and maldistribution of allocated sums, particularly in the case of the development budget. Again, a widely held, but incorrect, view is that primary education is virtually free in Bangladesh, that is, the government bears all expenses, particularly in government and registered/recognised schools and madrasas. Whereas the study by CAMPE shows that this is not the case at all. In reality, educational opportunities in the country are not properly linked to the social realities. Some institutions (e.g., government institutions as opposed to non-government ones) and some social classes (e.g., the richer students as opposed to poor students) are served much better than others. Hence, the need for an in-depth investigation into the financing of primary and secondary education in the country has long been felt.

The nature of policy direction in education in Bangladesh has failed to bring about sustained development and implementation of educational policies in the country. These policy formulations and the continued narrow political-ideological interests are hidden. Once a new government came to power, a new education commission or committee was formed to formulate a new education policy. It can be said that all of these commissions and committees were inevitably influenced by the respective ruling party's political ideologies and used as a means to short-term political gain.

The gradual shift in policy direction from state interventionism to neoliberalism has worsened the situation more. Due to increased demand for basic rights like education as the population is exponentially growing in Bangladesh, the public education system could not fulfil the demand of every citizen to cope due to scarcity of resources. Meanwhile, to fill up this gap between demand and supply, the profit-seeking private sector started stepping into the public sector like the education sector. The market-driven private sectors seek to maximise revenue through higher tuition costs. For example, most universities are market-driven and tuition-driven. By implication, the private universities offer only those degree programmes, which they can sell in the market at high prices, that is, charging high tuition and other fees including campus development fees. Since no private universities get any financial support from the government, they raise all the funds necessary to operate, maintain, develop and expand the university from the students. Of necessity, they need to generate large surpluses to build campuses. In a sense, these universities require the current generation (students) to subsidise the education of future generation (students) who will attend classes in the buildings/classrooms to be built in the future with tuition money from the present generation (students) because part of the surpluses generated currently is used to buy and develop land on which campus buildings are to be constructed. Since tuition and fees are the only sources of revenue, the sustainability of a private university is the function of how carefully the academic programmes offered are selected, and how the tuition structures are designed.

The social construction of education and human sociality, therefore, are important factors to set the policy directions for education. People do not want education to be a commodity rather they consider it as their basic human need, which must be satisfied by the state, and even the state is compelled to provide it in accordance with the constitution. Hence, a policy must be taken to provide education equally to all citizens since it is their basic human right. As citizens, they aspire to get equal educational access along with equal employment opportunities. Many countries received invaluable independence from these costly aspirations of its people. The political settlement, therefore, calls for egalitarian reforms where policies will be directed towards establishing equality through enhanced public financing and increasing public consumption through redistributing resources. Policies should be concerned about how society perceives education and hence policies should be formulated and implemented upon the aspirations and perceptions of society because policy is made for people and made by people.

So, now the question is what type of policy should be taken to promote equality in the education system and which model can be an inspiration in this regard? One of the best models across the world, which is the Finnish education system, can be taken as a standard since it is an educational system, which is fully subsidised and egalitarian in almost all ways.

Fifty-three years back, Finland was at risk of becoming the economic stepchild, with a terrible education system. Now it has turned its education systems into such a better position over the past half century that it has become an example for many other countries of the world. In Finland, school provides not just educational services but social services. In Finland, education is free at all levels from pre-primary to higher education. In pre-primary and basic education, the textbooks, daily meals and transportation for students living further away from the school are free for the parents. The Finns, the Northern European nation, mandates that their kids – who do not begin studies until age 7 – have 15-minute outdoor free-play sessions for every hour of their five-hour school day. Although grades are not given until fourth grade (and schools do not require any standardised tests until senior year), their students' achievement is undoubted. At upper secondary level and in higher education, the students themselves or their parents purchase their own books. At upper secondary level, the students have the right to a free meal and in higher education, meals are subsidised by the state.

Adult education is the only form of education that may require payment. To ensure the opportunities to study for everyone, there is a well-developed system of study grants and loans. Financial aid can be awarded for full-time study in an upper secondary school, vocational institution or institution of higher education.

The Finnish education system has hardly dead ends. Learners can always continue their studies at an upper level of education, whatever choices they make in between. The practice of recognition of prior learning has been developed to avoid unnecessary overlapping of studies. The main objectives of adult education policy are ensuring the availability and competence of the labour force, providing educational opportunities for the entire adult population and strengthening social cohesion and equity. The objectives should support efforts to extend working life, raise the employment rate, improve productivity, implement the conditions for lifelong learning and enhance multiculturalism. Educational institutions organise education and training intended for adults at all levels of education. Efforts have been made to make the provision as flexible as possible to enable adults to study alongside work. Adult education comprises education and training leading to a degree or certificate, liberal adult education and staff development and other training provided or purchased by employers as well as labour market training, which is mainly targeted at unemployed people. Liberal adult education offers non-formal studies. It promotes personal growth, health and well-being by offering courses relating to citizenship skills and society and in different crafts and subjects on a recreational basis.

In both general and vocational education, there are also separate educational paths for adults. In vocational training, competence-based qualifications are specifically intended for adults. In higher education, adults can study in separate adult education programmes offered by universities of applied sciences. Finland is bilingual, and every student learns both Finnish and Swedish. Every Finn who wants to be successful has to master at least one other language, often English, but she also typically learns German, French, Russian and many others. Language learning is considered an important factor in Finland (Ministry of Education and Culture, Finland, 2017; O'Neill, 2016; Choi, 2014).

Equality in education requires equality in distribution of power and equality in public consumption of educational resources. This equality can be brought into the society by redistributing resources from rich to poor through tax. The incidence of poverty in Bangladesh is still one of the highest in the world where about one-third (31.5 per cent) of its population is still living below the so-called poverty line (BBS, 2010). The number of people living in poverty has increased due to rising disparities in the distribution of resources within the country. The Gini coefficient of income has increased from 0.451 to 0.458 at national level with a growth rate of 0.16 per cent during 2000–2010 and it is known that the value of Gini coefficient stands within 0 to 1 while 1 denotes the most unequal state. This inequality is contributed by tax avoidance, less investment in human development and weak governance structure. The Government of Bangladesh, to meet the ever-increasing expenditure on public sectors, highly depends upon taxation. Although the collection of tax revenue has increased from 2008 to 2012, it is surprising to see that the tax gap has also increased every year along with this, the income and expense gap is not decreasing over the year. One of the main reasons behind this mismatched situation is tax evasion (Hasan, 2014). Tax evasion is the tendency or efforts by individuals, firms, trusts and other entities to evade taxes by illegal means. To evade tax, taxpayers deliberately misrepresent or conceal the true state of their affairs to the tax authorities to reduce their tax liability, and include, in particular, dishonest tax reporting (such as declaring less income, profits or gains than actually earned, or overstating deductions). According to the National Board of Revenue (2012), Bangladesh's tax–GDP ratio is comparatively lower than that in many other countries where less than 1 per cent of the population pay tax. Along with this, tax compliance is low and tax evasion is persistent.

Another tool to promote equality in education is enhancing equality in public consumption through public spending. According to the data of World Development Indicator, Bangladesh was ranked 155th among 161 countries in 2014 in terms of public spending in the education sector. UNESCO stipulates that the budgetary allocation for education should constitute at least 6 per cent of the GDP and 20 per cent of the total budget while the allocation for education in the national budget was only two per cent of the GDP in the outgoing fiscal year. Of 171 billion BDT to the education ministry in fiscal 2015–2016, around 126.77 billion BDT was non-development expenditure and 40 billion BDT was spent for development purposes, according to budget documents which means a large portion of the education budget is spent on non-development purposes, mainly for teachers' salaries and allowances, leaving limited scope for investment for improving the quality of education. Education expenditure is quite low in Bangladesh (only 2 per cent of total GDP) compared to its neighbouring countries, except Sri Lanka (Figure 5.1).

This low tax–GDP ratio contributes to low spending on the public sector including education and health. In many cases, it has been observed that the state-run educational institutes have scored better in providing quality education but their number is so low that many students do not get the opportunity to enrol in those, and that is where the private sector meets the unmet demand. Hence, the low budget allocation in the education sector is to be blamed according to many studies. As the size of the national budget is getting bigger every year, the budgetary allocation to the education sector also rises. However,

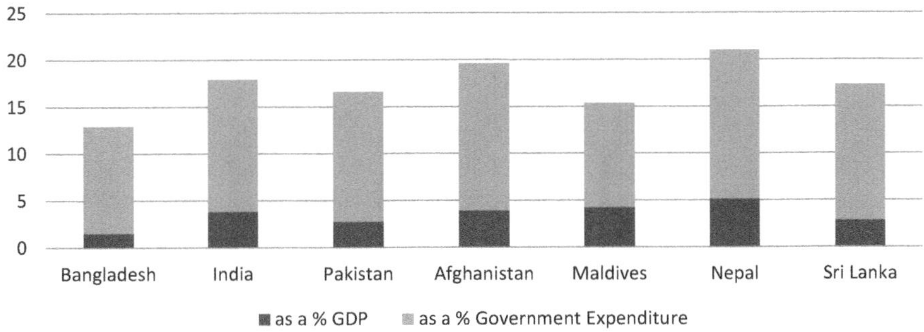

Figure 5.1 Public expenditure on education by nature of spending, 2014–2015

Source: BANBEIS (2020)

the sector's share in the national budget has declined over the years. The share of the education budget in the total outlay decreased to 11.6 per cent in fiscal 2015–2016 from 15.9 per cent in 2006–2007 budget, according to an analysis of the Centre for Policy Dialogue (CPD) and Campaign for Popular Education.

Less public spending on education means low quality and limited access to free education as limited public spending does not leave any scope to enhance the quality of education by setting up necessary physical infrastructures (e.g., laboratories and libraries), providing training to teachers, by improving the curriculum or by enlarging the size of classroom and thus it cannot provide access to all citizens (especially the disadvantaged groups) to almost free public education. Unequal access to education and low quality creates a state of inequality and social division of labour as people lag behind in terms of achieving human capital. Low human capital leads to unemployment and underemployment and thus people cannot afford a decent salary and standard of living. In this regard, it is noteworthy that countries with high human development spend a larger portion of their GDP (5.3 per cent in 2012) on education than many other countries (Figure 5.2).

The spirit of privatisation and neoliberalism in Bangladesh have disregarded these aspects of education, and also created a new form of social stratification. Along with this, the primitive accumulation and weak institutional arrangements create a system for tax evasion, which concurrently leads to a budget deficit in the education sector. Low public financing and limited resources do not allow to improve its existing low quality of education. Lack of access to quality education triggers the rate of unemployment and underemployment whereas state-provided education can ensure equal access and employment opportunities. The unproductive educated youths get frustrated and involve themselves in criminal and disgraceful activities. On the contrary, the main challenge faced by adolescents and young people is lack of skills. Many do not gain sufficient secondary education and there is not enough vocational

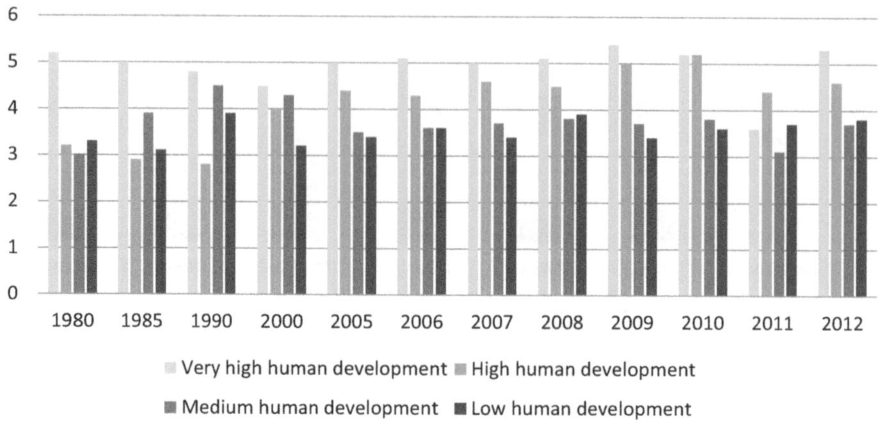

Figure 5.2 Public expenditure on education as a percentage of GDP

Source: UNDP (2015)

training available to compensate. More specifically, there is neither easy access to equivalent non-formal education programmes to complete basic education nor skills development programmes to transition into. The reality for most adolescents and young people from poor families is that they end up among the ranks of the rural underemployed. If adolescents and young people do not gain the skills they need, there is a danger that the country will not fully realise the demographic dividend resulting from a growing labour force and low dependency ratios (GoB, 2015).

Hence, it is evident now that a system of egalitarianism is required to create equal access to quality education and desired employment opportunities for all citizens irrespective of sex, race, ethnicity, religion, cultural orientation and disability. In this regard, public expenditure financing can be used to provide a minimum level of benefits for citizens, addressing unacceptable deficits in welfare with a particular focus on the poor, those in the informal and subsistence sectors and those without employment, such as domestic workers. Social insurance schemes should enable those who have sufficient income to invest in an additional level of protection against life cycle risks, such as old age, as well as illness and work-related injuries. Social security schemes enable people to engage more actively in the labour market. One is that people are provided with investment capital, which is enhanced by greater access to credit since banks and microfinance institutions are more willing to lend to social security recipients. However, the guarantee of a regular transfer also changes the worldview of recipients. It provides them with a minimum income platform that infuses their lives with predictability. Indeed, there is evidence of families receiving social transfers showing enhanced entrepreneurial behaviour by being more willing to invest in riskier but higher return activities (GoB, 2015). Thus, to ensure a state of equality in Bangladesh, strong governance and institutional arrangement need to be enforced to enhance taxation and investment in human development. Subsequently, proper taxation improves public financing, which will eventually quicken the implementation of social policies and thus strengthen governance. Proper taxation also distributes wealth and income from rich to poor, which escalates accountability, participation and equality, which leads to good governance.

Education and Government Expenditure: A Simulation

An econometric approach based on panel data is used for the identification of the channels through which social spending affects growth, as well as the full effects of higher spending over time on education. The simulations assess the impact of the following policy interventions: (1) an increase in education spending of one per cent of GDP.

To perform the simulations, a mathematical model has been used, which has the following form:

$$g_{it} = \alpha_1 i + \eta_1 it + \beta_{11} lnln(y_{(it-1)}) + \beta_{12} 2n_{it} + \beta_{13} sk_{it} + \beta_{14} Ed_i(t-1) + \beta_{15} He_i(t-1) + \beta_{16} \Delta Ed_{it} + \beta_{16} \Delta He_{it} + \sum_{m=8}^{n} \beta_{1m} (\Omega_{it}{}^{m}) + u_{it}$$

$$I_{it} = \alpha_{2i} + \eta_{2it} + \beta_{21} lnln\left(y_{it-1}\right) + \beta_{22} n_{it} + \beta_{23} Edu_{it} + \beta_{24} Hea_{it} + \beta_{25} Balance_{it} + \beta_{26} LowdefBalance_{it} + \beta_{27} p_{it} + \beta_{28} Highp_{it} + \beta_{29} Lowgov_{it} + u_{it}$$

$$Edu_{it} = \alpha_{3i} + \eta_{31} lnln(y_{it}) + \beta_{32} Popu15_{it} + \beta_{33} Hea_{it} + \beta_{34} urban_{it} + \beta_{35} QualityY_{it} + \beta_{36} EduSpending_{it} + \beta_{37} EduSpending_{(t-1)} + \beta_{38} EduSpending_{it} \times Lowgov_{it} + \beta_{39} EduSpending_{(t-1)} \times Lowgov_{i(t-1)} + \beta_{310} female_{it} + u_{it}$$

Here, Equation *1.1* is for calculating GDP, Equation *1.2* for investment ratio and Equation *1.3* for education capital.

Variables	*Description*	*Variables*	*Description*
g	real per capita GDP growth	*Trade*	trade openness
α	country-specific effect	*Balance*	fiscal balance
η	time-specific effect	*LowdefBalance*	low deficit fiscal balance
β	coefficients of the variables	*p*	inflation
y	per capita income level	*High*	high inflation
n	population growth rate	*diot*	changes in terms of trade
sk	investment ration in the growth equation	*Lowgov*	poor governance

(Continued)

(Continued)

Variables	*Description*	*Variables*	*Description*
Ed	education capital in the growth equation	*Popu15*	school-age population
Ω	control variables which include trade openness, fiscal balance and change in terms of trade	*Urban*	urbanisation
u	error terms	*Quality*	quality of educational system
I	investment ratio	*EduSpending*	education spending
Edu	education capital	*Female*	gender equality
		Fertility	birth per woman in a year

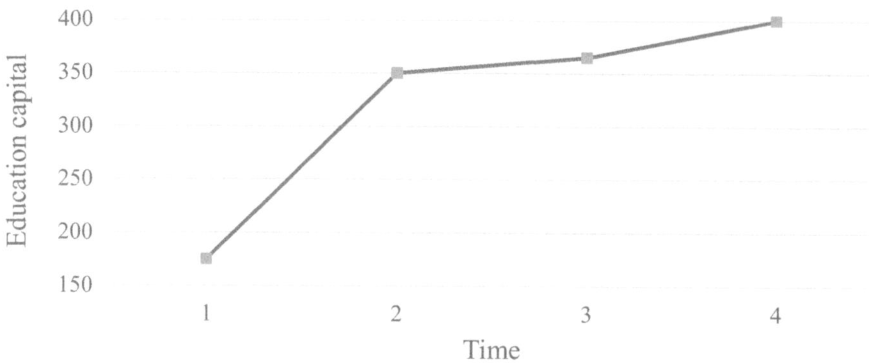

Figure 5.3 Simulation result for education

Source: Prepared by author

The dataset to calculate the effect of education spending comprises of data of eight South Asian countries: Afghanistan, Bangladesh, Bhutan, India, Maldives, Nepal, Pakistan and Sri Lanka. The goal is to show the impact of education spending on education, as proxied by the composite primary and secondary school enrolment rate (Figure 5.3).

The simulation suggests that one per cent change in the GDP will result in the composite enrolment to increase to 175 per cent for the South Asian countries. Over time, an increase will lead to higher composite enrolment.

Impact of COVID-19

Renovating educational management has become inevitable to make productive outcomes from this sector. It is suggested that an education commission will be formulated which will focus on the prime objectives of education skill development, innovation and building citizenship capacities. The commission will focus on research and development in education. It is undeniable that research is indispensable to prosper in innovation. In this backdrop, the commission will work to increase research capabilities and practices in higher educational institutions. It will create a skilled workforce in compliance with ongoing demand so that sufficient skilled workforce can be supplied in line with the fourth industrial revolution.

Along with a shutdown of economic activities, schools and educational institutes had been closed due to the pandemic for an uncertain period. Education is still not accessible for a larger section of people. There is huge inequality between the number of rich and poor students in the academic arena, mostly at tertiary level of education. Sixty-five per cent of the total students of public universities are represented by the 20 per cent richest class. The poorest 20 per cent constitute only 5 per cent in public universities (World Bank, 2019). In private universities, 57 per cent of the students are from the richest 20 per cent class while only 5 per cent are from the poorest 20 per cent class and 3 per cent are from lower-middle-income groups (World Bank, 2019). The current pandemic has introduced another version of inequality: access to the Internet while several institutions are taking classes virtually. Most of the students abiding in the rural areas are unable to attend classes, which are being held via virtual network. They do not have proper Internet facilities in the rural areas, let alone remote areas. Online education is only available to the students living in the capital and in other metropolitan areas mostly, due to a lack of coverage and affordability of Internet connection in remote areas.

The state directives of closure of all educational institutions have resulted in examinations being halted and postponed. Board examinations at the higher secondary tier have been postponed, which is likely to set back university admission dates. Meanwhile, the risk of session jams is looming large over the state of public universities, putting students' graduation and future prospects in grave uncertainty. This may in turn have serious ramifications for the youth employment situation that is already worsening due to job cuts, loss-making businesses and lack of employment creation. Such an intense setback during a time of demographic transition may cost the economy in the long run (Figure 5.4).

The current pandemic has unveiled the necessity of public health education. Fighting against this public bad would be easier if there was proper awareness regarding health and hygiene. Apart from taking dilatory actions, the government is struggling to educate people regarding the fatality of the disease and precaution against it. Most of the people have not taken the pandemic seriously at the preliminary level because of a lack of public health concern and consciousness. It has become visible that people seldom know about infection diseases, how they get spread and how they should be tackled. There should have been special provision for public health education in the current budget, which is not traced thoroughly in reality.

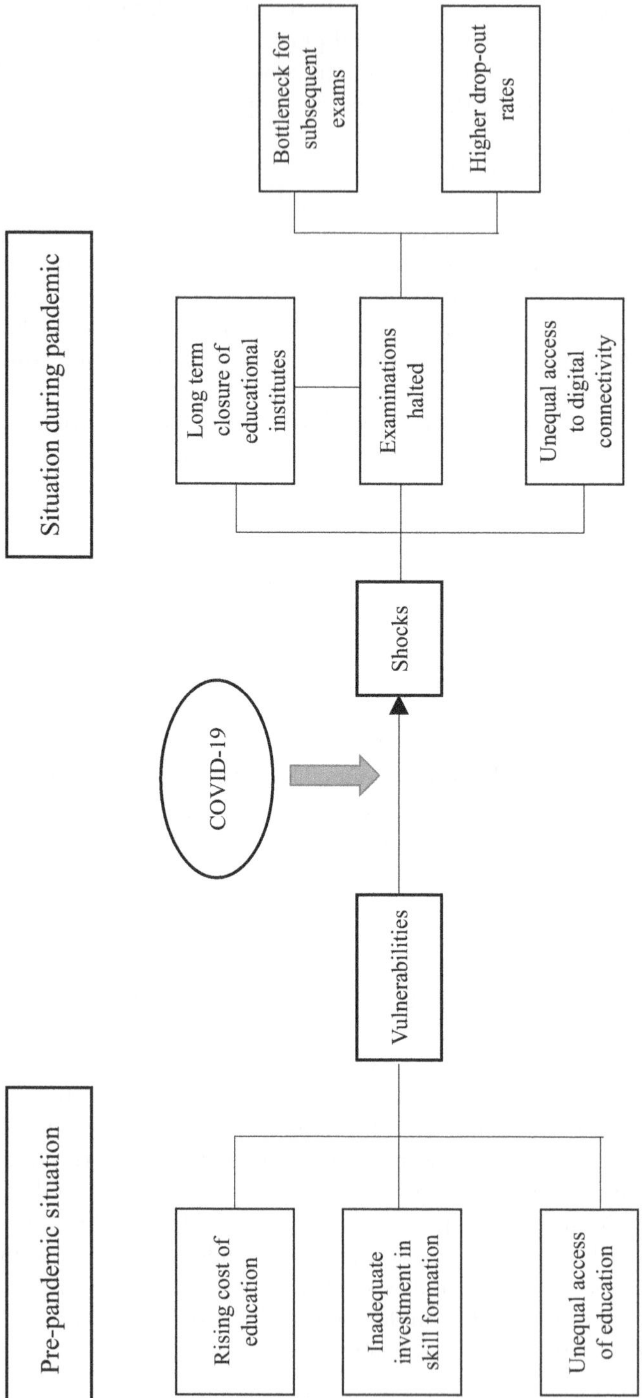

Figure 5.4 COVID-19 shocks on education

Policy Roadmap

Social policymaking in the education sector entails a four-pronged approach. This comprises of a vibrant public society, financing the public provisioning of universal education, supported by economic policies and countervailed by strengthening the role of institutions (Figure 5.5).

First, creating a vibrant public society will require policies for enhancing citizenship education, normalising the teachings of citizenship responsibility and rights in order to strengthen the social contract between the state and the citizens. Enhanced citizenship education will therefore improve macroeconomic indicators such as tax–GDP ratio by increasing tax compliance among the citizens. The establishment of a public society will be driven by the level

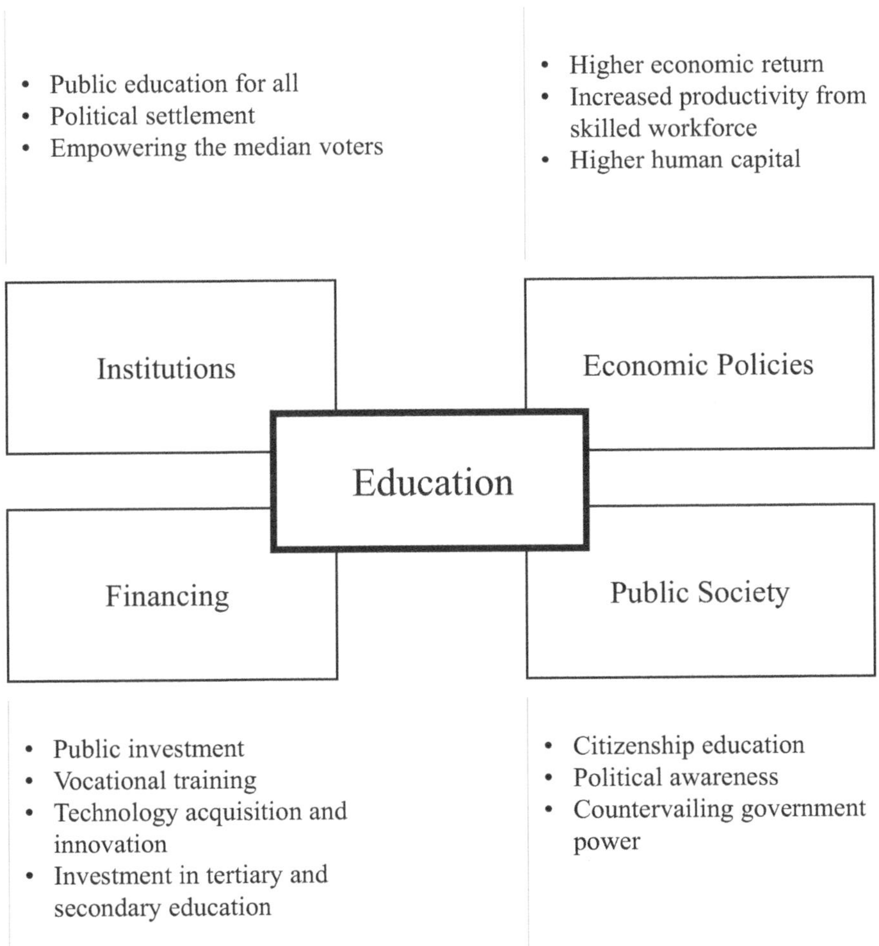

Figure 5.5 Social policymaking roadmap for universal education

of political awareness that exists among the citizens. Public society should be strengthened in a manner that it is enabled to act as a countervailing power against the decisions of the state to ensure proper check and balance between the state, political settlement and citizens.

Second, financing the public provisioning of education will involve large-scale public investment, particularly in the intellectual, cognitive and physical development of the human workforce to lead to long-term skill formation for expanding the productive capacity of the economy. The process can be aided by focusing on labour-intensive policies, vocational training and increased investment in secondary and tertiary levels of education. At these levels, public investment will improve skill development, research and knowledge generation, leading to innovation and technology acquisition.

Third, fiscal and monetary policies will be required to support the aims of productive capacity expansion through education. The economic policies will therefore need to be aligned towards the goals of social policies for education. The fiscal policy will support technology acquisition through higher public investment, which will result in increased productivity of the skilled workforce.

Lastly, the role of institutions – both formal and informal – requires strengthening, such that the power relations and political settlement favour the needs of the median voter, instead of the clientelist groups. The achievement of this intention will require social policymaking to ensure public education for all citizens by improving accessibility and affordability, and thereby erasing the inequalities in education. Universal education will help empower the median voter through citizenship education, skill formation and long-term productive capacity gains, enabling higher income and more equitable socio-economic outcomes.

Summary

Education is a fundamental human right, which is indispensable for the exercise of all other human rights. As a tool to sustain the economic growth of a country, education has a much wider impact than simply improving earnings or employment opportunities, which is why it is a component of the human development index. It has been observed that in all countries with comparable data, adults with lower literacy skills are far more likely to report poor health, have less trust in their fellow citizens and perceive themselves as objects – rather than actors – in the political process. The countries that fail to equip their residents with the proper skills and technological progress are unlikely to translate into sustained economic growth pathway, and large swaths of the population risk languishing on the margins of society.

The current approach to understanding education is dominated by varieties of neoclassical traditions, namely human capital approach and public choice theories while the governments across the world is undertaking market-centric reforms in education as a part of ideological project of neoliberalism, being principally designed by the multilateral banks initiated through structural adjustment reforms. However, the neoclassical understanding is that the education is to be provided by the market, which may result in excludability, externality and entry barriers for the students. To create market provision in education, proper regulation and quality assurance must be provided by the government. Otherwise, there would be no competition and high cost and low quality of education lead to unemployment and underemployment. The idea of Akerlof (1970) and Spencer (1973) on job market signalling and screening is used in the study to depict the scenario of market failure due to the inadequate public funding. The Post-Keynesian approach described the necessity of state intervention, for example, subsidy and taxation in education. Nevertheless, this approach overlooked the fact that a fragile and centralised power structure of government might create a situation of tax avoidance and thus lower the capacity of government. Due to the limitations of existing literature stated, this chapter proposed a new theoretical approach where education is considered as a need, not a demand, along with the necessary and sufficient conditions for universal provisioning of education.

It is undeniable that the education sector in developing countries is largely financed by private provision along with the state which has created access for many people. However, the emerging and often disregarded issues encompass the rising cost of education, deteriorating quality, shrinking budget allocation and increasing unemployment and underemployment. The weak institutional arrangement prevailing in these countries creates a system for tax evasion, which concurrently leads to a budget deficit in the education sector. Low public financing and limited resources do not allow governments of these countries to improve their existing inferior quality of education. The gender disparity in case of education and employment has worsened the situation further.

References

Akerlof, G.A. (1970). Quality uncertainty and the market mechanism. *Quarterly Journal of Economics*, 84(3), pp. 488–500.

BANBEIS Reports from. (2020). *Bangladesh education statistics*. Ministry of Education.

BBS. (2010). *Household Income and Expenditure Survey 2010*. Dhaka, Bangladesh: Bangladesh Bureau of Statistics.

Campe. (2007). *Education Watch 2006: Financing primary and secondary education in Bangladesh*. Dhaka: Campaign for Popular Education.

Choi, A. (2014). *What the best education systems are doing right*. Retrieved 22 April 2022 from https://ideas.ted.com/what-the-best-education-systems-are-doing-right/

GoB. (2015). *National Social Security Strategy (NSSS) of Bangladesh*. Dhaka: Government of the People's Republic of Bangladesh.

Hasan, R. (2014). The tendency toward tax evasion in Bangladesh. *World Journal of Social Sciences*, 4(3), pp. 149–161.

Hossain, N., Subrahmanian, R., and Kabeer, N. (2002). *The politics of educational expansion in Bangladesh*. Retrieved March 27, 2022, from https://opendocs.ids.ac.uk/opendocs/handle/20.500.12413/3929

Lawson, N., and Spours, K. (2011). Education for the good society: The values and principles of a new comprehensive vision. In N. Lawson and K. Spours (Eds.), *Education for the good society: The values and principles of a new comprehensive vision* (pp. 8–13). London: Compass – Direction for the Democratic Left Ltd.

Ministry of Education and Culture, Finland. (2017). *Finnish education in a nutshell.* Government of Finland.

National Board of Revenue. (2012). *Annual Report 2011–12.* Dhaka: National Board of Revenue.

New Age. (2015). *Pvt Univ students demand repealing of 15pc tax.* Retrieved December 1, 2021, from New Age www.newagebd.net/article/139802/pvt-univ-students-demand-repealing-of-15pc-tax

Nixon, J. (2011). *Higher education and the public good: Imagining the university.* London: Continuum International Publishing Group.

O'Neill, J. (2016, July 27). *10 best countries for education around the world.* Retrieved December 1, 2021, from Global Citizen website: www.globalcitizen.org/en/content/best-countries-education/

Seel, A. (2007). *Social inclusion: Gender and equity in education swaps in South Asia: Synthesis report.* United Nations Children's Fund.

Shibata, M. (2004). Controlling national identity and reshaping the role of education: The vision of state formation in Meiji Japan and the German Kaiserreich. *History of Education,* 33(1), pp. 75–85.

Spencer, K.A. (1973). *Agromyzidae (Diptera) of economic importance* (Vol. 9). Dordrecht: Springer Science & Business Media.

UNDP. (2015). *Human Development Report 2015.* United Nations Development Programme.

World Bank. (2019). *Bangladesh tertiary education sector review.* Washington, DC: World Bank.

Part III

Healthcare

6 Debates on Provisioning of Healthcare in Developing Countries

Introduction

In the story of the ant and the grasshopper, the grasshopper is a jovial little fellow playing the flute to his hearts' content during summer, while he watched an army of ants toiling laboriously transporting large quantities of food to their nest. The grasshopper, oblivious as he was to the impending winter and snowfall, belittled the ants' denial to consume the present warmth of summer. Short-sighted as the grasshopper was too probable future challenges that may arise, he took no measure to enable himself to adapt to those encounters. Within this analogy, the inability of the state to look beyond the current situation and strengthen the absorption capacity of institutions and the people when exposed to unprecedented systemic shocks may very likely end in the miseries akin to that of a starving grasshopper in the cold.

The idea of public health was similar to that of the story in Ancient Roman and Greek civilisation where preventive health measures like cleanliness and hygiene reduce health risks. Public health thus is not a new idea rather it has existed for a long time. It gained renewed interest after the "Spanish flu" pandemic in the early twentieth century. Countries started adopting healthcare policies that took care of their citizens by providing access to healthcare. Great Britain first explored the idea of a public health system in the nineteenth century. However, Soviet Russia was the first country that initiated public healthcare legislation in the early 1920s. European countries then followed suits and strengthened their healthcare sector.

The developing countries including Asian and African countries had little development in the health sector under colonial rule. The impact of it is still felt today as the inequality in healthcare has grown exponentially between the developed and developing nations. At the onset of another pandemic in the twenty-first century, push for a more inclusive and accessible healthcare in the form of universal health care has become inevitable. Universal health care provides access to healthcare to all citizens regardless of their economic activity. Cost of healthcare has been a burden on the citizens in both the developing and the developed world. As such, universal health care can reduce both horizontal and vertical inequalities all over the world.

DOI: 10.4324/9781003284222-9

Universal health care has its core in international politics, ethics and universal laws. Article 25 of Universal Declaration of Human Rights 1948 states that everyone has the right to revel in a standard of living that is adequate for health including medical care and the right to security during disability or sickness. Mothers and children require special care according to the declaration. In the same year, the constitution of the World Health Organization declared, "the enjoyment of the highest attainable standard of health is one of the fundamental rights of human beings without distinction of race, religion, and political belief, economic or social condition". There are mainly two motivations at work behind healthcare facility; first of all, it is a universally agreed basic need of any human being and the second one is, poor health causes negative externalities, from individuals to the society, from poor countries to rich countries; therefore any society has and should have a vested interest in providing healthcare to its members. Two basic aspects of poverty are often neglected in health policymaking; in developing countries, most of the people are poor and cannot afford to buy health services. The other aspect is governments in less developed countries have budget constraints. The question therefore is whether a nation should focus on health services provided by public provision or a combination of public, private and NGOs. Many may argue for private sector health provision through public financing but there is a strong incentive for the private sector to show inflated cost of the services. Besides, there may arise pressure from lobbyists to provide for the needs of the middle and upper class rather than the poor. Most importantly, there is demonstrated evidence that such provision may leave many behind in accessing healthcare. Therefore, the last hope for the poor people is government clinics and hospitals. The private provision is not a solution to reach the poor with healthcare services. Rather, the public sector has to come up with these services even though they have revenue deficits and organisational shortcomings. For extremely poor countries, aid by donor agencies can be a source of financing (Sachs, 2017).

History of healthcare in most of the developing countries can be traced back to before the colonial era. The institutions formed in the colonial era persist in policymaking in the developing countries. For instance, the healthcare of Bangladesh went through various stages mostly defined by the rulers. Before British rule, the Indian subcontinent depended upon traditional medical treatment. The Vaidyas (a Sanskrit word meaning "doctor" or "traditional physician") practiced Ayurvedic methods of treatment during the Hindu period. The Unani (Hekimi) methods, Perso-Arabic traditional medicine, were added to Ayurvedic system during the Muslim period. Simultaneously, folk treatment was also prevalent along with these two methods. East India Company introduced modern medical treatments in the subcontinent. Modern medical treatment has since been made available to the mass through public and gradually private provisioning. The 1971 war of independence of Bangladesh had an important role in starting national development processes, which were characterised by social mobilisation, institutional pluralism and civil dynamism, creating space for many stakeholders, government, non-governmental organisations

(NGOs), informal providers, international donors and commercial enterprises. In health-service delivery, all these stakeholders combined to pursue a pro-equity strategy, concentrating direct action on high-priority health issues such as family planning, immunisation, oral rehydration therapy, tuberculosis, vitamin A supplementation and others (Chowdhury et al., 2013).

In Bangladesh, the private sector and NGOs emerged due to limited capacity of the government in providing healthcare to all. Private sector comprises both formal and informal healthcare services. Formal healthcare providers in the private sector consist of both modern and traditional services through hospitals, laboratories and drug stores. Informal healthcare in the private sector is largely dominated by untrained medical providers of modern, traditional and homeopathic medicines. Informal healthcare is mostly based in the rural areas whereas the formal services provide healthcare largely in the urban areas. Inaccessibility and poor quality of public healthcare service in rural areas paved the way for NGOs to rise as "third sector" in Bangladesh. Increased funding from the donors in the 1990s helped the sector expand (Ahmed et al., 2017). External funding in healthcare in Bangladesh has been hovering around 8 per cent of the total health expenditure in the last decade (WHO, 2020).

As South Asia houses some of the world's largest populations, one of its greatest public health management challenges is overcoming the small number of health professionals available per capita. The region again has one of the worst ratios in the world, second only to sub-Saharan Africa. The situation could be ameliorated if graduate medical students were trained and appointed. At public hospitals, the service delivery of doctors, nurses and other staff is inexplicably inadequate due to over capacity with limited supply, which compels people to seek treatment at private hospitals. The cost of public healthcare is significantly lower than private healthcare, which is often not affordable by a considerably large population. The comparatively better quality of healthcare in neighbouring countries like Thailand, Singapore, India etc. is enticing both high- and middle-income groups, implicating drainage of resources.

A framework for universal health care in developing countries, with illustration of a country case of Bangladesh, is derived through a review of health policy and provision-related theoretical and empirical literature. The journey towards a system of universal health coverage is political. The political challenges in some cases are specific to a developing country context. It also represents the legacies of inherited colonial health systems, together with (neo-colonial) advices stemming from international policy regime, shaped by global political economy. A thorough understanding of political settlement eases the process of moving towards universal health coverage systems in developing countries. Besides a theoretical framework in the subsequent section of the chapter, the following chapter contains propositions to understand the ground realities of healthcare systems in developing countries, and proves these propositions empirically. The final chapter of this part ends with a road map for transformative change. All chapters encompass examples from countries that are moving towards universal health care.

Governing entities in the health sector can operate at different levels: global, national, subnational and local. Health provision, be it public or private, can be provided through both formal and informal channels. A minimum of three agents are in play for health provisioning – clients, providers and regulators.

Citizens are the "clients" of service providers and ideally should be able to hold the provider accountable for services. Accountability is expected to come through governments, regulators and other agencies. These may involve insurance providers, professional bodies, academic and training schools, accreditation agencies, donors and international development partners.

For example, the adoption of UHC policies in Turkey and Thailand benefited from strong executive leadership from the ministers of health and the heads of state, who worked to create broad popular support. In Brazil and Thailand, social movements had a catalytic role in putting UHC on the political agenda and in encouraging government leadership to adopt and implement reforms (Harris, 2012; Harris, 2015). In all cases, new programmes built on experiences and institutions provided opportunities to build capacity for managing and developing programmes.

While the 1898 invasion of Cuba was ostensibly intended to defend Cuban independence from Spain and stabilise trade relations in the region, Cuba had long been viewed by the United States as a hotbed of yellow fever and a source of the recurrent yellow fever epidemics that ravaged the American South. As Mariola Espinoza has convincingly argued, the invasion of Cuba was intended to put an end to this hemispheric threat of contagion. Responsibility for the elimination of yellow fever in Cuba quickly fell to Colonel William Gorgas. The army sent Gorgas to command a hospital for US yellow fever patients in Cuba in 1898 (Packard, 2016). Nigeria and its development partners have made several efforts to address the country's health needs. To date, investments to scale up polio immunisation campaigns and malaria control have been particularly large (IHME, 2015; PMI, 2014; WHO, 2014). Beyond disease-specific programmes, Nigeria has also enacted policies to improve access to and quality of healthcare. In 2014, the National Health Bill was passed, aiming to strengthen Nigeria's primary health care systems, bolster monitoring and evaluation capacities, and move towards universal health coverage through improved financial protections (Wollum et al., 2015).

Modern healthcare system in Bangladesh is partly developed because of increased government spending. The modern healthcare system grew from the colonial rule of Great Britain and after the partition, Pakistan continued the same system. Centralised system of healthcare of Bangladesh is largely a continuation of past policies taken by the rulers (Mahmood, 2010). "Bhore Committee" was the first step towards formulating a healthcare system which was formed in 1946. This committee formulated a health policy which integrated both curative and preventive services as well as established rural healthcare infrastructure. During the Pakistan regime, several policies were initiated such as rural healthcare centres, Malaria Eradication Programme and Family Planning Programme.

The healthcare delivery system in Bangladesh started its journey with the existing medical colleges, district hospitals and health centres from the Pakistan era. The high population in the country prompted the government to form a separate family planning division under the Health Ministry. The First Five Year Plan (1972–1978 and then extended to 1980) was drafted in accordance with the Alma Ata Declaration of 1978 and sought to improve healthcare by focusing on primary health care. The following two Five Year Plans focused on the human resources for health. The third and fourth planning periods (1986–1998) formulated sector-specific programmes including child health, diarrhoea and respiratory diseases and immunisation programmes (Anwar et al., 2015). Institutional and structural reforms in the health sector started taking place in the late 1990s after pressure from donors like the World Bank to promote parity and efficiency (Vaughan et al., 2000; Buse and Gwin, 1998). The reform gained pace after the approval of the Health and Population Sector Strategy (HPSS) in 1997, with privatisation, deregulation and liberalisation as the core of the agenda.

A Review

The mainstream theories of different kinds of health provisioning are associated with certain limitations which fail to provide the theoretical basis for universal health care for all. In order to construct the framework for developing countries, these limitations need to be addressed. The objective of this section, thus, is to generate a theoretical construct, based on the basic framework outlined in Chapter 2. It can provide a coherent analysis of the social construction on health-seeking behaviour of the individuals, concentration of healthcare in hands of the elite, and consequential inequality in terms of access to, and distribution of, healthcare resources, adversely impacting the society in general and the economy in particular.

States are expected to intervene or step in on issues of healthcare because the challenges associated with access to healthcare is fundamentally related to income. Given the required structural transformation of developing countries, mainly through rapid industrialisation, is dependent on a healthier workforce as well. A short supply in, and absenteeism of, skilled workers impose a huge financial burden on industries, which ultimately results in reduced income and delayed transformation. During the process of industrialisation, the infectious diseases replace with life-style maladies such as cancers and cardiovascular conditions. The change in the disease burden is also linked to increased life expectancies due to drop in mortality, particularly amongst the children, resulting from improvements in literacy, food supply and sanitation, which are caused by relatively higher disposable income, positively associated with the pathway of structural transformation. Even with greater than before income, these ailments are often too expensive to treat, making them affordable only to the wealthy section in a country. Thus, making healthcare available and accessible for all has become a primary concern for any government. For example, the transformed countries such as Singapore and South Korea have reaped the benefits of public healthcare expenditure in the provision of in-patient healthcare. The arrangements they undertook made citizens realise the true benefits of public provision in the most expensive components of healthcare services. Therefore, understanding health-seeking behaviour, economics of provisioning and policy process of expenditure is of tremendous importance.

For maintaining the similarity across the book, the theories and associated approaches are clustered into two categories: market-centric and political economic branches. The variety of theories related to the provisioning of healthcare through market-centric approach are organised under different schools, thoughts and branches such as neoclassical economics, neoliberalism, public choice, etc. Neither of these theoretical foundations are satisfactory enough to ensure the universal access to, and availability of, healthcare. The commodification of healthcare through market provision impedes the universal access of citizens through creating artificial scarcity and accumulation of resources to a few. Henceforth, private sector-centred neoliberal policy reforms do not bring any desired outcome but rather leave negative impacts on social well-being of the individuals, hitting hard the bottom of the pyramid, who comprises the most of the population. These drawbacks emanate from assuming political factors as exogenous by the neo-classical economics and idiosyncratic treatment of political process by the political choice theorists, with ideological overtones.

Health services can be provided by both the private and public sectors. The bone of contention arises when these relate to universal health care, meaning that the households with no ability to pay for healthcare must be served too. Because of constraint associated with ability to pay, the private sector is unable to provide universal health care, if the cost is not paid for by other means. Moreover, there are well-known market failures, besides market concentration, due to the private sector's thrust for profit, which breaks down the proverbial production at a level where marginal revenue (MR) is equal to marginal cost (MC).

There are attempts within the market centric approaches to address such failures. The British anti-Keynesian welfare economist, A. C. Pigou, in *The Economics of Welfare (1920)* argues that regulation is required to benefit the public through solving collective action problems when the private market fails to allocate the resources properly. The Pigouvian public interest theory believes that the government should correct these through regulations like providing subsidies or imposing taxes. The public interest theory is based on the assumptions that the government has the information of the market and the government can correct all the errors of the market without any cost. The economic theory of regulation argues that legislation is a good demand and supplied like other goods and thus legislative protection will be served to the interest of the group that generates greater benefit regardless of total social welfare. The theory also holds that political actors behave like businessmen and try to serve their own interest. The theory considers the decision-making by bureaucrats and politicians based on rational economic behaviour (Butler and Macey, 1996). The main criticisms of the public interest theory too concentrate on such peculiar assumptions. The market has a tendency to produce imperfectly specially when it is a public good and government regulation is not enough to solve the issue alone because of "rational" economic behaviour by the legislature and bureaucrats. Despite such, at the core, the market-centric approaches promote the values of individualism with arguments in favour of market pricing and commodification of healthcare. The only way therefore can be providing public goods by the government itself.

The neoclassical school which advocates for market provision also refers health to as public goods which are both non-excludable and non-rivalrous in such that individuals cannot be effectively excluded from consumption and where use by one individual does not shrink availability to others. These goods are associated with information asymmetry and price distortion which lead to market failure.

The neoclassical welfare perspective of healthcare posits that providing healthcare to everyone will ensure not only individual well-being but also societal welfare through positive externalities. The individualistic nature of neoclassical theories, however, acts contradictorily as the onus of maximisation of self-interest-based behaviour of citizens creates negative externalities in society. Hence, welfare is not maximised (Donaldson and Gerard, 1993).

The neoclassical school even acknowledges the role of factors like education, income and environment on health but they barely model these and the theoretical core primarily centres on individual preferences and utility function as objective function. The subjective nature of utility function is thus weakened due to the lack of focus on societal factors.

Public goods like healthcare provide a very important example of market failure, in which market-like behaviour of individual gain-seeking does not produce efficient outcomes to reach all segments of society. There are, however, clear structural reasons why market-driven healthcare and competition do not in fact promote efficiency or quality (Rice, 1997). Market competition does not make for better care as most patients do not have enough knowledge to make informed choices – a situation called information asymmetry in the healthcare "market".

Government regulation is required in a commercialised healthcare market because of high transaction costs. For example, one study finds the administrative cost in private sector as staggering 31 per cent of the overall expenditure, whereas in public healthcare, the cost is only 6 per cent of the expenditure (Leys, 2010). Supply and distribution of drugs and medical equipment in bulk in the public healthcare system allows economies of scale and the bulk purchase at the same time keeps the cost of medicines low (Hodgson, 2007).

Market provision keeps a section of the population out of healthcare. Higher marginal cost in providing healthcare to the most inaccessible and to those with pre-existing conditions is not assumed to be profitable by the private system, and these exclusions impede attainment of universal care (Allotey et al., 2012).

The high marginal cost of healthcare can only be absorbed by the public system. Private healthcare systems avoid such patients due to the higher cost and risk associated with it. Thus, a public healthcare system is necessary to offset the burden of the population and promote equity in the society.

Within the neoclassical school, human capital theory, which advocates investment in health, has acquired a centre of attraction within the mainstream economics. The idea of health as a form of human capital has a long history (Mushkin, 1962). Grossman (1972) develops a model in which illness prevents work, and thus the cost of ill health is lost labour time. A major difficulty in measuring the economic effect of health is the two-way causality between wealth and health (Smith, 1999). Another difficulty is the lack of consensus on what is meant by health. Different studies use different health measures: self-assessments of health, biomarkers, medical records, limitations on physical functioning, and anthropometric measurements have all been used as indicators of health. These measurement approaches may fail to provide a complete picture of an individual's health status, giving rise to a problem of measurement error. In addition, it is necessary to separate the effect of investments in health from the effect of natural or genetic variation in health (Schultz, 2002).

Childhood health has a significant impact on adult health when controlling for parental influences and education (Case et al., 2005). Yet another approach is operated to establish causality by way of using instrumental variables. For example, Schultz (2002) uses adult height with childhood health and nutrition to argue that each centimetre gain in height due to improved inputs as a child in Ghana and Brazil leads to a wage increase of between 8 and 10 per cent (Strauss and Thomas, 1998, provide a survey of studies in this area).

Hookworm and malaria in the United States in the 1910s and 1920s and in many countries of the American South were pandemic prior to eradication. Controlling for normal wage gains in areas that were not infected, the children, not exposed to these diseases due to their eradication, had improved incomes as adults relative to those born before eradication (Bleakley, 2003). This body of research on health and human capital generally supports the idea that health affects worker productivity. However, it lacks a good appreciation of which types of health intervention are most important and what rate of return can be achieved by investing in health as a form of human capital. In many developing countries, relatively inexpensive activities designed to prevent the spread of infectious disease (for example, vaccination) can increase health outcomes at low cost, suggesting a high rate of return. By comparison, treating chronic non-infectious diseases in developed countries is often costly. There is evidence that susceptibility to chronic disease in later life is determined by health and nutrition status of foetus and infancy (Barker, 1992), suggesting that early health investments are crucial for productivity of adults.

The Public Choice theory is another variety within the broad church of neo-classical school. The basic behavioural assumption of public choice stands the same as for any other traits of market-centric approaches like individualism, rationalism and profit-maximisation. This theory explains how public goods like healthcare are demanded and supplied, explaining the role of the government which works as a marketplace where citizens trade taxes for public goods. However, if the government is considered as a marketplace, there would be market failure in terms of public provisioning which then contradicts with the neoclassical understanding of public goods. This self-interest model does not explain much other humanistic behaviour such as the redistribution activities of government. Subsidy, increase in budgetary allocation, health allowance for the labour, etc. go beyond the rational self-interest of the government.

These utilitarian approaches do not focus on healthcare separately rather understand the overall utility maximisation of a society. Besides, these consider total utility or benefit and are not concerned about the distribution. These tolerate large disparities in order to achieve a higher level of utility (Ruger, 2006).

Communitarian theories of justice, on the other hand, argue for a relativist form of justice as a shared expression of values in a given community. The principles are constructed internally in a society. Communitarians take community values as absolute principle, if health service is considered as a necessary service that needs to be supplied by the government or not will be determined by the values and norms of a society. Ezekiel Emanuel proposes that the ideal system in a communitarian approach is of allowing the deliberate and democratic communities to develop their conception of good life and justice. That means if the society carries the value that public provision of healthcare is necessary, there must be provision of public healthcare (Ruger, 2006).

Libertarian perspective however holds a negative conception on public provision of healthcare. This particular theory of justice is advocated by Robert Nozick in his *Anarchy, Sate, and Utopia* (1974). According to the theory, taxation on the wealth of the rich in order to serve the poor diminishes the right of liberty for the rich. This theory therefore advocates for national laws that ensure negative freedoms in a society and reject the redistribution or equal distribution principle. The theory puts too much emphasis on negative freedoms but ignores positive ones. It also fails to address that the miseries of the poor people are not due to only their own negligence rather a product of inequalities in a society (Ruger, 2006).

Based upon ideas of this brand of justice as well as those of public choice theory and neoclassical economics, the market-centric neoliberal reform agenda advocates for cuts in public spending in education and healthcare; the removal of price controls and subsidies, particularly on food; the privatisation of public enterprises. The neoliberal project rests on two main planks. The first is increased competition, which is to be achieved through deregulation and the opening up of domestic markets, including financial markets, to foreign competition. The second is a smaller role for the state to be attained via privatisation and limiting the ability of governments to run fiscal deficits and accumulate debt. There has been a strong and widespread global trend towards neoliberalism since the 1980s.

However, this political project can be criticised on several grounds. Karl Polanyi (1944) pointed out the emergence of market liberalism – the idea that markets are self-regulating emerged as a means of managing the problems of industrialisation. This directly led to the depression, fascism and so on. Market liberalism is based on the view that markets are self-regulating and that markets operate separately from and above or outside society. However, Polanyi argues that markets have always been embedded and the goal of a fully self-regulating market that is disembodied is a utopian project. It cannot exist. There is, however, also considerable evidence that rolling out of neoliberal policies and programmes across the globe (Peck and Tickell, 2002) has been highly uneven (Harvey, 2006).

Amartya Sen (1999) has formulated capability approach, which is closely connected to the Aristotelian and Rawlsian views of justice. The capability approach is based on several claims. The major proposition is that equality can be ensured in many ways. Different theorists have defined equality in different ways in critique of that Sen asked, equality of what? Arguing that the correct focus for evaluating how well off people is their capability to live a life, not their resource wealth or subjective well-being, Sen states that wealth, income, schooling and healthcare provide a person to function. Capability approach, thus, focuses on capability of a person to lead a worthwhile life. It incorporates well-being and freedom to pursue well-being (Sen, 2000). In his formulation, capability relates to function in two ways. First, some capabilities like being able to eat well, clothe well, take part in social activities constitute a person's well-being. Later, this well-being provides the person freedom to pursue further well-beings. The second one is capability to function, the opportunity to exercise freedom for well-being. Sen argues that capability can be measured in two ways: what a person is actually doing and what are the alternatives available. Like the Aristotelian view, Sen's capability approach also believes in people functioning for well-being according to their own conception of well-being, not the conception that society set for its individuals (Ruger, 2006).

In John Rawls's liberal view, people have ignorance on their circumstances that determines the range of minimum level of primary goods and services. Primary goods are given to people with fair equality of opportunity. Rawls (1971) talked about the natural lottery; the distribution of advantageous and disadvantageous attributes by birth and the social lottery and the distribution of social assets or deficit through family, schooling, environment etc. Rawls's theory focuses on means rather than ends, and falls short to recognise that human beings have different needs of resources since there are different definitions of being better or worse off. Rawls's theory is criticised for not considering healthcare as a primary good. According to Rawls, no society can guarantee health to its individuals. Later, he changed his theory slightly in *The Law of Peoples* (1993) where he considers healthcare as one of the primary goods (Ruger, 2006).

Different schools have prescribed different conditions for provision of healthcare. Neoclassical school considers it as a public good due to market failure. State, hence, should provide public goods and collect tax (Stiglitz, 2000). Other branches within this mainstream school have treated health as capital which needs to be developed. The public choice school has also assumed health as a marketable good. Boyoued by such theories, the neoliberal reform agenda executed cut in the government subsidy in healthcare and introduced private provisioning which led to poor and inequitable health coverage. The political economic approaches also emphasise on the correlation between the access to health and the inequality in the society. Nevertheless, the mainstream schools of thoughts are inadequate in dealing with provision of healthcare in developing countries as has been heightened by the COVID-19 crisis.

Stylised Facts

The idea of developing a new framework also hinges upon stylised facts, which are empirical regularities, discerned from the real world. Besides the review of literature of different schools of thought, stylized facts matter enormously in inducing an alternative theoretical framework that deals with the real world and allows for understanding the agents, drivers and elements for transformational changes in developing countries.

Health sector in developing countries still suffers from a shortage in medical workforce and infrastructures, which hamper the availability of healthcare to the masses. Compared to developed nations, health infrastructures like hospital beds and tertiary healthcare still remain much underdeveloped in developing countries. For instance, there are only 7.95 hospital beds for every ten thousand population in Bangladesh and 5.3 beds in India. Compared to that, Japan has 130.5 and Norway has 36 hospital beds for every ten thousand population. Same scenario exists in the case of the healthcare workforce. The number of doctors for the ten thousand population in Bangladesh stands at 4.9 and in India it is 7.6. The number for developed countries is much higher. In Scandinavian countries like Norway and Finland, there are more than 45 doctors for every ten thousand population. Density of skilled health professionals in countries like Bangladesh is merely 7.38 per ten thousand population against the WHO standard 44.5 to achieve SDG and universal health care targets (WHO, 2020). The staggering difference in healthcare facilities between the developed and developing nations is evident from widely differing healthcare outcomes. Developing countries mainly African and Southeast Asian countries have been far behind than European countries in indicators like maternal mortality and life expectancy.

Access to healthcare is constrained by lack of knowledge or awareness about the services, financial barriers (e.g., high fees), geographical barriers (e.g., long distance) as well as cultural barriers like gender. There are differences in terms of levels of care. For instance, access to primary care is less constrained due to geographical barriers, but tertiary or mid-level health services are concentrated in urban areas. Inadequacies of skilled professionals such as specialist doctors and nurses are also a feature of rural health services. There are disparities based on socio-economic conditions too. People with higher socio-economic conditions enjoy better provision of health services. Policies, if such exist, in addressing disparities and distribution are poorly applied in the health sector (Ahmed et al., 2015).

The unequal provisioning of healthcare service delivery is responsible for accelerating inequality and poverty in developing countries. High out-of-pocket expenditure is a common feature of developing countries. South Asia and Africa are the regions with highest out-of-pocket expenditure. Average out-of-pocket healthcare expenditure of households in South Asia is 40.12 per cent while for Africa the number is 36.61 compared to only 29.82 in Europe (WHO, 2020). At the same time, such a high out-of-pocket expenditure has led to impoverishment in both Africa and South Asia. Globally, household health expenditure has pushed 1.23 per cent of the population below the poverty line. In Africa, health expenditure impelled 1.51 per cent of the population below the poverty line. In Southeast Asia, huge out-of-pocket expenditure has forced 2.76 per cent of the population below the poverty line (WHO, 2020). This deters efforts to curb poverty and achieve SDG targets in developing countries.

Inequality exists within a country as well. Health service delivery and outcome vary in size, amount, degree or nature amongst economic groups. For example, in Bangladesh, the richest 40 per cent spend 60 per cent on out-of-pocket payment. Inpatient care is also pro-wealthy in both public and private hospitals. The richest quintile receives 30 per cent of the total subsidy while receiving healthcare services. The use of traditional health service providers is high, for poor citizens, at almost 6–8 per cent and the percentage is much higher for children. The poor from both rural and urban areas rely on non-qualified private health providers due to the high rate of out-of-pocket expenditure, resulting healthcare almost inaccessible for the poor. The sales persons in pharmacies function as the main health service provider. There exist other barriers such as lack of knowledge or awareness and long distance to health facilities which make the equity situation even worse (Ahmed et al., 2015).

The people's perception of, and experience in, health facilities are not pleasant. Some of their main complaints are unresponsiveness, long waiting time, misbehaviour and absenteeism of the service providers. Exclusion of marginalised people, lack of privacy, inadequate explanation of the disease and frail management are frequently reported by the users. On the other hand, providers of health services blame poor infrastructure (human and physical) and inadequate supply of necessities as the reason for dissatisfaction. The doctors however recognise poor administration that fail to provide reward or punishment (Ahmed et al., 2015).

LDCs can produce generic drugs under the TRIPS agreement. This has helped many developing countries to deliver drugs at lower prices. However, this has only remained within generic drugs and these countries can barely invest in scientific research. During the COVID-19 pandemic, the United States, Germany, United Kingdom, Russia and China were the only countries to have produced a vaccine. As a result, developed countries have been able to vaccinate a large population. Developing countries on the other hand have been left behind in terms of vaccination. The United States vaccinated 35 per cent and the United Kingdom vaccinated 27 per cent of the population by May 2021. On the other hand, Southeast Asian countries including Bangladesh vaccinated less than 2 per cent of the population (Our World in Data, 2021). The inability of developing countries to produce vaccines has largely been due to patents withheld by the developed countries.

A Framework

Given the ground realities, the proposed framework has to adopt certain assumptions by breaking away from the mainstream to provide for universal healthcare while being cognizant that healthcare is by no means synonymous to health. First, healthcare is assumed as a basic human need which is different from the economic term "demand". Demand in the orthodox economics is the quantity of consumers, who are willing and able to buy products at various prices during a given period of time. Demand for any commodity implies the consumers' willingness and ability to pay for it. On the contrary, the need for healthcare is universal, irrespective of the capacity to pay for availing the services. "Demand"-based healthcare system asks for ability to pay for services, keeping a great majority out of the reach of the system while charging exorbitant prices, financed through out-of-pocket healthcare expenditure of households. Such cost negatively affects the income of household, especially in developing countries where still almost a quarter of the population remains under the conventional poverty line. A decent measure would have found an increased share. Disease always acts as a shock for households. As a result, such a shock pushes more households below the poverty line. In this scenario, a right-based provision of universal health care is a minimum requirement to ensure equitable access to healthcare. Public provisioning of healthcare may reduce the burden on the population. Such universal access will require reforms not only of formal institutions but also of informal institutions such as norms, values, etc., which are responsible for healthcare-seeking behaviour.

The framework interconnects as to how the state, citizens and community as a whole can cooperate in order to create a healthy life for individuals (Figure 6.1). State is assumed to be responsible for public provision of healthcare, making it accessible, affordable and effective. Leaving the healthcare to the private sector leads to inaccessibility for certain segments of the population. Private firms, without consumer-driven government regulation, will resort to price distortion and thus sell healthcare at a higher price, even without quality. Such behaviour hinders towards attaining universal health care. Public provision of healthcare thus not only keeps the market stable but also has the ability to reach all segments and ensure access to healthcare which is a fundamental human right and also a basic right enshrined in the constitution.

Citizens are responsible for norms, behaviour and hygiene practices related to preventive healthcare measures. The cultural attitudes, health literacy and social cohesion of a community determine the healthcare-seeking behaviour. Traditional and rural societies opt for traditional methods of healthcare. Higher

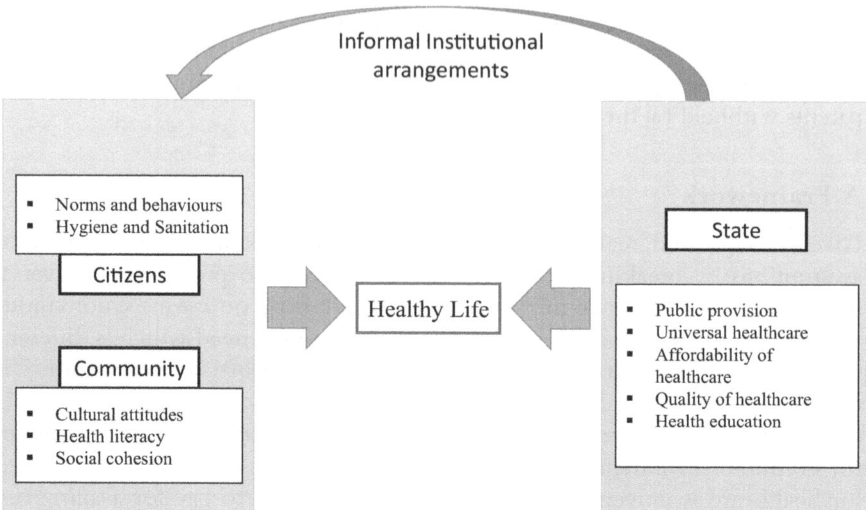

Figure 6.1 Citizens, state and healthy life

Source: Prepared by author

health literacy among the urban population and concentration of services in urban centres demonstrate a positive relationship with formal and modern healthcare. The service is governed by the institutions and arrangements put forth by the state. Institutions determine the nature of the relationship between the public and the healthcare system.

Summary

Healthcare is identified as a basic human need which is different from the economic term "demand", which will be empirically validated in the following chapters, making a distinction from the orthodox theoretical foundations. The alternative framework identifies state and citizens as the key agents in determining the level of ensuring access and affordability of healthcare. While state is entrusted with the public provisioning of healthcare, active citizenship induces the healthcare-seeking behaviour of the population. When both state and citizens work effectively in tandem, the outcome is optimum for the population.

Health should not be reduced to medical care rather to be understood as a state of complete physical, mental and social well-being and not merely the absence of disease or infirmity. The framework also centres on provisioning of universal health care as opposed to universal health coverage by analysing access, healthcare-seeking behaviour, price setting, market provisioning etc.

References

Ahmed, S., Alam, B., Anwar, I., Begum, T., Huque, R., and Khan, J.A.M. (2015). *Bangladesh health system review* (Vol. 5, No. 3). Manila: World Health Organization, Regional Office for the Western Pacific.

Ahmed, S., Tarique, K.M., and Arif, I. (2017). Service quality, patient satisfaction and loyalty in the Bangladesh healthcare sector. *International Journal of Health Care Quality Assurance*, 30(5), pp. 477–488.

Allotey, P., Yasin, S., Tang, S., Chong, S.L., Cheah, J.C.H., and Reidpath, D.D. (2012). Universal coverage in an era of privatisation: Can we guarantee health for all? *BMC Public Health*, 12(1).

Anwar, I., Nababan, H.Y., Mostari, S., Rahman, A., and Khan, J.A. (2015). Trends and inequities in use of maternal health care services in Bangladesh, 1991–2011. *PLoS One*, 10(3), p. e0120309.

Barker, J.C. (1992). Cultural diversity – changing the context of medical practice. *Western Journal of Medicine*, 157(3), p. 248.

Bleakley, H. (2003). Disease and development: Evidence from the American South. *Journal of the European Economic Association*, 1(2–3), pp. 376–386.

Buse, K., and Gwin, C. (1998). The World Bank and global cooperation in health: The case of Bangladesh. *The Lancet*, 351(9103), pp. 665–669.

Butler, H.N., and Macey, J.R. (1996). Externalities and the matching principle: The case for reallocating environmental regulatory authority. *Yale Law & Policy Review*, 14(2), pp. 23–66.

Case, A., Fertig, A., and Paxson, C. (2005). The lasting impact of childhood health and circumstance. *Journal of Health Economics*, 24(2), pp. 365–389.

Chowdhury, A.M.R., Bhuiya, A., Chowdhury, M.E., Rasheed, S., Hussain, Z., and Chen, L.C. (2013). The Bangladesh paradox: Exceptional health achievement despite economic poverty. *The Lancet*, 382(9906), pp. 1734–1745.

Donaldson, C., and Gerard, K. (1993). *Economics of health care financing*. Basingstoke: Macmillan.

Grossman, M. (1972). On the concept of health capital and the demand for health. *Journal of Political Economy*, 80(2), pp. 223–255.

Harris, J. (2012). *A right to health? Professional networks, HIV/AIDS, and the politics of universal health coverage*. PhD Dissertation. Madison, WI: University of Wisconsin.

Harris, J. (2015). "Developmental capture" of the state: Explaining Thailand's universal coverage policy. *Journal of Health Politics, Policy and Law*, 40, pp. 165–193.

Harvey, D. (2006). Neo-Liberalism as creative destruction. *Geografiska Annaler: Series B, Human Geography*, 88(2), pp. 145–158.

Hodgson, G.M. (2007). An institutional and evolutionary perspective on health economics. *Cambridge Journal of Economics*, 32(2), pp. 235–256.

IHME. (2015). *Financing Global Health 2014: Shifts in funding as the MDG era closes*. Seattle, WA: Institute for Health Metrics and Evaluation.

Leys, C. (2010). Health, health care and capitalism. *Socialist Register*, 46, pp. 1–28.

Mahmood, S.A.I. (2010). Public procurement and corruption in Bangladesh confronting the challenges and opportunities. *Journal of Public Administration and Policy Research*, 2(6), pp. 103–111.

Mushkin, S.J. (1962). Health as an investment. *Journal of Political Economy*, 70(5, Part 2), pp. 129–157.

Our World In Data. (2021). *Data dashboard*. Our World In Data.

Packard, R.M. (2016). *A history of global health: Interventions into the lives of other peoples*. Baltimore: Johns Hopkins University Press.

Peck, J., and Tickell, A. (2002). Neoliberalizing space. *Antipode*, 34(3), pp. 380–404.

PMI. (2014). *President's malaria initiative: Nigeria malaria operational plan FY 2015*. Washington, DC: PMI.

Polanyi, K. (1944). *The great transformation*. New York: Farrar & Rinehart.

Rawls, J. (1971). *A theory of justice*. Cambridge, MA: The Belknap Press of Harvard University Press.

Rice, T. (1997). Can markets give us the health system we want? *Journal of Health Politics, Policy and Law*, 22(2), pp. 383–426.

Ruger, J.P. (2006). Toward a theory of a right to health: Capability and incompletely theorized agreements. *Yale Journal of Law & the Humanities*, 18(2), p. 3.

Sachs, R.E. (2017). Administering health innovation. *Cardozo Law Review*, 39, p. 1991.

Schultz, T.P. (2002). Wage gains associated with height as a form of health human capital. *American Economic Review*, 92(2), pp. 349–353.

Sen, A. (1999). *Commodities and capabilities*. Oxford: Oxford University Press Catalogue.

Sen, A. (2000). *Development as freedom*. New York: Anchor Books.

Smith, J.P. (1999). Healthy bodies and thick wallets: The dual relation between health and economic status. *Journal of Economic Perspectives*, 13(2), pp. 145–166.

Stiglitz, J.E. (2000). Formal and informal institutions. *Social Capital: A Multifaceted Perspective*, 2000, pp. 59–68.

Strauss, J., and Thomas, D. (1998). Health, nutrition, and economic development. *Journal of Economic Literature*, 36(2), pp. 766–817.

Vaughan, J.P., Karim, E., and Buse, K. (2000). Health care systems in transition III. Bangladesh, Part I. An overview of the health care system in Bangladesh. *Journal of Public Health*, 22(1), pp. 5–9.

WHO. (2014). *Global polio eradication initiative: Financial resource requirements, 2013–2018*. Geneva: WHO.

WHO. (2020). *The global health observatory*. Geneva, Switzerland: WHO.

Wollum, A., Burstein, R., Fullman, N., Dwyer-Lindgren, L., and Gakidou, E. (2015). Benchmarking health system performance across states in Nigeria: A systematic analysis of levels and trends in key maternal and child health interventions and outcomes, 2000–2013. *BMC Medicine*, 13(1), p. 208.

7 Universal Health Care

Provisioning and Accessibility

Introduction

The chapter investigates public and market provisioning of healthcare through analysing variables such as access to quality care, health-seeking behaviour and price setting. It introduces a number of propositions as determinants of universal health care, covering both the demand and supply sides. The chapter examines individual and social behaviour towards seeking healthcare to comprehend the demand side while the supply-side discussion entails a rigorous comparative analysis of provisioning of healthcare by different means, including the public and private sectors. The path towards a system of universal health care is a complex one, interjected with systemic challenges, which emanate from the legacies of inherited distortionary health systems, predatory power of clientelist network over state, regulation and market at local, national, regional and global levels and concomitant interconnectedness with national and international political settlement and policy regimes.

National progress towards universal health care is intertwined with steps in the direction of a so-called health financing transition, characterised by rising per head health spending and an increasing use of pooled health funding. This trend has been accompanied by overall improvements in health status indicated, for example, by rising life expectancy and downward trends in child mortality rates. The empirical challenge is to assess the extent to which these observed relations are causal. In the context of crisis, increasing healthcare demands, and continuous technological innovation, health budgets are coming under acute pressure, particularly in low-income countries, where there is already constrained spending capacity. The intention of making healthcare more affordable is to induce a greater use of appropriate services. In principle, enhanced access to care could be achieved through expansions in either publicly or privately pooled financing. For developing countries, market provisioning of healthcare services and price setting on the basis of healthcare perceived as "demand" instead of need have structurally limited accessibility for populations unable to afford the high costs of private healthcare. As a result, dependence on market provisioning for health for an extended amount of time has rendered the health-seeking behaviour hesitant and unwilling for lower-income populations.

DOI: 10.4324/9781003284222-10

Socially Embedded Values

Socially embedded nature of the individuals, in terms of habits, beliefs and social conventions, determines health-seeking behaviour comprising consumer preferences and healthcare consumption. Cultural beliefs and practices often lead to self-care, home remedies and consultation with traditional healers in rural communities. These factors result in delay in treatment-seeking and are more common amongst women, not only for their own health but especially for children's illnesses. Different socio-cultural backgrounds tend to differ in the extent to which they delay seeking medical help. Cultural differences in delay of healthcare-seeking are attributed to a diverse set of factors, ranging from knowledge and beliefs regarding causes of the disease, associated symptoms, curability, consequences, and level of trust in physicians. Female members of some groups may be reluctant to be examined by male physicians and even the anticipation of this happening may contribute to delays in or complete avoidance of healthcare-seeking. People associating their symptoms with traditional or folk beliefs may be reluctant to seek medical advice because they perceive that healthcare providers lack cultural sensitivity.

Cross-cultural variations of a given psychological phenomenon are commonly attributed to the culture and socially embedded nature of the individuals. Because culture can be very broadly defined as a set of structures and institutions, values, traditions and ways of engaging with the social and non-social world that are transmitted across generations.

The horizontal axis shows the healthcare demanded and the vertical axis shows the individual preference for health (Figure 7.1). Socially embedded nature of individuals in the diagram is horizontal implying that nature

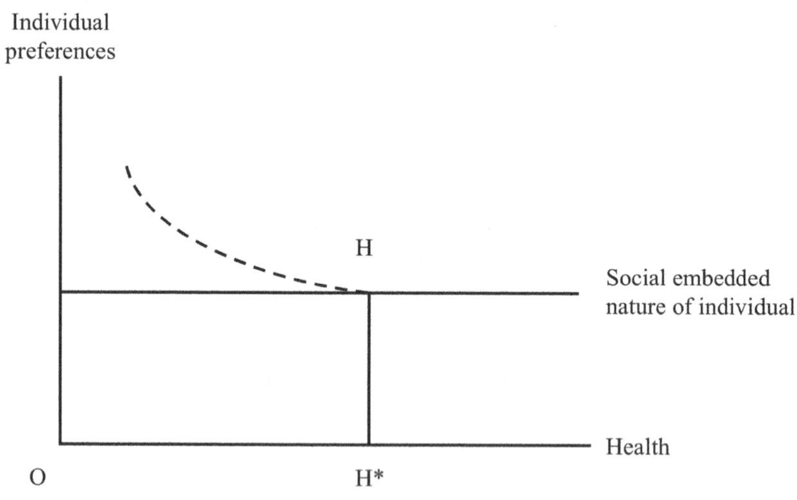

Figure 7.1 Socially embedded nature of individual affecting health-seeking behaviour

Source: Prepared by authors

is exogenously determined. Individual preferences fall according to socially embedded nature in terms of health-seeking behaviour. Since preferences are contingent upon socially embedded nature, it reaches point H incurring the healthcare services at point H^*. Therefore, the intersection point of H^* of the preference curve and the line of socially embedded nature determines the level of healthcare. This embedded nature of society obstructs preferences and claiming of proper healthcare services in the society.

Healthcare seeking behaviour is complex, and consumers rely on habits, routines, rules of thumb, social conventions and/or exhibit myopia. Thus, the formation of consumer preferences and their links to health and healthcare consumption points to the principle of non-independence, which refers to the socially embedded nature of the individual.

Healthcare seeking behaviour cannot be described in some system of differential equations because they are pretty complex. Suppose in a complex system the parameters to change healthcare behaviour are habits, routines, social conventions, myopia and rules of thumb.

X = healthcare seeking behaviour
H = habits
r = routines
s = social conventions
e = exhibit myopia
rt = rules of thumb
Y = socially embedded nature of the individual

Healthcare seeking behaviour depends on all habits, routines, social conventions, myopia and rules of thumb. In different societies, these are different and so is healthcare-seeking behaviour.

Again,

$$h = f(Y)$$
$$r = f(Y)$$
$$e = f(Y)$$
$$rt = f(Y)$$

which means that all these parameters are dependent on one's socially embedded nature. This implies that ultimately healthcare-seeking behaviour is actually directed by one's socially embedded behaviour. That is,

$$X=f(Y)$$

The various features of societal norms, values, customs and culture act as organising constructs of health-seeking behaviour, which influences individuals' preferences and determines the level of healthcare.

Individuals in a society seek healthcare services based upon their ideology, social status and socially embedded nature. Household income, education and ethnicity continue to be strong determinants of people's ability to access quality healthcare – and this is true of all countries analysed. Socio-economic status, hence, is a strong determinant of the health-seeking behaviour of individuals. Based on the health-seeking behaviour, two types of medical treatment can be identified prevailing in urban and rural Bangladesh. Different healthcare services differ in their philosophy and concept as to the causes of disease, their approach to healing, methods of treatment, and composition and preparation of medicinal products. As they exist in Bangladesh, they can be broadly classified into (i) traditional and (ii) modern systems.

Traditional system has been defined by the World Health Organization as a collection of knowledge and practice which relies on practical experience and observations in diagnosis and treatment. These practices have been in use from earlier generations and use natural substances including plants and animals, social and religious beliefs (Ghani, 1990). Ayurvedic and Unani systems are common traditional systems. Traditional systems are still in practice in Asian and African countries. Such practices though have gone through immense modernisation in recent times and have been competing with the modern allopathic healthcare systems and as such are a recognised healthcare system over the world.

Ayurvedic and Unani systems are still much prevalent in Bangladesh with over 6,000 registered and 10,000 unregistered practitioners. Ayurvedic healthcare is taught in five institutions in Bangladesh whereas Unani system is taught at ten institutions. The number of patients though have reduced in the traditional systems because of modern healthcare systems. Only 0.76 per cent of patients still consult Ayurvedic and Unani healthcare in the country (BBS, 2019).

Homeopathic system originated in Europe but is hugely popular in Asian countries. This system was originally developed from an allopathic system and usually uses plant-derived medicines. Distribution of patients in this sector is 2.36 in Bangladesh. Rural areas have higher distribution with 2.47 per cent compared to 2.02 per cent in urban areas (BBS, 2019).

Modern System is the globally used system of healthcare which not only includes the treatment but also prevents diseases through immunisation and hygiene. Technology has ushered in a new era in the modern healthcare system as it includes equipment in diagnostics and treatment. Technology is also used to produce medicines in this system. Healthcare thus requires sophisticated hospitals and medical centres. Healthcare professionals go through rigorous training to become medical caregivers. Modern healthcare sees different roles of caregivers varying from doctors to nurses to technicians. In order to function properly, the modern healthcare system requires a significant number of healthcare professionals. Developing countries usually face a dearth of both medical professionals and technological infrastructures. At the same time, this has the greatest number of patients.

In terms of service points of the modern healthcare system, pharmacies and dispensaries are the most used ones with 33.11 per cent of the population seeking healthcare from there followed by non-qualified doctors with a share of 22.50 per cent. Rural areas with 25.06 per cent of the population tend to consult non-qualified doctors whereas only 14.81 per cent of the urban population consult such doctors. On the other hand, the urban population seeks healthcare more from the qualified doctors compared to the rural population.

The distribution of medical practitioners shows a wide disparity between urban and rural areas in terms of MBBS doctors. Urban areas see more than double allopathic practitioners than rural ones (74.4 per cent in urban areas and 30.1 per cent in rural areas). The number of homeopathic and traditional practitioners is also higher in urban areas but the disparity is much less (Table 7.1).

Distance to healthcare facilities plays a major role in deciding particular services in both urban and rural areas. Short distance is followed by quality of treatment and the expenditure of service in terms of a patient choosing a particular service. Some variations exist between the urban and rural areas. Rural populations tend to look for reasonable expenditures more than urban populations in terms of choosing healthcare service. On the other hand, quality of healthcare impacts the decision of choosing healthcare more in urban population compared to rural population (Table 7.2).

Individuals tend to avoid treatment citing many factors varying from preconceived notions to physical accessibility to healthcare. In both urban and rural areas, the prime reason for avoiding treatment is that the individual thinks that the problem is not serious (Table 7.3). Such thinking is more dominant in urban areas than rural areas. Rural population on the other hand considers high

Table 7.1 Percentage of availability of medical practitioners

Medical practitioners	*Urban*	*Rural*
Allopathic/MBBS	74.4	30.1
Homeopathic	76.8	50.2
Unani/Ayurvedic	48.8	35.2

Source: BBS (2014)

Table 7.2 Reasons behind choosing particular health service

Reasons	*Urban*			*Rural*		
	Total	*Female*	*Male*	*Total*	*Female*	*Male*
Short distance	38.73	36.68	41.27	36.66	35.90	37.55
Reasonable expenditure	19.01	18.34	19.85	23.03	22.81	23.29
Doctor available easily	9.62	9.38	9.91	11.06	10.89	11.27
Female doctor available	0.64	1.09	0.08	1.29	2.05	0.20
Medical equipment available	1.59	1.51	1.69	1.46	1.51	1.41
Quality of treatment is good	25.25	27.16	22.88	21.39	21.46	21.31
Referred by other doctor/service person	1.11	1.32	0.85	0.92	0.92	0.91
Suggested by friends/relatives	2.24	2.63	1.75	2.48	2.67	2.26
For good reputation	1.57	1.65	1.47	1.62	1.57	1.68
Other reasons	0.24	0.24	0.25	0.82	0.22	0.14

Source: BBS (2019)

Table 7.3 Reasons behind non-treatment in terms of gender

	Urban		*Rural*	
	Female	*Male*	*Female*	*Male*
The problem was not serious	65.84	71.37	51.73	54.11
High expenditure of treatment	10.79	9.00	21.18	18.43
Non-support from family	1.74	3.00	7.15	5.74

Source: BBS (2019)

expenditure as a block towards getting treatment. This notion is held more by females than by males. Rural households also avoid treatment as they receive less support from family compared to urban households.

The urban areas prefer modern healthcare systems more than the rural areas, which still keeps their belief in traditional and homeopathic systems.

Private sector in Bangladesh has two broad groups: formal and informal. Qualified medical practitioners providing healthcare in an organised manner falls into the formal group whereas the informal group consists of healthcare workers having no formal qualifications and working in rural areas mainly.

Along with private clinics and hospitals, the number of diagnostic centres in the private sector is growing. In 2012, approximately 5,122 laboratories and other diagnostic centres were registered with the Ministry of Health and Family Welfare (MOHFW, 2012). In the private for-profit sector, there are some large diagnostic centres in the cities providing laboratory and specialised radiological tests. Some of these facilities maintain a high standard. In the non-profit private sector, there are centres like the International Centre for Diarrhoeal Diseases and Research, Bangladesh (ICDDR, B), which has a modern laboratory providing research facilities and extending laboratory services to the general community.

The NGO sector in Bangladesh has gained international limelight due to their involvement in the development. As of 2014, 2,471 registered NGOs are working in the health and nutrition sector in the country. NGOs play a significant role in promoting healthcare in the rural communities which has helped the country achieve milestones in family planning and maternal and child health. NGOs managed 9 per cent of the total health expenditure in 2007.

As both state and market are working in the health sector, a comparison can easily be made based on their pricing and quality of services. The quality of services provided by the hospitals is contingent on market incentives: because private hospitals are not subsidised and depend on income from clients, they are supposed to be more inclined than public hospitals to provide quality services and to meet patients' needs better. By doing so, they will not only be able to build satisfied and loyal clients who will revisit the same facility for future needs, the clients will also serve as a source of referrals to recommend the private establishments to friends and family, thereby sustaining the long-term viability of private hospitals. In public hospitals, on the other hand, there is supposedly little or no market incentive to motivate the staff to take extra initiative or effort to improve the condition of patients and ameliorate their suffering. Tax subsidies and other sources assure these organisations of their survival. Harsh as this may sound, evidence of the private sector's lack of responsiveness, dedication or quality assurance in media reports is often stark. The premise of orthodox approach is that market incentives would explain differences in the perceived quality of services provided by public and private hospitals. This contention was reasonably supported: private hospitals have been known to reduce quality by reducing inputs, to disregard social pricing considerations or, worse, to try to increase their profits by providing services that are unnecessary or even harmful. It is disquieting to note, however, that as the quality of healthcare is not at satisfactory level, many patients, who can afford it, are seeking treatment alternatives in other countries. Not only does this burden the nation's foreign exchange resources, customers seeking healthcare abroad have also been known to suffer collateral miseries that are associated with travel, accommodation, meals and related needs. For any major mishap necessitating a longer stay than originally planned, these inconveniences could easily be magnified several-fold (Andaleeb, 2000).

Discrepancies in the public health system, hence, influencing people irrespective of their affordability to seek healthcare at market systems even in foreign markets.

Firms and Price Setting

The market for healthcare is imperfect. There are significant entry barriers and few large firms control and set prices. Since the sellers enjoy some form of "protection" from others' entries into the market, they have the "liberty" to fix a higher mark-up when they decide their retail price. For instance, a few drug companies dominate the market. Hence, the health market functions as an oligopoly.

The vertical axis contains both the cost and price of healthcare and the horizontal axis measures the quantity of healthcare provided and demanded in the market (Figure 7.2). In an oligopolistic market, D represents the downward-sloping demand curve which is relatively elastic and MR represents the marginal revenue curve which is twice the slope of the demand curve. MC represents an upward sloping marginal cost curve that intersects the MR curve at Q_0 which is the profit-maximising point where firms provide products and hence the price is set at P_0. In an otherwise perfect market, the equilibrium would have been where the D curve intersects the MC curve. $MC=D$ is the competitive market price where the price is Pc and quantity is Qc intersecting at the equilibrium point E_1. In the oligopoly market structure, the firms eventually reduce the total output to profit-maximising Q_0 amount, exercise the market power, charge a spiralling price from Pc to Po and accumulate a huge amount of resource rent. The total rent accumulated by the sellers is $PoPcCE_2$. Therefore, the price is not set through bargaining or auctioning rather the oligopolies set the price level according to their market power. At the same time, these firms reduce the quantity from Qc to Q_0.

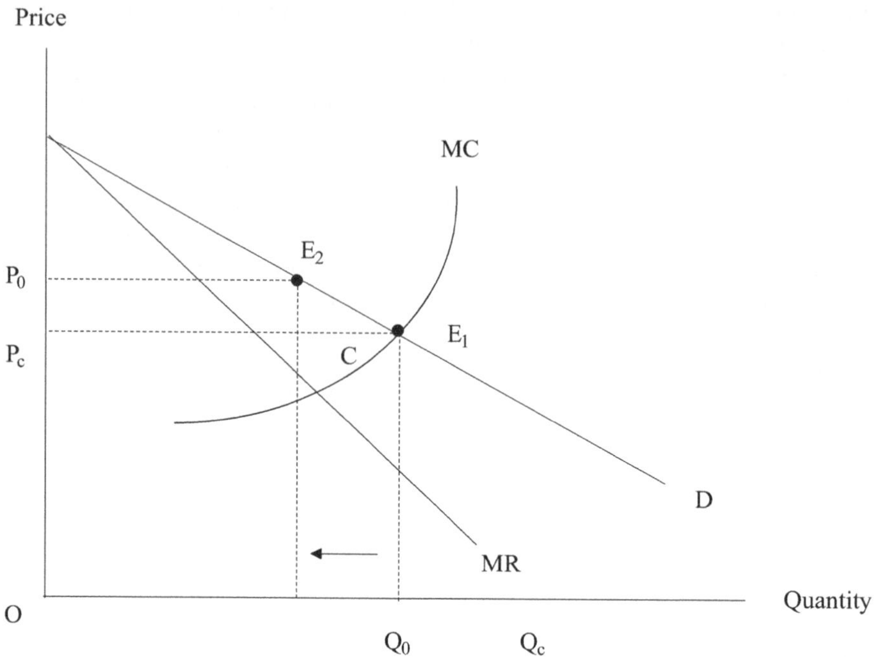

Figure 7.2 Oligopolistic health market structure

Source: Prepared by author

Here, health service price setting depends on market structure, administered pricing, cost-plus pricing and full-cost pricing. Suppose that

P=price setting
A=administered pricing
C=cost-plus pricing
F= full-cost pricing

Therefore,

$$P=f(A, C, F)$$

and

$$P \propto A \quad (1)$$
$$P \propto C \quad (2)$$
$$P \propto F \quad (3)$$

and

$$A \propto 1/R \quad (4)$$
$$C \propto 1/R \quad (5)$$
$$F \propto 1/R \quad (6)$$

Equations (*1*), (*2*) and (*3*) illustrate that price increases if A, C and F increase and price decreases if A, C and F decrease. Also, Equations (*4*), (*5*) and (*6*) clarify that A, C and F depend inversely on regulation R. So, it implies that the effective regulation in the market can reduce the price.

Market Provisioning and Universal Access

Market-provisioned health services hinder the possibility of universal access creating artificial scarcity and distorting price. Health is a basic human need. It is, therefore, a universal right. When healthcare is provided universally through public provisioning, everyone is supposed to get access to services. The market provisioning of health services considers it as a demand instead of a universal right. Such a conceptualisation of demand, referring to a consumer's desire to purchase goods and services and willingness to pay a price for a specific good or service leads to exclusion since everyone is not capable of paying for healthcare, despite the fact that every person requires access to healthcare services when need arises.

The horizontal axis displays the number of beneficiaries from healthcare and the vertical axis captures the price and individual benefit of healthcare. The concave curve depicts not only an inverse relationship but also an increasing trade-off between price and beneficiaries since the number of beneficiaries falls by the same margin as price increases. When price is zero, people will benefit from the free healthcare. High price is set by few firms as stated earlier. Those who have the ability to demand from the market at a set price can have access to healthcare. Market provision thus allows only N people to get access to the healthcare services as they are able to buy services from the market while others remain excluded (Figure 7.3). The market provisioning of healthcare services may impose negative consequences upon the economy, for example, in the forms of malnutrition and weak health conditions among the labour force, resulting in deprivation, poverty and inequality.

Suppose, in a society where population is divided into two categories: rich and poor. Moreover, assume that there is a particular price level for a particular healthcare service at a particular time which the poor cannot pay for anymore. Also, consider that

A = artificial scarcity and price distortion
B = price level beyond a particular level
R = rich
P = poor

Now consider the following truth table:

A	B	R	P	$R \cap P$
T	T	T	F	F
F	F	T	T	T

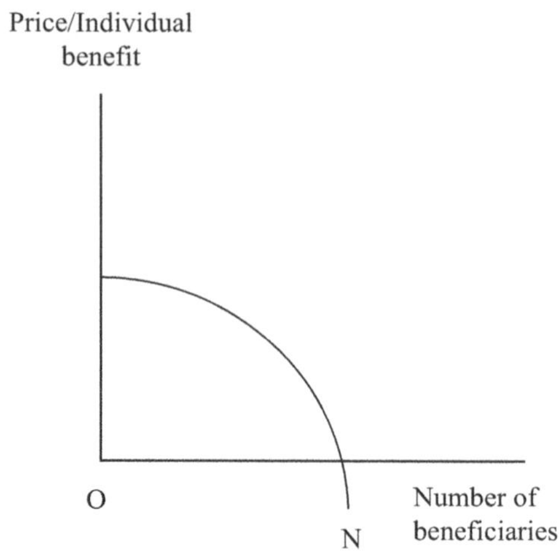

Figure 7.3 Market provisioning of health and exclusion

Source: Prepared by author

In the first row, when *A* is the case, the price level goes beyond that particular fixed level. So even though the rich can pay for services (the value of *R* is true), the poor cannot (the value of *P* is false). Therefore, when *A* is true, $R \cap P$ is false, implying that both the categories in that society cannot access services. In this scenario, the universal access to service does not occur.

In the second row, when *A* is false, price level stays under that particular fixed level (value of *B* is false). Therefore, the rich can pay for services (the value of *R* is true), so does the poor (the value of *P* is true). When *A* is false and $R \cap P$ is true, both the categories in that society have access to services, and the universal access is attained in this scenario.

The market provisioning creates an artificial scarcity and price distortion, and results in concentration of access to healthcare to a few. Universal access to the basic needs of human beings' health, one of the significant goals of Sustainable Development Goals (SDGs), is not ensured through market provisioning.

Universal Health Care (UHC) encompasses that people have access to needed quality healthcare services without any financial hardship. Certain developing countries such as Bangladesh have made some progress in health indicators. However, there is still inadequacy and disparities in access to services by various social groups. In this regard, financial barriers are a major concern. Such barriers arise when the cost of healthcare is met by an individual's regular income, irrespective of their capacities. Out-of-pocket (OOP) payments for accessing healthcare is one of the most regressive ways of financing healthcare and is responsible for pushing a substantial number of households into poverty annually in Bangladesh (Bangladesh Health Watch, 2011).

Equity in access to, and utilisation of, healthcare is an important goal for any health system and an essential prerequisite for achieving UHC for any country. The cases of Bangladesh, a developing country with out-of-pocket expenditure, and Japan, an advanced country with quality public provisioning, are taken as examples to investigate into the extent to which health benefits are distributed across socio-economic groups and how different types of providers contribute to (in)equity in health benefits. Health benefits from three types of formal providers are analysed (public, private and NGO providers), disaggregating into rural and urban populations of Bangladesh. Eventually, the distribution of benefits is compared to the distribution of healthcare needs (proxied by "self-reported illness and symptoms") across socio-economic groups of the country.

This scatter plot diagram exhibits the relationship between current health expenditure per capita and the inequality in life expectancy. There is high inequality in life expectancy, meaning population in the lower spectrum of income have lower life expectancy than those with higher income. Partly because the segment with greater income has access to better healthcare. Japan, on the other hand, records the lowest inequality in life expectancy, pointing towards that the government provision of healthcare is equitably distributed and accessible (Figure 7.4).

Country Spotlight: Accessibility Barriers in Bangladesh

Health services in Bangladesh have remained predominantly financed by households' out-of-pocket payments (OOPP). Direct payment for the purchase of

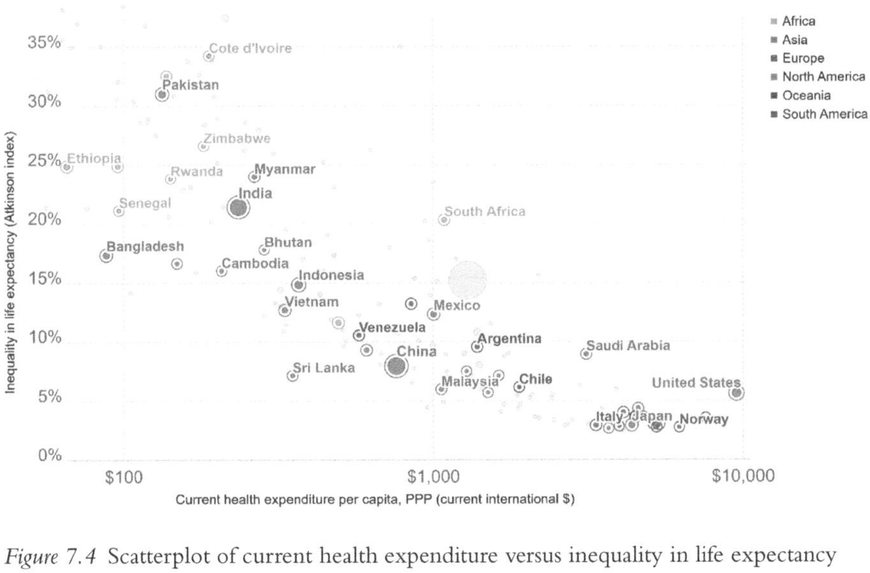

Figure 7.4 Scatterplot of current health expenditure versus inequality in life expectancy

Source: Our World in Data (2020)

pharmaceuticals and medical goods is the predominant contributor to OOPP, either through self-purchase or on the advice of a formal or informal healthcare provider, followed by the hospital cost and cost of medical diagnosis. OOPPs are mostly direct payments made at private sector and NGO facilities and to informal providers.

The growing reliance on OOPP leaves the population at risk. In 2016, at the national level, 85.42 per cent have reported that they met the medical expenses from their regular income, 13.35 per cent informed that such incurred from household savings while 2.03 per cent borrowed from friends and relatives. There exist variations with regard to means of financing medical expenditure for rural and urban patients. In the rural area, 79.08 per cent of the patients have spent from regular income, as against 85.42 per cent for the urban patients. In the rural area, 13.82 per cent of the patients have used household savings as against 11.37 per cent for urban patients. In rural areas, 2.35 per cent of the households have loaned from friends and relatives while such was 0.67 per cent for the urban households (BBS, 2010). The OOPP has remained the principal source of healthcare financing in Bangladesh, making 63.3 per cent of total healthcare expenditure.

Health cost, hence, can put households, especially the poor, into debt trap as many households tend to borrow money to meet the health expenditure. They have faced serious pains with healthcare financing and one in 10 households met with financial catastrophe while one in 20 non-poor households slided down under the poverty line due to healthcare costs (Islam et al., 2017). On average, the poor households have paid out about 11.0 per cent of their total household budget on healthcare and face a high incidence of financial hardship as a result of out-of-pocket healthcare payments.

When market provides healthcare, it depends on revenue collection and hence is more attentive to cost and profit (Table 7.5). It also provides service to people on the basis of demand which means people's affordability. In order to maximise profit, the private health sector charges high prices. This price is paid out of

Table 7.4 Sources of financing medical expenses

	National	*Rural*	*Urban*
From regular income	37.81	34.78	45.2
From household savings	28.28	26.56	32.47
Selling of household accessories	1.12	1.21	0.88
Selling of livestock	3.53	4.58	0.98
Selling of agricultural products/trees	1.16	1.56	0.18
Selling of permanent assets	1.52	1.9	0.6
Mortgaging land and assets	1.24	1.61	0.36
Borrowing from friends/relatives/office	12.1	12.7	10.63
Borrowing from money lender	2.49	2.73	1.89
Donated by friends and relatives	8.73	10.19	5.16
From other resources	2.03	2.18	1.67

Source: BBS (2019)

Table 7.5 The comparative evaluation of public and private provisioning

	Healthcare-provisioned by state	*Healthcare-provisioned by market*	*In Bangladesh*
Equity and access	Targets services for poor and vulnerable populations Attentive to geographic disparities	Individuals who can pay favoured; the poor and vulnerable excluded or ignored Services concentrated in population centres	Poor do not get quality services from public health and hence they look for costlier private healthcare Public health sector has extended up to Upazila level and below whereas private health sector is urban-centric as urban areas are populated and full of rich people
Customer orientation	Limited attention to customer convenience and comfort Indirect accountability for customer satisfaction	More attentive to customer convenience and comfort More direct accountability for customer satisfaction but may exclude poorest and sickest	Customer service in public health sector is not satisfactory at all, whereas, private health sector is very customer-oriented but poor cannot afford them or has to pay high cost which creates financial burden
Financing	Access to tax revenues Weak incentives to be cost-effective from sales or contracts conscious or cost-efficient	Dependent on revenue flows Attentive to cost and price	Public health sector is funded by government allocation which is very low, while, healthcare in market derives high profit from its revenue flows Healthcare and medicine are subsidised in public health sector whereas healthcare in market is attentive to cost and price since it is not subsidised

Source: Adapted from Preker and Harding (2003), World Bank

regular income of general people which is a financial burden for poor or low-income groups. The low public resources and profit maximisation nature of the private sector, hence, pushes the mass poor of Bangladesh into lack of access to healthcare or into financial crisis due to out-of-pocket payments or huge debt. The inadequacy of public funding and market intervention, hence, has become obstacle to access healthcare or quality healthcare for the poor in Bangladesh.

Health Expenditure and Economic Life

The level of healthcare spending is likely to have causal and consequential effects on both the level and distribution of health and the broader economy. Health is not simply a commodity like any other, and as a component of human potential, health is a crucial ingredient of economic growth and social development, entailing an acceptance of the need for an equitable distribution of, and access to, healthcare resources. The importance of health is to be strategised as an ingredient of socio-economic development, underscoring the necessity of equitable distribution of healthcare with adequate public expenditures for cumulative social well-being.

Suppose that

G = economic growth
H = healthy population
A = healthcare expenditure

$$dH/dt = \alpha A \quad (1)$$

$$dH/dt = \beta H \quad (2)$$

$$dG/dt = \beta H \quad (3)$$

with initial condition $A(0)>0,\ H(0)>0$.

where α= growth of healthcare expenditure
β= growth in the number of healthy population
Case 1: when $\alpha=0$

In Equation (*1*), the healthy population remains constant. As a result, in Equation (*2*), the growth of the number of healthy populations is zero. As a result, Equation (*3*) states that the growth remains as it was initially.

Case 2: when $\alpha>0$

In Equation (*1*), the healthy population increases. As a result, in Equation (*2*), the growth of the number of healthy populations also augments and in Equation (3) a positive growth in the economy is observed.

Case 3: when $\alpha<0$

In Equation (*1*), the healthy population decreases. As a result, in Equation (*2*), the growth of the number of healthy populations also declines. As a result, Equation (*3*) exhibits a negative growth in the economy.

Health expenditure has a positive impact on the health outcome, and such can, for example, be measured by life expectancy. Health expenditure by the government enhances the health infrastructure in a country, playing an active role in snowballing the life expectancy. Health expenditure and per capita health expenditure show significant positive impact on life expectancy in Bangladesh (Mahumud et al., 2013). Developed countries have shown a highly significant impact of expenditure on life expectancy as well. Sub-Saharan countries have also shown similar results (Novignon et al., 2012). Health expenditure also depicts a positive impact on under-five mortality rate (Bokhari et al., 2007).

This scatter plot diagram illustrates the relationship between current health expenditure per capita and the life expectancy at birth for several developed and developing countries (Figure 7.5). Japan ranks among the top-performing countries in this regard with high health expenditure and the highest life expectancy in the model. At the lower end of the spectrum, Bangladesh remains with one of the lowest health expenditures per capita in the model, along with Tanzania, Uganda and Pakistan, albeit with a higher life expectancy at birth than these countries. This incongruence points to the fact that because government expenditure on health is low, the high life expectancy may be the result of private healthcare provision. It may be implied that this dependence on private provision of healthcare is likely to be leading to health inequalities between those who can afford private healthcare and those who cannot. Wealthy people tend to seek healthcare abroad than the public hospitals because of the perceptions of poor quality and unreliable health services in public hospitals (Andaleeb, 2000). In particular, people were most dissatisfied with waiting time, cleanliness, privacy of treatment, and the standard of in-patient food. The healthcare system has barely gone through reforms since independence. As a result, patients dissatisfied with the poor healthcare services look for healthcare in foreign countries. This phenomenon has resulted in what is known as health tourism (Mahdy, 2009).

Without any alternative, the poor suffers the most as publicly funded primary health care services are plagued with absenteeism of service providers, lack of diagnostic facilities and essential drugs (Hasan, 2012). The shortage of doctors in rural Bangladesh is plaguing the obstetric reproductive healthcare services (Anwar et al., 2009). This must, however, be emphasised that the shortage or

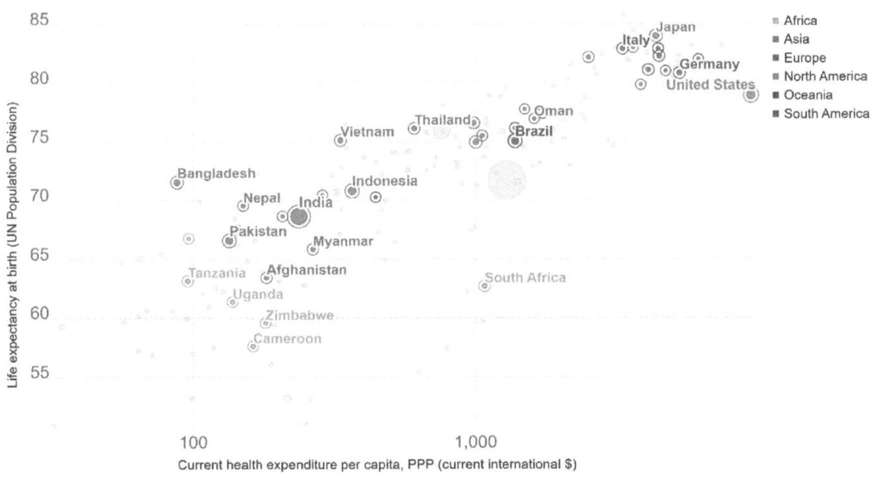

Figure 7.5 Scatterplot of current health expenditure versus life expectancy

Source: Prepared by author (Our World in Data, 2020)

unavailability of doctors or other health staff is not merely due to absolute manpower shortages. The doctors also remain busy with private practice at their private chambers, private clinics and local pharmacies.

In recent years, Bangladesh made noticeable progress in expanding healthcare facilities. From 1975 to 2007, public hospitals expanded from 131 to 670 and private beds increased from 15,452 to 33,818. Particularly, the availability of these facilities per person has improved. Additionally, from 1985 to 2009, the availability of hospital beds improved, from one bed for roughly 3,600 people to one bed for 1,900 people. Health workforce rapidly grew as well over time. The number of registered doctors rose from about 10,000 in 1980 to nearly 50,000 by 2009. This improved the availability of medical personnel per person consequently. The availability of doctors increased from one doctor for 6,600 persons in 1985 to 1,721 persons in 2018. Similarly, the availability of nurses also improved from one nurse for 15,000 persons to 2,427 persons. However, a significant structural change occurred when the private sector started playing an increasing role. The number of private hospitals/clinics expanded from about 150 in the early 1980s to over 2,200 at present; whereas, the number of public hospitals only increased from 510 to 647. Despite private clinics being small in size, the difference in the number of beds, compared to the number of hospitals, is insignificant. Currently, almost half of the hospital beds are accounted for by private clinics. It is necessary to ensure adequate availability of health services, as well as realise people's right to health. The services must be accessible and affordable for those in need, without prejudice.

Accessibility should be estimated in two dimensions – physical and economic. Physical accessibility to healthcare facilities upgraded greatly in the last 20 years. Bangladesh came under the Primary Health Care (PHC) services in 1990 with a mission to build one union sub-centre (USC) or health and family welfare centre (HFWC) in every union. Additionally, a health complex in every Thana (Upazila) and a general hospital or tertiary facility in every district (59). The health policy introduced in 1998 also considered community clinics at village levels. Although the healthcare system covers the entire population, physical accessibility has always been limited. The district towns are covered along with most of the Upazila headquarters (as of April 2009, 413 Upazilas out of 481 had a health complex). At the next level below, there were only about 1,300 Union Health and Family Welfare Centres for 4,403 unions, and out of 20,000 wards only about half had a community clinic.

Among all the categories of public health expenditure, child health expenditure (curative and preventive combined) was the most pro-poor – 54 per cent of all subsidies went to the poorer half of the population. This is the only category for which per capita subsidy is higher for the poor, even in urban areas. Subsidy per capita is the highest for the poorest quintile and declines monotonically for richer quintiles. However, this does not imply that the poor received higher subsidies per child. Regardless of the amount of subsidy received by a poor child, it is no mean achievement in a country where the richer segment captures the lion's share of most subsidies.

The equality achieved is mainly due to rapid expansion of immunisation services by the government in the last two decades. They are its main provider and hold over 90 per cent of all immunisations. Hence, there is no difference in the access of the poor and the non-poor – as measured by whether a child received at least one major vaccine. However, a difference exists as to whether a child has received all. The ratio of children receiving all vaccines (as in 2007) is 88 per cent for the non-poor and 80 per cent for the poor. The only other service the poor had equal access to is ante-natal maternity care. In 2000, nearly 90 per cent of the pregnant women, who were poor, attended government ante-natal facilities at least once, as compared to the non-poor which were around 79 per cent. In contrast to urban areas, 88 per cent are among the poor and 65 per cent are among the rich.

Poor people's access to the public's ante-natal care and immunisation services was roughly equivalent to that of the rich. This goes for attending delivery and postnatal care, along with all kinds of curative services. Government's role in providing curative services is limited; hence whatever is provided goes unfairly to the non-poor. Only 1.2 per cent of the poor availed government facilities for curative care, the month prior to the 2000 Household Income and Expenditure Survey, compared to the non-poor which were 2.3 per cent (World Bank 2003).

Unfortunately, the gap between the rich and the poor is widening with time. Successive rounds of the Bangladesh Health and Demographic Survey reveal that the proportion of children in the poorest quintile covered by medical treatment either has remained virtually unchanged or has gone down completely in three major childhood diseases – viz. fever, diarrhoea and acute respiratory infection (ARI) diseases. Only in the case of diarrhoea, the problem is partially mitigated by the increased coverage of Oral Rehydration Therapy (ORT). For others, there is no such relieving factor. By contrast, for the richest quintile, medical treatment coverage expanded in absolute terms for all. Inequity is rising towards access to maternal care too. For example, the poorer women's access to a medically trained person for ante-natal care, delivery assistance and postnatal care are much lower than richer females.

For women and children, the growing inequality can be observed in private facilities as the private sector is already biased towards the rich. Although the expansion of health facilities in Bangladesh is due to the private sector's development, it is evident that the curative healthcare system has failed to promote equitable fulfilment of the right to health.

Healthcare provision in the private sector is inequitable; which is understandable as the richer segment would only be able to access services of the private sector. The perspective of the right to health has to consider whether public health facilities can provide a fair substitute, which the poor can also benefit from. Unfortunately, the public sector is unable to offer such an alternative yet; which acts as a major impediment in Bangladesh.

Financial hardship for the poor due to health expenditure increases when public facilities are inadequate. Out-of-pocket payment increases when the households do not get access to subsidised public health services. Health financing is underfunded in Bangladesh; the government spends less than one per cent of gross domestic product (GDP) on health which is the lowest among South Asian countries (Zaidi et al., 2017). The country is simultaneously experiencing a double burden of diseases, low health service coverage, and a lack of financial risk protection mechanism in its health system.

The dual healthcare system of public and private health services coexists in three main levels – primary, secondary and tertiary levels – with a degree of divergence based on the level of profit (MOHFW, 2012). The public sector is largely used for outpatient, inpatient and preventive care while the private sector serves mainly in terms of outpatient and inpatient curative care. The public primary, secondary and tertiary care are provided through various types of health facilities such as general hospitals, specialised hospitals and health clinics. Public health services are heavily subsidised by the government. For instance, primary care services at health clinics are delivered almost free of charge, with each patient being charged a nominal fee of 13 BDT (equivalent to 0.17 USD in 2011) for a single outpatient visit (Bangladesh Health Watch, 2012). Private health providers mainly focus on curative services including general practitioner clinics, medical centres and private hospitals, with many folded charges compared to the public sector. The country has neither a national health insurance scheme nor a well-developed private insurance market unlike many countries with high concentration of private facilities. There are a number of small-scale NGO-based community insurance schemes, often operating in conjunction with micro-financing schemes, but these cover less than one per cent of the total population and target mainly poor populations (WHO, 2011). Thus, the private sector mostly remains within the reach of the rich. The proportion of health spending of the poor that goes to the private sector is higher than that among the rich.

It is also striking to note that outpatient visits to the pharmacy/drug seller make up for the largest share of outpatient visits for both the poor and the non-poor. Only 9 per cent of the outpatient visits of the poor are delivered in public facilities (Figure 7.6). This percentage is even lower than the one observed for the non-poor.

Universal access again faces hindrance in the country due to spatial disparity. Average medical expense per patient in Bangladesh in 2010, at an aggregate level, in the preceding 30 days was 397 BDT. This was 400 BDT in the rural area and 386 BDT in the urban area. In the rural area, the cost incurred per male patient was 421 BDT as against 381 BDT for female. On the other hand, in the urban area, on an average a male patient spent 349 BDT compared to 415 BDT by a female. In all areas, the expenditure for hospitals/clinics was the highest. At the national level, an average of 1,728 BDT was incurred as hospital/clinic fee. There also exist rural–urban variations in terms of distance and means of transportations to access health service. Among the rural patients, 52.87 per cent have to walk to the healthcare facilities. During

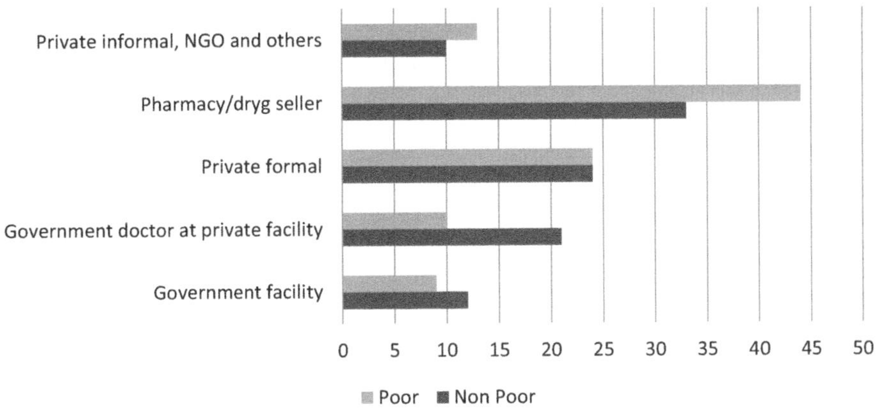

Figure 7.6 Distribution of curative visits by type of provider, for the poor and non-poor

Source: Cited in World Bank (2005)

the survey, 14.43 per cent of the rural patients used rickshaws or vans, a small, three-wheeled cycle, pulled by one person, while 10.53 per cent went by auto-rickshaws, a motorised three wheeler hired in the manner of a taxi. In urban areas, 45.12 per cent walked to the facility on foot, followed by rickshaws by 31.40 per cent and rickshaw vans by 8.48 per cent. In rural areas, the highest time spent by the patients to get to the healthcare provider was 279 minutes travelling via engine boat, which is powered by a diesel engine used for agriculture (BBS, 2010). These variations illustrate a significant degree of obstruction faced by rural households in accessing health services more than urban households.

The country's human resources for health are at crisis level. Uneven distribution of the health workforce, and issues of retention and overwork, will require innovations in capacity building, incentives and task shifting. The lack of effective regulatory systems also contributes to poor quality services, with a large informal sector catering to the poorest in society. As of 2020, there were only around five physicians and three nurses per 10,000 populations (Ahmed, Hossain et al., 2011), with particular shortages in hard-to-reach areas (Government of Bangladesh, 2012). Even with the growth in training institutions, absolute shortages of health workers continue. The deficiencies stem from low salaries (the entry-level salary is inadequate for a family of 5, a common family size), inadequate supply of human resources for health (HRH), inordinately slow recruitment, inappropriate skill-mix and difficulty in staff retention, particularly in remote areas (El-Saharty et al., 2015).

Since a large number of people in Bangladesh live under the poverty line and fall into the category of low-income or low-middle-income group,

Table 7.6 Proportion of nursing personnel and medical doctors per 10,000 population

Countries	*Nursing and midwifery personnel (per 10,000 population)*	*Medical doctors (per 10,000 population)*
Australia	125.508	35.672
Bangladesh	3.163	4.974
Burundi	8.526	0.500
China	26.621	18.647
Congo	7.462	
Cuba	77.286	79.541
Germany	132.352	41.944
India	21.079	7.590
Japan	119.502	24.115
Norway	181.559	26.983
South Korea	71.203	23.037
Senegal	3.127	0.711
Tanzania	5.843	0.140
Uganda	14.686	0.954
United Kingdom	82.245	27.563
United States	145.480	25.881

Source: WHO (2020)

the health cost is unbearable with their meagre regular income. And the availability of government provisioning and the quality of public healthcare services are not satisfactory. The rich can seek better healthcare in private hospitals or in any foreign country. Several community initiatives for ensuring low-cost services exist, while a number of private insurance companies offer individual and group insurance to private persons and corporate clients. These health insurance initiatives cover a very small share of the total population (Ahmed et al., 2016), leaving the majority out of the system, with high dependence on out-of-pocket expenditure and leaving the majority without access to quality healthcare, marginalising and excluding the poor. The comparative analysis of health provisioning by state and private sector needs to be understood in the backdrop of ensuring universal and affordable access to healthcare.

Summary

The chapter analyses access to quality care, health-seeking behaviour, price setting, market provisioning etc. to ascertain the conditions for transformation. The journey towards universal health care is troubled with political challenges, including the legacies of inherited health systems, international policy regimes and global political economy. The demand side of healthcare comprises of individual and social healthcare seeking behaviours. The supply-side entails the provisioning of healthcare by different entities, with predominance of private sector, highlighting the differences in outcomes in terms of equity and access, orientation and financing. The market provisioning caters to individuals who can afford to pay for the services, marginalising those without adequate disposable incomes and living in peripheral regions. The ground realities warrant for transformational changes through universal healthcare.

References

Ahmed, S., Hoque, M.E., Sarker, A.R., Sultana, M., Islam, Z., Gazi, R., et al. (2016). Willingness-to-pay for community-based health insurance among informal workers in urban Bangladesh. *PLoS ONE*, 11(2), e0148211. https://doi.org/10.1371/journal.pone.0148211

Ahmed, S.M., Hossain, M.A., RajaChowdhury, A.M., and Bhuiya, A.U. (2011). The health workforce crisis in Bangladesh: Shortage, inappropriate skill-mix and inequitable distribution. *Human Resources for Health*, 9(1), pp. 1–7.

Al Mahdy, H. (2009). Reforming the Bangladesh healthcare system. *International Journal of Health Care Quality Assurance*, 22(4), pp. 411–416.

Andaleeb, S.S. (2000). Public and private hospitals in Bangladesh: Service quality and predictors of hospital choice. *Health Policy and Planning*, 15(1), pp. 95–102.

Anwar, I., Kalim, N., and Koblinsky, M. (2009). Quality of obstetric care in public-sector facilities and constraints to implementing emergency obstetric care services: Evidence from high-and low-performing districts of Bangladesh. *Journal of Health, Population, and Nutrition*, 27(2), p. 139.

Bangladesh Health Watch (2012). *Bangladesh Health Watch Report 2011: Moving Towards Universal Health Coverage*. Retrieved March 22, 2022, from http://dspace.bracu.ac.bd/xmlui/bitstream/handle/10361/2897/BHW_Report_2011.pdf?sequence=1&isAllowed=y

BBS. (2010). *Household income and expenditure survey 2010*. Dhaka: BBS.

BBS. (2014). *Bangladesh demographic and health survey, 2014*. Dhaka: BBS.

BBS. (2019). *Household income and expenditure survey 2016*. Dhaka: BBS.

Bokhari, F.A., Gai, Y., and Gottret, P. (2007). Government health expenditures and health outcomes. *Health Economics*, 16(3), pp. 257–273.

El-Saharty, S., Sparkes, S.P., Barroy, H., Ahsan, K.Z., and Ahmed, S.M. (2015). *The path to universal health coverage in Bangladesh: Bridging the gap of human resources for health*. Washington, DC: World Bank. Retrieved from https://openknowledge.worldbank.org/handle/10986/21633.

Ghani, A. (1990). *Introduction to pharmacognosy*. Nigeria: Ahmadu Bello University Press Ltd.

Government of Bangladesh. (2012). Expanding social protection for health: Towards universal coverage health care financing strategy 2012–2032. *Health Economics Unit (HEU), Ministry of Health and Family Welfare (MOHFW)*. Dhaka. Retrieved December 1, 2021, from Socialprotection.gov.bd website https://socialprotection.gov.bd/en/2014/03/22/expanding-social-protection-for-health-towards-universal-coverage/

Hasan, M. (2012). Quality of primary health care services in rural Bangladesh: Patients' perspectives. *OIDA International Journal of Sustainable Development*, 3(8), pp. 69–78.

Huque, R., Rabbani, A., and Hamid, S. (2011). *Bangladesh Health Watch Report 2011*. Dhaka: BRAC. Retrieved from https://doi.org/10.13140/RG.2.1.4520.7522

Islam, M.R., Rahman, M.S., Islam, Z., Nurs, C.Z.B., Sultana, P., and Rahman, M.M. (2017). Inequalities in financial risk protection in Bangladesh: An assessment of universal health coverage. *International Journal for Equity in Health*, 16, p. 59. https://doi.org/10.1186/s12939-017-0556-4.

Mahmud et. Al. (2013). Impact of life expectancy on economics growth and health care expenditures in Bangladesh. *Universal journal of public health*. 1(4), pp.180–186.

MOHFW. (2012). *Expanding social protection for health: Towards universal coverage – health care financing strategy 2012–2032*. Dhaka: Health Economics Unit, Ministry of Health and Family Welfare.

Novignon, J., Olakojo, S.A., and Nonvignon, J. (2012). The effects of public and private health care expenditure on health status in Sub-Saharan Africa: New evidence from panel data analysis. *Health Economics Review*, 2(1), pp. 1–8.

Our World In Data. (2020). *Data dashboard*. Our World In Data.

Preker, A.S., and Harding, A. (2003). Innovations in health service delivery: The corporatization of public hospitals. Washington, DC: World Bank. Retrieved from https://openknowledge.worldbank.org/handle/10986/15145

WHO. (2011). *World health statistics 2011*. Geneva, Switzerland: WHO.

WHO. (2020). *The global health observatory*. Geneva, Switzerland: WHO.

World Bank (2005). *NGO Contracting Evaluation for the HNP Sector in Bangladesh Evidence and Policy Options*. Retrieved March 22, 2022, from https://documents1.worldbank.org/curated/en/654651468206957854/pdf/37838.pdf

Zaidi, S., Saligram, P., Ahmed, S., Sonderp, E., and Sheikh, K. (2017). Expanding access to healthcare in South Asia. *BMJ*, 357(j1645), pp. 1–4.

8 Institutions and Transformation of Healthcare in Developing Countries

Introduction

The state and nature of institutions – formal and informal – provide a nuanced understanding of the healthcare sector in order to transform from its current fragile state in developing countries, particularly exposed by COVID-19. The public goods provision failure in health due to underfunding originates from a misconstrued ideology that market is the organising principle and society is equivalent to market. Rather, pointing out that the market is subordinate to social, political and cultural norms, the chapter carves out a pathway for use value-generating public provisioning in healthcare. This necessitates a stakeholder mapping to exhibit how the power relations – from above, lateral or from below – influence the preferences in allocation of resources in healthcare sector, budgetary policies and public-oriented regulations for transformation since composition and distribution of power determine allocation, and power associated with vertical and horizontal collusions may result in primitive accumulation and discriminatory policies.

Healthcare is unlike other social or public services, and the provision of universal health care (UHC) is complex and varies between countries, even between those with institutional comparisons. Therefore, there is no one-size-fits-all approach to the provision of universal health care across countries, but is rather dependent on the institutional infrastructure and environment, along with the state of public society and human sociality in the particular country. This calls for a holistic view of society through a multi, inter, trans-disciplinary enquiry, including, amongst others, economics, management, sociology and psychology. However, the mainstream approach to healthcare provision is still prevalent, underwritten by rational choice theories that reverberate with the neoclassical assumption of rational decisions made by health-seekers. The neoclassical approach or neoliberalism has influenced governments around the world to adopt market centric healthcare provision. Theories of rationality and agency have also influenced the recent incarnations, namely the public choice theories and new institutional economics for designing structures within and between organisations.

DOI: 10.4324/9781003284222-11

On the other hand, the accumulation and distribution of healthcare resources depend greatly on the political settlement, power and state of public society involved in the decision-making process. Political settlement is understood here as the balance of power and institutions that underlies the political order (Di John and Putzel, 2009; Khan, 2010; Laws and Leftwich, 2014). Political settlement in a country determines the ability of the state to implement universal health care effectively.

Declaration from the Alma Ata conference in 1978 sets the foundation stone for universal health care. The conference underscores the importance of public health as a driver of economic and social development and rests responsibility of the health of the general populace on governments. The World Health Organization has acknowledged that implementation of UHC to an extent is political.

> *All countries can do more to raise funds for health or to diversify their sources of funding, to reduce the reliance on direct payments by promoting prepayment and pooling, and to use funds more efficiently and equitably, provided the political will exists*
>
> (Etienne et al., 2010).

The effective implementation of UHC involves "reframing the debate, identifying and creating political opportunities, and mobilising resources" as "adopting UHC is primarily a political rather than a technical issue" (Stuckler et al., 2010). The redistribution of health resources to implement UHC reforms inevitably requires political trade-offs, conflicts and negotiations (Fox and Reich, 2015). Similarly, Bump (2010) argues that UHC is "intensely political" because it involves "a renegotiation of the social contract and changes who gets what and who bears financial responsibility".

In particular, in moving towards UHC, questions arise over how to compel individuals, particularly wealthier individuals to contribute to shared health financing pools when it may run contrary to their individual interests to do so (Reich, 2015) as poorer population have less political power to influence policies (Etienne et al., 2010).

Stability and Healthcare Provision

Making progress towards UHC means engaging with deeply political questions. First, the reduction in the share of out-of-pocket (OOP) expenditure has been possible due to the government's capacity to raise revenue (Fan and Savedoff, 2014). Government's capacity to augment the domestic resource mobilisation, including policy decisions pertaining to tax structure, is ultimately a political decision (Besley and Persson, 2013). Second, pooled funding arrangements like insurance schemes or tax-funded publicly provided care redistribute healthcare resources from the healthy to the sick and from the rich to the poor. Introducing mechanisms that involve taxes is a function of political settlement and will invariably be resisted by particular interest groups (Etienne et al., 2010). Third, improving the standards of healthcare and service delivery is another political task (Council et al., 2013). Finally, weak institutions, poor infrastructure, deep-seated relations of patronage and rent-seeking in developing countries act as a barrier to health reform and implementation of UHC (Fox and Reich, 2015).

Four variables, assumed here, influence policy at each of the four phases: interests, institutions, ideas and ideology. In order for UHC reform to make it onto the national policy agenda, a number of factors need to assimilate together at the appropriate moment and context, representing "a convergence of an ongoing problem with a political window (occasioned by political and economic transitions) and an available policy solution" (Bump, 2010). The countries that have made substantive progress towards UHC have done so through "organic, domestic processes, which necessarily reflect local historical, cultural and institutional legacies. The elevation of health reform to the national political agenda clearly depends on the preferences of governments for health improvement as opposed to other activities" (Participants at the Bellagio Workshop on Political Economy of Global Health, 2015). The prevailing political ideology in a country also affects the degree to which the private rather than the public sector is used as the vehicle for health financing and service delivery (Fox and Reich, 2015).

The presence of democratic institutions appears to have some bearing on the political dynamics surrounding UHC reform. For example, the experiences of Germany, the UK and South Korea all bear out the observation that democratic pressure on policymakers can be an important factor in determining the allocation of tax resources for public health (Stuckler et al., 2010). It is also argued that democratisation does not necessarily lead to greater probability of expanded health coverage through popular pressure from newly enfranchised voters based on the experience of health reform in Mexico, Korea and Taiwan since health reforms are often preceded by a transition to democracy, and the actual expansion of UHC is typically led by elites and politicians rather than mass demands (Fox and Reich, 2015).

Political settlement analysis (PSA) is a relatively recent political economy approach to the study of UHC. At the heart of PSA is the idea that a society's institutional structure and the policies that flow from it reflect the interests of powerful groups in society, echoing the insights of classical political economists and early twentieth-century elite theorists, including Marx, Mosca, Pareto and Michels. There is also an explicit focus on the role of economic rents in securing the conditions for political stability. In other words, political settlements are formed and peace reigns when a society's institutions distribute rents in a way that is acceptable to powerful groups. Certain political settlements may be characterised by a common understanding of the rules of the game, including bargaining, manoeuvring and negotiation (Laws, 2012). Such takes place not just among elites but also between elites and their followers in wider society.

Composition and distribution of power determine allocation of resources in the health sector, budgetary policies and regulations. Concentration of power may result in confiscation of resources by a few and poor health outcome while distribution of power amongst the median voters may ensure high-quality provisioning of healthcare (Figure 8.1).

Allocation of budgetary resources for the healthcare sector is subject to a specific type of political settlement and power relationship with the in-built human trait of that society. This calls for exploring the interrelationship of political institutions and powerful agents within the whole society. The persistence of centralised power structure in the postcolonial developing countries has led to concentration of power to a few. Thus system of accumulation in developing countries is principally primitive in nature. Such accumulation is pervasive, particularly in cases of accessing, distributing as well as controlling over resources and provisioning of subsidies from resources of state. The biases created in favour of the rich and powerful could be somehow lessened by giving the poor access to such resources through the regulatory mechanisms. Absence of dynamic regulatory regimes and weak enforcement capacities reduce the poor's access to the existing resources. Hence, poverty is reproduced or the condition becomes more precarious. Due to the lack of coherence and/or complementaries in formulation of policies and implementation, bringing every segment of society under decent healthcare services thereof becomes complex.

Suppose

X= allocation of resources
Y= distribution power
Z= ACTIVE citizenship

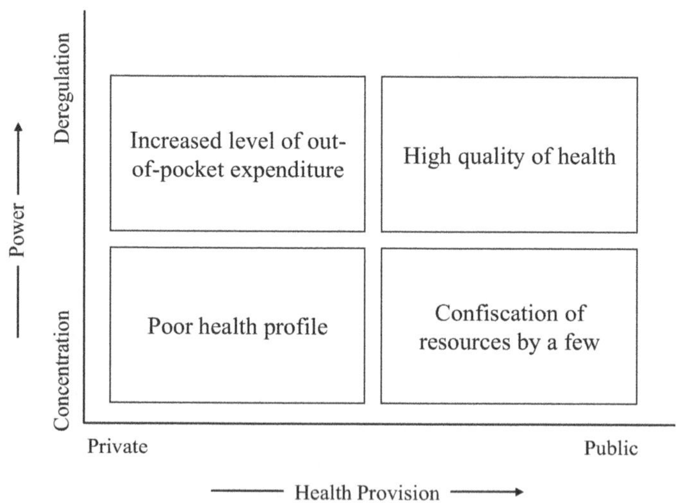

Figure 8.1 Game theory matrix

Source: Prepared by author

Here in a particular society, the allocation of resources will depend on distribution of power, that is, $X=f(Y)$. And distribution of power totally depends on active citizenship.

$$dL/dP=\delta P \tag{1}$$

Here,

δ = cooperativeness of that society
C = number of people with intention to cooperate in that society
L = power
P = population of that society

Equation (*1*) implies that change of power with respect to people or among people depend on the rate of cooperativeness among the people. In other words, the allocation of resources is dependent on cooperative behaviour of the people of the society which is otherwise demonstrated through active citizenship, a means to hold power to account.

Health is regarded as a fundamental human right and the government is bound by the constitution to provide healthcare to all segments of the population. Yet, the reality is far from the promises. For instance, Bangladesh on an average spends 3.5 per cent of the GDP in the health sector against the five per cent threshold suggested by the WHO. As a result, the out-of-pocket expenditure has been rising in the country and currently is 67 per cent (WHO, 2019). The health insurance is still miniscule in the country and so the public has to bear such a huge burden. In order to achieve and sustain UHC, Bangladesh has no alternative but to significantly increase public funding for the health system, simultaneously promoting equity and adhering to implementational effectiveness.

Transformability and Healthcare

In China, the central government is responsible for providing healthcare facilities. The main principle is every person must be entitled to healthcare services. Health authorities such as "National Health and Family Planning Commission and Local health and Family Planning Commission" have primary responsibility in organising and delivering healthcare services. It went through a cycle. With the takeover by the new regime in 1949, the health sector radically changed to all public from the most private services in the collective era, followed by a transition toward more private financing and delivery of health care in the post reform era in 1990s. Later, China undertook a reform in its healthcare system. The New Rural Cooperative Medical Care System (NRCMCS) was introduced in 2005 to provide health services to the poor people of China at a low cost. In China, the annual per capita health service cost is 50 Yuan per person which is about seven USD. Of the 50 Yuan, 20 Yuan is paid by the central government, 20 Yuan by the provincial government and the rest 10 Yuan is paid by the patient as of 2007. The service has covered 80 per cent of the total rural population of China. The coverage by the government depends on the location and the quality of service; if a patient takes service from rural clinics, 70–80 per cent cost is paid for by the government while 60 per cent of cost is provided if he or she goes to the urban clinics. If one chooses to access services from specialist doctors, 40 per cent cost is covered. In 2013, China had financed 5.6 per cent of its GDP on health with 30 per cent financed by local government and 36 per cent by publicly financed health insurance (Mossialos et al., 2015). The government versus private expenditure in China shows that the government spends almost 56 per cent of the total cost for healthcare and the rest 44 per cent comes from the private sector.

In Germany, health insurance is mandatory for all permanent citizens either through the statutory health insurance system (HIS) or by substitute private health insurance. The price of statutory health insurance depends on an individual's income, not his and her condition of health. Most of the university hospitals are state-owned, municipalities also play a role in providing healthcare. In 2013, total health expenditure was11.5 per cent of GDP among which 73 per cent was done through the public and 58 per cent was done through HIS. Sickness fund is compulsory for all the employees. Employees with a higher-income range may choose to be enrolled in private health insurance (PHI) or may voluntarily stay in HIS. In 2014, 8.8 million people were covered by substitutive private healthcare. HIS covers preventive services, inpatient and outpatient care in hospitals, mental healthcare, dental care, physical therapy etc. Out-of-pocket spending was calculated to be 13.6 per cent in 2013 (Mossialos et al., 2015). The government versus private expenditure in Germany shows that the government spends almost 77 per cent of the total cost for health.

In the UK, the state is responsible to provide healthcare services to all the people free of cost without any discrimination through *National Health Service* (NHS). In 2013, the UK spent 8.8 per cent of its GDP on health. In 2012, 10.9 per cent of the UK population opted voluntarily for private healthcare. The NHS mostly provides all forms of healthcare, including preventive, inpatient and outpatient services, immunisation services (Mossialos et al., 2015). The government spends almost 83 per cent of the total cost of healthcare, making it one of the highest in the world.

Sustainability and Health Shocks

COVID-19 points out public goods provision failure in health, social security etc. because of underfunding in use value-generating public provisioning. On the contrary, capital or exchange value-generating sectors were prioritised. The use-value producing public goods is indispensable for augmenting capabilities of citizens to transform economic structure, political settlement and organisation of society. For transformative changes, fulfilling the basic needs of citizens must be the foundation of the policy framework in any state which cares for legitimacy (Figure 8.2).

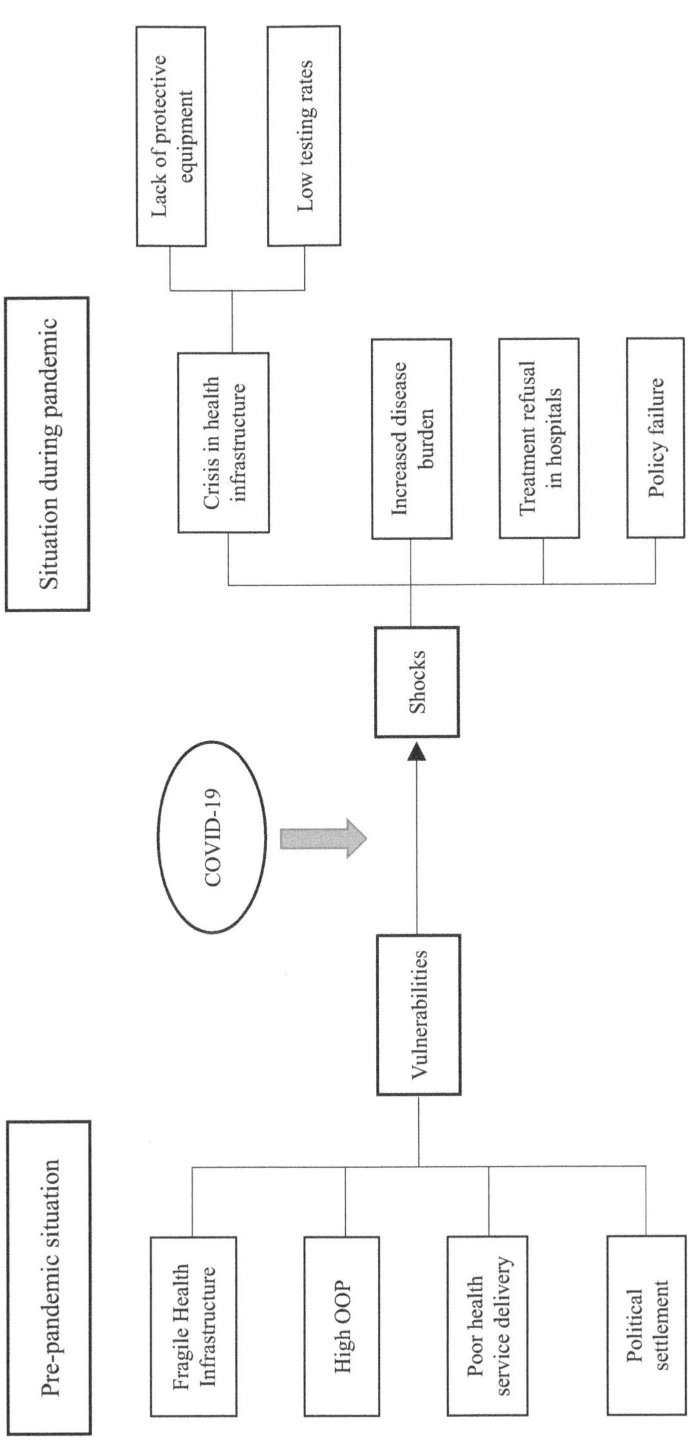

Figure 8.2 COVID-19 related shocks

Source: Prepared by author

Healthcare sector is in the state of peril long before the advent of the global pandemic because of trivial budget allocation, inadequate equipment, infrastructural deficiency, low-quality service and high out-of-pocket expenditure in most of the developing countries. The underlying fragilities in the health sector have been further exacerbated by the Coronavirus crisis. It has indeed revealed the feebleness of the infrastructure and intensified the ills in magnitude, worsening the sufferings of the citizens.

The pandemic has aggravated with it a worsened disease burden. Since the onset of the contagion, both public and private hospitals have been encountering an influx of both confirmed and suspected cases of the virus. A false binary of admitting patients with COVID-19 symptoms opposed to protecting existing patients with non-communicable diseases had also led to numerous cases of treatment refusals by hospitals resulting in great agony for the citizens. As the contagion magnified to community transmission, hospitals and healthcare facilities have offered treatments only minimally to non-infectious diseases, as most of their resources were directed towards COVID-19 patients, losing functioning of all forms of treatments.

The tendency to refuse treatments on part of hospital staff may be attributed to a lack of overall readiness to deal with the crisis brought on by a pandemic. Hospital personnel lacked protective gear for personal safety, adequate isolation units for keeping infectious patients separate from other patients with non-communicable diseases, adequate intensive care units, ventilators or even oxygen cylinders required for COVID-19 patients. The risks posed to frontline personnel and other patients who were immune-compromised far outweighed the hospital's responsibility in admitting a critical patient in several instances. The delay in testing and reports for the virus, due to a shortage of testing kits and testing labs, has only intensified the distress, as hospitals had been restricting the admission of patients without a COVID-19 clearance.

Poor quality of treatment and care in public hospitals for COVID-19 patients has been a major deterrent in health-seeking behaviour, pushing more people towards private healthcare, which still remains largely unaffordable, and hence inaccessible, leaving the low-income population in the lurch.

A peculiar change in health-seeking behaviour has emerged out of the depths of unpreparedness, dysfunction and chaos in the healthcare sector during the pandemic. Hospitals are viewed as the epicentre of the contagion by most citizens. The relative lack of preparedness, the inefficacy in successfully containing the infection through the use of disinfection and social distancing, and the anxieties owing to the lack of care in isolation units have in reality drifted people away from seeking healthcare at hospitals unless in an emergency. There have been reports of entire isolation centres lying empty in public hospitals as citizens are keeping away at will in fear of getting infected, poor treatment and anxieties of staying isolated.

A false binary has been construed through the policy choices of the government that puts people's lives and livelihoods at opposite ends of the balance. The health concerns and following non-pharmacological interventions affect different groups with different levels of intensity, owing to the existent inequalities of income, opportunities and access. Simultaneously, it has the potential to affect different sectors of the economy differently, discriminating between physically interactive and physically disjointed sectors. The non-pharmacological intervention in curbing the contagion was ordained in the form of a general holiday, or otherwise understood as a rather relaxed form of state lockdown. Due to its nature, state directives of self-isolation could not be reinforced strictly on the citizens, and the gradual but premature reopening of economic activities showcased the preferred intent of saving livelihoods over lives.

It is conspicuous that health management is not adequately balanced between the lower rungs in the infrastructure and the ones above them, that is, although a degree of primary care has been there, the higher tiers of healthcare remained largely unaddressed.

The complexities encircling the healthcare sector, the most crucial sector in battling the pandemic, are not rooted in the issues of costs, but also in fragilities of infrastructure. One of the most typical difficulties often encountered by the average citizen when seeking healthcare is that doctor's consultations are felt to be short and inadequate. A leading cause behind this is that the doctor–patient ratio in comparison to the population. As a result, the healthcare-seeking behaviour is moulded in a pattern where patients often have to opt for other, non-traditional, informal sources of treatment of ailments, such as consulting pharmacists, technicians of dispensaries or compounders. Another significant statistic is that the percentage of seeing a kabiraj/hakim/ayurvedic is higher than seeking treatment from NGO health workers or doctors. The meagre coverage of healthcare expenditure in turn worsens the cost burden for the new poor population and contributes to further pauperisation. At the same time, healthcare structure has plunged in heavy disease burden, worsened by the second and third waves. Doctors, nurses and technicians are dealing with the new infection cases whereas a significant part of non-communicable diseases has remained unattended. This discrepancy has already taken a drastic shape due to unavailability of proper treatment for non-communicable diseases. Most of the hospitals are not treating patients suffering from non-infectious diseases. As a result, it increases the rate of morbidity and mortality not only from COVID cases but also from non-communicable diseases.

Moreover, processes related to the diagnosis of sickness are marred with cumbersome and expensive practices, further diverting the healthcare-seeking behaviour of citizens. These complexities arise due to collusion among healthcare providers that exploit the absence of public-provisioned diagnostic services that cover the needs of the population as a whole. Adding to it, the public procurement of medical equipment is a process that is fraught with embezzlement, overvaluation of prices and influence peddling by power-exercising networks. These practices have led to inadequate medical equipment, diminishing the capacity to manage clinical conditions, made more evident during the surge of the pandemic. Simultaneously, the incapacity of a healthcare provider at one level due to insufficient resources cannot be compensated by another provider at a higher level because the infrastructure does not entail a referral system.

Policy Roadmap

Developing countries are in need of a radical transformation in the healthcare sector, especially after the global pandemic that has dealt an unequal blow to these countries. The fragility of the healthcare sector in developing countries has been exposed, at least in four key areas of the healthcare sector: infrastructure, financing, social care and institutions (Figure 8.3). In all these, developing countries need an overhauling to ensure equal access and affordability to healthcare.

The first order of business for developing countries is to establish universal health care that would ensure access to healthcare to the last mile. Rebuilding the health infrastructure can start from integrating the current health systems which include formal and informal healthcare. Improving the quality of healthcare faces impediments due to the lack of healthcare professionals and physical infrastructure. The margin between developed and developing countries in terms of infrastructure is wide. It cannot be reduced in a small period of time. The developing countries also do not have the capacity to absorb a sudden injection of infrastructure. Hence, the infrastructure can be widened over the long run. Developed countries have a monopoly on healthcare research and technology like medicines and vaccines. This has become widely visible during the pandemic. As a result, there is a disparity among two sets of countries. More than ever, developing research and innovation are required to tackle any future pandemics.

Healthcare spending in developing countries has been miniscule compared to developed countries and is the primary cause of the dilapidated healthcare sector. There is no alternative to increasing healthcare spending. The WHO has set the standard of five per cent of GDP to be spent on healthcare, at the minimum. In reality, the actual spending is way less in developing countries. For instance, Bangladesh spends less than one per cent of its GDP on healthcare. Health insurance can establish equity in healthcare. Health insurance has the capability to provide affordable and quality healthcare to the poorest section of the population, if they are underwritten by the government.

Cultural norms play an important part in healthcare-seeking behaviour in developing countries. Health education in developing countries has become important since the emergence of the COVID-19 pandemic. The pandemic required strict measures like social distancing, face coverings and hygiene, which were mostly ignored in developing countries due to prejudice and carelessness.

Healthcare is indeed a social care, where certain age groups require specialised care. Social care has economic benefits as well. Such care tends to increase the living condition of the population.

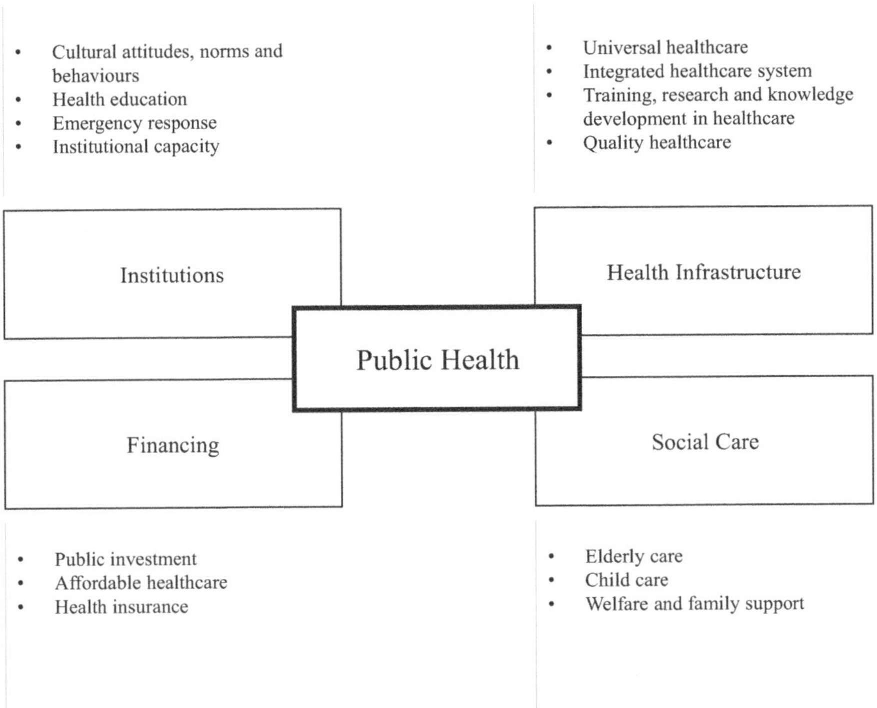

Figure 8.3 Policy roadmap

Source: Prepared by author

Summary

There is a fundamental contradiction between poor people's aspiration for accessible quality of essential healthcare services and the elite's strategy to supply such services. Nevertheless, ensuring universal health coverage is a fundamental challenge for a country without which the human development, economic and employment goals of the government may be hindered. Despite considerable thrust in providing healthcare, a significant number of people in developing countries are still deprived of healthcare.

Access to both kinds of services – universal form of services (i.e. services are to be made available to all citizens on a uniform basis regardless of income, status or power such as universal health care) and those services where income, position or influence have the capacity to leverage particular individuals or groups – is affected by financial circumstances, creating different levels of access and situations in which the poor from different segment are disadvantageous from the outset.

The developing countries are not well on the track to achieving universal health care as well as the percentage share of the health budget in total budgetary allocation is slowing down due to contraction in the economy, caused by the pandemic and subsequent cost of living crisis. The public expenditure is fairly low. Besides, most of the public expenditures are not linked with sectoral and national policies. The World Health Organization suggests that the health budget should be at least 15 per cent of the national budget for the developing countries. However, 15 per cent allocation of budget for the health sector is apparently further down the line as there are many other sectors competing for higher budgetary allocation to chart out the path to recovery and reconstruction. Thus, it might be quite difficult to achieve an equal society that people aspire for since hundreds of years, unless the top priorities are strategically curved out by governments. Most importantly, tackling structural barriers such as market failures, unresponsive public services, prejudice and discrimination are important too since these act as the hindrances for the people at large to access to universal healthcare.

Most of the schemes by governments are ad hoc and shortterm in nature which are far from sustainable solution in provision of equitable healthcare. Without a whole system wide transformation, backed by adequate health budget, only a few government initiatives as well as safety net programmes will not be enough to reach all segments of society. In the absence of universal healthcare, the sustainable development goals, including the aim of zero poverty and reduction in inequality, may remain as an elusive and distant dream. The government needs to revise regulatory strategies and approaches to control the rising drug and health service prices. As for most of the people, the system of healthcare is complex and inaccessible to quality services since the provision is driven by a hierarchical framework of power. A change in the total milieu of healthcare requires a transformation of social relations, a progressive public society with power concentrating in median voters for universal health care.

References

BBS. (2019). *Household Income and Expenditure Survey 2016*. Dhaka: Bangladesh Bureau of Statistics.

Besley, T., and Persson, T. (2013). Taxation and development. In *Handbook of public economics* (Vol. 5, pp. 51–110). Amsterdam: North Holland Elsevier.

BNHA. (2017). *Bangladesh National Health Accounts 2016*. Dhaka: Health Economics Unit, Ministry of Health and Family Welfare.

Bump, J.B. (2010). *The long road to universal health coverage: A century of lessons for development strategy*. Seattle, WA: PATH and Rockefeller Foundation. Retrieved March 22, 2022, from https://www.formosapost.com/pdf/The-Long-Road-to-Universal-Health-Coverage.pdf

Council, K.D., Wilson, J.C., Harris, B.M., O'Keefe, A.M., Henderson, C., Dixon, B., Merengwa, E., Nwazue, E., and Weaks, F. (2013). Improving health services for residents through community-based participatory research: A public housing leadership perspective. *Progress in Community Health Partnerships: Research, Education, and Action*, 7(1), pp. 89–93.

Di John, J., and Putzel, J. (2009). *Political settlements: Issues paper*. Discussion Paper. Birmingham, UK: University of Birmingham.

El-Saharty, S., Sparkes, S.P., Barroy, H., Ahsan, K.Z., and Ahmed, S.M. (2015). *The path to universal health coverage in Bangladesh: Bridging the gap of human resources for health*. Washington, DC: World Bank. Retrieved from https://openknowledge.worldbank.org/handle/10986/21633

Etienne, C., Asamoa-Baah, A., and Evans, D.B. (2010). *Health systems financing: The path to universal coverage*. World Health Organization.

Fan, V.Y., and Savedoff, W.D. (2014). The health financing transition: A conceptual framework and empirical evidence. *Social Science & Medicine*, 105, pp. 112–121.

Fox, A.M., and Reich, M.R. (2015). The politics of universal health coverage in low and middle-income countries: A framework for evaluation and action. *Journal of Health Politics, Policy and Law*, 40(5), pp. 1023–1060.

Khan, M. (2010). *Political settlements and the governance of growth-enhancing institutions*. Retrieved March 22, 2022, from https://eprints.soas.ac.uk/id/eprint/9968

Laws, E. (2012). *Political settlements, elite pacts, and governments of national unity*. Background Paper 10. Birmingham: DLP.

Laws, E., and Leftwich, A. (2014). *Political settlements: DLP concept brief 01*. Birmingham: University of Birmingham, DLP.

Mossialos, E., Wenzl, M., Osborn, R., and Sarnak, D. (2015). *International profiles of health care systems*. New York: Commonwealth Fund. Retrieved March 22, 2022 from https://www.commonwealthfund.org/sites/default/files/documents/___media_files_publications_fund_report_2016_jan_1857_mossialos_intl_profiles_2015_v7.pdf

Panitch, L., and Leys, C. (2009). *Morbid symptoms: Health under capitalism*. London: The Merlin Press.

Participants at the Bellagio Workshop on Political Economy of Global Health. (2015). Report from Bellagio: Advancing political economy of global health to understand and influence the drivers of universal health coverage, *Health Systems & Reform*, 1(1), pp. 20–21.

Reich, M.R. (2015). Universal health coverage is complex but achievable. *PharmacoEconomics & Outcomes News*, 735, pp. 7–29.

Stuckler, D., Basu, S., and McKee, M. (2010). Budget crises, health, and social welfare programmes. *BMJ*, 340. doi: https://doi.org/10.1136/bmj.c3311

World Health Organization. (2019). *Primary health care on the road to universal health coverage: 2019 monitoring report*. World Health Organization.

Part IV

Employment and Social Security

9 Disquisitions on Employment and Social Security

Introduction

In the popular American sitcom, The Flintstones, Fred Flintstone was a Stone Age caveman, portrayed as a blue-collar worker at a gravel pit. A frequently encountered scene between Fred and his boss Mr Slate, showcased as a stern and short-tempered caveman, involved Fred's dismissal from his job because of his silly slip-ups, only to be given back his job at the end of the episode. Underneath the fictional storyline lies the critical juxtaposition of early industrialisation in a Stone Age setting, hinting at the struggles of the Flintstones family and their blue-collar neighbours.

Aligned with the Yoruba proverb "by labour comes wealth", as well as the theoretical underpinnings laid by Smith's labour theory of value, or Marx's theory of labour power, this chapter solidifies that prosperity in economic standing is brought upon through labour. Guided by the notion that an increase in the powers of economic and political decision of labour is the eventual objective of social policymaking, this chapter argues for ensuring work for all for transformation as well as universal life-cycle-based social security system to absorb systemic shocks, including those resulted from pandemic and natural disasters.

The objective of this part is to understand the dynamics of labour market in developing countries, particularly focusing on Bangladesh, from the core of theoretical debates as well as develop an alternative explanation to causality of the stylised facts in the backdrop of existing policy regime, stemming from the orthodox theoretical underpinnings. Following the frameworks of the transformational pathway in education and health, the case for employment is strengthened through the use of necessary and sufficient conditions that merge intervening variables into the circular flow between households and firms.

Developing countries have perceived a corresponding process of economic growth driven by, and associated dispossession of, labour. A significant number of people live below the so-called poverty line. The labour has predominantly powered accumulation by way of low-waged-labour-centred-export, and for some remittance from migrant workers. Despite labour remaining at the core of such development, labourers are deprived in a number of ways. Against this backdrop, the key concern arises whether this type of accumulation by

DOI: 10.4324/9781003284222-13

dispossession enables the economy to create productive employment, reduce poverty and remove inequality.

The development of countries like Bangladesh is subject to international restructuring and international division of labour. Such a process is understood through the broader term of "globalisation" and certain bodies of literature branded this as neoliberalism. The augmentation of the ready-made garment (RMG) sector is a glaring illustration of such international division of labour. The rising cost of labour in advanced industrialised countries paved the way to relocate their production processes to low-cost labour locations in the South. Like other labour-intensive products, the RMG moved to East Asia in the 1960s, during that time, the government declared a New Industrial Policy (NIP), which represented a pronounced ideological shift towards neoliberal orthodoxy as the country embarked upon Structural Adjustment Reforms (SAR) at the instruction of IMF and World Bank in the Reagan/Thatcher epoch. The reforms in the labour market advanced mostly the male labour force to become progressively "flexible" and "feminised" (Titumir, 2013). The international reformation of the garment industry, built on the premise of low-cost labour, stimulated the rising demand for female labourers in formal employment while decreasing household budgets led to an upsurge in the supply of job-seeking women in Bangladesh. The increased participation of women in the labour market is not an outcome of self-serving allegations that the neoliberal reforms have provoked opportunities for greater female employment than before. Labour regulation, once rejected by the neoliberal school, has started surfacing again in the mainstream. Labour regulation does not decelerate the growth rather it positively affects it. Government intervention in the labour market can reduce income inequality (Storm and Capaldo, 2018). Labour laws supporting worker rights and voices tend to raise the collective bargaining capacity, which results in gain in productivity because of the increased motivation of the workers (Deakin et al., 2014). Labour laws can help formulate employment in developing countries through the provision of social security, collective bargaining and dispute resolution, which in turn can ensure economic security of the employees (Deakin, 2016).

Since the 1980s, the government undertook neoliberal reform programmes to accelerate growth through wide-ranging policies to improve competitiveness, enhance economic efficiency and dismantle state interventions to create conditions for promoting export-led growth. As a part of the process, significant reforms have been implemented including the introduction of deregulatory measures to facilitate increased participation of the private sector (Mujeri and Khondker, 2002). A section of the neoliberals is involved too in waging war against labour unions. One of the noteworthy features of privatisation has been the introduction of measures to bring liberalisation and openness to the economy (Volscho, 2012).

This chapter provides a framework, derived through a review of employment-related theoretical and empirical literature. The journey towards a universal system of employment is contingent upon political settlement specific to a developing country context. A well understanding of political settlement enables the process of moving towards employment as a rights-based approach in developing countries. A theoretical framework, hence, is needed to understand the circumstance of the labour.

A Review

The classical school combines ideas on income, wage and employment. Employment is the engagement of a person in occupation with working hours every day and wage rate. In most of the cases, classical economic thinking is driven by French economist Jean-Baptiste Say (1767–1832) and which is come to be known as Say's law, "supply creates its own demand". The classical economists deny the intervention of the state. They conclude that the economy is always fully employed. But, even if unemployment results (with surplus labour) at any particular wage level, this can be solved by accepting lower wages. This helps the unemployed labour go back to their job. Full employment exists when everyone who is at the running rate of wages wishes to be utilised. The individuals who are not willing to work at the current wage rate are not unemployed in light of the fact that they are deliberately unemployed. Hence, full employment is a circumstance where there is no possibility of involuntary unemployment as people are arranged to work at the existing wage rate but they do not find work.

Classical economists begin with assumptions like full employment, laissez-faire, perfect competition and self-adjusting labour and product markets. Here, total output of the economy is divided between consumption and investment expenditures, wages and prices are perfectly flexible and savings are automatically invested and equality between the two is brought about by the rate of interest. They perceived that deviation from full employment is a sign of unusual incidence in the economy and assumed unemployment to have been caused by either of the two: *First*, lack of information among people about where the jobs were or frictional unemployment. *Second*, people might insist on being paid more than they can make.

According to classical theory, the real wage is set by bargaining between the worker and employer and employment is determined by this real wage rate. The level of unemployment reflects the real wage set above the market-clearing level. In a condition where unemployment exists, they give the solution of a wage cut to get back to the previous full employment situation. Classical and neoclassical economists identified wage variations as determinants for maintaining the level of employment (Apergis et al., 2005).

Assuming supply creates its own demand, Say argued that in the economy there will be no overproduction of any commodities and services and no demand deficiency for goods because income received by a person is spent for purchasing of goods and services. As a whole, total production in the economy equals its total income earned. Economy is considered self-adjusting by dint of invisible hand. Some of the assumptions that the classical model took are the existence of pure competition, flexible wage and price, rationality (self-interest) and non-interfering government. According to them, whatever individual saves is totally invested (saving=investment). Therefore, aggregate income will be equal to its aggregate investment and lead to level of full employment. If, for example, saving is lower than investment, the rate of interest will be high or vice versa. This will continue until saving and investment get static at a full employment level.

The classical economists posit that price is related to supply of money, giving birth to the quantity theory of money. Greater the quantity of money, the higher is the price. The level of national income and employment, thus, depends on the aggregate production function and the supply and demand for labour.

In applying Say's law that supply makes its own demand, a presumption was made that the whole wage earned by the family units will be really spent. Saving represents a withdrawal of some income from the consumption stream. This will bring about insufficiency of demand or use on yield of products created. Thus, if a part of income is saved (that is, not consumed), supply of output produced would not create sufficient demand for itself. This will bring about a deficiency of aggregate demand which will cause fall in output and employment and the rise of involuntary unemployment.

Classical economists, however, denied the possibility of deficiency of aggregate demand even when a fraction of income is saved by the households. They showed that Say's law that supply creates its own demand for goods is held even in the existence of saving. Savings by households are invested by businessmen, that is, investment expenditure will be equal to savings of households. Income earned from production will be partly spent on consumer goods and partly on investment in capital goods. The amount which is not spent on consumer goods is saved and investment expenditure on capital goods by firms equals this savings. Therefore, there is no deficiency of demand or expenditure and circular flow of income goes on uninterrupted. Thus, supply goes on creating its own demand and Say's law is upheld. Further, rate of interest is determined by supply of savings and demand for investment. The investment demand is fixed to be a decreasing function of the rate of interest. If the rate of interest increases, so does the savings and vice versa. The changes in rate of interest cause investment and supply of savings to become equal.

John Maynard Keynes (1883–1946) in his *General Theory of Employment, Interest and Money* published in 1936 made an anterior attack on the classical postulates. He developed a new economics which brought about a revolution in economic thought and policymaking.

The *General Theory* was composed against the foundation of classical thought. By the "classicists", Keynes signified, "the adherents of Ricardo, those, that is to say, who received and idealised the hypothesis of Ricardian economic analysis". Keynes disavowed traditional and orthodox economics which had been developed over a century and which dominated economic thought and policy before and during the Great Depression. Since Keynesian economics is based on the criticism of classical economics, it is necessary to know the latter as embodied in the theory of employment.

Classical theory, though passed through a glorious age, came under attack and proven to be somewhat unrealistic, irrelevant and out of date as it failed to provide a grounded solution to the greatest economic crisis of 1929. Keynes found the basic assumption of classical thought of full employment unrealistic. He considered unemployment as a normal phenomenon and disregarded any possibility of reaching equilibrium. On the contrary, his ideas referred to underemployment conditions to be more realistic. Keynes also found the classical long-term equilibrium to be highly unlikely; as an alternative, he put greater emphasis on short-term equilibrium. For him, "in the long run, we are all dead". There is a possibility of changes in the context, thus what is real/practical today may seem obsolete in recent future. Fluctuation is inevitable.

Moreover, classical thoughts of economics greatly rely on Say's law that regards that supply always creates its own demand, thus there would be no general overproduction or glut and disequilibrium. Keynes conceived of the idea that the whole part of the money earned is not necessarily used up on consumption goods, or through the procurement of producers' goods or invested; rather very often and also inevitably money is saved and hoarded to give rise to the individual's cash balances which comes from the sense of security for future. Therefore, there can be a shortage of aggregate demand. Hence, even if there is a general rise to additional supply that may not always add up as an additional demand.

Further, if it continues this way, the haves will have more than fortune which cannot be entirely consumed thus leading to the intention of savings and on the other hand, the have-nots with their too little money income could not even maintain their bare minimum, which in both ways means a deficiency in aggregate demand with respect to additional supply, thus strengthening the possibility of general glut. Keynes objected to the classical idea of saving and investment equilibrium which is adjusted through the fluctuation of interest rate and all the disequilibrium hence as temporary condition. To Keynes, equilibrium between saving and investment are obtained through changes in income rather than in the interest rate. And thus of course, only further government spending can increase the possibility of better income prospects and interest rate adjustment has little to do with it.

Keynes disregarded the classicists' approach as unrealistic to the problems that gave rise to the contemporary thoughts of capitalist economy known as "laissez-faire". He also intensely opposed Pigou's plea for a return to free, perfect competition, a neo-classical variety stemming from his mentor in Cambridge, Alfred Marshall. To solve the problem of unemployment, he suggested betterment of prevailing inconsistencies in capitalist's economy while Keynes asked for a reform to the capitalist system.

Keynes pleads for a progressive welfare state instead of the smaller effect of moderation in the system itself. Besides, a progressive welfare state may not be adopted through a general fixation of bare minimum subsistence. In this regard, he asked for governmental intervention to bring about adjustment in the economy as a whole, as the system is not self-adjusting as presumed by the classicists.

Keynes was also critical of Pigou's viewpoint, furnished in *Theory of Unemployment*, that a general fall in wages at times of economic depression automatically reinstate full employment when and only if the market apparatus is freely working devoid of any kind of obstruction from trade unionism and government. Nonetheless, Keynes thinks otherwise. According to him, a general fall in wages would rather deteriorate the employment condition itself as the decline in wages will eventually decrease aggregate demand for goods as with the lower income the labourer will demand less. Keynes regarded the wages as not only the cost of production but also the income of the workers. As a result of general decrease in aggregate demand, it will thus affect the level of production to be reduced further. Unemployment issue will further aggravate rather than improve anymore.

Keynes did not believe in the capacity of the economic system to automatically reach optimal levels. For employment and investment to increase, he urged for state intervention through fiscal and monetary policy. His ideas were, when the economy moves to recession, the central bank should reduce interest rates to borrowers, which will instigate borrowing and investment and when that accumulation occurs throughout the economy the business confidence will grow and pull the economy out of recession. Deficit spending (spending more than revenue collected) was his tool of fiscal policy. Main insights of Keynesian explanation of business fluctuation and unemployment are, *first*, a general theory must account for the persistence of unemployment. *Second*, it will also account for fluctuations in unemployment. *Third*, distinguish carefully between savings and investment (Greenwald and Stiglitz, 1987).

Cyclical behaviour of macroeconomic aggregates is underlined by disturbances in demand (influenced by Marshallian demand–supply model). His idea on employment was more or less based on high emphasis on state intervention to cure the ills of market. His ideas played a role as intellectual foundations for welfare capitalism. Two fundamental assumptions underline Keynesian theory of employment: *First*, inefficient aggregate demand is the real cause of unemployment. *Second*, discretionary monetary and fiscal policy (decreasing taxes or increasing government expenditure) can help eliminate unemployment by increasing aggregate demand.

Owing to the great depression affected by WWI and other indicators, Keynes found a fundamental critique of the existing form of classical solution of problems in economics. His solutions were rather simple and easily applicable (Hicks, 1936). He asked for replacing private investment with public investment. He insisted on the government to borrow money and spend on public work. This will create jobs and increase aggregate demand (purchasing power). Governments later can cut back when it recovers and expands (Yergin and Stanislaw, 1998). Keynes talked more about greater responsibility of the state in directing investment. As one of the spearheads of policymakers, he was instrumental in founding Bretton Woods Institutions – the World Bank and the International Monetary Fund (IMF).

Keynesian economics has also provided a sign of greater pertinence when it comes to the analysis of investment patterns in developing countries, with much distinctive from the classical analysis. The classical economists could not differentiate between the saving and investment decision while considering a default pattern that saving will automatically lead to investment. Keynes made a huge difference while distinguishing between these two. He argued that income determined saving and not the other way around. According to him, if investment goes up, income will increase and that will lead to a higher level of income and more to be saved. The rate of investment is determined by the rate of interest on the one hand and the marginal efficiency of capital on the other. Marginal efficiency of capital refers to the expected rate of return on investment while rate of interest refers to annual payback rate to the investment employed.

If businessmen become more and more pessimistic concerning the future prospect of yield, the marginal efficiency of capital declines, which adversely affects investment, thus more attempts are made to hoard the money capital that would otherwise be invested. If otherwise happens, there would be more propensity to invest, thus higher levels of aggregate supply which may fall short to the level of aggregate demand hence producing a glut production. Either way, the level of aggregate demand and aggregate supply may not stay at the point of equilibrium.

Keynes showed that growing public investment in terms of increasing the possibility of higher level of employment is likely to stimulate private investment rather than reduce it, which is of much relevance to the developing countries' perspective contrary to classical economics, which advocates laissez-faire policies. In developing countries, governments intervene in the way of adopting suitable fiscal and monetary policies to stabilise prevalent economic prospects and to stimulate not only private investment to achieve rapid growth but also to ensure growth with price stability.

Development economics, however, was found after WWII, with certain distinction from neoclassical and Keynesian economics. Owing to the shortfall of these two, the structuralist approach also emerged. Population, technology, institutions and entrepreneurship are endogenous in development economics while these were considered exogenous in neoclassical economics. Rosenstein Rodan (1943) found that 25 per cent of population in developing countries were unemployed and this waste of labour could be solved through bringing capital to labour or vice-versa. But this was challenged by Albert Hirschman (1958) with his postulation, widely known as unbalanced growth theory, stating that the task of development policy is to maintain disequilibria. According to this model, industrialisation (through backward and forward linkages) of a certain leading sector would pull the rest of the economy. Investment at the limited number of locations (stimulant industry) will lead to neighbouring effect on other industries and regions (Peet and Hartwick, 2009)

The counter revolution to Keyenesianism was spearheaded by Milton Freindman in *A Theory of the Consumption Function (1957)* and *A Monetary History of the United States, 1867–1960,* with Anna J. Schwartz, 1963. With George Stigler and others, Friedman was among the intellectual leaders of the neoclassical Chicago school of economics, which rejected Keynesianism in favour of monetarism until the mid-1970s. The school then based its on the concept of rational expectations by its leading protagonists, including Gary Becker, Robert Fogel, Thomas Sowell and Robert Lucas Jr. Contrary to the idea of Keynesian thinking, Freidman asserted that inflation can be controlled by limiting the amount of money in the national economy and rejected government fiscal policy as a tool of demand management. He also argued that the Great Depression originated in a catastrophic failure of government. New classical macroeconomics builds on the idea of rational expectations that outcomes that are being forecast do not differ systematically from the market equilibrium results.

Inspired by Chicago School, there was also counter-revolution in development theory in the 1970s and 1980s, arguing that adoption of such industrialisation strategies has led to unproductive industrial investment in developing countries and led to misguided intervention by the state into economic life (Johnson, 1971). Bauer (1981) accused development economics as "intellectually corrupt" for its overemphasis on large capital investment. Lal (1980) extended this counter-revolution stating that in an imperfect world imperfect market mechanisms will do better than imperfect state planning. Developing countries, according to him, are not special cases as described. Thus, by the mid-1980s, the whole notion of development economics became discredited in conventional circles. To them, the market becomes distorted when government intervenes. Thus, the government is seen as detrimental to the economy. They further believe that, like the new classical school, government intervention in the market could lead to large deficits, increased debt and higher interest rates, which would eventually force the economy into a state of destabilisation.

Monetarist economists, of which the most notable of course is Milton Friedman, used the concept of the natural rate of unemployment hypothesis to argue that economies are more stable than previously thought. Friedman (1977) argued that the permanent trade-off between inflation and employment as expressed by the Phillips curve does not hold. Rather, each economy has a specific rate of employment called "non-accelerating inflation rate of unemployment" (NAIRU).

The Phillips curve inspects the relationship between the rate of unemployment and the rate of money wage changes. It was named after A.W. Phillips (1914 – 1975), a New Zealand economist who spent most of his career at the London School of Economics (LSE), who inferred the observational relationship that when unemployment is high, the rate of increase in money wage rates is low in his paper, *The relation between Unemployment and Rate of Changes in Money Wages in the United Kingdom, 1861-1957*. This is on account of labourers being hesitant to offer their services at not exactly the predominant rates when the demand for work is low and unemployment is high so wage rates fall gradually. Then again, when unemployment is low, the rate of increase in money wage rates is high. This is on the grounds that when the demand for labour is high and there are not many unemployed, employers will offer wage rates up quickly. The second element which impacts this backward relationship between money wage rate and unemployment is the way of business movement. In a time of rising business movement when unemployment falls with expanding demand for work, the managers will offer up wages. Alternately in a time of falling business action when demand for work is diminishing and unemployment is rising, managers will be hesitant to concede pay increments. Maybe, they will decrease wages. Anyhow, workers and unions will be hesitant to accept pay cuts amid such periods. Thus, bosses are compelled to release labourers, along these lines prompting a high rate of unemployment. Therefore, when the labour market is depressed, a little lessening in wages would prompt an expansive increment in unemployment. When the money wage rate is 2 per cent, the unemployment rate is 3 per cent but when the wage rate is high at 4 per cent, the unemployment rate is low at 2 per cent. In this way, there is a trade-off between the rate of progress in wages and the rate of unemployment. This implies that when the pay rate is high the unemployment rate is low and the other way around. Later, several economists have extended the Phillips curve analysis.

Friedman asserted that there was no compelling reason to expect a stable downward-sloping Phillips curve to explain the trade-off between inflation and unemployment Inasmuch as there is inconsistency between the expected rate and the actual rate of inflation, the downward-sloping Phillips curve will be found. When this inconsistency is uprooted as time goes on, the Phillips curve gets to be vertical. To clarify this, Friedman presents the idea of the normal rate of unemployment at which the economy regularly settles as a result of its structural imperfections. It is the unemployment rate below which the inflation rate increases, and above which the inflation rate decreases. At this rate, there is a propensity for the inflation rate neither to boost nor to lessen.

James Tobin (1972a and 1972b) proposed a negotiation between the negatively sloping and vertical Phillips curves. Tobin accepts that there is a Phillips curve within limits. In any case, as the economy grows and jobs develop, the curve turns out to be considerably more delicate and vanishes until it becomes vertical at some critically low rate of unemployment. At the critical rate of unemployment level, it is impossible to offer more employment because the job seekers have wrong skills or wrong age or sex or are in the wrong place. With respect to the normal part of the Phillips curve, which is negatively sloping, wages are sticky downwards because labourers resist a decline in their relative wages. For Tobin, there is a wage-change floor in excess supply situations. In the range of relatively high unemployment to the right of the critical rate of unemployment, as aggregate demand and inflation increase and involuntary unemployment is reduced, wage-floor markets slowly reduce. When all sectors of the labour market are above the wage floor, the level of critically low rate of unemployment is reached.

Samuelson and Solow (1960) championed the Phillips curve as a policy tool. Rather than focus on the relation between the rate of change in nominal wages and the unemployment rate as Phillips did, they estimated the relationship between the rate of inflation and the unemployment rate for the twenty-five-year period from 1934 to 1958. The notion of the Phillips curve as a menu of choices from which policymakers could choose quickly became an important consideration in economic policy, suggesting to the degree to which monetary and fiscal policies can be used to control inflation without high levels of unemployment. It gives a guideline to the government about the rate of inflation, which can be accepted, with a given level of unemployment. For this purpose, it is important to know the exact position of the Phillips curve.

While explaining the natural rate of unemployment, Friedman (1966) stressed that the only scope of public policy in influencing the level of unemployment lies in the short run in keeping with the position of the Phillips curve. He spoke out about the possibility of influencing the long-run rate of unemployment because of the vertical Phillips curve. The trade-off between unemployment and inflation, as per him, does not exist and has never existed. However, inflation might be rapid, but unemployment always tends to fall back to its natural rate, which is not some irreducible minimum of unemployment. It can be lowered by removing obstacles in the labour market by reducing frictions. Therefore, according to his counter argument, public policy will have to improve the institutional structure to make the labour market reactive to changing patterns of demand. Moreover, some level of unemployment must be accepted as natural because of the survival of a large number of part-time workers, unemployment compensation and other institutional factors. Another implication is that unemployment is not a fitting aim for monetary expansion. Therefore, employment above the natural rate can be reached at the cost of hastening inflation, if monetary policy is adopted.

Natural rate theory suggests that there is a limit to unemployment below which it cannot go. It is 5 to 7 per cent in the United States and below this rate will lead to rising inflation (Weiner, 1986). Thus, the natural rate of unemployment is stated as the rate of unemployment at which the actual rate of inflation equals the expected rate of inflation. It is thus an equilibrium rate of unemployment towards which the economy moves in the long run. In the long run, the Phillips curve is a vertical line at the natural rate of unemployment.

Weiner believes that this is not the optimal unemployment and can be changed at any time. This natural or equilibrium unemployment rate is not fixed over the long run. Rather, it is determined by a number of structural characteristics of the labour and goods markets within the economy. These may be minimum wage laws, inadequate employment information, deficiencies in workforce training, costs of labour mobility and other market imperfections. Anyhow, what causes the Phillips curve to shift over time is the expected rate of inflation (Weiner, 1986). He considers that removing labour market imperfection through microeconomic policies, the natural rate itself can be lowered. Therefore, the natural rate of unemployment is the rate at which there is no tendency to accelerate or decelerate inflation. At this point, the economy's inflation is constant over the years.

It is clear that Phillips curve is not stable, but shifts over time as expectations of workers and firms are adjusted over time. While measuring this theoretical concept, Gordon (1976) identified three features of this natural rate: *First*, the actual unemployment rate is hardly the same as the natural unemployment rate. *Second*, the natural rate is higher in relative sense. *Finally*, it goes upwards over time. Policymakers can bring the economy to a new natural rate with the new Phillips curve. Weiner (1986, p. 8) identified five labour market imperfections that hinder natural rate to get low. Those are mismatch in labour skill, location mismatch, institutional barriers, imperfect flow of information and disincentives in transfer of payment.

According to the classical perspective, full employment is natural and can be achieved through market forces. However, Keynes did not see the probability to achieve full employment and found unemployment as real fault of capitalism (Wray, 2009). Before Keynes, the classical economist promoted the concept of reserve army in order to discipline labour. Keynes showed in his *General Theory* that firms only produce the amount they want to sell and firms will not be induced to hire more workers than they need even if the wage rate is down due to unemployment. According to him, unemployment is not because of a defective labour market like a sticky wage or low skill (Wray, 2009). Rather unlike classical economists, he saw this as lack of deficient effective demand and could be solved by creating more jobs that will increase demand capacity. In addition, it requires social policy coming out from government intervention. Like the 1930s, it was again in 2008 when economists supported Keynes' ideas of Keynes for fiscal stimulus to get the nation around the globe back to its normal functioning.

Many found Keynes abortive during the stagflation (high inflation combined with high unemployment) of the 1970s. But they failed to understand that he was urging to create jobs in order to improve effective demand even if by digging holes during the time of recession. The context that he was focusing on was the depression and it is now clear that other than depression or deep recession, employing workers and paying them for useless work will only raise inflation (Tcherneva, 2008). Therefore, Keynes was in favour of target spending, especially in sectors or areas that are underperforming in order to achieve social goals (Keynes, 1936). The New Deal job programme by President Roosevelt's regime is one example of targeted programmes.

Given the critique posed on Keynesian thought by new classical economists, there has been a birth of a new branch within the mainstream, who are variously labelled as neo-Keynesians, new Keynesians and the Neoclassical Keynesian Synthesis. As the names suggest, the neo-Keynesians attempt to integrate Keynesian models into traditional or neoclassical economics, such as the Keynesian Cross model of Paul Samuelson and the IS–LM framework of

John Hicks and Alvin Hansen. They adopt the rational expectation hypothesis and the natural rate hypothesis of Milton Friedman. Therefore, new Keynesians are not overly enthusiastic about the ability of fiscal policy to counter negative business cycles. Moreover, their explanation of market failure stood on the modelling of wages and price stickiness (Dolenc, 2004). Unlike Friedman, authors pertaining to the "new consensus" or "new neoclassical synthesis" embrace the concept of a "vertical long-run Phillips curve.

The New Keynesians believe that the role of government is essential to address market failure and brought the ideas of imperfect information on the characteristics of workers to suggest efficiency wage theory, postulating that the only way the labourers can be motivated to be productive is the rise of wages given the interdependence of the wages of firms. They argue that the optimal wage of any firm depends on wages that the other firm pays. Second, they also suggest that imperfection in the capital market is derived from the existing information asymmetry. Such asymmetry can lead to equity rationing that can hold firms at the risk of bankruptcy. While the behaviour of the firm is judged upon, the willingness of it to take risk and unexpected changes at the base of working capital can depreciate the willingness. Third, credit rationing happens when potential risk considerations deter firms by limiting the amount that it is willing to produce. Therefore, its access to credit gets limited. Finally, asymmetry of information may restrict banks to lend more and this has a parallel impact on those firms who are willing to produce. Thus, the role of monetary authority will be to take initiatives that can stimulate banks to lend money (Greenwald and Stiglitz, 1987). The main dispute between the New Keynesians and the Neo-Classicists lies in wage and price adjustment. According to new classical macroeconomic theory, wage and price are flexible. The New Keynesians rejected their market-clearing method in the face of short-run fluctuation and thus are of view of sticky wage and price. They explain the involuntary unemployment and importance of monetary policy based on this stickiness (Mankiw, 2008). New Keynesian economists use the efficiency wage model to explain the market clearing mechanism of unemployment. According to them, wage reduction will cause decline in both productivity and profit. Rather they call for high wages that in turn makes workers more productive. By giving more wages, firms can stop workers from leaving the firm and can save the cost of new hiring as well as training workers (Stiglitz, 1984).

Some of the main policy implications of New Keynesian economics are as follows. *First*, there are feature of imperfections such as asymmetrical information among buyers and sellers, sticky rate of wages and prices and relatively high barrier of entry and exit, which could manipulate market structure, leading to widespread decline in demand, market failures, depression and rise in the level of involuntary unemployment. Hence, New Keynesian economics provides a rationale for government intervention in the form of active monetary and fiscal policies to prevent recessions, fall in output and employment and elevate aggregate demand to overcome a recession. *Second*, New Keynesian theoretical standpoints also find a general stand for prices and incomes agreements through bargaining between firms and unions. According to them, asymmetries and imperfections in the labour market tend to divide the market with respect to employment prospects. Imperfections of such kinds may possibly lead to high involuntary unemployment. To tackle this, prices and incomes policies should be formulated in such a way that it would increase the power of outsiders with respect to insiders by reducing the level of market imperfections. *Third*, another important implication of New Keynesian theory relates to the developing country in terms of corporate and government policies. It is mostly applicable when involuntary unemployment persists following an adverse economic shock, which is referred to as "hysteresis" or "lagged" effects. At the time of higher involuntary employment, the insiders (who are already employed) may use their bargaining power (mostly through reducing bidding level) to prevent outsiders from entering the labour force. This way, outsiders lose their influence on bargaining as they had already lost their union membership. In such a situation, when outsiders cannot enter the labour market, unemployment among them cannot exert pressure on wages, which remain sticky. *Fifth*, savers and investors are different with different motives. Much of the economy's saving is done by households while investment is mostly done by business firms based on profit expectations thus unlikely would ever be equal. This affects aggregate demand and causes fluctuations in income, output and employment in capitalist economies. Hence, it is not necessary that the economy will be in equilibrium at the level of full employment. This invalidates Say's law, since according to it overproduction and unemployment cannot occur. If the desired investment by entrepreneurs falls short of the amount of savings at full employment level of income, the equilibrium of the economy will be at less than full employment level resulting in involuntary unemployment.

The theories discussed require revisiting, particularly given the requirement of structural transformation in developing countries. Since new classical economics and its derivatives consider human beings to be "self-interested" rational agents who only want to maximise their profits, the policies based on this theoretical ground follow this assumption, which means self-interested policies must not have any cooperative, mutual or sharing orientations. The new classical school, therefore, ignores human sociality and fails to see human beings as cooperative and creative agents within society. As a result, policies become alienated from the masses and society (Titumir, 2022).

Public choice theory criticises Keynesian and post-Keynesian fiscal policy, arguing that politicians will make policies that will benefit them. Keynes and post-Keynesians failed to incorporate politics and political processes into their analysis (Buchanan, 1986). Since politicians seek to benefit themselves rather than the whole nation or national economy through fiscal and monetary policies, this theory argues that it creates a worse economic performance than occurs under a free market. Thus, it advocates the free-market approaches of new classical economics over interventionist policies by the government.

Keynes rejected the classical perspectives. His rejection of the classical view came from the fact that the doctrine of total withdrawal of the state from the market involves the possibility of the collapse of the capitalist system itself (Beaud, 1997). To Keynes, capitalism had no conceivable alternative, but his emphasis on government action in correcting the market economy made him the focus of much hatred within the capitalist community (Dowd, 2000). Despite its acknowledgement of the role of the state in the economy, Keynesianism provides no clear roadmap on how to enforce the role of the state and to what extent the state can intervene in the economy. It thus fails to incorporate politics and class as well as power relations into its analysis, which are the precursors in state policy formulation (Titumir, 2022).

Differing from new classical economics, post-Keynesians argued that state intervention is needed since the so-called free-market economy can hardly handle the swings, booms and busts in business cycles. Thus, Minsky calls for government steps to control these through regulation, central bank action and other tools (Minsky, 1974). Though they ask for the analysis of class and power relations of society and the role of the state in effective economic policies, they seldom explain the political settlement of postcolonial countries. It is, furthermore, argued that post-Keynesianism and eco-development share the same position regarding economic growth through the concept of radical uncertainty, and the importance of the precautionary principle (Berr, 2015). Despite its focus on intergenerational and intragenerational perspectives of development, again post-Keynesianism provides no clear-cut road map on how such decisions are to be made based on the political and class reality (Titumir, 2022).

The postcolonial state experienced a new wave of class formation due to changes in power and rule. The colonisers created a class that was obedient to the colonisers and enjoyed the facilities brought by the colonisers. These intermediate classes between the ruler and the ruled gained opportunity to bargain to have policies favouring them. These classes consisted of politicians, bureaucrats and intellectuals who assumed power in the political settlement in the postcolonial period. Therefore, the intermediate classes were directly involved with the state apparatus that allowed the interests of these groups to be prioritised over those of the masses. Given the multiple stratification among the intermediate classes in terms of power and wealth, it triggered competition among the different layers as well.

The relation between the different groups of the intermediate class in the process of primitive accumulation is also a very complex one (Titumir, 2022). These groups are driven by the need to maximise their personal interests, but at the same time, their actions are influenced by the decisions of other groups. As a result, the relations between the classes may either be collusive or competitive, comparable to an oligopoly. For instance, in order to optimise the receipt of benefits, bureaucrats and politicians may choose to form a coalition through which they can undertake complementary decisions that benefit both parties. These benefits, however, often come at the expense of other groups, such as the median citizen and the economy as a whole. Capital accumulation by the intermediate classes for the purpose of the concentration of wealth diverts investment and productive rents from technology and industry and leads to the creation of more unproductive rent by the state and political settlement. As a result, technology acquisition slows down the economy, hampering productive capacity. On the other hand, this class exploits the working class, not through its direct ownership of the means of production, but through its control of the state, which owns the means of production. The intermediate class is engaged in the process of primitive accumulation, and in this case, the most important factor is the holding of power of various dimensions. By using various types of power, the powerful group can acquire more wealth and income in various ways. On the other hand, the general people are being deprived of having access to both private and public goods. It is evident that by exercising power, the powerful groups have been converting public goods into private property. This gives them more scope to generate profit. Moreover, they avoid paying taxes mainly by using political power. Thus, what has undermined the state-led accumulation process is the inability to impose direct taxes on property owners. As a result, on the one hand, the general people have limited access to public

Table 9.1 Classification of theories

Approaches	*Concept about state and society*	*Concept about employment*	*Underlying gaps*
Neoclassical economics	State is an instrument to fulfil the self-interest of individuals. Believes in a laissez-faire economy with privatisation and a non-interventionist state.	– There is always full employment. – Unemployment is determined by real wage above market-clearing level. – Problem of unemployment can be mitigated through wage-price flexibility. – There exists voluntary unemployment.	– Full employment is an illusion. – Ignore the weak governance and the political transaction cost in developing countries. – Eliminates public spending on employment creation, which raises inequality in the society.
Keynesian and New Keynesian tradition	State is responsible for providing public services to all and ensuring minimum rights to its citizens.	– Full employment does not exist. – A cut in wages would not cure depression and unemployment, but would worsen them.	– Couldn't incorporate distributional aspects and social inequality in poor countries. – Prescribed a generalised policy suggestion while unemployment in developing countries is a unique case. – The unique aspect of political settlement in Third World countries is missing. – Human sociality is also missing.

Source: Prepared by author

goods, and on the other hand, economic development is being retarded due to inefficient revenue collection (Titumir, 2022).

This implies that where there is a clientelist type of political settlement, the powerful agents usually hold organisational power, which adversely affects the efficacy of rule of law and other formal institutions. As a result, the power holders have the scope to accumulate wealth in unfair ways. They do not have any incentive to use those resources in the productive sector as they know that in this type of political settlement, holding organisational power is more important than having economic power. Therefore, the distribution of power – the political settlement, accumulation of capital and class structure – come into the equation. The ideas of citizenship and order need to be considered for the purpose of state-building. The ideas of rights and social contracts need to be modified in the pursuit of the transformation of the state (Titumir, 2022).

On account of the deficiencies, there is a requirement for the advancement of new propositions, which could provide appropriate explanations of the determination of income and employment in developing countries. The structure of these countries warrants the need for a new framework, which not only elucidates the causal relations but also identifies the institutions that accelerates work for all and universal social security in the particular political and socio-economic context of a developing country. The new framework has to capture the nature of state and society, including the political settlement to comprehend as to how power relationships affect the institutional arrangements in formulating the attributes and components of citizen centric rights-based social policy. The key arguments and underlying problems of different major theories and approaches are summarised in Table 5.3, helping the alternative farmework to fill in the gaps.

A Framework

The institutional structure, underwritten by political settlement of developing countries, is crucial in the analysis of employment. This is emphasised by the normative egalitarian objective of categorising employment for all as a universal, inalienable and indivisible rights of citizens in a public society. Certain schools, predominantly the Keynesians, have underscored for state intervention, yet ensuring rights and justice is determined by the nature and dynamics of political settlement in a given country, necessitating also to undertake historical institutional analysis shaping the intersectional and interdependent trajectories for the desired transformative changes in developing countries. Secondly, there is a major problem with weaving self-interest into the fabric of neoclassical economics. Human beings are pro-social by nature and have inherent cooperative features. The analytical framework goes beyond Keynesian understanding of employment and confronts the arguments of the neoclassical economics by rejecting the idea that only market mechanisms can pave the way to the solution of chronic unemployment.

The framework uses political settlement to understand the distribution of power, while the idea of citizenship raises the question of legitimacy and public order. On the other hand, a normative value system incorporates human sociality as opposed to the assumption of self-interest made in neoclassical economics. These pillars are significant to understand the nature and scope of social policies, resulting in work for all and universal social security. The presence of both the aspiration for a public society and human sociality ascertains the equitable distribution of wealth and benefit in a society. If citizens do not aspire to a public society, the ruling political groups get bolstered, giving rise to clientelism. An absence of both leads to creation of rentier state and preponderance of rent-seeking (Titumir, 2022).

The social policies tend to serve the interests of the ruling class in the absence of public society. Powerful groups tend to grab the policies for primitive accumulation and rent-seeking in absence of a public society, leaving the general populace to face widespread exclusion, discrimination and exploitation. Rent-seeking primarily originates in the processes of institutional change, which leads to a change in the economic rights of individuals. The rentier state alters the social contract between state and citizens into one in which citizens do not possess the motivation to question the legitimacy of the government or uphold a countervailing power against the political settlements enacted by clientelist networks. The state, on the other hand, is not expected to demonstrate fiscal accountability towards citizens. In addition, clientelist networks end up receiving state-directed funds on their basis of loyalty to the regime, and it serves as the only source of economic gain, thus fuelling the political settlement between these networks and the state. Restructuring of rents is required to avoid the pitfalls of market failure and for the maintenance of compulsion into the fiscal policy. Moreover, enhancing productivity and growth involve not just the strengthening of some rents but also the weakening of others (Titumir, 2022).

The social policies are a function of checks, balances and human sociality, the absence of which may lead to widespread concentration of public resources, primitive accumulation and exploitation in society. Thus, securing equal access and benefit sharing require a public society and citizen-state, which can be realised through a proper system of checks and balances and human sociality in the state. Human sociality helps foster the aspiration and struggle for a public society and citizen-state. A society with checks and balances and human sociality secures equal access and benefit-sharing for citizens irrespective of class, caste, race or any kind of identity. Checks and balances establish an accountable and transparent governance system, which enforces the contract between the state and citizens. The opposite case – an absence of both checks and balances and human sociality – leads to widespread concentration of public resources, primitive accumulation and exploitation. The lack of transparency and accountability due to the absence of checks and balances allows the group in power to grab rents, and a lack of human sociality makes the social contract between state and citizens void. In the absence of human sociality but the presence of checks and balances, public society fails to materialise, giving rise to discrimination. When human sociality exists but checks and balances are absent, the state becomes coercive and exploitative. Macroeconomic policies in the absence of any or both create discrimination and exploitation (Titumir, 2022).

Failure to fulfil these sufficient conditions is likely to thwart the efficacy of transformation trajectory. Institutions safeguard productive rents for firms to undertake the expansion of productive capacity, and accordingly, the institutional capability determines the efficacy of these rents. This is due to the fact that often an unprecedented change in political and technological conditions, shift in institutional aims or a lack thereof may render productive rents inefficient over time. Both formal and informal institutions protect these rents, and therefore the institutional capability ensures that continuous discrimination of productive from unproductive rent is carried out in order to prevent inefficient rents seeping into the economy (Titumir, 2022).

Fundamentally, the framework is concerned with just and equitable distribution of economic goods and services which is both process- and outcome-oriented as opposed to positive economics which focuses primarily on outcome and stresses the importance of an egalitarian outcome. Within this framework, government intervention is not only desirable but also necessary as opposed to the neoliberal reform agenda, which has reduced the capacity of the state through liberalisation, deregulation and privatisation, professing that the market will deliver the results. It also captures elements of sustainable livelihoods, which is based normatively on the ideas of capability, equity and sustainability (Figure 9.1).

The framework responds to the structural realities of developing countries. In these countries, most of the population having entered into the labour market with poor wages are only creating a huge amount of "working poor". Furthermore, a huge amount of the employed population is also underemployed. These have also resulted in augmentation of income inequality. Typical incomes and adjustment of inflation, however, grew little while the cost of living has been mounting, descending the majority in struggle and hardship. African countries have been plagued by high unemployment as economies have become stagnant. Southeast and South Asian countries have yet to move up in the ladder of structural transformation. They have been unable to diversify their economy. Educational level still remains lower in these countries with governments mostly focused on ensuring access to primary education and enrolment.

While poverty reduction is on top priority in policy formulation, yet these countries are plagued by the poor, with limited access to durable assets, healthcare, education and institutional finance which may have helped boosting their basic needs. For sustainable poverty reduction, there is no alternative to employment generation. Developing countries have precarious records in generating enough employment. On top of it, the COVID-19 pandemic has worsened the condition. Due to COVID-19, global working hours were lost by 8.8 per cent or equal to 255 million full-time jobs. The

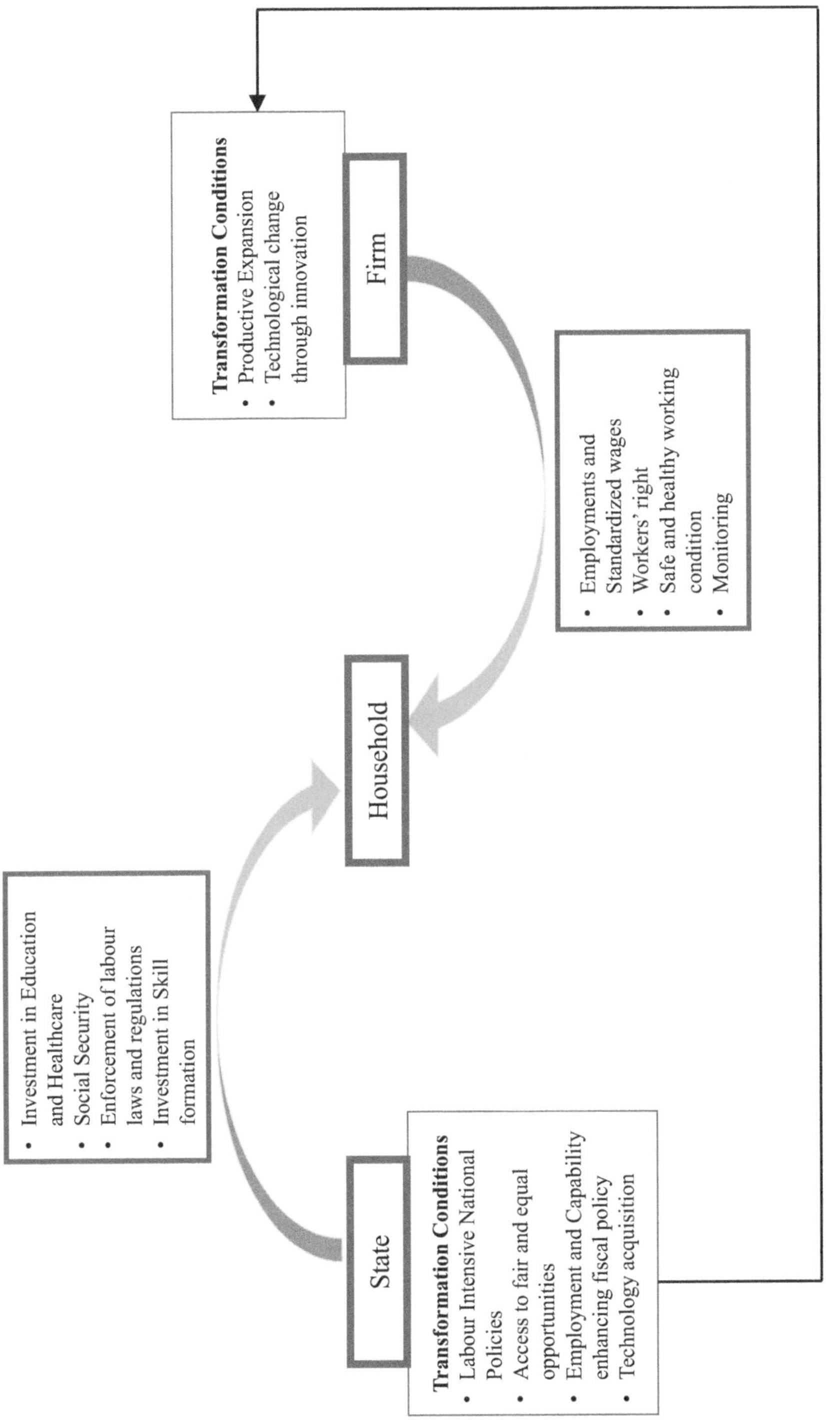

Figure 9.1 Transformational grid for employment

Source: Prepared by author

job loss during the pandemic amounts to 114 million (ILO, 2021). Developing countries, particularly lower-middle-income countries have faced the highest income loss.

The sustainable structural transformation of the economy is nowhere near. Agriculture still remains the primary sector of employment. In Africa, most of the work still remains around small mining and artisan work. For example, in Bangladesh, around 42.7 per cent of the labour force is engaged in the agricultural sector (BBS, 2017b), which is considered as lower-income elastic compared to the manufacturing sector. Currently, the average income in the agricultural sector and also the average labour productivity is very low. The informal sector employs the major share of the labour force, with low income and productivity amidst absence of compliance of workers' rights. For example, in Bangladesh, around 86.2 per cent of the labour force is in lower-income and lower-productive informal sectors (BBS, 2017a). In African countries, the average stands at around 85.8 per cent. The accelerated growth with productive employment, not an experience of growth without an expansion of jobs or the jobless growth, is the credible form of durable poverty reduction. This can be achieved in combination of both demand and supply sides of labour market policies, which are mainly driven by economic growth and growth in quality-adjusted labour force.

The population of youths or those aged between 15 and 24 globally stands at 1.3 billion, one-fifth of the world's population. More than half of this population is currently out of the labour force (ILO, 2020). A total of 267 million youths are out of education, employment and training. In South Asia, for example, youth unemployment stands at 18.7 per cent, much higher than the global average of 13.8 per cent (ILO, 2020). While governments have taken certain initiatives to increase enrolment in education, the number still falls much behind the developed countries. On top of it, youths in Africa and Asia are seriously disadvantaged with low skills. In sub-Saharan Africa and South Asia, only one per cent of youths are enrolled in vocational education. As a result, most of the youths are not trained for work. Hence, most of the employment of youths has gone to the informal sector. Ninety-five per cent of the youth employment in Africa is in the informal sector. These sectors fail to protect the life and livelihood of the youths (WEF, 2020). Despite the most population being in the economically active age, these countries are failing to reap the benefits of demographic dividend, a resultant from a shift in the age structure of the population of a country. The growing labour force has lower access to education, resulting in lower level of human capital formation, exhibiting a crying need for a technical and vocational education and training and associated policies to reduce the gap between poor–non-poor, men–women and underdeveloped and lagging regions by investing for higher growth to develop the labour force. It has also become a common scenario that graduates are frustrated with the burden of education, as there is concurrent joblessness amongst university graduates. There is also a dilemma of employability, arising out of skills mismatch, a discrepancy between the skills that are sought by employers and the skills that are possessed by job seekers. These act as hinderance for transformational change.

There is a need for paradigmatic shifts in policies and institutions for stimulation of the growth and acceleration of employment generation in developing countries. Such requires increased domestic private investment and foreign direct investment, yet the emphasis should not be only on raising the level of investment but also on the efficiency of investment through removal of a number of supply-side bottlenecks prevailing in these economies. A new synergy of macro, investment and trade policies with industrialisation as the core is a necessary condition to steer the process of sustainable structural transformation since developing countries demonstrate deindustrialisation, with varying degrees. Deindustrialisation is typically conceptualised as a decline in manufacturing as a share of total employment, having negative implications for long-run growth, given the special growth-pulling properties of manufacturing. The conceptualisation of industrialisation has to factor in changes in the levels and shares of employment in manufacturing, associated with concomitant changes in the share of manufacturing in GDP, the growth of manufacturing value-added, the labour intensity of manufacturing production and economic growth.

Summary

The discussion pertains to the dynamics of labour market in developing countries, dissects theoretical debates and develops an alternative explanation of causality to grid with the stylised facts, exhibited in the backdrop of existing policy regime, underpinned by the orthodox theoretical apparatuses. Following a detailed review of diverse traditions of theories on employment and identifying their drawbacks, a normative framework on *work for all* along with pragmatic solutions is proposed. The pathways for universal employment and universal social security are brought about through endogeneity of political settlement or social property relationships, and informal institutions, with a focus on nature and distribution of power in a given society.

The framework makes a departure from a narrow focus of increasing labour market flexibility – the subtle subtext of which is to lower wages and non-compliance of rights. Moreover, rights and wages, often the fruits of hard-fought bargaining, are also perceived to be part of the problem in the current orthodox thinking. In mainstream analysis, all too habitually workers are asked to bear the brunt of the costs of adjustment, in terms of soaring unemployment and plummeting wages, even when the labour market is not the core of the problem facing a country. Issues of workers' rights and entitlements, including the rights to participate in decision-making that affects their lives, are rarely raised.

Employment is a function of social and labour rights or social equity and collective well-being instead of individual's productivity and competitiveness. Any intervention must relate to men's and women's abilities to utilise their capabilities to realise their self-potentials while recognising that men's and women's abilities to utilise their capabilities depend on access to resources, entitlements, accountability and equality of opportunities. Thus, any programmatic intervention should entail just and favourable conditions of work underwritten by justice and social rights. Unless radical changes are undertaken for decent employment, structural transformation of a country will remain far fetched. Such requires major policy and institutional changes in both demand and supply sides of the labour market by substantially strengthening human development, especially through quality education and training programmes to enhance skills and encourage greater labour force participation underwritten by a rights-based approach to employment.

The nature of state policies is embedded in, and an integral part of, society, which is contingent upon the aspiration for a public society and human sociality. The social policies are supposed to ensure distributive justice and equal access to benefit when there is presence of both human sociality and a struggle for a public society.

References

Apergis, N., Miller, S.M., Panethimitakis, A., and Vamvakidis, A. (2005). *Inflation targeting and output growth: Empirical evidence for the European Union*. IMF Working Papers, 2005(089). Washington, DC: IMF.

Bangladesh Bank. (2008). *Recent employment situation and labour market developments in Bangladesh*. Policy Paper, 807. Retrieved from https://www.bb.org.bd/pub/research/policypaper/pp0807.pdf

Bangladesh Bureau of Statistics (BBS). (2017a). *Preliminary report of the household income and expenditure survey (HIES) 2016*. Dhaka: Bangladesh Bureau of Statistics.

Bangladesh Bureau of Statistics (BBS). (2017b). *Report on quarterly labour force survey 2016–17*. Dhaka: Bangladesh Bureau of Statistics.

Bauer, P.T. (1981). *Equality, the third world, and economic delusion*. Cambridge, MA: Harvard University Press.

Beaud, M. (1997). *Economic thought since Keynes: A history and dictionary of major economists*. New York: Routledge.

Berr, E. (2015). Sustainable development in a post Keynesian perspective: Why ecodevelopment is relevant to post Keynesian economics. *Journal of Post Keynesian Economics*, 37(3), 459–480.

Buchanan, J. (1986). Budgetary bias in post-Keynesian politics: The erosion and potential replacement of fiscal norms. In J. Buchanan, C. Rowley, and R. Tollison (Eds.), *Deficits*, pp. 180–195. Oxford and New York: Basil Blackwell.

Deakin, S. (2016). *The contribution of labour law to economic development and growth*. Centre for Business Research. Cambridge: University of Cambridge. Retrieved from https://www.cbr.cam.ac.uk/wp-content/uploads/2020/08/wp478.pdf

Deakin, S., Fenwick, C., and Sarkar, P. (2014). Labour law and inclusive development: The economic effects of industrial relations laws in middle-income countries. In *Institutional competition between common law and civil law* (pp. 185–209). Berlin and Heidelberg: Springer.

Dickens, W.T. (2009). A new method for estimating time variation in the NAIRU. In *Understanding inflation and the implications for monetary policy: A Phillips curve retrospective* (pp.

205–228). Retrieved from https://mitpress.universitypressscholarship.com/view/10.7551/mitpress/9780262013635.001.0001/upso-9780262013635-chapter-6

Dolenc, P. (2004). Keynesian economics. In S.B. Hussain (Ed.), *Encyclopedia of capitalism* (Vol. 1). New York: Facts on File, Inc.

Espinosa-Vega, M., and Russell, S. (1997). History and theory of the NAIRU: A critical review. *Economic Review: Federal Reserve Bank of Atlanta*, 82(2), pp. 4–25.

Friedman, M. (1977). Nobel lecture: Inflation and unemployment. *Journal of Political Economy*, 85(3), pp. 451–472.

Friedman, M. (1966). Comments on 'The case against the case against the guideposts' by Robert Solow". In G.P. Shultz, and R.Z. Aliber (Eds.), *Guidelines, informal controls, and the market place*. Chicago: University of Chicago Press.

Gordon, R.J. (1976). Recent developments in the theory of inflation and unemployment. *Journal of Monetary Economics*, 2(2), pp. 185–219.

Greenwald, B.C., and Stiglitz, J.E. (1987). Keynesian, new Keynesian, and new classical economics. *Oxford Economic Papers*, 39(1), pp. 119–133.

Hicks, J.R. (1936). Keynes' theory of employment. *The Economic Journal*, 46(182), pp. 238–253.

Hirschman, I.I. (1958). *On multiplier transformations*. United States Air Force, Office of Scientific Research.

International Labour Organization. (2020). ILO Monitor: COVID-19 and the world of work. *Updated estimates and analysis*. Int Labour Organ.

International Labour Organization. (2021). *ILO monitor: COVID-19 and the world of work*. Updated Estimates and Analysis, seventh edition. Int Labour Organ.

Johnson, H.G. (1971). The Keynesian revolution and the monetarist counter-revolution. *The American Economic Review*, 61(2), pp. 1–14.

Kates, S. (2009). *Say's law and the Keynesian revolution: How macroeconomic theory lost its way*. Cheltenham, UK: Edward Elgar Publishing.

Keynes, J.M. (1936). The supply of gold. *The Economic Journal*, 46(183), pp. 412–418.

Lal, D. (1980). A liberal international economic order: The international monetary system and economic development. Retrieved April 20, 2022, from https://ies.princeton.edu/pdf/E139.pdf

Mankiw, N.G. (2008). What would Keynes have done? *New York Times*. Retrieved from https://www.nytimes.com/2008/11/30/business/economy/30view.html

Mujeri, M., and Khondker, B. (2002). *Poverty implications of trade liberalization in Bangladesh: A general equilibrium approach*. Dhaka: Bangladesh Institute of Development Studies.

OECD. (2000). *V. revised OECD measures of structural unemployment*. Paris: OECD.

Peet, R., and Hartwick, E. (2009). *Theories of development: Contentions, arguments alternatives*. New York: Guilford Publications.

Rosenstein-Rodan, P.N. (1943). Problems of industrialisation of eastern and south-eastern Europe. *The Economic Journal*, 53(210/211), pp. 202–211.

Samuelson, P.A., and Solow, R.M. (1960). Analytical aspects of anti-inflation policy. *American Economic Review Papers and Proceedings*, 50(2), pp. 177–194.

Stiglitz, J.E. (1984). *Theories of wage rigidity (No. w1442)*. National Bureau of Economic Research.

Storm, S., and Capaldo, J. (2018). *Labor institutions and development under globalization*. Institute for New Economic Thinking Working Paper Series No. 76. Retrieved March 22, 2022, from https://ssrn.com/abstract=3228805

Tcherneva, P.R. (2008). *Keynes's approach to full employment: Aggregate or targeted demand?* (No. 542). Working Paper. Retrieved from https://www.levyinstitute.org/pubs/wp_542.pdf

Tobin, J. (1972b). 'Friedman's theoretical framework'. *Journal of Political Economy,* 80(September/October), pp. 319–337.

Titumir, R.A.M. (2013). Accumulation by dispossession: State of labour in Bangladesh. In Titumir, R.A.M. (Ed.), *Accumulation and alienation: State of labor in Bangladesh 2013.* Dhaka: Shrabon Prokashoni.

Titumir, R.A.M. (2022). *Fiscal and monetary policies in developing countries: State, citizenship and transformation.* Oxon and New York: Routledge.

Volscho, T.W. (2012). Neoliberalism, Piven and Cloward's bargaining theory, and wages in the United States, 1965–2006. *Journal of Sociology and Social Welfare,* 39, p. 55.

WEF. (2020). *Global risks report.* World Economic Forum.

Weiner, S.E. (1986). The natural rate of unemployment: Concepts and issues. *Economic Review,* 71(January), pp. 11–24.

Wray, L.R. (2009). *The social and economic importance of full employment.* Retrieved from https://www.levyinstitute.org/pubs/wp_560.pdf

Yergin, D., Stanislaw, J., and Bothwell, R. (1998). The commanding heights: The battle between government & the marketplace. *International Journal,* 53(2), pp. 362.

10 Work for All

Skills, Productivity and Wages

Introduction

This chapter analyses both the market and non-market determinants of employment, exhibiting that the lack of investment for expansion of productive capacity and skills formation results in unemployment and underemployment. Additionally, prevalence of low skills, unbounded supply of labour and limited productive capacity accrues lower return to labour compared to capital, and leads to low levels of savings amongst labourers, resulting in perpetual reproduction of inequality. Moreover, labour extraction, increased allocation of more resources to monitoring, higher than the market wages, and the compliance of workers' rights altogether increase productivity. It suggests for structural transformation from informal to formal sector employment, with mission-oriented industrialisation strategy, which creates multiplier effects as well as accelerates. For example, technological catching up, particularly in this age of fourth industrial revolution, is a much-sought mission to enhance productivity and gain competitiveness. A nationwide industrial regeneration scheme in developing countries is a good candidate too. Such multipliers can accelerate all - aggregate demand, consumption, investment and net-exports. Secondly, the actions to connect vulnerable workers to employment requires paying attention to specific needs of the population (i.e., female and the physically challenged) in the form of universal social security as well as facilitating human capital formation, including skills for employability.

In the first half of the nineteenth century, economists put forward a theory which Karl Marx later called the "compensation theory" (Marx, 1867). This theory comprises different market compensation mechanisms that are triggered by technological change and can counterbalance the initial labour-saving impact of process innovation (Vivarelli, 2014). The compensation theory has several components. A compensation mechanism "via new machines" displaces workers in industries through innovation but again creates jobs in production of new machines (Say, 1803). A compensation mechanism "via decrease in prices" displaces the workers as well. But innovations lead to a decrease in production costs resulting in a decreased price. Lower prices of products increase demand which then creates additional production and

DOI: 10.4324/9781003284222-14

employment. A compensation mechanism "via new investments" increases employment in the economy through investment arising from the gap of time between a cost decrease and a subsequent fall in prices previously mentioned. This mechanism established the hierarchy in compensation mechanisms of technological unemployment first brought in by Ricardo (1821). The formation of new capital was considered a condition sine qua non. If capital is not supplied in tandem with the additional workforce, other mechanisms would not work.

The compensation mechanism "via decrease in wages": As with other forms of unemployment, the direct effect of labour-saving technologies may be compensated through a proper price adjustment in the labour market. In a neoclassical framework, with free competition and full substitutability between labour and capital, a decrease in wages would lead to an increase in the demand for labour. The compensation mechanism "via increase in incomes" comes from the Keynesian and Kaldorian streams. In a Fordist mode of production, unions take part in the distribution of the products from technical progress. A portion of the cost saved because of technical change emerged as increased income and subsequent increase in consumption. The increased demand leads to rise to employment, and such causation automatically offsets the initial job losses caused by innovations (Boyer, 1990; Pasinetti, 1981).

The compensation mechanism "via new products" moves away from the traditional role of technology in the production process. Rather, technology can generate jobs through the creation of new economic branches.

> Entirely new branches of production, creating new fields of labour, are also formed, as the direct result either of machinery or of the general industrial changes brought about by it.
>
> (Marx, 1867)

This provides a theoretical basis for digital transformation as an "open access opportunity for all". Digital revolution has not emerged from a vacuum. Ceaseless amalgamation of human knowledge and skills, funded primarily by tax payers, reached this level. Yet, publicly-funded innovations are constantly being usurped by a few tech giants, instead of those remaining as public or common goods. Secondly, these behemoths are profiting out of a rather radically changed workplace where producers are also transformed into consumers. The oligarchies are getting their work done by a few numbers of remunerated employees compared to traditional companies while bulk of production is created voluntarily by unpaid users who are too reduced as their consumers, amassing huge amount of surplus by two distinctive ways, besides much of innovations being subsidised by public exchequer. One is seized as economic rent from volunteer producers while the other is generated out of sales of goods and services to them. The economic rent is generated from unpaid labourers, a factor of production, for which costs needed to bring them into production, are not paid. Thirdly, the digital markets are conceptualised as institutions to provide consumers with material well-being. Yet mounting academic research demonstrates evidences of consumers being systematically exploited through illusion, manipulation and deception due to asymmetric information, psychological weaknesses and unequal power. Digital markets, rather than being benign, allegedly intrinsically "phish" consumers as "phools". Such oligarchic system, if not regulated at every level, run risks of rendering people at large exploited and marginalized, instead of allowing them to enjoy freedom and self-fulfilment.

Developing countries have limited capacity in innovation and public investment in R&D. These countries have to rely on international trade and technology transfer from developed countries for new technological innovations. Almost all the technological changes in developing countries are brought through import (Acemoglu, 2003; Keller, 2004; Piva, 2003). However, whether these innovations actually bring any changes to employment depends on the absorptive capacity of a country. The capacity to absorb is subjected to the level of innovation and new technologies as well as public support in fostering those innovations. Countries with higher absorption capacity can induce technology in a much better way to augment employment. Nevertheless, developing countries in most cases face lack of competition and fail to remove the institutional rigidities, which may impede the effectiveness of price and income compensation mechanisms (Abramovitz, 1986; Lall, 2004).

The vital aspect of economic growth and employment generation is the structural transformation of an economy. The transformation occurs when resources, both labour and capital, shift from less productive sectors to a higher productive sector. Most commonly from the agriculture sector to the manufacturing sector. The transformation may occur within the sectors like from less mechanised industry to a highly mechanised industry. The sustainability of economic growth hinges upon both outside the sectors and within the sector transformation. For developing countries, the rate of the transformation is still in progress with agriculture still dominating the economy. Hence a shift of resources into the manufacturing sector and secondary industry is required for economic growth and employment generation. This not only raises the size of the economy but also increases productivity as technological progress, spillovers, and scaling up occurs due to the transformation.

This is further vexed by historic tracking of developing countries moving away from manufacturing into services at a faster pace than those observed in cases of developed counterparts. This process of premature "de-industrialization" is evinced by indicators such as lesser share of employment of manufacturing along with its value addition to economy compared to those of service sectors. There is a long-held consensus that manufacturing is the primary channel of modernization and creation of employment, especially by absorbing unskilled labourers. The stories of development in pre-and-post Second World War bear testimonies in this regard as under employed from agriculture are pulled into manufacturing, thereby increasing consumption spending and resulting into growing national income.

Productive Capacity and Skills Formation

Lack of investment for productive capacity expansion and skill formation results in unemployment and underemployment. A high level of investment in expansion of productive capacity results in high employment opportunity. The vertical axis in the diagram captures the productive capacity and the level of employment is denoted in horizontal axis. The expansion of productive capacity depends upon the level of investment (Figure 10.1). With expanded investment in productive capacity, new employment opportunities also rise. Productive capacity stands at point P^* from the point P due to increase in investment. This expansion of production boosts employment from E to E^*.

Job creation is a function of expansion of productive activity and skills formation. Suppose that the employment opportunities by a limited number of companies at a particular time in a particular society are constant. In addition, assume that once the wage level reaches above equilibrium it does not come down naturally for a particular time.

Suppose,

J = job creation
P = expansion of productive capacity
S = skills formation

$$dJ/dt = \alpha P + \beta S \qquad (1)$$

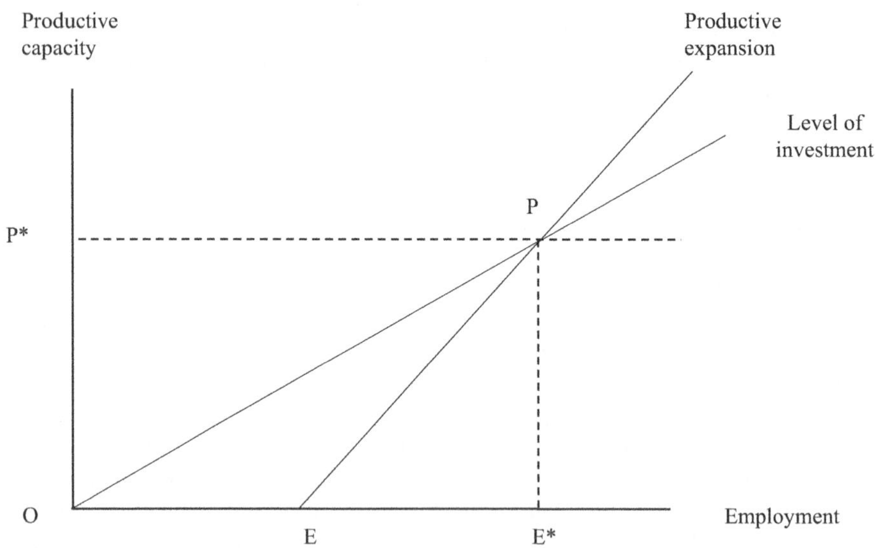

Figure 10.1 Productive capacity expansion and employment

Source: Prepared by author

Growth in jobs

$$dJ/dt = \gamma J \quad (2)$$
$$dE/dt = \gamma \quad (3)$$

with initial value $J(0)>0$, $P(0)>0$, $S(0)>0$. And α, β, γ are the growth rate of expansion of productivity capacity, skills formation and job creation, respectively. Also $\alpha, \beta, \gamma \geq 0$.

Case 1:

When $\alpha, \beta=0$, it means that expansion of productivity capacity and skills formation did not occur. Therefore, the level of employment remains as it was initially. So, in Equation (*2*) the growth will be zero, that is, $\gamma=0$. Consequently, in Equation (*3*) the employment in a particular society at a particular time will remain constant. So, when the wage will go above equilibrium, it will follow the pattern,

Employment $\propto$ *1/ (increase in real wage)*

Therefore, when real wage increases, some people might lose their job.

There is a scenario here, suppose that in that particular society at that particular time, there are two types of people seeking employment.

E_1 = who loses job due to movement of real wage above the equilibrium
E_2 = new graduates

So, L = people needing employment = E_1+E_2

$$dL/dt = \alpha_1 E_1+\alpha_2 E_2 \quad (4)$$

Here α_1 = rate of increase of people who lose their jobs due to real wages being above the equilibrium.

and α_2 = rate of increase of new graduates

Therefore, Equation (*4*) exhibits the rate of increase of population requiring jobs. With skills formation and expansion of productivity capacity remaining constant, L will keep increasing, creating a joblessness situation in the economy at that particular time.

Case 2:

Suppose that α, β is increasing, in Equation (2), the growth rate of job formation will also increase consequently increasing the rate of employment.

There are two types of sectors – (i) a sector in which already employment is available, and supposing that such is constant, and (ii) a newly created sector. If constant + $\gamma > \alpha_1 + \alpha_2$ is ensured, it does not matter even if real wages go beyond equilibrium, implying the necessity to increase the value of γ which depends on the increase of

J = job creation and
P = expansion of productive capacity.

The countries that witnessed growth has largely been possible due to expansion of productive capacity and utilisation of the labour force. For example, historically, agriculture had been the dominant sector in Bangladesh and employed well over 70 per cent of the working population after the independence in 1971. Two events were particularly important in shifting the labour dynamics in the country. First, the readymade garments sector sprung up in the 1980s and was built upon the abundance of labour. The sector did not require high level of skills and hence tapped into the unskilled and semi-skilled labour force. Second, overseas employment opportunities in the Middle Eastern countries opened at the same time. This sector also relied on unskilled and semi-skilled workers. This worked in favour of the large number of unskilled workers in the agricultural sector in rural areas who migrated to urban areas and abroad for employment. The structural transformation in the economy began at that stage and only accelerated in the following decades. Readymade garments sector also had a long-lasting impact on female employment. This sector also caused migration of unemployed females from rural areas to cities. The shift from the low waged agricultural sector to the higher waged industries and the overseas employment resulted in an increase in private consumption. The outcome of this increased consumption was a sharp reduction in poverty, especially in rural parts of the country (Titumir, 2021a).

For developing countries, there is a crying need for growth of labour-intensive productive capacity in order to stave off increasing unemployment and a decelerated decline in the incidence of poverty, exacerbated by the COVID-19. Despite considerable thrust on poverty alleviation, a significant number of people lived below the poverty line, and there is a new poor. For instance, the poverty rate, which had decreased in recent years in Bangladesh, may exhibit an upward movement for the first time since 1992. Poverty has gone beyond a straightforward headcount ratio during the pandemic, indicating the differential impacts on groups without entitlements – of the new poor, of small businesses, of female-headed enterprises – in terms of income erosion, unemployment, food security and nutrition. The fallout is however not limited to the informal sector or rural areas. Rights are not protected even in the formal sector, as employees face income erosion, as they have been sent on furlough without any subsequent financial support from the government. The pauperisation process is likely to accelerate due to natural disasters, such as cyclone Amphan and the decade's worst floods, which have left numerous communities stranded and despondent in the middle of the pandemic (Titumir, 2021b).

The world of work is precarious, given more than three fourth employment is in informal sector, characterised by lower than minimum wages, unfair dismissals and extreme vulnerability to joblessness since such jobs remains outside the jurisdiction of labour laws. Social protection provisions are marred by problems of fragmentation, errors of inclusion and political patronage-based targeting. If the new poor population is taken into consideration, the intended number of beneficiaries for these safety net programmes is insignificant when compared to those requiring support. The lack of inclusive social safety nets has given rise to shortcomings in constructing the list of recipients, allowing a leeway for ineffective management of resources, extortion and abuse of power (Titumir, 2021b).

The rate of joblessness, particularly youth unemployment, is rising at a significant rate, making it a global crisis, though its social and economic characteristics vary considerably in size and nature from one country and region to another (ILO, 2012). In Bangladesh, the nature and extent of employment of the youth is an important indicator of the additional employment generating capacity of the economy. Alternatively, the extent of unemployment of youth labour indicates the failure of the growth process to create enough jobs for the new entrants to the labour force and, consequently, the loss of potential income and welfare (Bangladesh Bank, 2008). Moreover, the national rate of wage is still below the poverty bar of 1.90 USD per day. Low wage, lack of employment opportunities together with new poor would cumulatively reign in the rate of recovery in developing countries, screaming for a transformative structural change.

Factor Mobility, Wages and Inequality

Factor mobility with prevalence of low skills, unbounded supply of labour and limited productive capacity accrues lower return to labour compared to capital, and leads to low levels of savings amongst labourers, resulting in perpetual reproduction of inequality.

Developing countries are in a situation with unemployed professional, skilled, semi-skilled and less-skilled labour force. The huge amount of workforce needs to be engaged in employment to ensure their participation in the economic development of the countries as well as to improve their living standard. That is why factor mobility, level of skills and expansion of productive capacity are crucial. Factor mobility with incidence of low skilled huge supply of labour and limited productive capacity generates lower wages (Table 10.1).

Migration plays a dynamic role in developing economies mainly in two major ways through reduction in unemployment and increased inflow of remittance. The lower inflow of remittance leads to dwindling levels of savings amongst

Table 10.1 Factor mobility and productive capacity

		Productive capacity	
		Ineffective	*Effective*
Factor mobility	**Low-skilled**	Perpetual reproduction of inequality with low wage	Less bargaining power of labours
	Skilled	Violation of labour rights with low return on labour	Fruitful gain from labour migration leading to more savings and investment

labourers, resulting in unending reproduction of inequality. On the other hand, mobility of skilled workforce with effective labour rights in an environment of expanding productive capacity results in higher wage and consequential augmented savings. The issue is illustrated through the case of Bangladesh.

In 2020, Bangladesh received 21.7 billion USD from remittance which accounted for 6.6 per cent of the GDP. Developing countries are among the top 10 remittance receivers. The share of remittance received varies largely between the developed and developing nations. Share of remittance in the GDP in lower-middle-income countries is 2.5 per cent whereas in high-income countries the share is just 0.3 per cent. In the period 2003–2015, remittances grew by 14 per cent annually in current USD terms (Table 10.2) and by almost 17 per cent in BDT terms. Remittances share of GDP grew more than double in Bangladesh compared to the South Asian countries. Nepal, another South Asian LDC, receives remittance worth 24 per cent of its GDP. Most of the income comes from low skilled works.

Bangladesh ranks sixth among migrant origin countries, but is ninth among the top 10 remittance receiving nations, implying that sending more workers abroad while earning less in remittance. Major competitors in the overseas job market – including Sri Lanka, Pakistan and the Philippines – gain much from the skilled workforce they send abroad. The average monthly remittance sent by a Bangladeshi expat is USD 203.33 while a Filipino worker earns on an average USD 564.1, which is more than double compared to a Bangladeshi. The monthly average income of a Pakistani expat is $275.74 and $395.71 for an Indian and $532.71 Chinese citizen. Among the Bangladeshi migrants, only 36 per cent are skilled while 45 per cent are skilled from Philippines 47 per cent from Sri Lanka and 43 per cent from Pakistan. Moreover, higher-skilled workers send more money than the less skilled migrants and that an increase in skills increased the amount remitted by up to USD 255 per month between 2009 and 2019. Migrants' skills determined how remittances were invested and saved, with skilled migrants requesting family members to invest remittances into savings accounts whereas unskilled migrants generally used remittance to pay off loans. Higher skilled migrants were employed in better paid jobs and

Table 10.2 Remittances as a share of GDP

Remittances as share of GDP	
Bangladesh	6.7
India	3.2
Pakistan	9.9
Nepal	24.1
Vietnam	6.3
South Asia	4.4
OECD	0.8
High income	0.3
LMIcs	2.5

Source: World Bank (2020)

were more likely to send higher remittances for longer periods than lower skilled migrant workers (IOM, 2020).

The most important barrier for labour mobility is national borders, though distances in space, culture, and language are inherent impediments to mobility. The compelling economic evidence on the economic gains and social benefits of migration sits awkwardly with stark political opposition to immigration. The tax equivalent of an international border is over 150 per cent for young unskilled workers from most developing countries, more than three times larger than those imposed by physical and cultural dimensions of distance. The average income gain for a young unskilled worker moving to the United States is estimated to be about USD14,000 per year. If there were doubling the number of immigrants in high-income countries by moving 100 million young people from developing countries, the annual income gain would have been USD1.4 trillion. This global welfare gain is held back by restrictions on international flows of labour (World Bank, 2018).

While much weight is often given to highlight and celebrate the achievements in economic growth in Bangladesh, a critical look points out the loopholes in the existing growth pattern of the country. Sizable portion of the population still remains under poverty and trends in inequality are increasing as observed by different measures of poverty gap and inequality indices (Legatum Prosperity Index, 2016; Osmani, 2018; Unnayan Onneshan, 2014). Remarkably, the high economic growth in Bangladesh has been accompanied by increasing income inequality in the labour force. The return on labour has declined over the recent years, making inequality an inevitable outcome of the process. A careful analysis reveals that during the decade of 1985/86 to 1995/96, the real wage increased at an average rate of 1.26 per cent annually whereas the growth in labour productivity was 2.88 per cent, while the real wage growth rate and labour productivity growth rates were 1.16 per cent and 2.42 per cent respectively (Table 10.3).

Quite significantly, this trend has reversed during the most recent decade since 2005/06 to 2015/16 when the real wage increased only at a rate close to zero (0.03 per cent) despite further boost in the labour productivity growing at rate of 3.59 per cent on average. This indicates that due to declining real wages, in spite of increasing labour productivity, the situation of income distribution is

Table 10.3 Annual average growth rate of GDP, employment, labour productivity and real wage (per cent)

Period	*1985/1986–1995/1996*	*1995/1996–2005/2006*	*2005/2006–2015/2016*
Real GDP growth	4.21	5.56	5.89
Employment growth	1.33	3.14	2.3
Labour productivity growth	2.88	2.42	3.59
Real Wage growth	1.26	1.16	0.03

Source: Osmani 2018

exacerbating, further disfavouring the working class. Since the mid-1980s, the growth rate of real wage increasingly lagged behind the growth rate of labour productivity, and this implies the share of labour in the national income is decreasing consistently. This explains the trend of rising inequality as captured by other traditional measures like the Gini-coefficient and the Palma ratio.

The surplus labour was transferred to the manufacturing, primarily to the RMG sector. This provided a competitive advantage in the sector which later became the driving factor of the economy (Helal and Hossain, 2013; Osmani et al., 2015). At the same time, the country missed out on utilising the demographic dividend, as the manufacturing sector is still reliant on RMG and has failed to produce advanced products.

Taken as a whole, Bangladesh experienced little growth in real wage with low return to labour and rising inequality in labour income. Growth in labour productivity has also witnessed a slow rise in recent years with around half of the labour force employed in low productivity agriculture (Figure 10.2a). Compared to China, Bangladesh fares lower in labour productivity.

Productivity and Labour Extraction Function

Labour extraction, if increased by allocation of more resources to monitoring or increasing employment rent, induces increase in productivity, given that human labour is the only common characteristic shared by all goods and services exchanged on the market, either as a source of wealth of nation or the development of capitalism as a system of exploitation. For increasing the output of a firm, which comes from increased labour productivity, the ratio of output per worker, employers have to allocate more resources to monitoring workers through employing supervisors to reduce labour shirking with a view to increased extraction out of labour. Even from the neoclassical arguments of labour efficiency (total labour cost divided by gross revenue) and labour productivity (gross revenue per worker) cannot be ensured, the labour will start to shirk the work and hence reduce the output. In order to keep the output in a steady state, employers extract labour through monitoring. This has also given birth to varieties of theories such as efficiency wage, which stipulates that increasing wages can lead to expanding productivity. In other words, labour extraction or exploitation of labour leads to escalating output. Productivity, thus, can be improved through appropriate adjustments to a farm's input mix, primarily by increasing labour productivity through supervision, higher wages and increasing human capital per worker and by adopting new technology, amongst others.

Inherent power structures, institutional arrangements of developing countries affect the employment opportunity, basic income scheme and social security of people. State is responsible for the distribution of resources, basic rights and facilities to its people. The role of the state machinery is to provide income-earning facilities to citizens and invest in their skills and development. However, in developing countries, because of accumulation behaviour of powerful agents, citizens

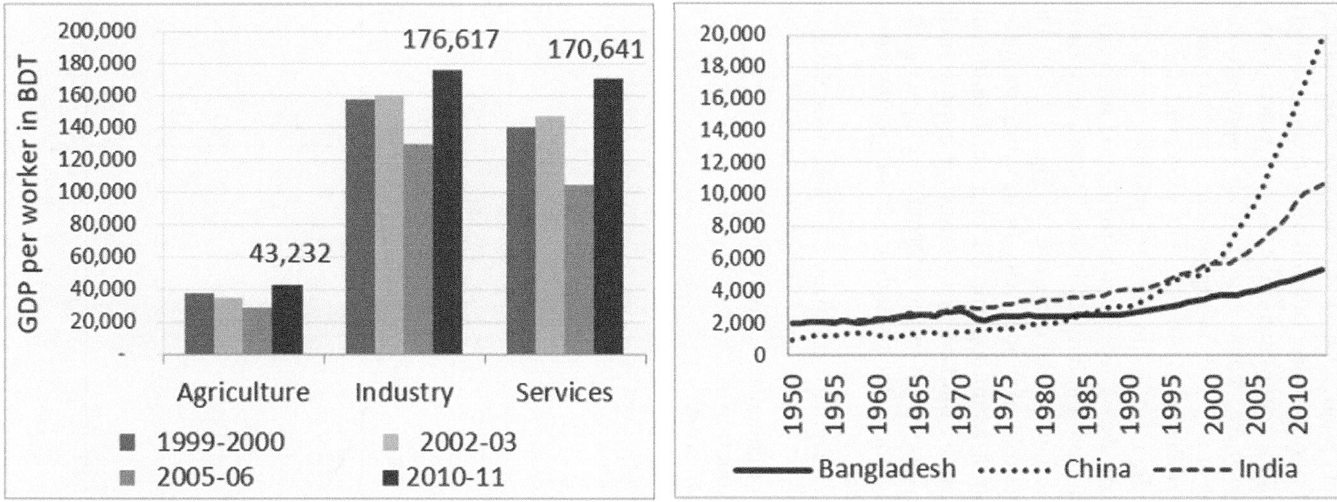

Figure 10.2 (a) GDP per worker by broad economic sector (in BDT) (b) Labour productivity in Bangladesh, India and China

are deprived of employment opportunities. Thus, labourers are dispossessed through patron–client politics. One of the fundamental challenges and the reasons for dispossession of labour in Bangladesh is the growing gaps between the creation of employment and the requirements for the new entrants into the labour force, besides underemployment. There is a growing disproportion between the rate of growth in employment and unemployment, implying fragility of absorption capacity and vulnerability of labourers to low wages and non-adherence of rights.

For illustrating the relationship between productivity and labour extraction, assume that the vertical axis depicts monitoring and supervision while the horizontal axis portrays productivity of labour. When investment in supervision increased from *O* to *I*, productivity rises to *P* (Figure 10.3). The point *I* denotes the maximum threshold of productivity from strong monitoring and supervision. After that point technological catching up, training and skills development of the workers are fundamental for further improvement in productivity. At the same time, investment in monitoring and supervision will have a marginally diminishing effect due to higher cost of spending on monitoring than the output produced.

Suppose that an imaginary company "*A*" produces chocolates. Assume

N = number of chocolates at particular time
L = labour extraction
W = amount of work
M = resources related to monitoring.

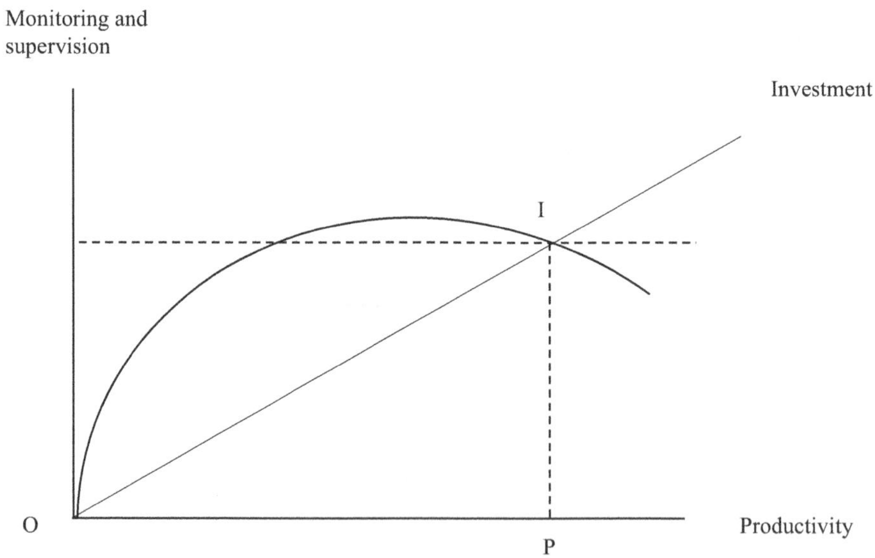

Figure 10.3 Extraction of labour and productivity

Source: Prepared by author

For the purpose of elucidation, suppose that, the company has put up some closed-circuit television (CCTV) cameras and computers to monitor the work of labourers. In addition, a condition is that if a person wants to take a job in that factory, s/he must work for eight hours and the work will be monitored by CCTV cameras. If more monitoring, including techniques and resources, are added to the factory, the labourers will further increase their work.

$$dW/dt = \alpha M \quad (1)$$
$$dW/dt = \beta W \quad (2)$$
$$dL/dt = \beta W \quad (3)$$
$$dL/dt = \gamma L \quad (4)$$
$$dN/dt = \gamma L \quad (5)$$

with initial conditions,

$w(0)>0,\ L(0)>,\ N(0)>0.$

and $\alpha, \beta, \gamma \geq 0$ and α, β, γ are growth rate of resources related to monitoring, amount of work, labour extraction, respectively,

Case 1: $\alpha=0$

If resources related to monitoring do not change in Equation (*1*), the rate of growth of amount of work, β remains zero in Equation (*2*). Therefore, in Equation (*3*), the rate of change in labour extraction remains constant. Consequentially, in Equation (4), the growth rate of labour extraction, γ is zero. As a result, the number of chocolates at a particular time remains the same as before.

Case 2: $\alpha>0$ and increasing

When resources related are deployed for increased monitoring in Equation (*1*), the rate of growth of amount of work, β also exhibits escalations in Equation (2). Simultaneously, in Equation (*3*), there is an upturn in the rate of change in labour extraction. Hence, the number of chocolates produced surges with the growth rate of labour extraction, γ in Equation (*4*).

Labour extraction is induced by providing the labour force with increased wages and incentives. Provision of social security, insurance, etc. may raise the output. Developed countries, thus, have higher labour productivity with lower work hours per person engaged due to higher wages and universal social security. The developed countries have achieved the transformation through wages and social security measures to increase the productivity of the labourers, besides continuous advancement in technologies. They have not opted for reduction in wages and/or primitive exploitation of labour rather invested in human capital and technologies.

Developing countries, on the contrary, have higher work hours per person engaged compared to the developed nations. The productivity of the workforce is also much higher for the developed nations (Figure 10.4). Higher work hours in developing countries is the result of labour-intensive mode of

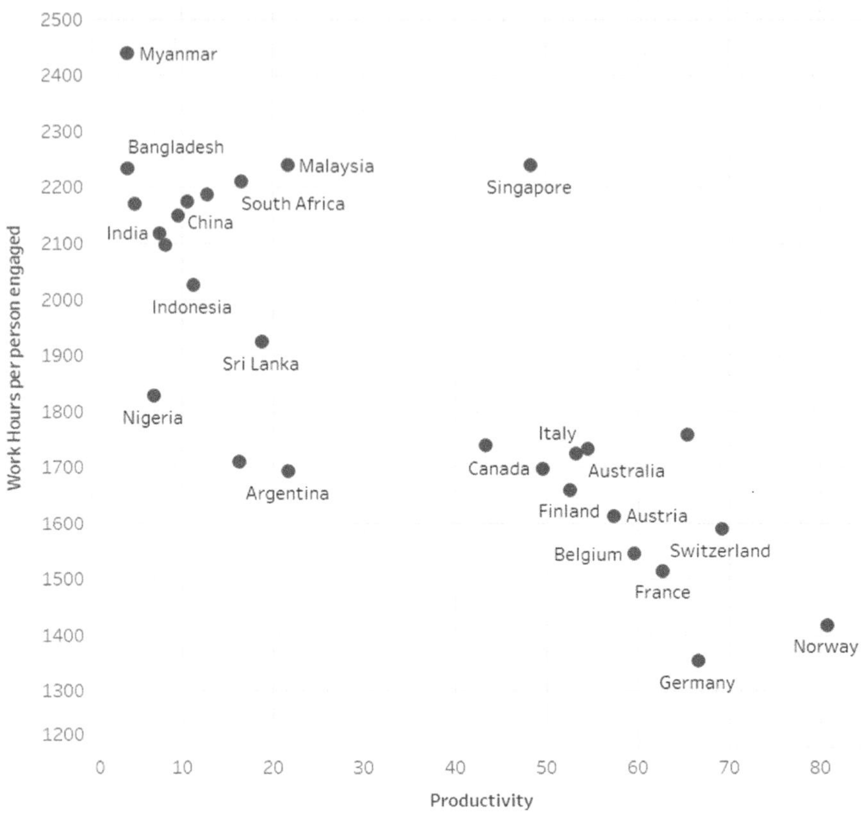

Figure 10.4 Labour productivity in selected countries

Source: ILO (2020)

production and the lack of regulations and labour rights. This demonstrates the primitive accumulation behaviour of the powerful. Thus, labourers are dispossessed due to the patron–client politics. Labour extraction through monitoring may raise the work hours but may reduce productivity in the long run because of lack of rights and entitlements. Developed countries provide social security, labour rights and the negotiation power of the labour through unions, which raise productivity with lesser working hours. The rights to work for all and social security are also in tandem with the human rights and sustainable development goals (SDGs). The SDG 8 underscores about "sustained, inclusive and sustainable economic growth, full and productive employment and decent work for all" while different human rights covenants call for social security at every stage of life for everyone.

Spotlight: Employment Trends in Bangladesh

The economy of Bangladesh could not create jobs compared to the increased labour force. As a result, there was an increasing rate of unemployment throughout the years. The labour force grew from 36.1 million in 1995–1996 to 62.1 million in 2013. On the contrary, the number of unemployed persons increased during the same period from 1.3 million in 1995–1996 to 2.60 million in 2010 and stood at 2.6 million in 2016. The number of employed enlarged from 34.80 million in 1995–1996 to 59.5 million in 2016 (Table 10.4). Although the unemployment rate in 2016 decreased slightly to 4.2 per cent than 4.3 per cent in 2013, yet such is not a full picture due to a folly in the national statistical agency's definition of employment, which counts a person as employed if s/he was working one or more hours with or without pay during a reference period. Essentially, the level of employment suffers from large-scale disguised unemployment, meaning too many workers are filling too few jobs, characterised by low productivity and mostly following in to informal labour markets.

The absolute size of the employed labour force decreased to 37.6 per cent in 2016 from 39.39 per cent (approximately 23.3 million) in 2013 (BBS, 2017). There is a growing concern due to mounting ratio of unemployed, implying the fragility of absorption capacity and vulnerability of labourers to low wages and violation of rights. Henceforth, ensuring jobs for all has remained elusive in absence of expansion of productive capacity.

Although the share of the working-age population, aged between 15 and 64, is around 67 per cent, the proportion of the inactive population, persons who are not employed or unemployed, is still 41.5 per cent of the population (Table 10.5). Since an economically inactive population is dependent on family income, denoting a much higher dependency burden than what is implied by the theoretical dependency ratio (BBS, 2017). Inactive population in the youth age group is very high, with the proportion of youths in neither education nor employment or training (NEET) is 26.1 per cent in Bangladesh. The gender

Table 10.4 Employment and unemployment trend in Bangladesh

Population in labour force (in million)					*Employment to population ratio (per cent)*	*Unemployment rate (per cent)*
Year	*Total population*	*Labour force*	*Employed*	*Unemployed*		
1995–1996	121.8	36.1	34.8	1.3	29.6	3.60
1999–2000	129.8	40.7	39	1.7	31.4	4.18
2002–2003	133.4	46.3	44.3	2	34.7	4.32
2005–2006	138.8	49.5	47.4	2.1	35.7	4.24
2010	147.9	56.7	54.1	2.6	38.3	4.59
2013	154.1	60.7	58.1	2.6	39.4	4.28
2016	158.5	62.1	59.5	2.6	37.6	4.2

Source: Labour Force Survey, 2002–2003, 2005–2006, 2010, 2013, 2016

Table 10.5 Unemployment by age group and gender

Unemployment rate by age group		*Male*	*Female*	*Working-age population per cent*
15–17	10.5	10	12	26.3
18–24	10.11	8.9	12.4	
25–29	6.7	4.9	10.0	
30–64	1.9	1.0	4.2	36
65+	0.9	0.6	2.4	4.7
Total	4.2	3.0	6.8	67

Source: BBS (2017)

gap in NEET rates is particularly large in countries like Bangladesh, where 47 per cent of young women are NEET, compared to 10 per cent of young men in the age group of 15–24 (ILO, 2020). The large proportion of inactive non-student population reinforces the underutilisation of labour prevalent in the country. The youth unemployment rate in the Asia and the Pacific region has risen since 2012 and is estimated at 14.1 per cent in 2020, compared to 13.7 per cent globally (ILO, 2020). In developing countries, NEET are relatively higher compared to the developed nations, resulting in huge loss as the potential of millions is not being properly tapped for failing to create not enough decent jobs for these young people. The precarity, a state of persistent insecurity with regard to employment or income, has become ominous after the downturn caused by COVID-19 in developing countries, with asymmetric recovery in comparison to the pace of advanced countries.

Unemployment is also higher among educated youths with secondary or post-secondary education. (BBS, 2017). In Bangladesh, unemployment is high among those with advanced levels of education. The number is higher for other developing countries as well. In the developed countries, however, the unemployment number is high among those with basic level of education and the number is significantly lower in advanced level of education (Table 10.6).

Unemployment among youths has been traditionally higher than for the rest of the workforce, and the gap appears to be increasing rapidly in recent years. The unemployment rate among older adults remains low and slightly decreased over time, whereas the rate for young workers increased between 2010 and 2016 for all population groups. The problem of rising unemployment among youth undercuts productivity and sustainable growth and is particularly vexing for developing countries as such may unleash social destabilization.

Youth unemployment is concentrated among workers with high levels of education. The unemployment rate among youths who have completed secondary school and above is over 10 per cent, and higher for females than for males; the unemployment rate among post-secondary-educated youth is close to 20 per cent (Table 10.7). Therefore, part of the increase in youth unemployment observed in recent years might be driven by a change in the educational composition of new labour market entrants. Better educated youths who enter

Table 10.6 Youth unemployment by level of education

Countries	*Basic*	*Intermediate*	*Advanced*	*Total*
Bangladesh	6.4	17.3	29.9	10.9
India	11.2	22.9	34.3	16.3
Thailand	1.7	2.5	5.3	2.6
South Korea	8	8.9	9.1	9
Norway	12.6	6.8	4.1	7.6
Sweden	30.7	9.3	6.4	12.9
Senegal	10.7	17.8	45.1	9.8
Uganda	7.9	8.7		6.5
United Kingdom	16.4	8.6	5	8.6
United States	11.8	7.9	3.3	6.4

Source: ILO, 2020

Table 10.7 Unemployed youth aged 15–29 in total unemployment, by education level (per cent)

Level of education	*Unemployment rate*		
	Total	*Urban*	*Rural*
None	4.7	3.4	5.2
Primary (Class I–V)	9.1	7.0	10.0
Secondary (Class VI–X)	25.4	24.4	25.7
Higher secondary (Class XI–XII)	20.2	21.6	19.7
Tertiary (all degrees or diplomas)	0.2	14.7	8.3
Others/unknown	0.3	0.2	0.3
Total	69.9	71.4	69.3

Source: BBS (2017), Labour Force Survey 2016

the labour market may have a high reservation wage, while high-paying jobs are unavailable given the slowdown in the labour market in recent years (Toufique, 2014).

Informal forms of employment consist of agricultural day labourers, urban street vendors, paid domestic workers, or at-home producers of clothing or other manufactured goods etc. A high proportion of informal workers are self-employed (ILO, 2002). The unorganised sector is characterised by low or irregular incomes, long working hours, small or undefined workplaces, unsafe and unhealthy working conditions, and lack of access to information, markets, finance, training and technology (Heintz and Pollin, 2003).

A declined rate of growth has been observed for the formal sector of Bangladesh throughout the last decade (BBS, 2017). Informal sector on the other hand grew positively for the same period. In 2016, about 86.2 per cent of the total employed persons aged 15 or older were in informal employment while only 13.8 per cent were in formal employment. Informal employment incidence was highest in agriculture sector (97.9 per cent of the total employment in that sector), industry sector (90.0 per cent of total employment in that sector) and service sector (70.6 per cent of total employment in that sector). A large number of people are employed in the informal sector with low levels of education. In terms of age group, 90.5 per cent of the youths aged 15–29 engaged in the informal employment and 83.8 per cent of the adults aged 30–64 engaged in the informal employment (BBS, 2017).

Moreover, the rate of participation in the formal and informal sectors also differed by gender. Male was engaged in informal sector more than three times (3.44 times) compared to female in 2002–2003 whereas the rate slightly decreased at two times (2.34 times) in 2013. The engagement of females in both formal and informal sectors increased compared to males for the mentioned period. In rural areas, 97.0 per cent of the females are in informal sector employment, with 90.6 per cent in urban areas. Of the national employment, only 4.6 per cent of females are employed compared to 17.7 per cent of the male in the formal sector.

Among the total population, 5.7 million and 35.6 million were male in the formal sector and informal sector, respectively (Table 10.8). For females, 1.6 million and 15.2 million were involved in the formal and informal sectors, respectively. Moreover, there exists urban–rural variation in employment. In the urban area, 24.9 per cent of workers were involved in the informal sector compared to 7.8 per cent in the rural area. On the other hand, in the urban area, 75.1 per cent was involved in the informal sector compared to 92.2 per

Table 10.8 Employment by formal and informal sectors

Year	*In million*		*In percentage*	
	Formal	*Informal*	*Formal*	*Informal*
2002–2003	9.2	35.1		
2005–2006	10.2	37.2		
2010	6.8	47.3		
2013	7.3	50.8	13	87
2016	8.2	51.3	12.8	86.2

Source: BBS (2017)

Table 10.9 Informal employment

Country	*Informal employment*
Bangladesh	86.2
Thailand	55.7
India	91.8
Myanmar	82.4
Uganda	90.7
Colombia	47.4

Source: ILOSTAT (2020)

cent in the rural area in 2013. Apart from this, low skills, subdued wages, high degree of vulnerable employment, lack of safety and protection at work further characterise the labour market in Bangladesh (Unnayan Onneshan, 2014). Growing informalisation of the economy affects the quality of employment and skills formation and indicates a depressed employment situation in the country (Titumir and Hossain, 2003).

Relative position of Bangladesh is similar to other developing nations. Neighbouring countries like India and Myanmar both have high levels of employment in the informal sector. Thailand on the other hand has a lower level of informal employment compared to Bangladesh.

Over the past four decades, notwithstanding many external and internal shocks, Bangladesh has increased its per capita income by fourfold. Bangladesh has been able to maintain healthy rates of growth in real GDP during the 2000s and first half of 2010s. Bangladesh's economic growth rates in recent years (more than 6 per cent) have been higher than most of the South Asian countries and many of the sub-Saharan African countries. The country has recently been upgraded from low-income country (LIC) to lower-middle-income country (LMIC) as per World Bank's classification. There is an aspiration of graduating from the LDC status to middle-income country by 2026 as per UN classification.

Economic growth in Bangladesh has not been complemented by accompanying growth in productive employment in the industrial sector with the exception in ready-made garments manufacturing factories. This is unlike the spectacular growth and economic transformation experienced by the East Asian countries which enabled them to capitalise on demographic dividend. For example, in South Korea between 1980 and 1990 the share of employment in agriculture halved from 34 per cent to 17 per cent with a 40 per cent decline in absolute share of employment in agriculture (Khan, 2005). In Bangladesh, the share of agricultural output has decreased from 21.8 per cent of GDP in 2003 to 16.3 per cent in 2013 – a 25 per cent decline over a decade, but during the same period the share of employment in agriculture has decreased only by 12.7 per cent and agriculture sector still accounts for half of total employment (45.1 per cent) in the country (Table 10.10).

Table 10.10 Distribution of output (per cent of GDP) and distribution of employment (per cent of total employment) by broad economic sectors

	2000	*2003*	*2005*	*2010*	*2013*	*2016*
Share of agriculture in GDP	25.5	21.8	20.1	17.8	16.3	14.8
Share of employment in agriculture	62.1	51.7	48.1	47.5	45.1	41.7
Share of industry in GDP	25.3	26.3	27.2	26.1	27.6	28.8
Share of employment in industry	10.3	13.7	14.5	17.7	20.8	20.5
Share of service in GDP	49.2	52.0	52.6	56.0	56.1	56.5
Share of employment in service	23.5	34.6	37.4	35.3	34.1	37.8

Source: BBS (2017) and World Bank Data

Over the same decade, the share of industry in GDP changed little (4.9 per cent increase during 2003–2013 decade) and share of service saw only slight increase as well. Nonetheless, the percentage of the labour force employed in industry doubled between 2003 and 2013 but still accounts for only one-fourth of total employment. The share of employment in the service sector has in fact witnessed a decline from its 2005 level which was growing in the previous decade. A further breakdown of employment growth in manufacturing subsectors demonstrates that employment growth in the ready-made garments sector accounted for much of the increase in employment (Raihan, 2016). In East Asian case, the employment elasticity of output growth was between 0.7 and 0.8 when real wage increased with rise in per capita income, but in case of Bangladesh, as some estimates showed, this rate may fall between 0.3 and 0.4 where employment elasticity with respect GDP growth is quite low and even declining (Khan, 2005). Other estimates show that overall employment elasticity is low in South Asian countries and this region experienced little structural transformation compared to East and Southeast Asia (Kapsos, 2005).

Economic diversification is commonly viewed as a necessary condition for a sustained and long-term growth of the economy and job creation. Diversification is argued to be playing an important role in structural transformation of the economy from producing low value-added products to high value-added products. Promotion of labour-intensive and high-productivity sectors, in both the farm and non-farm sectors, is therefore fundamental. This should be coupled with interventions to enhance productivity, jobs and incomes in traditional and informal activities where there are large pools of surplus labour.

Bangladesh is undergoing dynamic changes in its population age structure as stipulated by age structural transition model. The demographic transition and the consequent changes in the age structure of population of the country exhibit the highest concentration of the population looks to be shifting from children to working-age to elderly population (Figure 10.5).

The youth dominate with almost 52 per cent belonging to below 24 years of age and 32 per cent under 15 years of age. The country achieved significant reduction in the mortality and fertility rates even though the proportion of the youth population will remain high in the age composition of Bangladesh for at least next three decades due to what is called as population thrust effect. For instance, the proportion of the working-age population has increased 22.74 per cent from its lowest point of 51.9 in 1970 to 63.7 in 2010 and the UN projects a peak at 69.6 in 2030 followed by a latter period of gradual decline. In contrast, the proportion of young population (aged 0–14) has decreased 29.08 per cent from its highest point 44.7 in 1970 to 31.7 in 2010 and the UN projects around 20 per cent of the total population in 2040 after that it will decline further before getting steady during 2080s (UN, 2015). The future trend, however, indicates that the situation will reverse with a rapid increase in the number of the older population and a gradually declining young population. The projections reveal that the share of the old population will be doubled from its present size by 2035 becoming 9.4 per cent of the total population and will

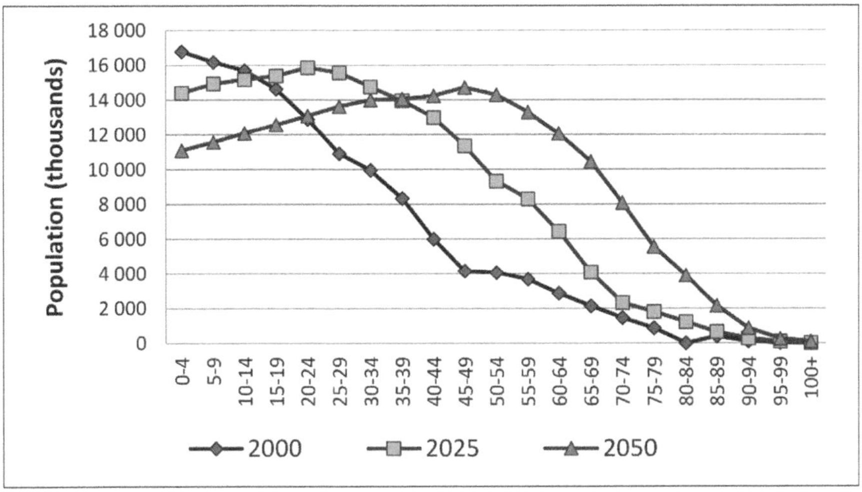

Figure 10.5 Shifts in population age structure in Bangladesh, 2000, 2025 and 2050

continue to increase at a faster rate becoming 16.2 per cent by 2050 and finally reaching at 31.4 per cent by 2100 (UN, 2015).

The population shift to prime working ages creates an upsurge in economically productive population who consume less than they produce and also save for their consumption in old age. The dependency ratio as a result gets to its minimum. Per capita income rises as the number of dependents per worker decreases. Among the working-age population aged between 15 and 64, there are two age groups – youth age group (aged between 14 and 24 years) and middle-age group (50 years and above). For the first group, the challenge is to ensure a smooth transition from education to employment by matching levels of skills with appropriate jobs in growing and productive sectors of the economy. Creating a favourable environment for savings and investment along with incentivising the middle age group, who tend to save more, requires prioritisation. An additional and growing size of labour force would not generate higher economic growth unless they are employed productively. Realisation of maximum potential economic growth is less likely to be achieved without a threshold level of capital deepening in the economy.

Whereas the consequent share of the working-age population will start to decline more visibly from 2040 and will decrease to 14.6 per cent by 2070 and after that the decline will continue but at a decreasing rate. It is predicted that due to declining and then negative population growth rate the number of working-age population will start to decrease mostly from 2040 and this trend will be intensified by acceleration of population ageing during the post 2050 period. These changes in the age structure are also evident from the gradually increasing median age of the population as it is projected to increase from 24 years in 2010 to 33.8 years in 2030 and 36.1 in 2040 with further increase in the next decades. Future projections show that by 2051, the share of the population of older ages will continue to rise relative to young- and middle-age populations due to lower or negative fertility rate and increasing life expectancy (Figure 10.6).

These projected trends in the next three or four decades are particularly essential to be taken into account in deciding the course of economic development of the country. First, the share of the young dependent population aged below 14 years is decreasing at a faster rate but the age group still comprises 29 per cent of the total population implying that a sizable amount of resources is needed to cater to their human capital development. Second, the share of the working-age population (15–64 years) is increasing considerably with a higher bulge in the young population aged below 24 years. This trend, as the projection suggests, will prevail up to 2050 giving large opportunities to reap benefit from a larger labour force while equally posing challenges of employment creation and absorption in productive sectors. Third, the share of the older population aged more than 50 and 65 years will, accordingly, start to increase significantly from the 2030s and the cohort will constitute a major proportion claiming for a large share of resources in terms of social security and old-age benefits for the next few decades. Appropriate policies are crucial for leveraging of full economic potentials from population changes during the intermediate phase. Currently being in the intermediate stage of demographic transition, Bangladesh has also experienced rapid growth in its labour force and its dependency ratio has reduced which is offering an opportunity for realising demographic dividend in the country and albeit with impending challenges to equip and utilise its growing labour force.

Demographic variables contribute to economic development through changes in population age structure. After estimating the relationship between changes in population age structure and economic growth among 127 countries for the period of 1950–2010, the World Bank finds that a percentage point growth of the working-age population led to a rise in per capita GDP growth by 1.1 to 1.2 percentage points (World Bank, 2016). This direct effect of the growing size of the working-age population on economic growth is termed as the first demographic dividend. Given Bangladesh is currently in the intermediate stage of its demographic transition and halfway through the productive or first dividend phase, the first demographic dividend with a window of opportunity started in 1975 and would end in 2040 (Mason, 2005). The magnitude of the first demographic dividend in Bangladesh, however, has been lowest among South Asian countries (Figure 10.7b).

In South Asian countries, demographic dividend contributed to a rise in per capita GDP growth by 0.80 per cent a year during the 1970–2000 period and during the same period Bangladesh experienced only 0.46 per cent dividend a year (Mason, 2005). Comparatively, Sri Lanka has gained the highest dividend in South Asia, but the magnitude of gains in economic growth due to demographic dividend is lower in Bangladesh than those of India and Pakistan.

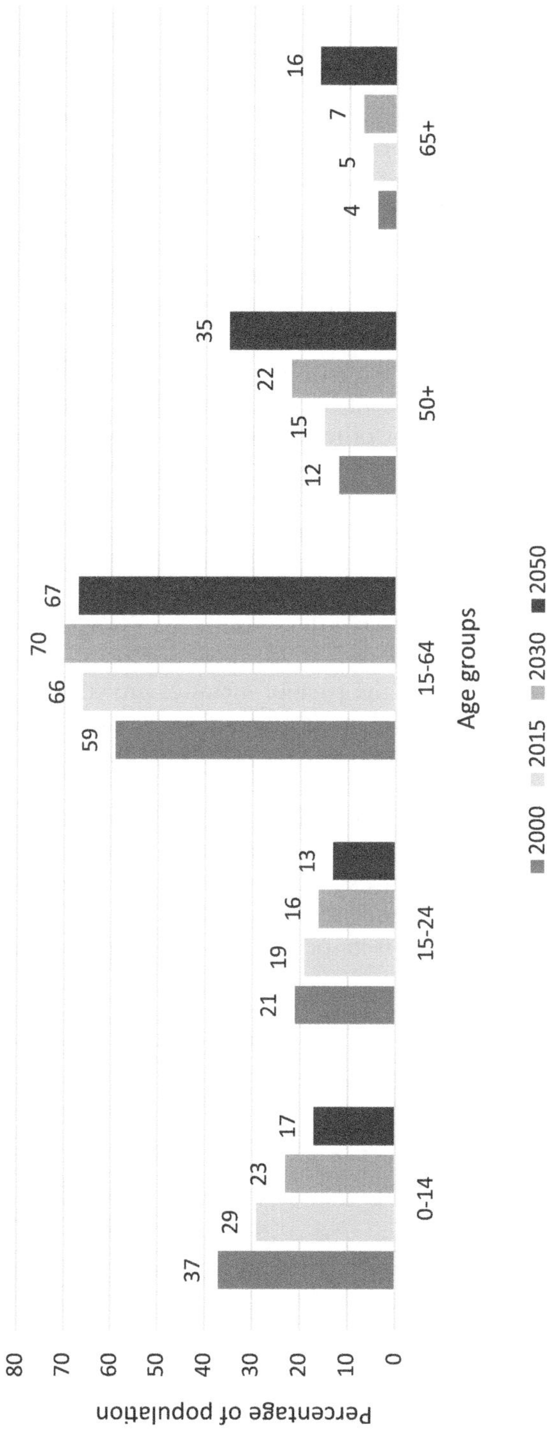

Figure 10.6 Percentage of total population by selected age groups in Bangladesh

Despite the relatively longer duration of dividend period, economic gains that have been realised in South Asia are lower and lower in Bangladesh than most of the East and Southeast Asian countries (Mason, 2005).

Bangladesh has enjoyed a long period of intermediate productive phase and is still left with more decades, but it could not fully exploit the advantageous changes in its demographic age structure to accelerate its economic development. The question that needs to be explained is as to why the magnitude of dividend has been so low in Bangladesh and how Bangladesh can maximise its gains from remaining years before demographic advantages turn negative. A selective assessment of the economy of Bangladesh might provide some insights in this regard.

Investment in social sectors like health, education, technology etc. is significant to develop skilled and trained human capital. The public expenditure on education and health, amongst others, at least explicates two effects – social and individual. For example, a more educated student is considered to earn considerably more income than a less educated while social benefits of education flow to the whole society as the payoffs of the education. Ironically, the national budget does not seem to pay heed to the impetus in terms of higher sector-wise allocation of resources. The declining trend in the allocations for social sectors may seriously threaten the sustenance of progress of social development indicators in which Bangladesh has demonstrated her success and consequential failing to accelerate the pace of inclusive growth in the country. In 2013, the public spending stood at 32.21 per cent of GDP in the developing and emerging economies, whereas Bangladesh stands only at 16.79 per cent of its GDP as public spending.

The low public investment in physical and social infrastructure in the backdrop of continued sluggish private investment may hinder achievement of the SDGs. The allocations of development expenditure for social sectors as percentage of the total development expenditure have recently undergone decreasing trends signalling inadequate investments in social development and posing challenges to

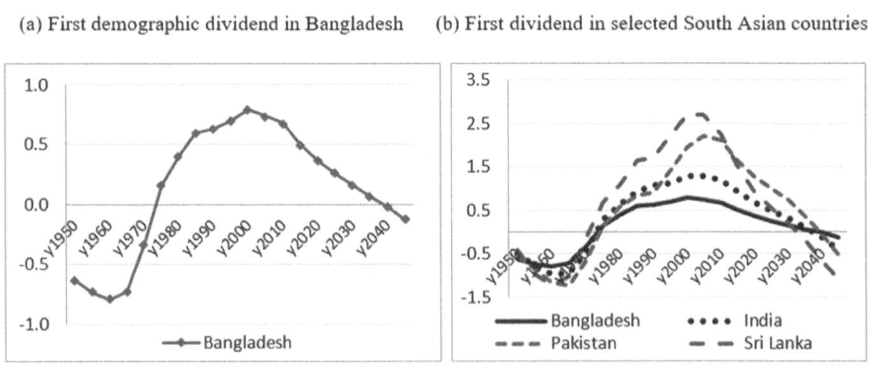

Figure 10.7 First demographic dividend in Bangladesh and other South Asian countries

the formation of human capital in the country. Public investment in the social sector is generally considered to play an important role in the economic development of a country by maintaining law and order, providing economic infrastructure, harmonising conflicts between private and social interests, increasing labour productivity through education and health and enhancing export industries (Al-Yousif, 2000). The implications are felt in every sphere of citizens' lives – work, transportation, healthcare, recreation, and educational facilities.

Bangladesh lags far behind other developing as well as its neighbouring countries in raising public spending adequately. The government's plans to increase the size of the government spending in relation to GDP in order to provide the basic economic and social services and improve the quality of public service delivery across the country have remained unachieved over the years. Improving education outcomes requires large investment for infrastructure and capacity building as well since more than one-fourth of the population is now in school-going age (0–14 years). Large difference in student–teacher ratio indicates that the country requires significant investment in development of education sector (Table 10.11).

The amount of public investment in the education sector is very low in Bangladesh and it has remained at only 2.2 per cent of GDP or even lower throughout the last several decades (MoF, 2017). In terms of international comparison, existing education infrastructure and current level of investment in education are quite low and insufficient for enhancing human capital. Because of insufficient funds, the progress in the education sector more or less has been limited to the intensification of enrolment in primary education or to the increases in literacy rate. Moreover, the number of educated unemployed is on the rise due to skills miss-match arising out of matching improvement in the quality of education vis-à-vis enrollment. The trend of allocations of public expenditure for education over the last few years has, however, been on the decline. On top of that, inefficient and corruption-ridden administration of the education system has resulted in poor implementation of existing budgets and policies in the country (Rahman et al., 2016). Overall, public expenditure in health and

Table 10.11 Student–teacher ratio at primary and secondary levels

	Primary pupil–teacher ratio			*Secondary pupil–teacher ratio*		
	1990	*2000*	*2013*	*1990*	*2000*	*2013*
Bangladesh	63.0	57.1	40.2	27.4	38.4	32.2
India	46.0	40.0	35.2	28.7	33.6	25.9
Nepal	39.2	38.0	25.6	31.1	30.2	29.2
Sri Lanka	29.1	26.3	24.4	19.1	19.6	17.3
Singapore	25.8	25.6	17.4	17.9	19.4	14.9
Malaysia	20.4	19.6	12.5	19.3	18.4	13.6

Note: Country data were taken from the nearest available years to 1990, 2000 and 2013

Source: Asian Development Bank (2015)

education in Bangladesh is much lower than the world average rate which is 6 per cent and 5 per cent of GDP, respectively, and even lower than average spending in low-income countries (Figure 10.8).

Overall attainment of education is low despite progress in recent years as one-fifth of the labour force has no educational qualifications. Female education at primary and secondary levels is higher but it remains low at tertiary level. A great majority of the rural labour force is uneducated and their proportion is almost five times higher than that of urban workers (Table 10.12).

Segregated data on highest educational attainment of population age groups of 15 years and only 40.4 per cent of 20–24-year-olds completed higher secondary level education in 2011 (Table 10.13). The proportion of graduates is

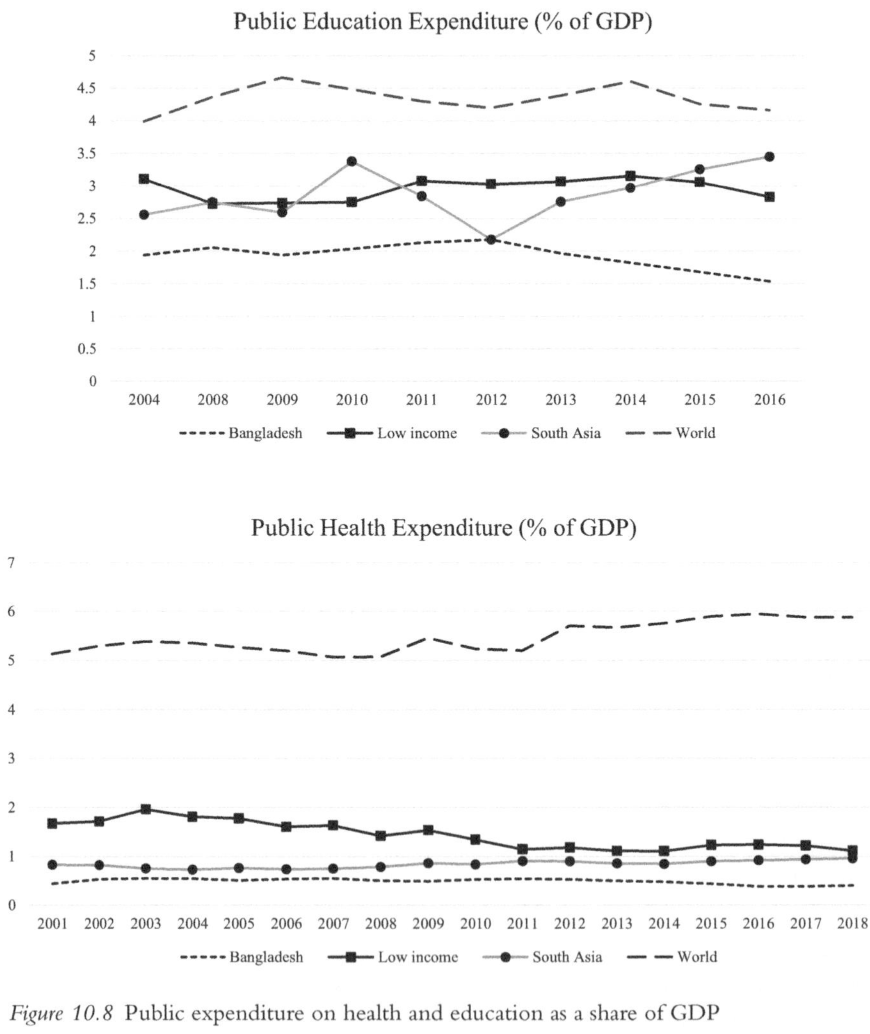

Figure 10.8 Public expenditure on health and education as a share of GDP

very low for all ages over 15 and constitutes only 9 per cent for age groups 20–29 in Bangladesh. More strikingly, about 58 per cent of the 50 years and above population has no education and 77.5 per cent for all populations aged above 40 years and more.

Since the country's Labour Force Surveys collect data only based on education qualifications and do not provide classification based on skill levels of the labour force. Alternatively, data from Bureau for Manpower Export and Training (BMET) on migrant workers give some indications that skills formation is not up to the expected level. For example, among total 568,062 manpower exported in 2011, professionals constituted only 0.2 per cent and skilled workers 40 per cent, whereas the share of semi-skilled and less skilled was 5 per cent and 55 per cent, respectively (BMET, 2012).

Table 10.12 Education of the population aged 5 and over in Bangladesh (per cent)

Level of education	*Total*	*Urban*	*Rural*
None	31.4	22.6	35.1
Primary (Class I–V)	22.7	20.4	23.6
Secondary (Class VI–X)	34.3	37.2	33.2
Higher secondary (Class XI–XII)	7.1	10.7	5.7
Tertiary (all degrees or diplomas)	4.2	9.1	2.2
Others/unknown	0.2	0.1	0.2
Total	100	100	100

Source: BBS (2017) Labour Force Survey 2016

Table 10.13 Educational attainment of population aged 15 and over by 5-year age group, 2011

	Highest class passed						
Age group	*No schooling*	*Primary*	*Junior secondary*	*Secondary/ higher secondary*	*Graduate*	*Master's or higher*	*Total*
15–19	1.6	23.1	28.4	46.8	0.2	0.0	100
20–24	2.2	26.6	26.9	40.4	3.7	0.3	100
25–29	3.4	30.2	25.4	33.8	5.3	1.8	100
30–34	5.2	32.2	22.7	31.0	6.2	2.7	100
35–39	7.4	35.5	21.6	27.6	5.6	2.3	100
40–44	9.5	35.9	20.2	26.5	5.7	2.2	100
45–49	10.4	37.3	20.0	25.9	4.6	1.8	100
50–54	13.3	39.0	17.8	24.4	4.3	1.3	100
55–59	13.6	39.3	17.2	24.4	3.9	1.5	100
60–64	15.1	41.1	16.3	22.8	3.7	1.1	100
65+	15.6	41.4	17.4	21.7	3.0	0.8	100
All ages 15+	7.1	32.7	22.7	32.0	4.1	1.4	100

Source: BBS (2017) Population and Housing Census 2011

Taking into account this prevailing pattern of low skill formation in the country, it is clear that there might be widespread skills gaps and mismatches of skills in many sectors of the economy. For instance, estimates suggest that around 62 per cent of young workers are undereducated as per the requirement of their jobs in mainly skilled agriculture, trades and other related fields (Toufique, 2014). According to Bangladesh National Skill Survey (2012), first of its kind, the estimated gap between demand and supply of skilled labour in selected manufacturing and trade sectors is approximately 1.458 million each year, which is a hugely large figure (NSDC, 2012). Putting together, educational attainment of the existing labour force is still low with lesser gains in income from additional schooling. Less skilled and semi-skilled workers constitute the majority of the labour force and there remains a widespread skills gap. Existing allocation, infrastructure and capacities of technical and vocational training is also limited. All these have clear consequences on the formation of human capital, which eventually builds foundation for rapid economic development during the age of structural transition through realising potentials of increasing labour supply.

An assessment of health and education scenario in Bangladesh, despite evidence of achievements in certain respects, rather reveals a grim picture of poor nutrition and persistent inequality in health, and low quality and rising disparity in educational outcomes. A major part of the young working-age population between the age range of 15 and 24 years continues to remain in education and their proportion has increased during recent years. Education and skills development of the youth age group immediately contribute to economic growth by enhancing the gains in employability, productivity and income earned by those who are already in or about to transition to the labour market and thus can increase the magnitude of demographic dividends (ADB, 2016).

Summary

Analysing both the market and non-market determinants of employment in light of the new framework, it exhibits that the lack of investment for expansion of productive capacity and skills formation results in unemployment and underemployment. Additionally, prevalence of low skills, unbounded supply of labour and limited productive capacity accrues lower return to labour compared to capital, and leads to low levels of savings amongst labourers, resulting in perpetual reproduction of inequality. Moreover, labour extraction, increased allocation of more resources to monitoring, higher than the market wages, and the compliance of workers' rights altogether increase productivity. It suggests structural transformation from informal to formal sector employment, including manufacturing. The actions to connect vulnerable workers to employment require paying attention to specific needs of the population (i.e. female and the physically challenged), facilitating educational transitions for youth, and lowering the costs of international migration for lower-income and marginally located workers. These must be implemented and delivered with expanding worker protection and social insurance.

Given the vast domestic demand, enhancement and diversification of productive capacity is the way forward. Such efforts are, in the long run, preparations for strengthening export competitiveness too. To strengthen and modernise the economy through diversification of industry sectors, the developing countries must develop a highly skilled workforce – its human capital – to keep pace with that diversification. Training and education can transform an unskilled and semi-skilled workforce. This would result in the creation of decent employment as well as moving away from informal sectors.

In order to establish a sustainable education system, transformative policy regime is essential. To maximise the social returns from education, higher emphasis and increased budget allocation are required. The primary target of education is to create a skilled workforce which can be increased through higher spending in secondary and vocational education where the rate of return is the highest. Nevertheless, technology and innovation transform the economies to a sustainable growth path.

Currently, most of the developing countries are in the midst of a demographic transition. For reaping the benefits of the transition, there must be higher and systematic investment along with necessary reforms in the education sector, enabling to move towards a transformative and sustainable development pathway.

Considerable challenges remain at the forefront in the efforts to improve the health status of the population, reduce health inequalities, improve the quality of care and public satisfaction with healthcare, and to increase the efficiency and sustainability of service-delivery agencies.

Equity in access to, and utilisation of, healthcare is an important goal for any health system and an essential prerequisite for achieving Universal Health Care for any country.

The chapter also identifies several fragilities, which need to be addressed in order to move towards work for all. The productive expansion of the economy as well as the enforcement of regulations by the government can be identified as the crucial factors to the transformability and sustainability. Transformation conditions depend on strong and functioning institutions.

References

Abramovitz, M. (1986). Catching up, forging ahead, and falling behind. *Journal of Economic History*, 46, pp. 386–406.

Acemoglu, D. (2003). Patterns of skill premia. *Review of Economic Studies*, 70, pp. 199–230.

ADB. (2015). *Key indicators for Asia and the Pacific 2015*. Mandaluyong City, Philippines: Asian Development Bank. Retrieved from https://www.adb.org/sites/default/files/publication/175162/ki2015.pdf

ADB. (2016). *Bangladesh: Looking beyond garments-employment diagnostic study*. Asian Development Bank.

Al-Yousif, Y.K. (2000). Do government expenditures inhibit or promote economic growth: Some empirical evidence from Saudi Arabia. *Indian Economic Journal*, 48(2), pp. 92–96.

Bangladesh Bank. (2008). *Employment promoting growth in Bangladesh: Monetary and financial sector issues*. Dhaka: Bangladesh Bank.

BBS. (2017). *Labour Force Survey 2017*. Dhaka: Bangladesh Bureau of Statistics (BBS).

BMET. (2012). *Bureau of manpower employment and training, government of the peoples' republic of Bangladesh*. Dhaka. Retrieved from www.bmet.org.bd

Boyer, R. (1990). *The capital labour relations in OECD countries: From the fordist "golden age" to contrasted national trajectories*. Working Paper CEPREMAP, 9020. Paris.

Heintz, J., and Pollin, R. (2003). *Informalization, economic growth and the challenge of creating viable labor standards in developing countries*. PERI Working Paper No. 60. Retrieved April 26, 2022, from https://scholarworks.umass.edu/cgi/viewcontent.cgi?article=1048&context=peri_workingpapers

Helal, M., and Hossain, M. (2013). Four decades of economic development of Bangladesh: An assessment. *Journal of the Asiatic Society of Bangladesh (Hum.)*, 58(2), pp. 335–362.

ILO. (2012). *Global employment trends for youth 2012*. Geneva: ILO.

ILO. (2020). *Global Employment Trends for Youth 2020*. Geneva: ILO.

ILOSTAT. (2020). *ILOSTAT*. Retrieved from https://ilostat.ilo.org/data/country-profiles/

IOM. (2020). *Migration, family remittances, assets and skills categories in Bangladesh*. Dhaka: IOM.

Kapsos, S. (2005). *Estimating growth requirements for reducing working poverty: Can the world halve working poverty by 2015*? International Labour Office.

Keller, W. (2004). International technology diffusion. *Journal of Economic Literature*, 42, pp. 752–782.

Khan, A.R. (2005). Growth, employment and poverty: An analysis of the vital nexus based on some recent UNDP and ILO/SIDA studies. Retrieved April 14, from https://www.ilo.org/employment/Whatwedo/Publications/WCMS_120683/lang--en/index.htm

Lall, S. (2004). The employment impact of globalization in developing countries. In *Understanding globalization, employment and poverty reduction*. New York: Palgrave Macmillan.

Legatum Institute. (2016). *The Legatum Prosperity Index 2016*. Legatum Institute. Retrieved from www.prosperity.com

Mankiw, N.G. (2008). What would Keynes have done? *New York Times*, p. 28. Retrieved April 14, 2022, from https://www.nytimes.com/2008/11/30/business/economy/30view.html

Marx, K. (1961). *Capital*. Moscow: Foreign Languages Publishing House, first edition 1867.

Mason, A. (2005). *Demographic transition and demographic dividends in developed and developing countries*. Retrieved April 14, 2022 from https://www.un.org/en/development/desa/population/events/pdf/expert/9/mason.pdf

MoF (Ministry of Finance). (2017). *Bangladesh economic review*. Dhaka: MoF.

NSDC. (2012). *Bangladesh skills snapshot 2012*. Dhaka: National Skills Development Council.

Osmani, S.R. (2018). Aspects of the poverty scenario in Bangladesh during 2010–2016. *Bangladesh Development Studies*, 26(3), pp. 1–31.

Pasinetti, L. (1981). *Structural change and economic growth*. Cambridge: Cambridge University Press.

Piva, M. (2003). *The impact of technology transfer on employment and income distribution in developing countries: A survey of theoretical models and empirical studies (Working paper no. 15)*. Geneva: ILO.

Rahman, M., Khan, T.I., and Sabbih, M.A. (2016). *Budget for education in Bangladesh an analysis of trends, gaps and priorities*. Dhaka: Centre for Policy Dialogue.

Raihan, S. (2016). *Structural change and dynamics of labor markets in Bangladesh: Studies on labor and employment.* Dhaka: South Asian network on economic modeling (SANEM).

Ricardo, D. (1951). Principles of political economy. in P. Sraffa (Ed.), *The works and correspondence of David Ricardo.* Cambridge: Cambridge University Press, vol. 1, third edition 1821.

Say, J.B. (1964). *A treatise on political economy or the production, distribution and consumption of wealth.* New York: M. Kelley, first edition 1803.

Titumir, R.A.M., and Hossain, J. (2003). Employability: A strategic framework for the informal sector in Bangladesh. *Journal of the Institute of Bangladesh Studies*, 26.

Titumir, R.A.M. (2021a). *Numbers and narratives in Bangladesh's economic development.* Singapore: Palgrave Macmillan.

Titumir, R.A.M. (2021b). Class, power and inequality in Bangladesh. In R. Al Mahmud Titumir, N. Georgeou, and A. Chowdhury (Eds.), *COVID-19 and Bangladesh: Response, rights and resilience.* Dhaka: University Press Ltd.

Toufique, K.A. (2014). *Labour market transitions of young women and men in Bangladesh.* Geneva: ILO.

UN. (2015). *Global assessment report on disaster risk reduction 2015 – Making development sustainable: The future of disaster risk management.* Retrieved from www.preventionweb.net/english/hyogo/gar/ 2015/en/gar-pdf/GAR2015_EN.pdf

Unnayan Onneshan. (2014). Recent trends of growth in agriculture, industry and power. *Bangladesh Economic Update*, 5(3).

Vivarelli, M. (2014). Innovation, employment and skills in advanced and developing countries: A survey of economic literature. *Journal of Economic Issues*, 48(1), pp. 123–154.

World Bank. (2016). *World Development Report 2016: Digital dividends.* Washington, DC: World Bank.

World Bank. (2018). Moving for prosperity: Global migration and labor markets. *Policy research report.* Washington, DC: World Bank.

World Bank. (2020). *World Development Indicators.* Retrieved from: https://data.worldbank.org/indicator/BX.TRF.PWKR.DT.GD.ZS?name_desc=false

11 Universal Social Security in Developing Countries

Introduction

The idea of social security is not a new one. The imposition of obligations on communities to pay taxes in order to provide for the poor can be traced back for hundreds of years in a number of different societies, including the Christian *tithe*, a custom of contributing a 10th of income for religious purposes, often under ecclesiastical or legal obligation and the Islamic *zakat*, one of the Five Pillars of Islam, ordering all Muslims who meet the necessary criteria to donate a certain portion of wealth each year.

In modern times, the formalisation dates back to 1889 when Otto von Bismarck, the chancellor of Germany initiated a social insurance programme. The idea behind the *social insurance* programme was to promote the well-being of German workers. It was also expected to work as an incentive for the workers to increase efficiency and motivation in their work, and to stave-off calls for more radical socialist alternatives. The next decisive stage in the history of social security came in the 1930s during the presidency of Franklin D. Roosevelt in the United States. Roosevelt launched the Social Security Act in 1935 to ease the enormous income and welfare loss of Americans during the worst economic crisis of the world. The programme that started only to provide immediate relief to the vulnerable population, went on to provide benefits to the elderly and then to those unemployed. Met with dire criticism from the conservatives, the programme still stands as one of the most important acts of the United States history which led to the creation of the Social Security Administration. On the other side of the Atlantic, social security gained dominance as countries were struggling from the destruction of World War II. The post-war United Kingdom government enacted a series of Acts, namely the National Insurance Act 1946, the National Assistance Act 1948, and the National Health Service Act 1946 to found the modern British welfare state, based upon the ideas contained in a government report, *Social Insurance and Allied Services* (1942), primarily authored by Lord Beveridge. The Beveridge Plan, published in the midst of World War II, proposed widespread reforms to address what he identified as "five giants on the road of reconstruction": "Want, Disease, Ignorance, Squalor and Idleness". Similarly in France, Pierre

DOI: 10.4324/9781003284222-15

Laroque, a French senior civil servant returning with General de Gaulle from exile in London, was appointed as the first Director General of social security in the setting up of ordinances founding and organising social security. From there on, social security has spread to almost every corner of the world. The vision of a welfare community that provided the people with social security from "cradle to grave" as a right for all citizens has largely been institutionalised by Nordic countries, and everybody is entitled to the same basic amount when faced with a "risk", such as sickness, work injuries or old-age.

Alas! Rangpur, the very birthplace of Beveridge, has the highest rate of poverty in Bangladesh with a rate of 47.2, almost double the average rate of 24.3, according to the government's Household Income and Expenditure Survey 2016 (BBS, 2019). The poverty rate of Rangpur has seen an increment of 4.9 percentage points from the previous 2010 report whereas all other divisions as well as the national poverty rate has demonstrated a declining trend. The poverty incidence in rural areas of Rangpur is 48.2 per cent whereas the urban poverty incidence is 41.5 per cent. The situation has further exacerbated, resulting in to new poor, by the outbreak of COVID -19 pandemic. William Henry Beveridge was born on March 5, 1879 in Rangpur, Bangladesh to Henry Beveridge, a civil service officer and district judge of colonial India, and Annette Ackroyd, who co-founded the Working Women's College in London.

The chapter contains a framework for universal life-cycle-based social security in light of catastrophic experiences of COVID-19, particularly encountered by day wagers and informal sector workers due to flawed target-based, fractured, fragmented social safety net programmes, plagued by exclusion and inclusion errors. The chapter makes the case for universal social security by undertaking a rigorous analysis of different targeted interventions and demonstrates that such programmes are costly, difficult to administer, politically vulnerable and produce segmented, uncoordinated welfare systems. Similarly, it exhibits that the market-based approaches have a less-than-satisfactory record in terms of protection, coverage, redistribution and gender equity as well as contributing towards economic development and stabilisation in developing countries. Furthermore, it showcases that "cost-saving" and "efficiency-enhancing" measures, such as user fees for social services are not transformational since underutilisation or lack of quality services constitute the greater public policy challenges in developing countries. Most importantly, attainment of zero poverty, outlined as SDG-1 of ending poverty in all its forms everywhere, requires a universal system since targeted interventions do not address the underlying causes of poverty while a substantial proportion of developing countries' population lives in poverty.

Jobless growth and resultant widespread unemployment have formed a sense of precarity in developing countries. The transformational pathway in employment is hence, to ensure work for all for transformation as well as universal (not targeted) life-cycle-based social security systems to absorb systemic shocks, including those resulting from pandemic and natural disasters. Disparate gender and class dimensions in skill formation, innovation, citizenship, universal health care and work for all will hamper the creation of a public society that serves the demands of every citizen equitably. The conceptualisation is backed by evidence, accompanied by rigorous undertakings on fiscal and monetary policies to underwrite those in praxis.

Like many developing countries, Bangladesh started its journey with a huge population and fragile economic and political structure since independence. The disadvantaged groups lag behind in society in terms of accessing to quality education, healthcare and employment opportunities. These deprivations enclose them into a vicious cycle of poverty and deprivation.

The COVID-19 pandemic has exposed the failure of universal basic needs, that is, health, education, social security, food, shelter and others. Conditions had worsened even before the onset of the pandemic. For example, the rate of poverty reduction in Bangladesh slowed down; in 2000–2010, the rate of decline was about 1.8 per cent, which dropped to 1.2 per cent in 2010–2016 (BBS, 2019). Furthermore, a pre-COVID-19 estimate by the World Bank suggests that the vulnerable population at risk of falling into poverty had increased to 55 per cent of the total population. The existing social protection and social safety nets are ineffective. Those selected as beneficiaries for the schemes, in many cases, are chosen politically, leaving the deserving unserved, with many cases of leakage and mishandling. Government responses have mostly aided those involved in formal sectors. However, informal sectors still remain out of any government benefits due to the targeted approach of social security. The significant logic behind entitling these public goods with "universal" is embedded in the failure of the social safety net schemes or other targeted approaches since these kinds of programmes, at least, create two problems. First, there might be "selection bias" while making a list of the beneficiaries. This bias gets exacerbated when political affiliation is considered as a hidden requirement and advantage to obtain the benefits. Some may get excluded and some may get overprivileged given his/her comparatively better economic status than that of the excluded one. Second, considering health, education and social security as part of any targeted scheme turns these into "relief". Education, health and social security are not charity for citizens of the country. These are each citizen's rights and entitlements which should be ascertained by the state for mass people.

The mean-tested approach in providing social security can be problematic. Mean-tested approach fails to provide a safety net to all citizens and can be economically inefficient to augment the social policy of a country (Atkinson, 1996). The objective of social security is to provide citizens the means to lead a dignified life. For example, the current set of policies in Bangladesh is more of a mix of social protection and safety net than a social security. The social protection policies are aimed towards some selected group of vulnerable population and the objective of such policies is to reduce the risk and vulnerability of the group at risk rather than the whole population. The social protection scheme in Bangladesh covered 27.8 per cent of households and programme beneficiaries were 28.7 per cent of the population. Most of the social protection programmes in the country have targeted beneficiaries and the primary objective is often the reduction of poverty. The benefits from protection programmes fail to provide any significant changes in the life of the beneficiaries. Such safety net programmes take the poverty line into consideration while beneficiary selection but leaves out those with low earnings. The international poverty line of USD 1.90 a day does not even ensure a decent living in Bangladesh. This threshold of poverty line only considers the biological need of a human. The social safety net programme in Bangladesh costs less than three per cent of the GDP. The Social Protection budget in the 2019–2020 fiscal year is 8.80 billion USD of which one-third was spent on pension programmes for the retired government officials. The lack of a comprehensive and universal social security programme in Bangladesh has exacerbated the inequality in society. In order to create equal opportunities for all of its citizens, a universal social security programme enhances the capability of citizens which in turn ensures decent life and thus eradicates risks and vulnerabilities. Such opportunities can only be created through the provision of benefits which not only fulfils the subsistence requirements but also enables the rights holders to improve their living in different parts of their lifespan. There are many tools of social security like social insurance, basic income, conditional cash transfer which can help achieve the above-mentioned objective. The key is universality, meaning benefits for all regardless of the status of employment or age of citizens.

A Framework

With a view to pull the population, including women and marginalised groups, out of the crisis, an explicit set of measures need to be undertaken. Providing adequate social security through various allowances and benefits is a crucial prerequisite for supporting the pandemic-affected population. If the new poor and vulnerable are taken into consideration, the number of beneficiaries from safety net programmes is trivial. Therefore, the chapter posits a five-pronged model for universal social security to cater to all citizens, including low-income households, women, elderly and the informal sector (Figure 11.1).

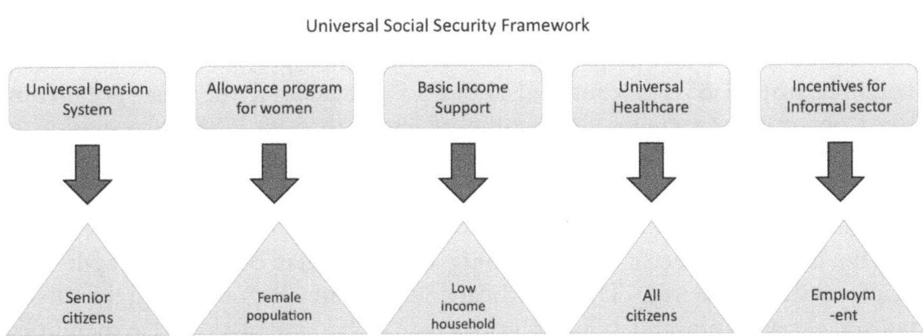

Figure 11.1 Universal social security

Source: Prepared by author

The importance of social security has increased manifold during the COVID-19 pandemic that has ravaged across borders. Governments across the world have initiated measures to tackle the income and job loss in the economy. The problem gets severe for the developing countries which have been working throughout the last decades to remove poverty. The pandemic is set to push back those efforts. Existing mean-tested approaches already have high exclusion and inclusion errors that question the efficacy of such measures.

COVID-19 pandemic has exacerbated the global unemployment and income scenario in a way never seen before. The pandemic has seen a job loss of 114 million in 2020. As such, the labour force participation rate has dwindled globally to 58.7 per cent. At the same time, the global unemployment rate rose from 1.1 per cent to 6.8 per cent. With all the unemployment and job losses, global labour income has declined by 8.3 per cent. The loss amounts to 3.7 trillion USD, around 4.4 per cent of the global GDP (ILO, 2021a). With the different waves of the pandemic hitting developing countries, the situation is getting only worse. Amidst widespread job and income losses, European countries in particular have fared well because of their highly developed social security systems being in place. Comprehensive social security system allowed these countries to swiftly take measures to deliver help to the people. At the same time, most of the countries, especially developing ones, had to respond almost from scratch to ensure access to those who have lost jobs or income. It obviously took some time for them to reach out to the vulnerable groups and hence, prolonged the hardship (ILO, 2021b). Even countries like the United States have suffered due to the same problem. While governments announced recovery plans, yet the stimulus took months to reach its desired population.

Globally, 61.2 per cent of the employment is in the informal sector. However, this does not provide a full picture. Of the global employment in the informal sector, 93 per cent are in emerging and developing countries. In developing countries, 69.3 per cent of the total employment is in the informal sector, compared to just 18.3 per cent in developed countries (ILO, 2018). The high number of informal employment entails less job and income security. This population is the first group to see a fall in income during a pandemic when economies go through lockdown. In Bangladesh, employment in the informal sector is around 85 per cent and about 15 per cent of the total population has a per capita average daily income of less than 5.88 USD. If provision of basic income grants were distributed through banking channels, liquidity in the hands of individuals could have increased consumption expenditure, leading to a surge in the total demand in the economy.

The healthcare sector in developing countries has been in a fragile state prior to the pandemic. The healthcare sectors are plagued by high out-of-pocket expenditure and poor infrastructure. The out-of-pocket expenditure in developing countries amounts to 500 billion USD. At the same time, this high expenditure pushes 90 million people into extreme poverty in developing countries annually (WHO, 2019). The pandemic is set to put the health sector further aback. The high out-of-pocket expenditure without social protection measures put the poor people in developing countries at higher risk from the pandemic. In Bangladesh, the health sector gets only 0.9 per cent of GDP in spite of recommendations by international organisations, such as the WHO, that four per cent of GDP should go to healthcare.

While the new Coronavirus infection spares no one, its socio-economic impact has exposed the longstanding discrimination that women face at home and in the economy. The poor are hit hardest, including migrant and domestic workers. Globally, more men are employed in the informal sector than women. However, in low and lower-middle-income countries, around 89.7 per cent of women work in the informal sector compared to 82.7 per cent of men (ILO, 2021b). It is not just the informal work that has been causing distress to the women. Women, in general, have to work in households as well, where the work goes unpaid. Nearly 60 per cent of women in Bangladesh work in the informal economy, with low wages and less in savings or safety nets. The majority of domestic workers are also women. As such, there is a need for a rethinking of social security benefits for the women, compensating their work at home.

The onslaught of the pandemic calls for a revamp in social security, particularly in developing countries. An income allowance or a basic income grant supports the population that earns less than the amount required to maintain a basic living. The allowance shall be for the 15–59 age group, living below the extreme poverty line. An unemployment benefit can be paid to a person over 22 years old and under the retirement age who is actively seeking employment and working 16 hours or less every week. Housing benefits can be provided for rented accommodation to persons with no income or very low income. The unemployment benefits would help the unemployed to maintain their consumption level.

The current economic crisis has resulted in economic suffering for the elderly since they are mostly unable to work, and those able to work are facing diminishing income. Benefits for elderly and pensions are already available in most of the countries. However, there remains a high exclusion error in elderly benefits. Rather than a mean-tested approach, there should be a universal provisioning of pension for all elderly population. This will result in a decline in poverty as well.

Social Security for All

The concept of a homogenous social security for all gathered momentum as the existing mean-tested policies are fraught with exclusion and inclusion errors. The mean-tested approach in providing social security can be problematic. Mean-tested approach fails to provide to all citizens and can be economically inefficient to augment the social policy of a country (Atkinson, 1996). The identification of beneficiaries also remains questionable in developing countries due to weak governance and political structures that eventually results in exclusion of those who need benefits or inclusion of those who do not require benefits (Razzaque et al., 2020; Titumir, 2021).

Exclusion or inclusion error does not deter governments from adopting targeted approaches. Targeted approach takes various shapes in different countries. The mean tests mostly provide benefits to people who are believed to have income or financial resources lower than a decided threshold. However, a popular mean test approach, Proxy Mean Test (PMT) has been adopted in most developing countries which is also supported by World Bank and other international agencies. Proxy Mean Test determines the level of welfare of a household to decide on the coverage based on statistical analysis (Kidd et al., 2017). Countries use different methodologies to determine the level. This is usually done by taking data from household surveys.

Countries opt such measures, arguably, for two reasons. First, government policies act as the most crucial factor in determining the type of social protection. For example, governments with more conservative ideas are usually against higher spending in social sectors and promote tax cuts which eventually decreases the capacity of spending. More liberal governments however promote more inclusive social policies. Social spending is funded through increased tax returns (Kidd, 2013). Second, lack of funds forces developing countries to adopt mean-tested policies as universal social security that covers 100 per cent of the beneficiaries is a costly venture even though such policies have been proven to eradicate poverty and improve living (Kidd and Khondker, 2013).

Mean-test approaches are criticised because of their exclusion and inclusion errors. This criticism stems from two reasons. First, the methodologies used to determine the beneficiaries and welfare level is done through surveys. The accuracy of the surveys affects the outcome of the methodologies and eventually the social protection system. Any significant lapse in the methodology may result in exclusion of true beneficiaries and may include non-beneficiaries. This is particularly a problem for developing countries. The quality of surveys is usually poor in developing countries due to weak infrastructures. Most of the methodologies in social security require poverty statistics in general to determine beneficiaries. However, developing countries have serious limitations in producing these statistics. In most developing countries, such surveys are done with an interval of ranging between three to ten years, which is a long time to provide accurate poverty status of a country (Alkire, 2014). Underestimation of poverty statistics may lead to exclusion of beneficiaries while overestimation may result in inclusion of non-poor in the list. Second, prevalence of corrupt practices negatively affects allocation and selection of beneficiaries of social protection (Delavallade, 2006). Political pressure to show better results from the social protection programmes as well as "vote bank politics" often forces governments to include households from higher-income percentiles. This causes inclusion of population who can lead lives without benefits, leading to deprivation of genuine beneficiaries (Farrington and Slater, 2006).

Mexico adopted *Oportunidades* or *Prospera*, a conditional cash transfer programme, as their flagship social protection programme. The programme was aimed towards the poor and ultra-poor to improve education, health and nutrition of the people. The programme has benefited approximately one-fourth of the population. This programme has been hailed as a role model and has been adopted in well over 50 countries all over the world. Impact on the beneficiary population has been proven unanimously (Lindert and Core, 2013). However, the programme has its fair share of failure as well. The poverty-based selection of beneficiaries has resulted in exclusion of 70 per cent of the poorest 20 per cent eligible population. Similarly, in Indonesia, the cash transfer programme excluded 93 per cent of the target population. In Cambodia, 56 per cent of the target population faced exclusion from the social protection programme (Kidd et al., 2017).

Pakistan launched Benazir Income Support Programme (BISP) as their indigenous solution to poverty. The programme is a usual cash transfer programme targeted to the poor population. However, this programme also had a high exclusion rate. The programme excluded 92 per cent of the target population, which was the poorest 20 per cent (Kidd, 2013). In India the vulnerable groups are often deprived of social assistance programmes due to politically powerful groups, who dominate the process of identification (Hirway, 2003; Mahamallik and Sahu, 2011). Around 60 per cent of the estimated target population are deprived of below-the-poverty-line (BPL) card, which is used to identify beneficiary groups of social security programmes (Ram et al., 2009).

The targeted approach taken by countries leaves out a large percentage of the vulnerable population. While countries have taken steps to increase spending

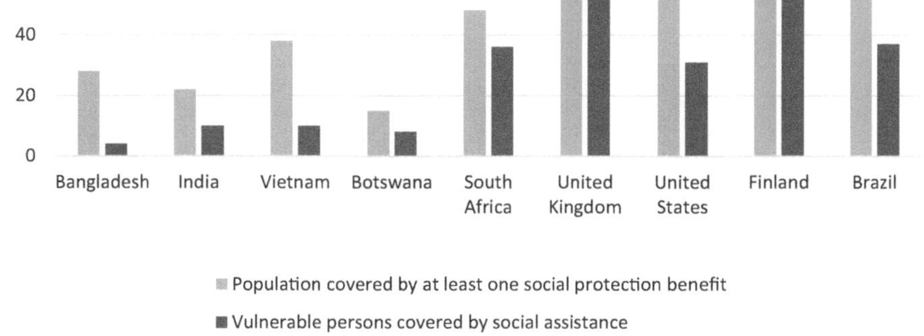

Figure 11.2 Social protection coverage

Source: ILO (2021b)

and coverage of social safety net and social protection schemes, the programmes have not been able to deliver the intended benefits because of mean-tested approaches. Bangladesh, for example, covers 28 per cent of the population with at least one social assistance benefit. However, social assistance covers only four per cent of the vulnerable population who require assistance (ILO, 2021b). Hence, the programmes become inefficient. The scenario is more or less similar in all developing countries. Developed countries like the United Kingdom and Finland on the other hand cover a huge portion of the vulnerable groups. Finland in particular protects all of her population with social assistance including vulnerable persons (Figure 11.2).

There exists a high exclusion and inclusion error in social security programmes in Bangladesh. These are basically social safety net programme under the National Social Security Strategy (NSSS). The programme is mainly aimed at alleviating poverty. Government in recent years extended the programme to take into account the urban poor which was previously left out of any social security programmes (Razzaque et al., 2020). The mean tested policies to address poverty however failed to create an impact due to low coverage and high exclusion errors. The targeting and delivery of benefits mainly work through the local governments where fraudulent praxis culminate into high targeting errors (Razzaque et al., 2020). In addition, low coverage of beneficiaries also results in an exclusion of vulnerable groups who require social benefits (Razzaque et al., 2020).

Around 71 per cent of the vulnerable population remains out of social security (Figure 11.3). The excluded are much higher in urban areas than rural regions partly because the programmes were initially launched in order to remove extreme poverty from rural belts. As a result, rural areas have lower exclusion error. On the other hand, rural areas are beset by a higher inclusion

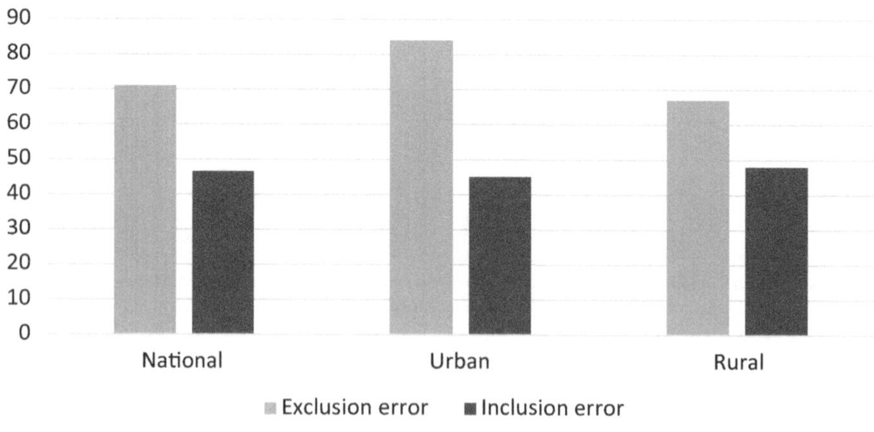

Figure 11.3 Targeting error of social security system in Bangladesh

Source: Razzaque (2020)

error compared to urban expanses. Nationally, the inclusion error stands at 46.5 per cent. Increasing the coverage can significantly reduce the percentage of errors. For instance, if 20 per cent of the population is covered, the error rates will vary between 44 and 55 per cent, when only 10 per cent of the population is covered, the error rates jump to diverge between 57 and 71 per cent (Kidd and Wylde, 2011). A universal coverage will reduce the errors.

Universal coverage would ensure access to social security for all and would leave no one out. For example, a targeting approach with lower coverage leaves a major part of the poor population out of social security. As the coverage increases, more inhibitants are enrolled into the system, but still, a sizeable mass remains beyond coverage due to methodological errors and racketeering in local governance structure. Instead, a universal coverage can eliminate the inclusion and exclusion errors. Life-cycle based universal coverage will ensure rights for all who are within the statutory threshold (Figure 11.4). Most importantly, the social safety net measures cannot reduce a massive poverty condition (Grosh et al., 2008).

Undoubtedly, developing countries have not been able to create fiscal space, allowing governments to provide budgetary resources for a desired purpose without jeopardizing the sustainability of its financial position or the stability of the economy due to faults with nature of fiscal and monetary policy making. Fiscal space is required for making extra resources available for worthwhile government spending. The nature of state building and consequential political

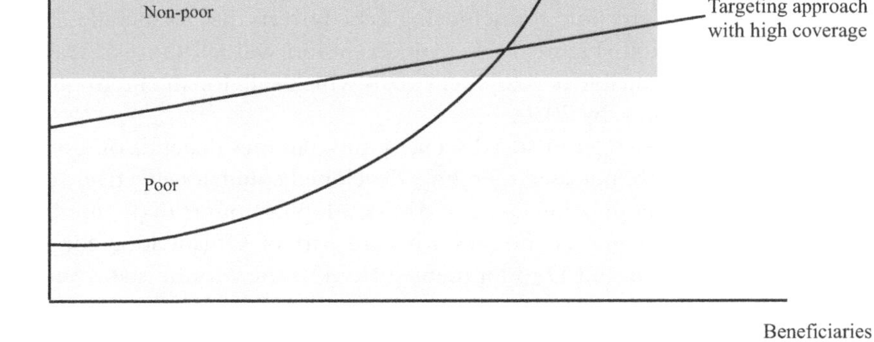

Figure 11.4 Universal coverage and targeting approach

Source: Prepared by author

settlement stand in the way to create fiscal space, amongst others, by impeding to pursue progressive taxation through raising income taxes to make it as the largest share of domestic resource, and cutting lower priority politically directed expenditure (Titumir, 2021, 2022). The level of inflow of overseas development assistance has remained a hallmark of unkept promises while the international aid structure has shifted in favour of loans from that of grants. The nature of the state has dictated to opt for a escapist route of resorting to mean-tested approaches.

While the PMT approach is based on poverty rates of a country, and if the methodology of estimating poverty rate in itself excludes a certain number of population, most importantly such cannot effectively remove poverty (Kidd and Wylde, 2011). In such cases, a universal social security provision can be much more effective, if the governments are committed to ending poverty in all its forms everywhere (SDG – 1). Even before COVID-19, baseline projections suggested that six per cent of the global population would still be living in extreme poverty in 2030, missing the target of ending poverty. The fallout from the pandemic threatens to push over 70 million people into extreme poverty. Income losses are expected to exceed $220 billion in developing countries, and an estimated 55 per cent of the global population have no access to social protection (UNDP, 2020). Without a life-cycle based universal social security, these losses will not only reverberate across societies, impacting education, food security, nutrition, human rights, but also will reverse decades of progress in the fight against poverty.

Social Security Spending

Social security spending directly influences the welfare of the vulnerable population. Shortages of funds lead to low percentage of coverage of social security in low-income and lower-middle-income countries. The non-coverage has been further aggravated by high errors due to the prevailing targeting approach in these countries. Thus, a programme that aims to provide benefits to everyone below the poverty line for achieving zero poverty has to include all the vulnerable population (Figure 11.4). Any exclusion will fall short of realising the first goal of sustainable development goals which calls for an end to poverty in all its manifestations by 2030.

Increasing the coverage of social security programmes depends on government spending. With increased spending, developed countries effectively cover the majority of the population compared to developing countries (Figure 11.5). Within the high-income economies who are part of Organisation for Economic Co-operation and Development (OECD), the Nordic states such as Finland, Norway rank top in coverage and spending. The Nordic welfare system is based on a high degree of universalism, meaning all citizens are entitled to basic social security and services. The universalism is derived from the political settlement of these countries in view of broad public support due to bidirectional causality. People are willing to pay relatively high taxes in order

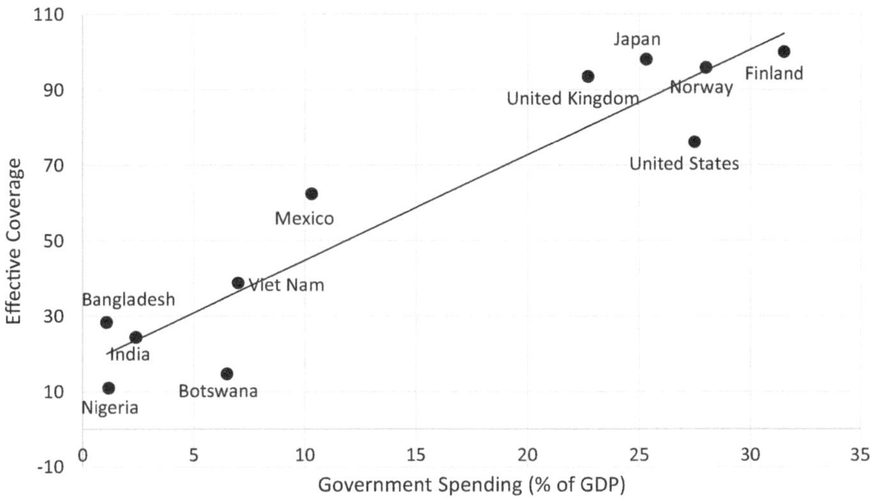

Figure 11.5 Social security spending versus coverage

Source: Authors' calculation

to fund welfare provision, and hence the public social expenditure in Nordic countries has remained around 30 per cent of GDP while average across the OECD countries is 20 per cent of GDP.

The public supports universalism and, in return receives life-cycle based support, irrespective of their position in the labour market. The welfare services include the requirements in every stage of life cycle in the forms of child benefits, parental leave, health services and hospitals, all of which are free at the point of delivery. The public sector also looks after sick and unemployed people and senior citizens. The basic institution is the societal value, which underpins the conviction that all humans are of equal worth, a characteristic of a public society. The distribution of power – political settlement – in these countries are driven by the median. Thus, the public society, which comprises median population, does not allow distribution to be skewed towards a small proportion of population, and therefore provides a better representation of a value. The collective idea of high standards of living and equal opportunities for all is all-pervasive in the Nordic countries. In practice, it has resulted in reduced economic inequality and attainment of high scores in all indices relating to economic social and cultural rights (ESCR) including the rights to adequate food, to adequate housing, to education, to health, to social security, to take part in cultural life, to water and sanitation, and to work as well as civil and political rights such as individuals' freedom from infringement by governments, social organizations, and private individuals. The ideal of free human beings enjoying civil and political freedom and freedom from fear and want can only be achieved through a political settlement, allowing everyone to enjoy civil and political rights as well as economic, social and cultural rights.

The developed countries end up spending up to a quarter of the GDP in providing social benefits while most of the developing countries spend less than 5 per cent of their GDP on social security (Table 11.1) due to the prevailing political settlement that takes refuge to illusion, opacity and concealment, manufacturing an endless sequence of discrete, repetitive, trivial, and meaningless information, offering little, if any, reflection of reality. The classic example of the political establishment is the use of per capita income. In a country, for example, if there exists a small number of high-income and a large number of lower income households, the average income becomes inflated due to skewed nature of income distribution. Such a statistics hide more than it reveals.

Bangladesh as a developing country spends much less on social security. The allocation for the Social Security and Welfare sector is 6.0 per cent of the national budget (Table 11.2).

Table 11.1 Social security spending in different parts of the world

Country	*Spending in social security (per cent of GDP)*
Bangladesh	1.7
India	2.7
Sri Lanka	6.5
Vietnam	6.3
Japan	23.1
Finland	30.6
Mexico	12.0
Nigeria	0.7
Botswana	6.6
United States	19.0
United Kingdom	21.5
Norway	23.9

Source: social protection.org, 2021

Table 11.2 Allocation for social security

Year	*Allocation for social security*
2010–2011	7.3
2011–2012	6.8
2012–2013	5.7
2013–2014	5.6
2014–2015	6.1
2015–2016	5.7
2016–2017	5.8
2017–2018	6

Source: Ministry of Finance, 2019

Such low allocation was attributed to the diversion of expenditure from the social sector to meet the rising payment because of principal and interest for the high public borrowing to finance the budget deficit arising out of political expediency (Titumir, 2021). Moreover, in Bangladesh, social safety net programmes (SSNP) have been developed and evolved on an ad hoc basis. The major shortcoming of these SSNPs is that they are short term in nature and only designed to address post-disaster situations, besides being dogged by inclusion and exclusion errors.

Estimating a precise cost for a universal social protection programme depends on various parameters such as the coverage areas, whether the amount of benefit will be in terms of the national poverty line, minimum salary, or USD purchasing power parity (PPP) per day and many other factors. Fortunately, the ILO has already developed a social protection floor calculator that can provide universal social protection cost estimates for a country in terms of the aforementioned parameters. This can be calculated in terms of national poverty line or Purchasing Power Parity (PPP) of 3.2 USD for lower-middle-income countries' lower poverty line, as mentioned by the World Bank (Figure 11.6). Here, an illustrative example is given for Bangladesh, which is by no means a comprehensive one.

Universal Child Benefit: Using this calculator, providing a universal child benefit of only 25 per cent of the national poverty line would cost 12.9 per cent of the GDP. This will account for around 11.40 billion USD for children below 15 years old. On the other hand, providing 3.20 USD PPP per day would accrue around 12.27 per cent of the GDP.

Universal Old-Age Allowance: A benefit to all persons aged 65 and over accounts for 2.18 per cent of the GDP. If the World Bank's recommendation of 3.2 USD per day for the lower-middle-income countries is followed, the required spending is 7.3 billion USD (2.07 per cent of the GDP).

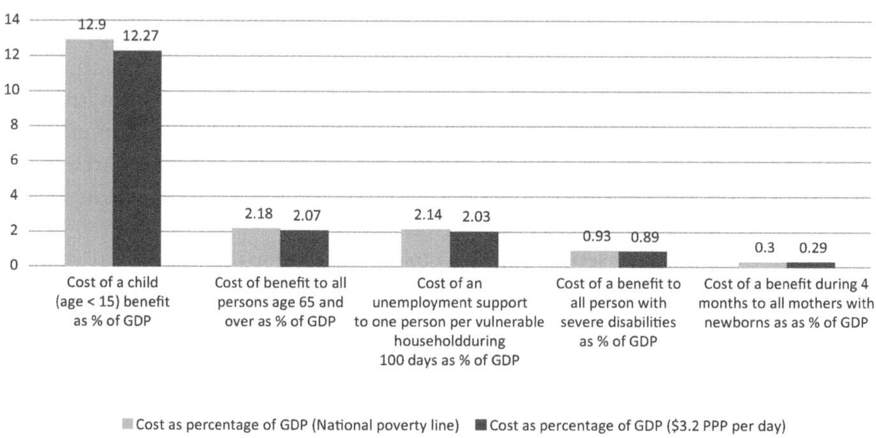

Figure 11.6 Estimation of universal social security

Source: Unnayan Onneshan (2021)

Universal Unemployment Benefit: An employment guarantee for one person per vulnerable household for 100 days would account for 2.14 per cent of the GDP (7.7 billion USD).

Universal Disability Benefit: People with disability (PWD) refers to people who require additional assistance for their mobility. A benefit scheme for this group, with 3.2 USD PPP per day, would cost around 0.89 per cent of the GDP.

Universal Maternity Benefit: The main purpose of this programme is to provide a cash transfer equivalent to 100 per cent of the national poverty line to mothers with newborns and all pregnant women for a period of at least four months. Considering 2.4 per cent fertility rate and 2.1 per cent fertile women, around 1.06 billion USD (0.30 per cent of GDP) is required.

A universal social security programme may cost around 20 per cent of the GDP. Bangladesh currently spends less than two per cent of GDP while the OECD countries average 20 per cent and the per cent goes as high as 30 in Scandinavian countries.

Summary

The absence of an effective social security system hinders the path of social development exerting an immense adverse impact on the low-income population particularly the poor and marginalised group in the society. It is, however, needless to say that governments in developing countries must focus on raising public expenditure through increased collection of revenue and allocating sufficient resources for such sectors as education, health, and social security and welfare in pursuit of achieving a sustainable society. Increased allocation would allow governments to go for universal life-cycle based social security that would eradicate the problems of exclusion and inclusion posed by the mean-tested approach. There is no denying the fact that poverty can be eliminated when money goes directly to those who need it. Targeting approaches with low coverage will not achieve the goal social security seeks to achieve. A universal social security programme may not only boost the economy through consumption smoothing but reduce leakage in the social sector. Nonetheless, monitoring of the social security programmes also needs to be carried out regularly in order to evaluate the effectiveness of the programmes in empowering the poor and marginalised population.

Social security represents society's current answer to the problem of economic insecurity. Social security measures have a twofold significance for every developing country. They constitute an important step towards the goal of a welfare state, by improving living and working conditions and affording the people protection against the uncertainties of the future. These measures are also important for structural transformation industrialisation as these enable workers to become more productive. These ensures that labourers are human beings who have both rights and duties not as a mere factor of production.

The social security is a function of political settlement. For a universal social security system in developing countries, far-sighted politics, steered by public society, are essential for transformation into a citizen-state. While complementarities and harmonisation between macroeconomic and social policies are indispensable, the delimitation of responsibilities between central and local governments to avoid fragmentation and effective coordination is fundamental. A new form accountable organisation, underpinned by effective implementation centred bureaucracy is a prerequisite to establish a universal system of delivery, accountable to citizens.

References

Alkire, S. (2014). *Towards frequent and accurate poverty data.* Retrieved April 20, 2022, from https://ophi.org.uk/ophi-research-in-progress-43b/

Al-Yousif, Y.K. (2000). Do government expenditures inhibit or promote economic growth: Some empirical evidence from Saudi Arabia. *Indian Economic Journal*, 48(2), pp. 92–96.

Atkinson, A.B. (1996). The economics of the welfare state. The American Economist, 40(2), pp. 5–15.

ADB. (2015). *Key indicators for Asia and the Pacific 2015.* Mandaluyong City, Philippines: Asian Development Bank, 2015. Retrieved from https://www.adb.org/sites/default/files/publication/175162/ki2015.pdf

BBS. (2019). *Report on household income and expenditure survey 2016.* Dhaka: Bangladesh Bureau of Statistics.

Delavallade, C. (2006). Corruption and distribution of public spending in developing countries. *Journal of Economics and Finance*, 30(2), pp. 222–239.

Farrington, J., and Slater, R. (2006). Introduction: Cash transfers: Panacea for poverty reduction or money down the drain? *Development Policy Review*, 24(5), pp. 499–511.

Grosh, M., Del Ninno, C., Tesliuc, E., and Ouerghi, A. (2008). *For protection and promotion: The design and implementation of effective safety nets.* Retrieved April 20, 2022, from https://openknowledge.worldbank.org/handle/10986/6582

Hirway, I. (2003). Identification of BPL households for poverty alleviation programmes. *Economic and Political Weekly*, 38(45), pp. 4803–4808.

ILO. (2018). *Women and men in the informal economy: A statistical picture* (third edition). Geneva: International Labour Organization.

ILO. (2021a). *ILO statistics.* Geneva: International Labour Organization.

ILO. (2021b). *World social protection dashboard.* Geneva: International Labour Organization.

Kidd, S. (2013). Rethinking 'Targeting' in international development. *Pathways' perspectives*, Issue 11.

Kidd, S., Gelders, B., and Bailey-Athias, D. (2017). *Exclusion by design: An assessment of the effectiveness of the proxy means test poverty targeting mechanism.* ESS – Working Paper No. 56. Geneva: ILO.

Kidd, S., and Khondker, B. (2013). *Scoping report on poverty and social protection in Bangladesh.* Unpublished report for AusAID: Australia, Canberra.

Kidd, S., and Wylde, E. (2011). Targeting the Poorest: An assessment of the proxy means test methodology. AusAid Research Paper, AusAid, Canberra.

Lindert, K., and Core, N. (2013). *Conditional & unconditional cash transfers.* Washington, DC: The World Bank, 36.

Mahamallik, M., and Sahu, G.B. (2011). Identification of the poor: Errors of exclusion and inclusion. *Economic and Political Weekly*, 46(9), pp. 71–77.

Ram, F., Mohanty, S.K., and Ram, U. (2009). Understanding the distribution of BPL cards: All-India and selected states. *Economic and Political Weekly*, 44(7), pp. 66–71.

Razzaque, A. (2020). *Rethinking social protection responses to the Covid-19 crisis: Issues and policy priorities for Bangladesh.* Background Paper prepared for the General Economics Division (GED), Planning Commission. Dhaka: Government of Bangladesh.

Razzaque, M.A., Asif Ehsan, S.M., and Bhuiyan, M.I.H. (2020). Barriers of accessing social protection programmes for the poor and marginalised. In *Compendium of social protection research in Bangladesh 2020* (pp. 56–117). Dhaka: General Economics Division (GED), Planning Commission. Government of Bangladesh.

Titumir, R.A.M. (2021, June 5). Will this peculiar form of fiscal conservatism reverse the downturn? *The Business Standards.* Retrieved from www.tbsnews.net/features/panorama/will-peculiar-form-fiscal-conservatism-reverse-downturn-256099

Titumir, R.A.M. (2021). *Numbers and narratives in Bangladesh's economic development.* Singapore: Palgrave Macmillan.

Titumir, R.A.M. (2022). *Fiscal and monetary policies in developing countries: State, citizenship and transformation.* Oxon and New York: Routledge.

UNDP. (2020). *Covid -19 Pandemic.* Retrieved from https://www.undp.org/coronavirus

Unnayan Onneshan. (2021). *From squeeze to expansion: Policy and institutional reforms for averting k-shaped recovery.* Dhaka: Unnayan Onneshan.

World Health Organization. (2019). *Primary health care on the road to universal health coverage: 2019 monitoring report.* Geneva: World Health Organization.

12 Institutions and Transformation for Universal Employment and Social Security in Developing Countries

Introduction

The chapter analyses the political impediments and institutional rigidities towards a universal employment scheme and social security. Inherent power structures and institutional arrangements of developing countries affect the employment opportunity and social security of people, and thus requires inclusion of human sociality, public society and political settlement, in the framework of analysis, as factors for transformation. Human sociality or its opposite – as is conceived here – self-interest is constructed by norms, a form of institution referring to unwritten rules of behaviour and values, a form of institution concerning the principles that guide normative position. Human sociality or self-interest, thus, is socially constructed. The dynamics of human sociality construct (or impede formation of) public society, where median households hold power. The nature of (public) society, dictated by degree of human sociality, results in particular form of political settlement. the characteristics of a political settlement allow for exploration into the dynamics of institutional structure, evolution of policy and associated developmental outcomes. Political settlement – composition and distribution of power – determines macroeconomic policies and investment decisions, which accelerate (disrupt) transformation. For a transformative change, for instance, the fiscal policy has to accelerate the rate of physical and human capital formations by expanding investments in public and private enterprises and by diverting resources from socially less-desirable outcomes, to achieve universal employment and equitable distribution of income and wealth. On the other hand, a predatory state implicates aggressive wealth accumulation by the governing elite using state resources for personal gain (Ayittey, 2005; Fatton, 1992). According to neopatrimonialism, an extension of the predation state theory, the resource is usurped through patron-clientel networks (Mkandawire, 2015; Bratton and van de Walle, 1994). The logic of such negative regime type, however, does not sufficiently explain the dynamics of post-colonial process of statebuilding nor does capture variations in sectoral outcomes within an economy.

The political settlement framework along with its intrinsic categories of human sociality and public society, on the other hand, is helpful to understand

DOI: 10.4324/9781003284222-16

the context of policymaking and resultant outcome, and hence allows for capturing social and economic policies in developing countries, which have largely failed to expand productive capacity and consequential generation of significant decent wage employment. Political settlement analysis refers to the distribution of power in a political system among the elite and other groups and how power is encapsulated in formal institutions. It is the country-specific power distribution and the set of institutions shape the policies and ensuing flow of the economic benefits (Khan, 2010; Whitfield et al., 2013; Booth, 2015). The political settlement framework permits identification of the sources of pressure by the ruling elite in their choices of policies and constraints in implementation.

Three main dimensions of relationships generate pressure and constraints for policy formulation and implementation. Horizontal relationships, or elite competition, occur among factions of a ruling coalition. Vertical relationships define the societal redistribution demands and generate top-bottom, client-patron networks as well as networks of key elite factions and their constituencies. External shocks such as the collapse of the oil market, forex crises, rise in cost of food imports and global economic slowdown also exert pressure on those in power. It is the nature of the political settlement that explains the success or failure of transforming the productive sectors, creating decent wage employment and establishing universal social security. For universal employment and social security, three conditions – stability, transformability and sustainability – are discussed in the following sections.

Stability Conditions

In developing countries, power structures are determined by balance of power between individuals and groups, which in turn are mostly governed by the accumulation of capital and involvement in resource-dependent networks. Political settlements are characterised by the nature of these clientelist networks that are focused on obtaining the use of public resources for private benefit, achieving economic outcomes through non-economic processes using the state apparatus, and thereby distorting macroeconomic and social policies to cater to the needs of the few.

Non-functioning and weak institutional policy arrangements of developing countries are subject to a specific type of political settlement and power relationship. The centralised power structure has persisted in the developing countries even in the post-colonial phase, leading to concentration of power amongst a few, with precarious civil and political rights for citizens. The concentration of power and the absence of civic rights culminate in fragile governance with an unequal society. Here, a causation between (abusive) power and (bad) policy outcome is illustrated in the realm of monetary and fiscal policies.

Monetary policy influences investment by changing the interest rate. If the interest rate is less, investment will increase. Yet the outcome can be imposed by a powerful agent.

Suppose,

I = investment
R = regulation
O = procedural order
r = rate of interest.

It is supposed to take the form:

$$I = f(R, O)$$

Here investment depends on rate of interest and order. Again, rate of interest and procedural order both depend on regulation, that is,

$$r = f(R)$$
$$o = f(R)$$

$$dO/dt = \gamma R \quad (1)$$
$$dO/dt = \beta O \quad (2)$$
$$dI/dt = 1/\alpha\, r+\beta O \quad (3)$$

Here it is considered that initially there is already some regulation and procedural order in that society, and $I(0)>0$.

Here in Equation (3), the rate of investment increases as the rate of interest decreases along with increased rate of procedural order. If the rate of interest decreases but the procedural order does not increase, the investment drops than before.

Equation (*1*) exhibits that procedural order augments with the rise of prudent regulation and such condition contributes towards increased investment in Equation (3).

Such can also be shown in the case of fiscal policy. Fiscal policy is primarily instrumented through public spending and taxation. Suppose,

S = public spending
T = tax-cut
R = regulation
O = proceduralorder

Increased government spending assumed to result in higher investment. But without a procedural order, the investment will eventually fall. Therefore,

$$I = f(S, O)$$

Both public spending and procedural order depend on regulation. So,

$$O = f(R)$$

$$S = f(R)$$

$$dS/dt = \in R \quad (1)$$
$$dS/dt = \alpha S \quad (2)$$
$$dO/dt = \in R \quad (3)$$
$$dO/dt = \beta O \quad (4)$$
$$dI/dt = \alpha S + \beta O \quad (5)$$

initial conditions, $S(0)>0$, $I(0)>0$.

$\in$ = rate of increase of regulation.
α = rate of increase of public spending
β = rate of increase of procedural order.

When $\in$ increases, the rate of public spending α and rate of order β also increases in Equations (2) and (4). As a result, in Equation (5), investment also increases.

In most of the developing countries, the economies are still emerging. Hence, there are higher contracting failures compared to the developed countries that already have an established ordered system. Besides, weak institutions give room for "clientelist political settlement" in developing countries. With low enforcement capacities of formal rules and regulations, such are bent according to the need of the few, holding power. As a result, policies are too a larger extent bowed to generate primitive accumulation, harnessed through extra-economic means including use of power and force, as opposed to crony capitalism, in which business profit out of collusion with the state, with latter bearing all risks. The accumulation is not aimed at employment-led growth, but also thrives out of endemic violation of labour rights and dispossessed workers of minimum wages.

A common scenario in the streets of developing world is strikes organised by labour groups and unions. Reasons for the industrial actions range from sudden job losses to non-payment of due salaries. Compensation less than survival wages has become a common grievances among labourers. With the international division of labour, the exploitation of labour has increased rapidly. The protests and strikes however seldom end in a win for the labourers. Governments in in many cases use force to suppress the protests. The industrial harmony amongst different stakeholders is low. The dissonance dates back to the colonial days and such has incarnated with neoliberal policies including privatisation and deregulation, degrading the conditions of workers through so-called flexibilisation, a form of employment relations that permit employers to increase or diminish their workforce, without no longer promising employees lifetime job security. The brute force of capitalism that exists basically arrived in developing countries from the colonial rulers. Therefore, neoliberalism has its roots in these countries in the interplay of colonial confiscation and dispossession of labour. The advent of neoliberalism led to the proliferation of many private sector entities.

The 80s and 90s saw the arrival of neoliberal policies, packaged as Structural Adjustment Programmes (SAP) in Asia, Africa, Latin America and the Caribbean. The International Monetary Fund (IMF) and the World Bank were the proponents of such policies with an aim to mass privatisation, market deregulation, balanced budget, and floating exchange rate regimes. Countries, tormented by balance of payment vulnerabilities triggered by the oil crisis, required external funding and had to swallow these policies in exchange. Asian and African countries were left with no other option but to abide by the programmes. However, the policies backfired for the developing countries. Countries that adopted SAP saw a collapse of social sectors like education and health as well as exhibited poor macroeconomic performance. As a result, these countries could barely meet the basic rights of the population which also later resulted in mass agitations in many countries (Naiman and Watkins, 1999). Soon the IMF replaced the SAP with another package, titled Poverty Reduction Strategies (PRS). The PRS was sold being mindful of the condition of individual countries as opposed to the criticisms of "one-size-fits-all" approach of SAP (Zack-Williams and Mohan, 2005). However, the strategy did little in improving the aggravated conditions.

The outcome of these neoliberal policies was felt strongly by the social sector causing unemployment and erosion of welfare programmes. The currency devaluation led to an increase in the cost of living across the countries (Edwards and Edwards, 2002). Continuous deregulation resulted in a decline in the enforcement of labour laws as the capacity of the government reduced over the period (Edwards and Edwards, 2002; Volscho, 2012). On the other hand, the proponents of such policies argued that debt relief provided through the programmes would enable the countries to improve social sectors and eradicate poverty (Hoogvelt, 2005). However, the outcome was different as African countries still mired in high poverty on one hand and a sharp increase in debt on the other.

The underdevelopment of the labour unions can also be attributed to the years of colonial rule and the political regime that succeeded the colonial empire. Exploitation by the colonial rulers often resulted in small protests and outbursts that were dealt with force. The nature of protests against the establishment has remained the same and so has the way to deal with the protests. At the same time, labour unions were politicised by the political parties. Two such notable examples in the case of Bangladesh are the Bengal National Chamber of Labour, and the Indian National Trade Union Congress developed by the Muslim League and the Indian National Congress, respectively, when the parties were in power in Bengal and other provinces in colonial India. After the partition, during both the Pakistani and Bangladeshi regimes, the labour unions were politicised again by the major political parties and military regimes. The politicisation of the labour unions has inhibited the federations to act as the voice for labours. Rather different fractions of labour unions fought against each other to protect their political masters.

Political leaders have also been actively involved in the business environment through ownership of firms and the vice versa has become the recent trend. In the case of Bangladesh, the share of RMG in GDP has grown over the years and so has the number of employees. A significant share of the parliamentarians are businessmen, with obvious dominance of ready-made garment (RMG) owners. As a result, businessmen-cum-politicians show little interest in labour unions, and labour unions have not been influential in protecting the rights of the labour in RMG (Khan, 2013, Islam, 2004). The sector faces regular criticism due to the poor quality of work environment and extremely low wages, without having functional unions and constant opposition to formation of unions. Labour unions in the RMG sector in Bangladesh have remained somewhat inconsequential and voiceless.

The failure of the labour unions in RMG also comes from the labours it represents. From the beginning, the sector has relied heavily on female workers, especially the migrant female workers who are compelled to work with low wages, without any alternative due to unavailability of jobs in rural areas amidst dire poverty. These women have to remain loyal to their employers largely due to their precarious economic conditions, coupled with docile nature and little knowledge of labour laws and rights. Given the labour extraction function implemented through tight work schedules, they are faced with hardly any time for mobilisation, exacerbated by another grim reality that these female workers are also required to take care of the family and associated household errands. As a result of all of these, labour unions could not grow in the sector and the owners have taken advantage of it through systematic exploitation and violation of workers' rights.

Bangladesh Labour Act 2006 incorporated a host of changes related to employment, minimum wages, trade union and overall working environment. The Act repealed 25 employment-related Acts and Laws. However, some of the changes were controversial and did not take international laws set out by ILO Conventions into cognizance. Some of the laws like restriction on trade unions in a new establishment, imposing extra work hours act against the interests and rights of workers. The government amended the Act in 2013. The amendment included improving workplace safety, freedom of association, and collective bargaining (Vogt, 2017). Yet such is still insufficient to ensure the formation of unions and enjoyment of rights, which form the basic stability conditions in the world of work.

Transformability Conditions

The process of transformation generally takes place in an economy through the transformation of a traditional agrarian society into an industrial one that fosters the growth of manufacturing sector, creating decent employment (Sullivan and Sheffrin, 2003). The factors that facilitate industrial modernisation are mainly accumulation of capital and investment, application of new technologies, large scale value adding production, and formal employment of skilled labour (Lewis, 2003).

There are the decades of debates along ideological lines on the industrial policy, particularly on the role of the state (Chang, 2011), with recent convergence towards pragmatic discussions on the design and implementation of industrial policy strategies. Such convergence can be categorised into four areas. First, there are many types of market failures, beyond the mere conventional problem of "externalities", like economies of agglomeration and coordination failures (Lin and Chang, 2009; Lin and Monga, 2012), which need to be addressed through industrial policy (Khan and Blankenburg, 2009). Second, the infant industry argument has been recently recast in new forms (Chang, 2002; Shaffaedin, 2005; Greenwald and Stiglitz, 2006; Dosi et al., 2009), belying the erstwhile perspective that markets work well enough to render industrial policy unnecessary. Third, the evidences accumulating over the years also suggest that industrial policy is not an idiosyncratic practice found only in East Asian "miracle" economies, but most of today's industrialised countries used at least some form of industrial policy, especially trade protectionism (Bairoch, 1993; Chang, 2002 and 2007; Reinert, 2007). Fourth, a successful design and enforcement of industrial policy strategies depends on the organization and structure of political power in that society, and that may or may not allow the effective opportunities and compulsions for rapid and effective technology acquisition and learning (Khan, 2013).

The concept of industrialisation can be understood with regard to such idea of classical political economy as the division of labour which renders both the organisational and intellectual aid in the production process (Slichther, 1961). The neoclassical growth theory postulates that output is a function of the stock of capital per capita (Solow, 1956). Increase in productivity, therefore, requires accumulation of capital at a pace faster than population growth (Swan and Trevor, 1956). A natural and inexorable convergence of growth and productivity across countries has been assumed by taking the diminishing returns to capital into account. When the stage of zero growth by capital accumulation is reached, further development is determined by a rate of technical change that causes industry to expand and economy to grow (Romer, 1996; Veloso and Soto, 2001). The postulate, however, received criticism since the expected paths of capital accumulation as well as anticipated convergence of growth across countries have not been observed (See Baumol, Nelson and Wolf, 1994; Veloso and Soto, 2001).

In response to the consideration of technological change as an exogenous factor generated outside the economic process, the endogenous growth theory puts forward that technological change is a result of the allocative choices of economic agents, thereby affecting productivity and growth patterns from the inside (Romer, 1996; Aghion and Howitt, 1998). Emphasising the significance of innovation and knowledge creation, the theory advocates the emergence of research and development as a new sector in the economy and the introduction of human capital as a factor of production (Lucas, 1998). While raw labour and physical capital are reckoned to be the critical inputs for production, skills and knowledge arise as the key factors that have to be accumulated to accelerate long-term growth and innovation (Veleso and Soto, 2001). The theory is, however, questioned since it lacks empirical verification (See Krugman, 2013).

As a part of a wider modernisation process, industrialisation is conceptualised in connection with the social change and economic development, and has been made related to technological innovation and large-scale production base of manufacturing, beginning with the development of large-scale energy and metallurgy production (Sullivan and Sheffrin, 2003). Against the backdrop of the emergence of modernisation thoughts in development discourse, Rostow (1960) rendering the stages of growth argues that development of more productive and commercial agriculture and cash crops not consumed by producers and/or largely exported together with enhanced investment in changes to the physical environment to expand production lead to industrialisation. Rostow's postulate is, however, challenged on the grounds of de-emphasising the differences between sectors i.e., capitalistic versus communistic societies and perceiving automatic growth by the time of maturity (e.g. Todaro and Smith, 2009).

Categorising an economy into two sectors – traditional sector characterised by agricultural-based, overpopulated and subsistence sector with zero marginal productivity of labour, and modern sector which is highly productive industrialised and capitalised – Lewis (1954) comes up with an exposition of how industrialisation occurs in the underdeveloped countries. As land fertility is limited and the productivity is low in underdeveloped regions, which are characterised by traditional sector, there exists surplus labour and a transformation of labour gradually occurs into the industrial sector. Production in industrial sector thus increases, leading to higher profit made and reinvested by the capitalist, causing the expansion of industry until the whole surplus labour in subsistence sector is absorbed. The propositions of the two sector model are, however, challenged, amongst others, on the grounds of reinvestment in labour saving capital equipment rather than labour (See Subrata and Misra, 1978; Todaro and Smith, 2009).

Import substituting industrialisation, which encourages the local production of industrial products, was advocated with a view to expanding infant industry and fostering industrialisation at national level (Salvator, 1976; Brian, 2003; Chang, 2002; Shaffaedin, 2005; Greenwald and Stiglitz, 2006; Dosi et al., 2009). The infant industry argument was buttressed through tariff protection against the imported commodity in order to allow domestic producers enough time to learn the industry, to achieve economies of scale in production and external economies of learning by doing which lower the cost and prices, resulting in increased profit for domestic producers which motivates the establishment of more industries. The postulates of import substituting industrialisation, however, draws several criticisms on grounds of high economic and social costs, small and isolated domestic market, power concentration in the hand of few business, and insufficient internal demand for the import substituting products (Franko,2007; Todaro and Smith, 2009).

Export promotion considered as an outward looking concept of industrialisation was billed as an alternative to import substituting industrialisation and several countries, namely Hon Kong, Taiwan, Singapore and Korea were shown as an example (Chacholiades, 2008). Export promotion emphasizing the development of industries whose main market is overseas is underpinned by the notion that industrialisation depends on availability of several factors that enable the production and distribution to take place at comparatively low cost (Belloc and Maio, 2011; Salvator, 1976). The monolithic view of portraying the Easy Asian countries' success only due to export orientation has been replaced by a growing convergence that the particular variant of industrial policy that each of these countries tried was compatible with internal power balances that allowed the state to create incentives and compulsions in critical areas rather than these countries' exceptional state capacities that are not achievable anywhere else nor the case of outward orientation (Khan and Blankenburg, 2009).

From a political economic perspective, industrialisation occurs through market mechanism where three variables, namely incentive, infrastructure and institutions, which are popularly known as the three "I"s, play the crucial role. Incentives guide the allocation of resources and the effort to develop new knowledge, whereas infrastructure generates desired capabilities through developing physical assets, human capital, and general technical structure, and institutions facilitate the process of industrialisation through efficacious policy responses (Lall, 1992).

It is also important to understand the stages of industrial development. In doing so a descriptive framework, with the following attributes, has been developed (Titumir, 2015).

Non-existence Stage: This stage, also can be termed as pre-industrial phase, consists of only one sector – agriculture - for survival. The phase is characterised by high birth and mortality rates resulting in no surplus and no capital accumulation leading to no investment and industrialisation. The labour force is engaged in agriculture where wage rate is very low.

Seedling Stage: The seedling stage of industrialisation begins as growth in population increases and the demand for food and clothing and agricultural production increases due to the presence of increasing returns to scale in the sector. Surplus in production creates some opportunities for trade and increases wage a little.

Start–up Phase: Being born, some small and medium scale industries start their journey and a few large industries like textile and iron mills emerge. The wage rate is comparatively higher in industry than in agriculture, resulting in transfer of labour from agriculture and the absorption of labour by the industries. Industrial production increases through division of labour within the sector leading to accumulation of capital, profits for owners, and reinvestment of profits.

Growth Phase: The growth phase of industrialisation experiences replacement of small and medium industries with the expansion of large and heavy industries. The improvement of transport system facilitates the trade beyond the boundary of nation, expanding the size of the market. More specialisation, innovation and technological advancement cause diversification of production and increase in output per capita. Higher wage rate in industries attracts more people to come to urban areas causing urbanisation.

Stabilisation Phase: The main feature of this stage is that production and profits tend to be stable over the years, while competition remains fierce. The industrial base is more diversified. People have disposable income for consuming high-value consumer goods, while the government invests in infrastructure in a large scale resulting in rapid development of transportation, mass consumption and sustainable rate of economic growth.

The First Industrial Revolution of 17th century changed the traditional production system with the invention of steam engine. The Second Industrial Revolution was driven by new sources of power such as electricity, oil and gas in the beginning of 19th century. The Third Industrial Revolution in the post-second world era heralded computer technology, semi-conductor and microchips, and other electronic and electrical devices, besides newer sources of energy like nuclear power. The penultimate one brought huge changes through likes of internet, mobile communication technology, etc. as well as massive progress in medical technologies, biotechnologies, pharmaceutical industry etc. Nevertheless, the changes and effects of Industry 4.0 on peoples' lives are in no match to the three revolutions.

Digital revolution has not emerged from a vacuum. Ceaseless amalgamation of human knowledge and skills, funded primarily by tax payers, reached this level. Yet, publicly-funded innovations are constantly being usurped by a few tech giants, instead of those remaining as public or common goods. Secondly, these behemoths are profiting out of a rather radically changed workplace where producers are also transformed into consumers. The oligarchies are getting their work done by a few numbers of remunerated employees compared to traditional companies while bulk of production is created voluntarily by unpaid users who are too reduced as their consumers, amassing huge amount of surplus by two distinctive ways, besides much of innovations being subsidised by public exchequer. One is seized as economic rent from volunteer producers while the other is generated out of sales of goods and services to them. The economic rent is generated from unpaid labourers, a factor of production, for which costs needed to bring them into production, are not paid. Thirdly, the digital markets are conceptualised as institutions to provide consumers with material well-being. Yet mounting academic research demonstrates evidences of consumers being systematically exploited through illusion, manipulation and deception due to asymmetric information, psychological weaknesses and unequal power. Digital markets, rather than being benign, allegedly intrinsically "phish" consumers as "phools". Such oligarchic system, if not regulated at every level, run risks of rendering people at large exploited and marginalized, instead of allowing them to enjoy freedom and self-fulfilment.

The revolution opens up an opportunity for developing countries to utilise huge unemployed youth and can transform from the current jobless growth trajectory to a job-creating economies. These countries have the potential to reap benefits of "demographic dividend". There is an alarming miss-match between creation of employment and new entrants to the labour market. E-readiness, comprising e-skills and e-literacy, is a fundamental requirement for a digital society.

Strategic skills are needed to understand pros and cons of digital revolution. Furthermore, matching education, training and awareness raising are crucial to make best out of this transformation. There are talents and potentials, but such call for harnessing in quality education and training institutions to match requirements. Skills alone cannot be developed by individuals rather comes from education systems and on-the-job trainings. The cycle has to start from primary education, strengthen in secondary and vocational spheres and further in tertiary level. A significant rise in public expenditure is required for enhancing capabilities, and that too have to be supplemented by the industry. Infrastructures have emerged as big challenge in developing countries to realise potentials of digital revolution. Introduction of new technologies such as analytics, development of networks and smart devices face impediments due to poor ICT infrastructure. The developing countries will not be able to march forward, if these remain a mere recipient of digital services, pioneered by other countries.

There is much adulation about big data. Big data is a non-rival public good. Yet there are examples of such being monopolized. In the new wave of changes due to digital transformation, new problems regarding public good management are emerging. In this regard, government provisions are needed to have citizens' command over data and make a dent to release from grips of monopolies. Moreover, the tech oligarchies remain out of reach of taxation. For example, these are operating in Bangladesh and earning billions of revenues, but are non-resident for the purposes of taxation. Some tech giants are also reluctant to have country offices in smaller countries, with much interest in having the company registered in tax heavens. Several countries, like Spain, France, and India have introduced "digital tax" and taxation on these companies could be a significant source of revenue for the government.

Blockchain is often ascribed as decentralized, distributed, and often times public technology and huge potentials are attributed as a means to development. Nevertheless, in an absence of regulatory oversights, there are volatilities due to scams and market manipulations in cryptocurrencies and such penalise investors like Ponzi schemes. Blockchain are touted to do away with intermediaries, but in some occasions traditional means such as banks provide services apparently at low cost to the end user. Blockchain requires large amounts of computing power to run complex algorithms, necessitating enormous amount of energy. This costs heavily on environment, particularly in the backdrop of climate crisis, causing higher vulnerabilities to developing countries. This calls for transformation of the system to a low intense energy user.

The current digital revolution is supposed to affect the whole ecosystem. The relations amongst human being, technology, nature and society may lead to massive transformation. All stakeholders within the system must have their just share such that no one gets alienated or exploited from the cycle.

While the necessary condition for transformability is expansion of productive capacity, primarily through industrialisation, the sufficient conditions in the forms of formal and informal institutions play the decisive role.

Public order, constructed by norms, values and social cohesion, driven by public society resulting from the particular form of human sociality, determine the direction of macroeconomic policies and leads to an equal society. Equalising and inclusive policies geared towards creating employment and provision of universal social security for all serve to ensure stability for growth and human well-being. For transformative change, institutions act as the driver since institutions reinforce public order among citizens, emboldened by norms, values and social cohesion, in order to create a more equitable society.

Human sociality, socially constructed norms and values, leads towards investing in job-intensive growth sectors, resulting in a stable public order in a society. Public order sustains in a harmonious way where citizens have the space to partake in the decisionmaking and in their well-being. It involves people's concern, sympathy, caring and respecting others. Humans are social beings, embedded with socially constructed norms and values, contradict the neoclassical idea of self-interest as the basis of rationality. The socially constructed norms and values prevent them from being animals, make them care for others, and think of the distribution of resources/wealth more equitably. It is needless to say that human sociality is a crucial factor in directing society's motive. Society, which has no social cohesion in-built in its nature, is less concerned to the greater benefit of its all people. On the contrary, a public society, with an intention of greater social cohesion, is willing to take measures for its people universally.

The mainstream economics, especially the orthodox neoclassical and new institutionalist doctrine, assume individuals as rational agents, guided by self-interest and are devoted to "maximising" or "economising" under conditions of scarcity. However, individuals take economic decisions not on the rational pursuit of selfish ends but on such things as kinship, group affiliation, religious beliefs, or political or other group loyalties. It is society, which schemes them to share, to unite, to care. This is explained in greater details by Bowles and Gints in their numerous articles and books where they viewed the human being as a reciprocal being (Bicchieri, 2010; Binmore, 2010; Gintis, 2011; Bowles, 2012.

Strong reciprocity (Bowels, 2012), which is the trait of social being, craves for propensity to cooperate and share with others, even at personal cost. With this trait, humans as social beings can maintain a stable public order where citizen gets the distribution of resources to ensure universal social security.

The self-interest seeking and the non-cooperation allow for concentration of public resources in the hands of few, leading to weak public order and resultant dispossession, including chronic underemployment in a society. Without a dominance of social being, self-interest seekers tend to maximise their own benefits by capturing the rent. Again, even if there exists the social being attitude among people in a society, without the required public order there would be less access to social security (Figure 12.1).

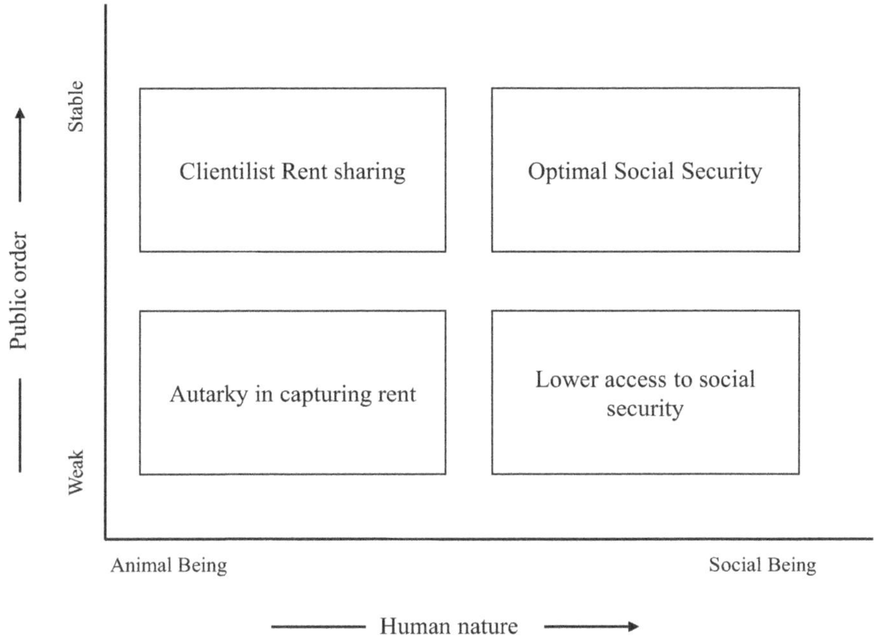

Figure 12.1 Public order and human nature

Thus, mutual cooperation between human beings leads to the direction of macroeconomic policies in income-generating investment. When classical stuck in their rationalist to self-interest-driven behaviour, rather humans together can make a better place to live through their cooperation, thus ensuring a public society with a universal social security.

Suppose that the population in the society is divided into two groups. One who is politically powerful and another who is not. Let α portion of the society is considered politically powerful and β portion is assumed politically not powerful. Further assume, governments distribute wealth and income in two ways, through taxation and public spending. Here, the portion of the population who are politically not powerful are obedient towards the government and they pay taxes regularly.

Let

$M = \alpha P$ = politically powerful population
$N = \beta P$ = politically not powerful people

L = political power
O = public order
γ = political activities of the political personnel
C = cooperative behaviour of people
μ = rate of cooperation

The more politically active someone is; the more political power he holds.

In the case of government spending,

$$S = \alpha P + \beta P = M + N$$

$$dM/dt = \gamma L \ (1)$$
$$dN/dt = c \ (constant)\ .\ (2)$$

Hence,

$$dS/dt = dM/dt + dN/dt = \gamma L + c \ (3)$$

But

$$L = f(O) \ (4)$$

and

$$O = f(C) \ (5)$$
$$dO/dt = \mu C \ (6)$$

Equation (*1*) implies that the more power one holds in the society the more they gain while in Equation (2) infers that the money remains constant for people not politically active, and thus, their wealth does not increase. Equation (*3*) implies that the distribution depends on power as dT/dt changes proportional to γ.

The political power is function of public order (Equation - 4) and public order is controlled by cooperation or the degree of human sociality (Equation – 5). Equation (*6*) implies that the more cooperative behaviours exist in a society, there are increased public order. Public spending is hence controlled by cooperation or the degree of human sociality.

Sustainability Conditions

The fulfilment of transformability conditions is likely to initiate society to look towards sustainability conditions, such that the stability and transformation achieved from equalising policies and transformational institutions can be safeguarded from unprecedented shocks to the society. An absence of prudent measures to achieve these sustainability conditions will render the economy and citizens vulnerable to unforeseen challenges, and eventually, overturn the benefits gained from the stability and transformation over the years.

The strike of the pandemic has brought economic activities throughout the world to a halt and recovery has been slow-paced. The slowdown in economic activities has exposed fault lines, triggered significant income erosion, gnawed away at standard of living due to the absence of adequate social protection. In many countries, governments are hard pressed in financing relief, rehabilitation, recovery and reconstruction from the pandemic. The socioeconomic fallouts are set to widen the gap between the developed countries and the LDCs further as the pandemic and the policies to control it have disproportionately affected poor populations both within and between countries. Some countries are recovering relatively quicker than others, owed to existing coping mechanisms – universal social protection, well-structured healthcare sector, fiscal capacity and technological advancement.

Recovery is deemed to be following either a U, V or W shape. Optimists project a rapid and quick recovery to the previous growth path, resembling a V-shaped curve. Nevertheless, the nature of the recovery relies on the process by which the recovery will be carried out. The determinants of recovery are set by the policies adopted by the government. Two different routes of recovery will be visible if the government adopts active restraint measures or if it ordains active inaction or business as usual measures in policy. In the framework of active restraint, four major conditions are assumed. These include: presence of public goods provision, redistributive policies and actions, macro-financial interventions and structural policy reforms. If these conditions are met, the resources and economic benefits and opportunities will reach all the citizens without being concentrated in the hands of a few groups. As a result, the recovery trajectory will not be discriminatory but will lead to a relatively low inequality equilibrium. But if these four conditions are not met in the government's recovery policy, the economy will traverse on a path of extreme discriminatory recovery and the recovery trajectory will gradually take the form of the English letter "*K*". *K*- shaped recovery path indicates that wealth is concentrated in the hands of some of the upper classes and on the contrary the poverty incidence continues to increase. The business-as-usual policies act as a form of active inaction which accelerates a rise in inequality, and hence polarisation, whilst a paradigm shift by design could act as an active restraint that curbs the degree of aggravation of inequality and polarisation

In Bangladesh, for instance, income erosion resulting from the losses in various sectors from the shutdown will create poverty in the country. The income erosion may result in 43.5 per cent of households having income less than the international poverty line. In the worst-case scenario, with the prolonged shutdown, the estimate suggests that 47.43 per cent of the households will have income below the poverty line. Systematic reopening of the economy with a focus on job creation and retention might see the percentage come down to 39.43 per cent (Unnayan Onneshan, 2020). Youth have suffered from the pandemic, with an estimate of job loss of one in six young people (ILO, 2020).

COVID-19 pandemic will exacerbate the existing vulnerabilities in the developing countries. Developing countries have higher employment in informal sectors. The informal sector lacks risk-mitigating measures for those employed. Weak enforcement of labour laws means that the labour force does not have required protection from the state. The levels of skills are already low in developing countries. Any shock adds injuries to an already existing wound. The COVID-19 pandemic has caused mass unemployment in these countries. Lower skilled labourers face most of the brunt, as there are few opportunities for them to seek employment elsewhere. An absence of state-mandated unemployment benefits or social security worsens the situation. Developed countries disbursed massive unemployment benefits as the pandemic hit (Figure 12.2).

Employment in the informal sector in Bangladesh is around 85 per cent and about 15 per cent of the total population has a per capita average daily income of less than BDT 500. As most of the employed population is in the informal sector, it leaves a large population out of the minimum wage jurisdictions and deprives them of basic amenities. Since a bulk of the population is dependent on daily wages to run their families, drastic measures like lockdown have led to even greater disasters at the individual and family levels. A survey of 5,461 households in rural and urban slums found that their average income decreased by about 70 per cent and food expenditure by 26 per cent (Rahman and Matin, 2020).

Due to the economic shutdown, 95 per cent of people have lost a colossal share of their salaries and 51 per cent of workers have no job currently due to the shutdown of economic activity and layoff (BRAC, 2020). In the ready-made garments sector, around 1 million workers from a workforce of

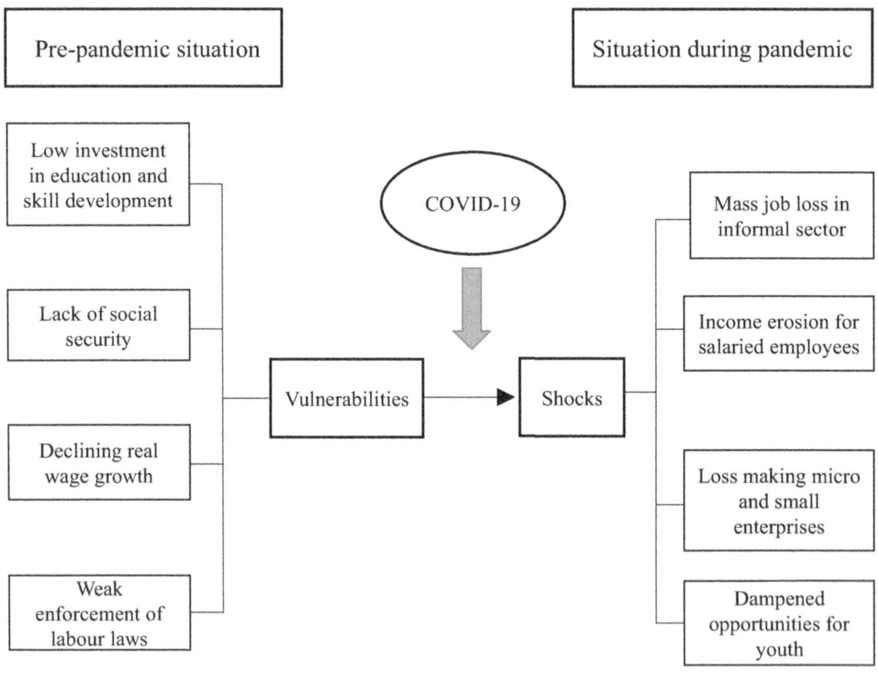

Figure 12.2 COVID-19 related shocks

Source: Prepared by author

3.5 million have been laid off because of the pandemic. According to an estimation, a percentage decrease in the GDP growth will result in a 0.93 per cent increase in the unemployment rate. Hence, the unemployment rate may rise more than 3 per cent because of the fall in GDP (Unnayan Onneshan, 2020). Large industries, including the RMG sector, have slashed many from work as the crisis prolongs. As a result, thousands of workers have lost jobs just from the RMG sector. In addition to large industries, a precarious situation emerged in cottage, micro, small and medium enterprises (CMSMEs) since two out of three private sector employees are involved. The CMSMEs elevates economic growth as well as generate employment opportunities since these are labour-intensive, requiring less time for production, small capital and low establishment costs. Due to stringent conditions laid out for availing the stimulus packages, small and medium enterprises have been unable to swiftly draw loans from the banking sector. In April 2020, total job postings in the largest online job searching sites declined by 87 per cent in Bangladesh implying thin employment opportunities (Ovi, 2020).

The economic slowdown indicates that future prospects for youth in employment are bleak. The ILO estimates that 27.39 per cent of the youth population were not in employment, education or training before the pandemic. In the aftermath of the lockdown, the scope of income-generating activities has shrunk for the youth. There is a large cohort of students who bear their own expenses from tutoring but the pandemic has left them out of work. Many had worked part-time in informal roles, which have been halted due to the pandemic. Moreover, the youth population is staring ahead into greatly reduced scope for employment as organisations scaled down their operations and are unwilling to hire new employees.

To add to the prevailing conundrum, millions of migrant workers, including half a million wage labourers, have returned home from overseas. Millions of other migrant workers have been waiting to return home unemployed. However, there will not be any employment opportunities for them at home right away. The number of unemployed individuals in rural areas in Bangladesh is around 7.7 million, which is expected to increase when those in disguised unemployment and those newly unemployed are added to the equation. As the destination countries have imposed a shutdown and travel ban, workers returned to their home countries strewn into extreme uncertainties. The global economic downturn has placed their job security in peril, hampering future earning potential.

There have been different crises in the world at different times and different approaches have been taken to recover from those crises. Not all approaches are same and these vary according to the context. The last major crisis was in the year 2009-2008, and a "New Consensus" policy framework emerged as a way out of that financial crisis. According to the new consensus, a lot of liquidity was provided against bonds as well as austerity policy measures were adopted. But while large corporations have benefited immensely, employment has not increased and risks and vulnerabilities in financial sector persisted.

Since the money did not go to the people but to the corporations, the policy framework adopted in the line of new consensus had failed and inequality increased more rapidly. In light of the past experience, in order to recover from the current recession, the cash must reach the last mile directly. Accordingly, seven principles for overcoming the crisis are listed here and if these are fulfilled, relatively a non-discriminatory recovery can be made possible. First, the cash must go into the pockets of every citizen regardless of current income, in the form of universal basic income. Second, provisions for universal public goods should be made adequate, such as education, health and social security. Third, policies must be taken for the majority instead of considering only the interests of a few, and in that regard, CMSMEs, which employ most of the people, need to be brought under financial incentives with emphasis. Fourth, diversification of products and their markets is crucial to augment competitiveness. Fifth, the production system must be green and clean in order to ensure sustainable and green development. Sixth, new investment and new employment must be created through fiscal policy rather than relying solely on monetary policy. Seventh, programmes and policies need to be mission oriented and public spending should be made to create multiplier effects on the economy, which will provide public goods and internalise externalities. A sustained mission driven strategy, comprising diversification, technological acquisition, competitiveness for being part of the international production network and expansion of domestic capacity is much warranted. Restoring the economy to a post-COVID scenario will require a concerted effort and mix of both monetary and fiscal policy measures.

The prevalence of a tunnel vision in determining allocations seems to favour clientelist networks and shows little consideration of the emerging nuances brought on by the struggles of workers, informal sector, small business owners and the majority of the citizens who still remain excluded during such trying times.

Table 12.1 Summarising conditions for stability, transformability and sustainability

	Stability	*Transformability*	*Sustainability*
Conditions	Policy and political settlements	Macroeconomic policies and human sociality	Employment, well-being and unforeseen shocks
Propositions	Both deregulation and decentralisation of power and civil rights have to be ensured simultaneously	Public order driven by human sociality, constructed by norms, values and social cohesion determines the direction of macroeconomic policies and leads to an equal society.	Benefits of decentralisation of power, equalising policies and public order should be safeguarded from being overturned by unforeseen challenges, such as COVID-19

Source: Prepared by author

Albeit a crash may be staved off by the stimulus packages announced, it will be to no avail if sustainability questions are not addressed. The condition - active citizenship - plays a crucial role to ensure accountability through checks and balances in sustaining the economy through provisioning of universal work and social security. The lack of such focused strategic roadmap to recovery, mindful of conditions for stability, transformability and sustainability, nonetheless exposes the inability to serve the needs of the many (Table 12.1).

Policy Roadmap

The economic growth seen by developing countries has not transformed into employment as the countries still see high unemployment and underemployment. At the same time, countries are now at the peak of their demographic dividend as the higher birth rate in the previous decades has now joined the workforce. Policies are required to utilise the most out of the demographic dividend. The following policy guideline provides a roadmap to boost employment (Figure 12.3).

First, industrial policies in developing countries must be formed with employment generation capacity as the key factor. Productive capacity remains very low in developing countries, much owed to the low technology base. Governments must frame policies that allow aggressive technology acquisition like East Asian countries. Technology is required for countries to move to sophisticated industries from low productive industries. At the same time, factor mobility has to be brought under policies that would allow the export skilled workforce. This would allow the remittance earning to grow. The slow rate of structural transformation needs to pace up that would create higher employment. Besides industrial policy, fiscal measures may result in a faster structural transformation. Fiscal policies often act as a barrier in promoting investment both local and foreign.

Currently, developing countries ensure productivity primarily through stringent work practices and not through rights and incentives. Developed countries have incentives in place to increase the output of the worker. Incentives like unemployment benefits not only provide temporary benefits but also motivate people to look for jobs. Universal social security act as an added incentive to the employed population. Those employed in the informal sector already face high risk and uncertainty, which can be offset by such social security.

Developing countries, in general, have poor conditions of work. The minimum wage is often not incorporated and even if there is one in place, the wage rate is extremely low. Working conditions are questionable. There must be strong labour policies and laws in place to protect the rights of the workers. The absence of active labour unions also suppresses their voice and hence results in exploitation. Strengthening the labour unions will raise the bargaining capability of the workers. Higher wage increases productivity and while it may add to the cost, the profit from higher productivity will far outweigh the increased cost due to labour extraction function.

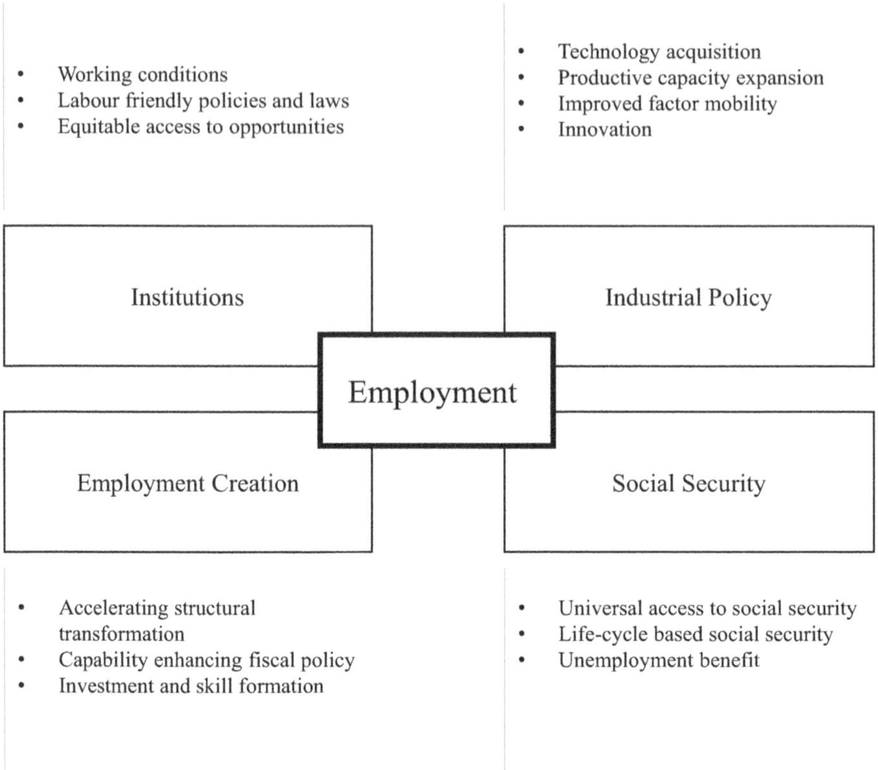

Figure 12.3 Policy roadmap

Source: Prepared by author

Summary

The advancement in the labour market is vital for bringing about desirable changes in growth outcomes and achieving success in poverty reduction. Achieving a reduction in poverty and inequality is a fundamental challenge in a country without which the human development, economic progress and universal employment will be hindered. Equitable income and resource distribution need to be ensured by public policies and investments for ensuring such a process of growth. Economic growth needs to be inclusive so that it can generate more income and employment opportunities for the poor. The key challenge is to expand decent employment opportunities through both wage and self-employment to absorb the growing labour force.

The neoliberal paradigm, however, as a practised agenda in Bangladesh, reduces the capacity of the state through privatisation and deregulation, accepting that the market will correct the inequality. Instead, the policies have given rise to widespread inequality. Lack of social safety nets and social sector programmes due to balanced budget policies worsen the condition of citizens. In order to correct the faults of the neoliberal policies, governments need to act and intervene in a manner that enhances the productive capacity to ensure full employment and reduce disguised unemployment. The rising inequality can only be addressed when citizens are provided with jobs that pay justly to the work.

Despite remarkable progress on poverty alleviation since the independence of Bangladesh, a significant number of people are still living below the poverty line. The rate of the employed population has been increasing and so has been the employment in the informal sector. Also, it is clear that a gap between ILO ratification and practices is there in reality. Reducing this gap to improve these circumstances as well as to ensure the labour rights and laws properly will be the core objective of the policymakers and the government. The existing policies and programmes need to be revised and redesigned to cope with the situation of labour injustice. Unless the government takes appropriate steps to establish labour rights, proper development along with a sustainable work environment will remain elusive.

The policy framework needs to promote an employment-friendly environment, encourage labour-intensive restructuring in both formal and informal sectors, facilitate the skill development of the labour force, and bring about appropriate changes in labour market policies. In addition, the policies must seek to fulfil the aspirations of the people in their working lives including opportunities, incomes, rights, voices, and recognition. The poverty reduction strategy would be sustainable if it is consistent with a well-articulated employment strategy that creates productive and decent employment opportunities so that workers of every level of skill, education, and training can get remunerative employment.

References

Aghion, P., and Howitt, P. (1998). *Endogenous growth theory*. Cambridge: MIT Press.

Apergis, N. (2005). *Inflation targeting and output growth: Empirical evidence for the European Union*. Washington, DC: International Monetary Fund. Retrieved April 20, 2022, from https://www.elibrary.imf.org/view/journals/001/2005/089/article-A001-en.xml

Ayittey, G.B. (2005). Why Africa is poor. In *Africa unchained* (pp. 1–32). New York: Palgrave Macmillan.

Bairoch, P. (1993). *Economics and world history – Myths and paradoxes*. Brighton: Wheatsheaf.

Baumol, W., Nelson, R., and Wolf, E. (1994). Introduction: The convergence of productivity, its significance, and its varied connotations, In Baumol, W., Nelson, R., and Wolf, E. (eds.) *The convergence of productivity: Cross-national studies and historical evidence,* pp. 3–19 Oxford: Oxford University Press.

Bauer, P.T. (1981). *Equality, the third world, and economic delusion*. Cambridge, MA: Harvard University Press.

Bhuiyan, M.M.R. (2017). Welfare state development in developing nations: The relationship between organised labour and international organisations. *Global Labour Journal*, 8(3), pp. 182–200.

Bicchieri, C. (2010). Norms, preferences, and conditional behavior. *Politics, Philosophy & Economics*, 9(3), pp. 297–313.

Binmore, K. (2010). Social norms or social preferences? *Mind & Society*, 9(2), pp. 139–157.

Booth, D. (2015). Thinking and working politically. *GSDRC professional development reading pack*. Retrieved April, 20, 2022, from http://www.gsdrc.org/docs/open/reading-packs/twp_rp.pdf

Bowles, S. (2011). Is liberal society a parasite on tradition? *Philosophy and Public Affairs*, 39(1), pp. 47–81.

Bowles, S. (2012). *The new economics of inequality and redistribution*. Cambridge: Cambridge University Press.

Bowles, S. (2012). Warriors, levelers and the role of conflict in human social behavior. *Science*, 336, pp. 876–79.

BRAC. (2020). *95pc people suffer losses in income*. Retrieved November 19, 2021, from Brac.net website: www.brac.net/latest-news/item/1284-95pc-people-suffer-losses-in-income

Bratton, M., and Van de Walle, N. (1994). Neopatrimonial regimes and political transitions in Africa. *World Politics*, 46(4), pp. 453–489. https://doi.org/10.2307/2950715

Chacholiades, M. (1990). *International economics*. New York: McGraw-Hill Publishing Company.

Chang, H-J. (2012). *Industrial policy: Can Africa do it?* IEA/World Bank Roundtable on Industrial Policy in Africa. Pretoria: South Africa.

Chang, H-J. (2002). *Kicking away the ladder – Development strategy in historical perspective*. London: Anthem Press.

Chang, H-J. (2007). *Bad samaritans*. London and New York: Random House.

Chang, H-J. (2011). Industrial policy: Can we go beyond an unproductive confrontation? In J. Lin, and B. Pleskovic (Eds.), *Annual world bank conference on development economics 2010, global: Lessons from East Asia and the global financial crisis*. Washington, DC: World Bank.

Deakin, S. (2016). *The contribution of labour law to economic development and growth*. Centre for Business Research, University of Cambridge. Retrieved April 20, 2022, from https://www.cbr.cam.ac.uk/wp-content/uploads/2020/08/wp478.pdf

Dosi, G., Cimoli, M., and Stiglitz, J. (Eds.). (2009). *Industrial policy and development: The political economy of capabilities accumulation*. Oxford: Oxford University Press.

Edwards, S., and Edwards, A.C. (2002). Social security privatization reform and labor markets: The case of Chile. *Economic Development and Cultural Change*, 50(3), pp. 465–489.

Fatton, R. (1992). Predatory rule: State and civil society in Africa. Boulder, CO: Lynne Rienner.

Gintis, H. (2011). Durkheim and the birth of economic sociology. *Economic Record*, 87(279), pp. 646–648.

Gordon, R.J. (1976). Recent developments in the theory of inflation and unemployment. *Journal of Monetary Economics*, 2(2), pp. 185–219.

Greenwald, B., and Stiglitz, J. (2006). Helping infant economies grow: Foundations of trade policies for developing Countries. *American Economic Review*, 96(2), pp. 141–146.

Heintz, J., and Pollin, R. (2003). *Informalization, economic growth and the challenge of creating viable labor standards in developing countries*. PERI Working Paper No. 60. Retrieved April 20, 2022, from https://scholarworks.umass.edu/cgi/viewcontent.cgi?article=1048&context=peri_workingpapers

Helal, M., and Hossain, M. (2013). Four decades of economic development of Bangladesh: An assessment. *Journal of the Asiatic Society of Bangladesh (Hum.)*, 58(2), pp. 335–362.

Hicks, J.R. (1936). Keynes' theory of employment. *The Economic Journal*, 46(182), pp. 238–253.

Hoogvelt, A. (2005). Postmodern intervention & human rights: Report of the commission for Africa. *Review of African Political Economy*, 32(106), pp. 595–599.

ILO. (2020). ILO: More than one in six young people out of work due to COVID-19. ILO: More than one in six young people out of work due to COVID-19. Retrieved November 20, 2021, from Ilo.org website: www.ilo.org/global/about-the-ilo/newsroom/news/WCMS_745879/lang-en/index.htm

Islam, N. (2004). Making of a nation, Bangladesh: An economist's tale. *Asia-Pacific Development Journal*, 11(2).

Johnson, H.G. (1971). The Keynesian revolution and the monetarist counter-revolution. *The American Economic Review*, 61(2), pp. 1–14.

Khan, M., and Blankenburg, S. (2009). The political economy of industrial policy in Asia and Latin America. In G. Dosi, M. Cimoli, and J.E. Stiglitz (Eds.), *Industrial policy and development: The political economy of capabilities accumulation* (pp. 336–377). Oxford: Oxford University Press.

Khan, M. (2010). *Political settlements and the governance of growth-enhancing institutions*. Retrieved April 22, 2022, from https://eprints.soas.ac.uk/9968/

Khan, M. (2013). *The political settlement, growth and technical progress in Bangladesh*. Copenhagen: Danish Institute for International Studies, DIIS.

Krugman, P. (2013). The new growth fizzle. *New York Times*. Retrieved April 20, 2022, from https://krugman.blogs.nytimes.com/2013/08/18/the-new-growth-fizzle/?mtrref=www.google.com&gwh=CEB4185CD71AD0B8D566E6A64B6885F9&gwt=regi&assetType=REGIWALL

Lall, S. (1992). Technological capabilities and the role of the government in developing countries. *Greek Economic Review*, 14(1), pp. 1–36.

Lewis, A. (1954). Economic development with unlimited supplies of labour. *The Manchester School*, 22(2), pp. 139–191.

Lin, J., and Chang, H-J. (2009). Should industrial policy in developing countries conform to comparative advantage or defy it? – A debate between Justin Lin and Ha-Joon Chang. *Development Policy Review*, 27(5), pp. 483–502.

Lin, J., and Monga, C. (2012). Comparative advantage – The silver bullet of industrial policy. Presented at the "Roundtable on New Thinking on Industrial Policy," organised by the International Economic Association (IEA) and the World Bank, 22–23 May 2012, Washington, DC.

Lucas R. (1998). On the mechanics of economic development. *Journal of Monetary Economics*, 22(1), pp. 3–42.

Mason, A. (2005). *Demographic transition and demographic dividends in developed and developing countries*. Retrieved April 20, 2022 from https://www.un.org/en/development/desa/population/events/pdf/expert/9/mason.pdf

Mkandawire, T. (2015). Neopatrimonialism and the political economy of economic performance in Africa: Critical reflections. *World Politics*, 67(3), pp. 563–612.

Mujeri, M., and Khondker, B. (2002). *Poverty implications of trade liberalization in Bangladesh: A general equilibrium approach*. Dhaka: Bangladesh Institute of Development Studies.

Naiman, R., and Watkins, N. (1999). *A survey of the impacts of IMF structural adjustment in Africa: Growth, social spending, and debt relief*. Retrieved April 22, 2022, from https://www.cepr.net/documents/publications/debt_1999_04.htm

Ovi, I.H. (2020, May 29). *Covid-19: Number of new jobs decline by 87% in Bangladesh*. Retrieved November 19, 2021, from Dhaka Tribune website: www.dhakatribune.com/bangladesh/2020/05/29/covid-19-number-of-new-jobs-decline-by-87-in-bangladesh

Rahman, H.Z., and Matin, I. (2020). *Livelihoods, coping, and support during COVID-19 crisis.* Dhaka: BRAC Institute of Governance and Development.

Reinert, E. (2007). *How rich countries got rich and why poor countries stay poor.* London: Constable.

Romer, P. (1990). Endogenous technical change. *Journal of Political Economy,* 98 (5), pp. 71–102.

Salvator, D. (1976). *International economics.* New York: Jhon Wily & Sons.

Shaffaedin, M. (2005). *Trade policy at crossroads – The recent experiences of developing countries.* New York: Palgrave Macmillan.

Storm, S., and Capaldo, J. (2019). Labour institutions and development under globalization. In *The Palgrave handbook of development economics* (pp. 553–587). Cham: Palgrave Macmillan.

Sullivan, A., and Sheffrin, S.M. (2003). *Economics: Principles in action.* New Jersey: Pearson Prentice Hall.

Swan, T.W. (1956). Economic growth and capital accumulation. *Economic Record,* 32(2), pp. 334–361.

Titumir, R.A.M. (2015). Industrialisation in Bangladesh. In A. Riaz, and M.S. Rahman (Eds.), *Routledge handbook of contemporary Bangladesh,* pp. 159–172. London and New York: Routledge.

Titumir, R.A.M., and Hossain, J. (2003). Employability: A strategic framework for the informal sector in Bangladesh. *Journal of the Institute of Bangladesh Studies,* 26.

Todaro, P.M., and Smith, S.C. (2009). *Economic development.* New York: McGraw-Hill.

Unnayan Onneshan. (2020). *Whither bending for life and livelihood: A rapid assessment of national budget 2020–21.* Dhaka: Unnayan Onneshan.

Veloso, F., and Soto, J.M. (2001). *Incentives infrastructure institutions: Perspectives on industrialization and technical change in late developing nations.* New York: Elsevier Science.

Vogt, J. (2017). The Bangladesh sustainability compact: An effective tool for promoting workers' rights? *Politics and Governance,* 5(4), pp. 80–92.

Volscho, T. (2012). Neoliberalism, Piven and Cloward's bargaining theory, and wages in the United States, 1965–2006. *Journal of Sociology and Social Welfare,* 39, p. 55.

Whitfield, L., Buur, L., Therkildsen, O., and Kjaer, A.M. (2013). The politics of industrial policy. In *Conference on "learning to compete".* Helsinki: WIDER.

Zack-Williams, T., and Mohan, G. (2005). Africa from SAPs to PRSP: Plus ca change plus C'est la Meme Chose. *Review of African Political Economy,* 32(106), pp. 501–503.

Part V

Conclusions

13 Social Policy Agenda for Developing Countries

The direction of social policy is deeply embedded in political settlement. The nature of the state and the state of public society determine the level of provision of public goods, distribution of resources and equitable opportunities of income and wealth. In absence of a public society, where the median voters hold power in political settlement, the state apparatus lacks of required checks and balances. As a result, the provisioning of goods and services in most of developing countries has been controlled by clientelist rent-seeking groups and have achieved opposite of what it desired: worsened the inequality, decreased real wage, fragile health sector and concentrated power. The COVID-19 crisis has unmasked the fractures, pre-existing structural rigidities and institutional fragilities in the economies of developing countries more than ever. The case for public provisioning has, thus, further gained traction due to the pandemic, which has swept away the livelihoods of a large section of population in developing countries.

Currently pursued policies and mechanisms by a majority of developing nations, particularly in post-colonial states of Africa, Asia, Latina America and the Caribbean, have not succeeded in achieving the desired objectives, rather inflated inequalities exponentially, despite public provisioning has been at the heart of the struggles and aspirations of decolonisation and independence of postcolonial states. These have not been able to transform the developing countries due to failings in locating the loci of transformation problem. On top of it, the COVID-19 pandemic, which has not only cost millions of lives around the globe and engendered unprecedented economic crisis, but also laid bare the weaknesses of the existing structures and institutions to absorb the consequences of exposure to shocks. This calls for searching for a new approach to examine the challenges.

The paradigm has to move away from the orthodox neoliberalism, rooted in neoclassical, public choice and new public management schools, linking social policies for transformation with citizenship. Thus, a transformational grid for social policymaking is about interconnectedness amongst public society, state building and public provisioning. A public society, a countervailing power, can establish accountability to its citizens by a state, which is by nature coercive and extractive. Thus, state building is not merely about reforms and structural

DOI: 10.4324/9781003284222-18

adjustment measures rather a relation between state and citizens. It becomes, therefore, imperative to understand the power relations in the political settlement, and for state building to be effective, the power has to lie with the median voters. Therefore, universal provisioning of education, healthcare and employment for citizens is contingent upon the direction of state building and formation of public society. It is needless to say that human sociality is a crucial factor in directing the society's motive as opposed to that of human being conceived as "self-interest" maximiser.

The public provisions in the social sectors are often non-functioning due to the weak governance and low allocation of resources in developing countries. Along with it, the imbalanced privatisation and commercialisation of knowledge and healthcare have made the situation worse. The low quality of education, the graduate unemployed youths, the increasing dropouts, etc. have proved that the things are not going well as they are presumed. Along with these, there are systemic issues like lack of access to quality education and health. The state of health in rural areas, as these countries are predominantly non-urban, is in an alarming condition. Lack of trained doctors, nurses and other facilities and prevalence of malnutrition, chronic poverty and huge demographic change are burdening the sector. Lack of employment opportunities particularly for the youth has been impeding economic and human development in developing countries, evident from the high rate of NEET (not in employment, education and training).

In developed countries, the social contract between the state and citizens is adhered through the rule of law, property rights and checks and balances. Thus, there are flows of public goods provision. In the education sector, life skills development of the population is emphasised through greater expenditure. Spending on research and development is high as governments focus on innovation, eventually leading to higher productivity. Citizenship education entails claiming the rights to economic welfare and social security, and to the right to live the life of a civilised being. In terms of healthcare, most of the developed countries have adopted the strategy of universal health care that ensures equal access to healthcare facilities for the people. Healthcare structures in most of the European countries are dependent on ample public financing of healthcare which ensures access to every citizen regardless of their levels of income, with view to mitigating health inequalities. As a result, health-seeking behaviour becomes more active in an absence of a market-centric approach in healthcare provisioning. While there is huge exclusions in developed countries with market-centric approach in provisioning of healthcare such as the USA, despite having adherence to the rule of law, property rights and checks and balances. A market-based provisioning of education and health care by no means can guarantee universal access to education and healthcare.

Universal provision of education and healthcare renders the labour force productive, skilled and innovative. Developed countries have a much higher ratio of formal employment in the economy that provides rights to the labour. Due to the existence and compulsion of labour laws and regulations imposed by formal institutions in developed countries, rights are upheld and exercised. This helps these high-income countries to maintain a certain degree of existing competitiveness over the developing nations.

Developing countries are governed by a kind of ruling elite who reproduces a concentrated form of power that creates an unequal distribution. The discrimination in distribution deprives the poor of basic social opportunities, worsened by the lack of accountability and the exertion of social coercion by the ruling elite, rendering the inequality persistent. The social contract between the state and citizens is not upheld due to unequal power relations. As formal institutions are weak in developing countries due to a lack of checks and balances, the means of providing public goods are rendered fragile. Due to unequal and concentrated power relations, the powerful breaks the distribution channels of provisioning of public goods and hinders the reach of welfare to the marginalised population. With besieged by neoliberal ideas of international organisations, lack of powerful checks-balances-centred formal institutions, and countervailing public society of their own, developing countries tend to adopt a market-centric approach for public good provision. The market-centric approach, in absence effective regulatory mechanism, allows for the ruling elites to be in control of such "market", with the power of setting of predatory prices and profiting out of shifting the burden of risks to the state.

An absence of public society in developing countries, despite years of aspiration and struggles for a just society, dates back to colonial rule of hundreds of years. The "divide and rule" and "divide and conquer" tacts hit hard on social values such as cooperation, cohesion and burden-sharing among societal beings through creation and perpetuation of antagonisms and sectarian divides on the lines of religion, ethnicity etc. After independence, these countries witnessed rise of intermediate classes, with a hunger for primitive accumulation. Intermediate classes are formed of classes that occupy an intermediate position and play a key role in the political process, but not as dominant as the capitalist class. Broadly, the intermediate classes comprise of rich and middle farmers, urban petty-bourgeoisies and educated middle classes, having a greater degree of organisational ability resulting from their better education and greater wealth. These classes are different from workers, poor peasants and the illiterate unemployed.

The rat race competition is motivated by usurpations of assets and there is an incentive to compete for accumulation of political power of the state. The cadres of the newly-elected government who were in opposition before the change of the guard take control from the cadres of the outgoing government who wait for their turn and continue to agitate against the government. This cyclical pattern of control, agitation, and return for control perpetuates the reproduction of the politics of confrontation. The material basis of this particular form of accumulation has, thus, given birth to a nexus amongst politicians, members of the administration, the law enforcing agencies and the judicial system in developing countries. Such a nexus is cyclical and transient, and always houses with the party/alliance in power.

The reproduction of the networked system lies in the ability to capture resources and consequential distribution, either directly to grassroots, or through creation of provision for central, regional and grassroots leaders. This requires pursuance of "winners-take-all" strategy and use of power and coercion over administrative, law-enforcing, judicial, and criminal justice systems. In this process the opposition members become totally deprived, waiting with high intent and figured strategies of how to multiply the loss incurred during the period of absence from power. The system thus has been able to create on its own a system of reproduction and welfare system for members belonging to factions of different parties, at the expense of ordinary citizens. The networked system of factions has even in some cases given birth and sustained a system of private force, parallel to the apparatus of the state, in order to steer the process of acquiring and maintenance of command over the captured resources, as such process warrants considerable expression of intimidation, coercion, and oppression.

The clientelist networks are grabbing the economy by dint of state power. The political process has evolved in a particular direction, corresponding to the characteristics of political activists and the incentive-structure to reproduce the political system. As such, the main pillars of the state, namely a functioning judiciary, an effective parliament and a civil administration to implement the political mandate for the people given by the people to the elected representatives of the people, are getting eroded. The motive of the ruling elite is simply to have a centralised state with concentration of power. The system has become authoritarian and cannot withstand even muted dissent and public scrutiny. These groups have moved away from neopatrimonialism towards a more networked political settlement. The outcome of such settlement is reflected in government policies regarding the provision of public goods such as education, health and employment. Public investment and employment creation therefore compromised, results in poor pace of poverty reduction and a rapid rise in inequality. The failure to bring the economy to order, therefore, results in unsustainable economic outcomes, which go to the pockets of few at the expense of many. These unequal and unjust economic outcomes are reflected in every sphere of the economy.

The mandate of social policymaking is to curb the growing inequalities in the forms of class, power and marginalisation through nation building, public society and public provisioning. When a state fails to effectively control and regulate the market for education, healthcare and employment, and ensure equitable distribution, it results in a rise in infant mortality, fall in literacy rates, epidemics like Ebola and AIDS as seen in the African nations, which adversely affect women, children, lower-income quartiles and marginalised communities. Inherently, failures in social policymaking pertain to the struggles of excluded groups that have lower levels of "power over" countering hegemonic pressures.

The outcomes of market-centric approach in the education sector imply that every individual does not have equal access to education. Albeit primary education has improved over the years in developing countries, ascending tiers of education still remain subpar. First, inadequate investment in secondary and higher secondary levels of education especially hinders the formation and development of life skills. Second, incongruences in the education infrastructure such as classroom size, teacher–student ratio and speed of adapting to new technology dampen the quality of education. Third, tertiary education lags behind in terms of enrolment and research and development, adversely affecting real chances of innovation. Funding for research is low, and in certain areas almost non-existent, forcing the economy to be trapped in low-return-labour-intensive processes. The huge inadequacy of citizenship education implies that citizens are not made aware of their own rights and responsibilities, therefore they fail to claim what is rightfully theirs. It also results in the want of triggering social cohesion, thus leading to hatred, hostilities and even to inter-sectional violence. In sub-Saharan countries, for instance, such sets off frequent civil wars and conflicts between tribes, resulting dictators in thriving in power. The conflicts lead to child labour, abuse and criminal offences.

Healthcare sectors in developing countries have overtly resulted in health inequalities, emboldened by the advent of a global pandemic. Government expenditure is excruciatingly low in the healthcare sector, as low as one per cent of GDP, resulting in a lack of access to publicly provided healthcare by the general public. The out-of-pocket expenditure remains high, restricting the healthcare-seeking behaviour of the people because of the high costs involved. The cost of healthcare is relatively higher in rural areas due to hidden costs of transportation, accessibility and quality of treatment. It is evident that there are no provisions for universal health care in developing countries. There is also an apparent lack of financing schemes such as health insurance, let alone publicly funded ones. The failure of public provision in these circumstances give rise to a market-centric approach in healthcare provision. Higher prices in the market increase healthcare costs, and for the population vulnerable to poverty, those living just above the poverty line, an incidence of a health shock is likely to be detrimental to the household, pushing them back into poverty. The existence of a private market in this sector is a diversion from the fact that healthcare is a need in itself, rather than a demand, indicated by the low healthcare-seeking behaviour of individuals.

The shortcomings of the education and healthcare sector bring about a labour force with low productivity and a smaller skillset that dampen future employment opportunities. The percentage of informal employment is around 70 per cent in developing countries, implying that the majority of the labour force remains devoid of labour rights and jurisdictions that could safeguard their earnings and decent living. The macroeconomic policies are not directed to be job-expanding and hence, unveil dearth of formal employment, with certain countries exhibiting a pre-mature deindustrialisation.

Jobless growth and resultant widespread unemployment have formed a sense of precarity in developing countries. The transformational pathway in employment is hence to be based on ensuring work for all as well as universal, and not targeted, life-cycle-based social security systems to absorb systemic shocks, including those resulting from the pandemic and natural disasters.

Transformational pathways for developing economies depend on education, health and employment. For the education sector, governments in developing countries must increase spending to ensure universal education for all. To create a skilled workforce, governments need to increase spending on infrastructures and technical and vocational education. To boost innovation, countries have to aggressively acquire technologies for further development in manufacturing industries. These policies are bound to increase labour return and boost overall economic output. Finally, the ultimate goal of reaching a public society lies in the ability to form citizenship in people. Citizenship education will raise awareness among citizens about political and human rights. Citizenship can only be achieved when the government has control over the education rather than the private market.

In the healthcare sector, there exists high out-of-pocket expenditure as well as exclusion. Even though public healthcare exists in many countries, it still remains insufficient. The private market in healthcare has resulted in higher costs. As a result, healthcare-seeking behaviour has deteriorated in developing countries. To ensure access to healthcare, governments in developing countries have to initiate universal health care through public provisioning.

The global pandemic and resulting job loss reinforce the notion of social security that will protect their livelihood. Developing countries have high informal employment and low social security provisions. As a result, employees suffer from the risk of losing their jobs. Minimum wage has to be replaced with the idea of the living wage. Living wage safeguards the living standard.

The failures in public provision in developing countries thus hinder the individual's capability for better living and the freedom to choose their own path in their lives based on the education, health and employment opportunities they receive. In the face of the worst pandemic in the last century, it is of utmost importance to protect the life and livelihoods of the people. Healthcare sector has suffered the most during the pandemic, particularly in developing countries. Economic shutdown to contain the virus has affected those in the informal sector. Unequal education between the rich and the poor has widened further during the pandemic.

It is the right time to overhaul social policies. The inability to choose a better, more dignified life and the dearth of a strong social contract leave citizens in a vicious cycle between inefficient public provision and handicapped life chances. The fundamental principles of a country's social policy originate from the aspirations of the people through their struggles. Hence, aspirational social policy is an understanding of the type of the society people want to live in. The evolution of social policy is deeply rooted in the direction of development, societal structure, and prevailing political settlement in a society. Universal provisioning, enabled by a transformational state and underwritten by a public society, is necessary for the elimination of poverty and the eradication of inequalities which have been plaguing developing countries.

Index

accountability 10, 17, 27–28, 40, 44, 46, 48–52, 61, 68, 132, 199, 281
Acemoglu, Daron 209
Akerlof, George 36, 66–67, 125
animal spirit 36, 66–67
Arrow, Kenneth 38

basic income 5, 216, 241–243, 272
Becker, Gary 63, 190
Blackship Turmoil 108
Bourdieu, Pierre 63
Bowles, Samuel 30–31, 37, 48, 68–71, 86, 266

capability approach 66, 138
citizenship capability 18
clientelism 199
Coase, Ronald 39, 62
Coase Theorem 39, 62
coercion 9, 27, 40, 44, 46, 49, 283, 284
communal solidarity 45, 109
compensation theory 207–209
corruption 10, 48, 67, 105, 113, 231
COVID-19 3–4, 120, 139–140, 167, 172–176, 200–222, 239–242, 248, 269–272, 277, 281
Curve, Phillips 190–194, 204

Daniels, Norman 31
demographic dividend 228
disease burden 133, 174
distribution of healthcare resources 133, 158, 168
Dorfman, Robert 34
Durkheim, Emile 29, 276

egalitarianism 7, 114, 198, 200
Engels, Friedrich 34
entitlements 27, 104
Esping-Anderson, G. 28

evolutionary game theory 71
externalities 62, 69, 81, 96, 130, 135, 261, 272

free market 33, 65–66, 68, 195–196
free rider 62
Friedman, Milton 190, 194
full employment 7, 185–188, 193, 195, 197, 275

Galbraith, James K. 63
general equilibrium 34
General Theory of Employment, Interest and Money 186, 188
Gini coefficient 15, 19–20, 116, 216
Gintis, Herbert 30, 37, 48, 68, 69, 70–72, 266
global polio eradication initiative 132
great depression 186, 188, 190

health and population sector strategy 133
healthcare policies 129
healthcare provision 157, 159, 161, 167, 168, 282, 285
healthcare seeking behaviour i, xviii, 141–142, 147, 164, 175–176, 285–286
health infrastructure 4
health shock 172, 285
historical discontinuity 111
human rights 6, 10, 16, 48, 59, 75, 78, 105, 124, 130, 220, 248, 286
human sociality 6, 7, 29–30, 63, 70, 72, 78, 104, 106, 108, 109, 114, 167, 195, 199, 204, 255–266, 268, 272, 282
Hume, David 71–73

informalisation 18, 21, 225
informal sector 5, 21, 74, 92, 96, 163, 202, 212, 223–225, 235, 239–243, 269, 272–273, 275, 286

innovation xviii, 19, 47, 75, 77, 81, 100, 120, 145, 176, 207, 239, 261, 274, 282
institutional challenges 64, 131, 145, 230, 239, 281
institutions 3, 5, 11, 17, 22, 26–34, 37, 39, 40, 42–48, 59, 85–86, 88, 108, 167, 255, 281
intensification of inequality 11, 13, 15, 17, 18, 23, 29, 45, 68, 76, 86, 129, 140, 155, 161, 213, 215, 241, 269, 275, 284

jobless growth 4, 202, 239, 264, 285

Keynes, John Maynard 26, 33, 66, 186–190, 193, 196, 198, 208
Keynesian welfare state 134
Krugman, Paul 262, 277

labour extraction 207, 216, 260, 273
labour market 28, 65, 84, 87, 93, 115, 118, 183–184, 191–195, 200, 203–204, 208, 221–223, 225, 234, 249, 265, 274–275
labour productivity 96, 202, 215, 231
labour rights 203, 213, 220, 258, 275, 285
laissez-faire 32, 34, 45, 185, 187, 189, 197
life expectancy 60, 96, 139, 145, 155, 158, 159, 228
limited access order 43
Lord Beveridge 238

market provisioning 61–62, 81–83, 105, 142, 146, 153–154, 164–165
Marx, Karl 28, 34, 41, 207
mean-test approach 244
microcredit 84

Nash equilibrium 72
National Health Bill 132, 171
neoliberalism 11, 24, 65, 84, 113, 117, 124, 137, 167, 184, 258, 281
neo-marxist 42
neopatrimonialism 255, 276–277, 284
new industrial policy 184
new institutional economics 27, 39, 45, 53–55, 167
new Keynesian school 193–195, 197, 205
New Rural Cooperative Medical Care System 171
North, Douglass 39
Nozick, Robert 70, 137
Nussbaum, Martha 66

oligopoly 68, 151, 196
open access order 43
out-of-pocket expenditure 14, 20, 87, 140, 155, 164, 168, 170–171, 174, 242–243, 285, 286

paradigm shift 4, 269
Pareto efficient 62
patrimonial capitalism 68
Phillips, William 190–194
Pigou, Arthur Cecil 134, 187, 188
Pigouvian tax 62, 78
Polanyi, Karl 41, 137
political settlement 5, 6, 22–23, 27–28, 43–44, 47–48, 77, 109, 123–124, 131, 145, 168, 170, 172–173, 184–185, 196–199, 203, 248–250, 255–256, 286
post-Keynesianism 53–54, 79, 204
poverty line 116, 140–141, 156, 163, 183, 212, 241, 243, 248, 251–252, 269, 275, 285
power of median voters 6, 27, 123, 170, 178, 281
price discrimination 81–83, 96, 105
price-setting 142, 145, 151–152, 164
principal-agent 10
principle of meritocracy 111
private healthcare 131, 136, 145, 157, 159, 172, 174
productive capacity 211
Proxy Mean Test (PST) 244
public choice theory 11, 27, 124, 136–137, 167, 195
public financing 16, 114, 117, 119, 125, 130, 282
public goods 3, 6–10, 18, 20–24, 26–33, 37–38, 40–42, 44, 46, 49, 51–53, 55, 62, 65, 69, 75, 80, 82–83, 105, 135, 137, 167, 172, 197, 240, 269, 272, 281–284
public health 121, 129, 131, 143, 144, 151, 157, 161, 162, 168, 169, 177
public society 3, 4, 6, 10, 13, 22, 27–29, 33, 40, 41, 44, 46, 49, 52, 61, 75, 77, 81, 104–106, 110, 123–124, 167–168, 178, 198–199, 204, 239, 249, 253, 255, 266–267, 281–283, 286
public spending 16, 45, 65, 83, 105, 116–117, 137, 197, 230–231, 253, 257–258, 268, 272
Putnam, Robert 64, 79

Rawls, John 7, 70, 138
Reagan, Ronald 184
Ricardo, David 32–33, 186, 208
rights-based approach 185, 204

Samuelson, Paul 11, 25, 34, 40, 55, 192–193, 205
Say, Jean-Baptiste 185
Say's law 185–187, 195
Sen, Amartya 66, 138
sheepskin effect 64
Smith, Adam 27, 32, 36
social capital 63–64
social care 176
social collectivism 109
social contract 3, 22, 81, 104, 123, 168, 198–199, 282, 286
social distancing 3, 4, 81, 174, 176
social division of labour 68, 109, 117
social insurance 118, 235, 238, 241
social insurance schemes 118
social minimum 70
social mobility 84
social protection 5, 17, 212, 240–241, 243–248, 251, 268
social recession 110
social safety net program 14, 16–17, 70, 239, 241, 246, 251
social security schemes 5, 118
social stratification 68, 87, 109, 117
Solow, Robert 34, 192, 205, 261
Stiglitz, Joseph 31, 62, 138, 188, 194, 261, 262
structural adjustment reforms 11, 125, 184
structural transformation 133, 195, 200, 202–204, 207, 209, 212, 226, 234, 252, 273
sustainable development goals 139, 154, 220, 230, 239, 248
S4YE 92

technology acquisition 47, 75, 81, 124, 197, 261, 273
Terakoya 112
Thatcher, Margaret 184
Tobin, James 191
Todaro, Michael 262, 278
trade-related aspects of intellectual property rights 39, 40, 48
transformational path 4, 81, 108, 183, 239, 285–286
Treatise of Human Nature, A 71

underemployment 65, 91, 93, 117, 125, 187, 207, 210, 218, 234, 266, 273
unemployment 4, 5, 17, 19, 33, 65, 74, 76, 83, 91–93, 99, 117, 125, 185, 207, 238, 255, 285
universal child benefit 251
universal disability benefit 252
universal health care 4, 129, 145, 167, 176, 235, 282, 285–286
universal maternity benefit 252
universal old age allowance 251
universal pension system 241
universal rights 153
universal social security 198–207, 219, 238, 256
universal unemployment benefit 252

Weber, Max 9, 27
welfare capitalism 188
welfare state 28, 187, 238, 252
work for all 183, 198, 207, 239, 285